D1542896

THE FAMILY
IN
ANCIENT ROME

NEW PERSPECTIVES

EDITED BY
BERYL RAWSON

CORNELL UNIVERSITY PRESS
Ithaca, New York

OAK PARK PUBLIC LIBRARY

© 1986 by Beryl Rawson
All rights reserved. Except for brief quotations in a review, this book, or parts thereof, must not be reproduced in any form without permission in writing from the publisher. For information address Cornell University Press, 124 Roberts Place, Ithaca, New York 14850.

First published in 1986 by Cornell University Press.

Library of Congress Cataloging in Publication Data
Main entry under title.

The Family in ancient Rome.

"Result of a three-day seminar held at the
Australian National University, Canberra, in July
1981"—Introd.
    Bibliography: p.
    Includes index.
    I. Family—Rome—Congresses.   2. Women—Rome—
Congresses.   I. Rawson, Beryl.   II. Australian
National University.
HQ511.F35   1986   306.8'5'09376   85-18976
ISBN 0-8014-1873-9

Printed in Great Britain.

306.85
F198

22.25

Cornell University Press

8-4-86

CONTENTS

TABLES

CONTRIBUTORS

Mrs Edyth Binkowski Research Assistant, Australia National University, Australia

Ms Jan Blayney Lecturer in Classics, Victoria University of Wellington, New Zealand

Professor Keith R. Bradley Associate Professor of Classics, University of Victoria, B.C., Canada

Professor J.A. Crook Professor of Ancient History, Cambridge University (St John's College)

Ms Suzanne Dixon Lecturer in Classics, University of Queensland, Australia

Professor W.K. Lacey Professor of Classics, University of Auckland, New Zealand

Dr Beryl Rawson Reader in Classics and Dean, Faculty of Arts, Australian National University, Australia

Professor P.R.C. Weaver Professor of Classics, University of Tasmania, Australia

INTRODUCTION

This book is the result of a three-day seminar held at the Australian National University, Canberra, in July 1981. It is not, however, a volume of 'Proceedings'. Papers have been selected, revised and edited to provide cohesion and logical internal development. Although these chapters cannot cover all aspects of so large a subject, the first chapter and the bibliography provide an introductory discussion of general features of Roman family life and of previous and current work in the field; and a concluding chapter incorporates significant points from the seminar discussion to highlight problems and directions for further work.

This is not, then, the final word on 'The Roman Family': a larger, more comprehensive volume is a project which will take some years yet. But the subject is of such interest, and so little material on it is readily available, that a volume is desirable now, to guide scholars in other fields and students to what has already been done, to give examples of specialised current research which illuminates the subject, and to point the way to future research.

In Chapter 1, Rawson discusses previous work and its limitations, and presents a generalised picture of the main features of 'The Roman Family' in the last century BC and the first two or three centuries AD: size, membership, relationships between members, broken families, the role of education.

Crook's chapters deal with the legal evidence, which is fundamental to the study of many aspects of Roman society but which is surprisingly unfamiliar even to other Roman historians. (His self-deprecatory n. 1 in Chapter 2 underestimates the need for such a background chapter. Seminar participants found it invaluable.) Crook already extended knowledge of Roman law and its social implications in his *Law and Life of Rome* (1967), whose Chapter 4 is especially relevant to family studies. His present discussion, in Chapter 2, of women's role in wills and in the acquisition and transmission of property throws light on Romans' concept of 'the family' — how the network of kin was extended and how continuity was maintained. Women increasingly had control over their own property, and in the second century AD gained the right to bequeath to their own children.

In Chapter 3, Crook questions the motivation of a decree of the first century AD which prevented women from going surety for someone else's debt. This limitation on women's financial freedom seems at variance with other legal and social developments of which we know. Crook suggests that it was neither anti-feminist nor overprotective of women, but that it protected women from a very particular error of judgement which could occur in the wake of recent increases in their freedom of action.

Dixon's chapter continues the theme of property disposition and its effect on women and children. She argues from Cicero's correspondence that in the late Republic (mid-first century BC) social expectations and conventions were at least as important as law in making arrangements for the maintenance of children and for dowry after divorce.

Lacey's chapter forms a link between public and private. He argues that *patria potestas*, the authority of the (male) head of household, was the fundamental institution underlying the structure of Roman society. It not only affected most aspects of family life, but its assumptions also underlay political practice and procedure. The Roman state was, in effect, a family.

Weaver, Rawson and Bradley move the focus more to the household and the individual. In a society where marriages or unions frequently involved partners of different legal status and where the nuclear family household could not always be maintained, what was the effect on children?

Weaver examines relationships between free women and slave men. Children of such unions were normally freeborn, but the *senatusconsultum Claudianum* (AD 52) made some exceptions to this. The exceptions seem to be male children in the imperial household: they may have been being reserved for administrative careers — lucrative and influential careers, although officials remained slaves until at least the age of 30.

Rawson examines children of more humble status. She shows that a stable family life could exist even for slaves and those of recent slave status, but considers in more detail those children whose natural parents were unwilling or unable to raise them as their own. Attitudes to infanticide and exposure and to orphans, illegitimates and adopted children are touched on, and a close analysis made of 'foster children' who are referred to as *alumni* or *vernae*.

Introduction

Bradley was not present at the original seminar, but his work was known to participants and we are grateful to have his contribution to this volume. His chapter discusses the widespread use of wet-nurses in Roman society; possible reasons for the practice; and what it reflects of parental attitudes.

Blayney's brief chapter sets out ancient theories of conception, with particular reference to the 'doctrine of the two seeds' (giving an effective role to the female seed), sex differentiation and heredity. Upper-class Romans had access to these theories, but this did not exclude belief in ineffective methods of contraception.

A brief conclusion draws together the main lines of argument which have emerged and attempts a projection of future work to be done in the study of the Roman Family.

In section (I) of the Bibliography Binkowski and Rawson discuss available sources under various headings: general works on Roman society, works on comparable societies, particular aspects (children, death and burial, demography, education, housing, law, marriage, medicine, nomenclature, *patria potestas*, religion, slaves and freedmen, social classes, women).

Thanks are due to all who participated in the original seminar, especially R.A. Bauman, Keith Hopkins and E.A. Judge who contributed papers. Although these scholars reserved their papers for publication in different forms elsewhere, their role at the seminar has improved the quality of this volume in many ways. We all were grateful to the Humanities Research Centre for sponsoring the seminar.

I owe personal thanks to many colleagues and friends. Lily Ross Taylor set me on this research path more than 20 years ago. For nearly as long, Paul Weaver has shared ideas, encouragement and problems with me. Of colleagues in my own department, Robert Barnes deserves special mention for his unfailing and encyclopaedic bibliographical help. The Australian Research Grants Scheme and the ANU Faculties Research Fund made a part-time Research Assistant post possible, a post filled successively by three assistants whose invaluable help I warmly acknowledge: Simon Wild, Lee Sturma and Edyth Binkowski.

1 THE ROMAN FAMILY

Beryl Rawson

(1) '. . . the institution of the Roman family was strengthened by a healthiness, a solidity, a spirit of uprightness and self-restraint superior to that of perhaps all other ancient people.' 'From the point of view of purely human morality [as opposed to Christian-inspired], Roman marriage was virtually perfect.' (Paribeni 1948:75, 22)

(2) 'At the beginning of the Christian era, marriage and family conditions in Rome were in a very bad way indeed. The domestic virtue of the conquerors of the Mediterranean world was gone.' (Zimmerman 1947:395)

And a combination of (1) and (2): (3) 'How far removed [in the second century AD] from the inspiring picture of the Roman family in the heroic days of the Republic! The unassailable rock has cracked and crumbled away on every side.' (Carcopino 1940:100)

All three statements share the assumption that the family is a central and basic institution in society and that the health of a community can be measured by the stability of its family life. In (1), a scholar in Mussolini's Italy was seeking to illustrate the superior virtues of the Italian people and to find the root of these in the family structure of the ancient Romans. (2) and (3) are both preoccupied with a 'decline and fall', and (2) would date this somewhat earlier than would (3). The writer of (2), a modern sociologist concerned with claims of a 'decline of familism' in modern western society, was trying to come to a better understanding of his own society by looking at the course of family history in other societies. (3) is from a general social history of ancient Rome, first written in 1939 and based largely on the writings of upper-class Romans: it is the usual stereotype.

Such generalisations persist, in spite of the specialised work done in Roman social history in recent years. The most recent general book on Roman education, by Bonnèr, (1977) is an illustration (see Bibliography under 'Education'). How is it that such different generalisations can be made about the family in ancient Rome, or that so many writers can accept and perpetuate the picture of a sudden disintegration of 'the family' without showing surprise or curiosity that an institution supposedly so strong and stable for centuries could founder so easily? No real attempt has ever been made to explain or document the stereotype. This is the more surprising now that it is recognised that the political power and cultural achievements of Rome continued long after the point at which most writers date the 'decay' of the family (first century BC to first century AD).

If the family was indeed so central an institution in Roman society, surely its disintegration must have been reflected in other aspects of Roman life. But the impact of the family on wider social values, structure and practice is almost never analysed. Influences in the reverse direction, from general social changes to the family, are often adduced as causes of the family's breakdown, e.g. Roman society's increasing wealth and foreign-born slave numbers, and the coming of a long period of peace. Such factors, baldly stated, are no longer convincing explanations for supposed moral decline. Prosperity in itself need not be an evil force. If Rome failed to find good uses for her new wealth, if its effects were indeed corrupting, especially in the family context, this needs to be demonstrated, and for which classes; it cannot be assumed. We would now recognise it as simplistic to praise war as a noble binder-together of a nation or to attribute moral decline to peace. And the prejudices inherent in phrases such as 'slave morality', 'eastern morality', and 'female licence' are all too obvious. Thus a Roman history textbook used by several generations of students, containing statements like the following, no longer commands respect: 'The new ideals which had come in from the East where home life was hardly known, overlaid on the Roman reluctance to suppress the female sex, ended in the spread at Rome of a moral licence which finally destroyed its victims' (Last, in Bailey 1923:231). Echoes remain in more recent and more reliable books (e.g. Johnston 1957:44; Wilkinson 1975:70 — 'Luxury and moral degeneration', a sub-heading under 'The Impact of Greece').

So the three statements which introduced this chapter, though typical of much of what has been written on the Roman family, are no longer satisfactory, and do little to help us understand the way people behaved and related to one another within the family unit or how the family and society at large interacted. They are based on too limited or selective a body of evidence (hence the different generalisations possible); they take for granted an idealised past; and (2) and (3) make unsupported assumptions about a severe discontinuity in Roman culture, basing moral judgements on this. Future studies of the Roman family must, in the first place, give us a detailed and systematic examination of all the available evidence; they must then attempt to interpret this evidence with the help of insights and techniques developed by other disciplines in recent times.

Reasons for the lack of satisfactory studies of the family in ancient Italy are several. For any society, studies of the family are fairly recent (see Thirsk 1964; Hareven 1971). They have often been beset by the prejudices and *a priori* assumptions about the family which are part of our cultural tradition. For ancient Italy, there have been limitations due to the comparatively small quantity of evidence available, the type of evidence usually selected, and the purpose of the scholars or historians who have written on the subject. The evidence used has been drawn largely from Latin literature, which was written almost entirely about the upper classes and for the upper classes (and usually by the upper classes). Moreover, the situations and characters from that literature which have dominated readers' attention have been the colourful, the flamboyant and the scandalous. There is, however, a large body of non-literary evidence available, e.g. the law, inscriptions, coins, works of art, remains of dwellings and city centres, and all the other fruits of archaeology. Much of this can throw light on the people and activities of a much wider section of the population than the upper classes of Latin literature. The following chapters draw on Roman law, epitaphs and a range of literature (including letters and technical medical texts): they give a glimpse of Roman society at several levels.

For any ancient society, of course, there will always be frustrating gaps in the evidence available and thus some questions which we cannot answer. One must be frank in acknowledging these.[1] But new methods have been developed for reconstructing the family life of mediaeval Europe, and the work being done in that field should encourage us to hope that even from fragmentary evidence we can form a much more rounded picture than was once thought possible.[2]

The Bibliography discusses in more detail previous work which has a bearing on the Roman family. The few books whose titles have indicated a specific interest in the Roman family (Lacombe, Paribeni) have never enjoyed a wide reputation and are now badly outdated. In general social histories of Rome the treatment of the family, when it has had any place at all, has been superficial, some comprising a paraphrase of or series of quotations from classical authors, others a narrative of 'daily life', describing various institutions and ceremonies. Favourite sub-headings relate to the ceremonies of marriage and betrothal, birthdays, funerals, festivals and games, to practices of upper-class education and of dinner parties, and to the institutions of slavery and religion. Some give a good account of the material setting of the Roman family but seldom relate this closely to the kind of life lived within that setting. They all fail to offer any real insight into the fundamental basis of the family — what made it work (or not work), what were the interrelationships of various members, what were their expectations — or into the place of the family in the total social structure. We are told something of the general (aristocratic) ideals of Roman culture — *virtus, dignitas, auctoritas, gloria, pietas, gravitas*[3] — but neither how the child was socialised to conform to these ideals nor what the reasons were when the child or adult failed to implement them.

The most substantial work on the family has been done in the field of Roman law. Most of the legal textbooks set out what the requirements and capacity were for a legal Roman marriage, what were the legal consequences of such a marriage and its dissolution, what rules applied to dowry, and what were the status, rights and limitations of the *paterfamilias* (head of household), women, children, freedmen and slaves. Corbett (1930) was for long the most specific and detailed for family matters, although it was concerned with only the law of marriage. Watson (1967) is more recent and comprehensive. These legal reference books are indispensable for the specialist who wishes to make a serious study of the Roman family, but most of them are too technical for the lay reader, and deal only with the formal relations of Roman society. John Crook's *Law and Life of Rome* departed from the usual presentation of Roman law in an attempt — most successful on the whole — to relate the laws to the broader social context in which they applied. There are indications that other Roman law scholars are becoming inter-ested in 'using the institutions of the law to enlarge understanding of the society and bringing the evidence of the social and economic facts to bear on the rules of law' (Crook 1967b:7), and this is to be warmly welcomed. Crook's chapters below continue in this vein, and Dixon and Lacey make considerable use of legal evidence in wider contexts.

There will always be a need to investigate the wider field of behaviour where law is irrelevant or ignored. Through no fault of the legal writers themselves, their books have tended to confirm the partial picture of Roman society presented in more general books. The law code is of necessity much concerned with delicts, and matters such as divorce and disputes over dowry and inheritance figure largely. In particular, Augustus's legislation to punish adultery, celibacy and childlessness has been given, perhaps, undue prominence in discussions of Roman society. The 'informal' Roman marriage has also been misinterpreted. Thus the stereotype of a disintegrating family structure has found some support here. Moreover, Rome's law, like its literature, is largely concerned with the upper classes, and this has coloured many of the works referred to above. Those writers who have tried to take some account of the lower classes have seldom had an intimate enough knowledge of the relevant evidence and have thus drawn false conclusions.[4] A considerable amount of specialised work on inscriptions especially, and on the implications of the form of the Roman name for social class and family relationships has been done in recent years and it is to be hoped that the effects of this work will soon appear in more general and accessible books.[5] Chapters 6–8 below are based on this kind of evidence.

In one particular respect, there has been valuable work being done on the Roman family for many years. The close interrelation between family relationships and political groupings has been recognised since early in the twentieth century. In 1912 Matthias Gelzer published *Die Nobilität der römischen Republik* (translated into English in 1969), in the Preface to which he wrote that he had 'tried to investigate more closely the composition of the ruling class and the foundations of its predominance'. Seeds in this book germinated into Friedrich Münzer's *Römische Adelsparteien und Adelsfamilien* (1920), a much fuller study of the interrelationship between families and political factions in the Roman nobility. Since then (but, in English, especially since the publication in 1939 of Ronald Syme's *Roman Revolution*) there has been an important and fruitful school of 'family history' (often called prosopography) which has interpreted much of the public life of ancient Rome in terms of marriage alliances and the extended family. This has been given impetus because of certain aspects of political life at Rome: there were no political parties in our sense; political groupings were fluid and changing, and yet there do seem to have been stable cores. It has proved an attractive hypothesis to explain these cores in terms of family alliances, and in spite of attacks on the more extreme exponents of this approach it is an interpretation of Roman history which is now fully established. This kind of family history must inevitably, however, deal only with the upper classes — those with direct political influence. It is now generally recognised that social class can have an important effect on the nature of the family in any society: what is true for one class is not necessarily true for another. The very concept of class, however, is seldom unambiguous, and in Roman society the juridical hierarchy of status — freeborn (including senators, equestrians and ordinary plebeians), freed (i.e. ex-slave) and slave — is not always synonymous with that of power or prestige.[6]

Not only social class but time and place can be determinants of family structure and behaviour. This chapter will limit itself to a period of approximately three centuries: the last century BC and the first two centuries AD.[7] (The Republican period is usually taken as ending about 31 BC. The period following is known as the Principate, or Imperial period — when one man, the *princeps* or emperor, controlled the Roman world.) As a result, specifically Christian evidence will not be discussed. Although Christian families were already in Rome by the middle of the first century AD, their influence was slight: Rome was essentially a non-Christian society in the period to be discussed. The bulk of Christian evidence does not pre-date the fourth century. Discussion will also be focused on the city of Rome. Although Rome's law and many of her customs were widely adopted in the rest of Italy, there are essential social differences between an urban, cosmopolitan centre of up to 1½ million people and smaller rural centres.[8] The formal structure of the Roman family can be taken to apply to the rest of ancient Italy, and many Romans travelled frequently between Rome and other Italian towns. But individual behaviour and experience may have varied considerably for city and country people: life in the country was probably simpler than in the city; diversions and material facilities were fewer; slave numbers and proportions appear to have been lower.

General Features

In view of what has been said above, and of other factors which influence some part of a population more than other parts, it may seem foolhardy to speak of 'the Roman family' as such. Nevertheless, some general features do emerge from a variety of evidence, and these can be set out here and used as a framework for the more detailed accounts that follow. These general features can be assumed to apply in some sense to all members of Roman society unless the contrary is stated. But it should often be obvious that the economic and political motivation for some aspects would have been lacking in the lower classes. For instance, the senior male probably commanded a certain respect in his family at all levels of society; but in poor families and some mixed marriages he may not have had the economic power or legal status to exert much influence. Moreover, the considerable social mobility of Rome's population probably made many members aware of Augustus's regulation of mixed marriages; but poor and humble families are not likely to have feared the penalties or looked for the rewards of Augusts's legislation on marriage and child-producing. Nor is it likely that a concern for inheritance complicated their family structure, nor would the hope of political power dictate the contracting and dissolving of their marriages.

The nuclear family was small, but what the Romans meant by a *familia* could be much larger. The Roman *familia* consisted of the conjugal family plus dependants (i.e. a man, his wife, and their unmarried children, together with the slaves and sometimes freedmen and foster-children who lived in the same household). It was not an extended or joint family (i.e. it did not normally include more remote relatives or several conjugal groups or even several generations of the stem family).

The formal head of the legally recognised family, the *paterfamilias*, was the oldest surviving male ascendant, and his authority over his descendants lasted until his death, unless formally dissolved by a legal act.

Thus women and grown children could have a very inferior legal status. In practice, they enjoyed considerable independence.

Women remained members of their family of origin, in some senses, even after marriage.

There appears to have been (at least in the upper classes) some conflict between marriage ideals and practice, and some tension between male and female expectations.

Marriage and the natural family unit retained their importance, despite the frequency of broken families (through death, divorce or slave conditions).

The moral legislation passed by Augustus continued to have considerable influence on upper-class families, even if it failed in its primary purpose.

Legitimate children belonged to their father's family and bore his family name. Illegitimate children belonged to their mother's family and bore her family name (if she had one).

Extra-family groups and influences sometimes replaced the functions of the family.

Education and family influences interacted to sustain the strength of family traditions.

The continuance of the family name (the *nomen*) was of great importance.

Size and Membership

The term *familia* could, in its widest sense, refer to all persons (and property) under the control (*patria potestas*) of the head of the family (*paterfamilias*). More often, however, it referred to a household, and this was normally the conjugal family plus dependants (who were not usually blood relations). The size of the *familia* varied greatly, depending largely on the wealth of the head of the household. For rich and poor, in Republic and Principate, the nuclear family was generally small; anything more than two or three children (who survived infancy) excited comment. In the second century BC, Cornelia, the mother of the Gracchi brothers, bore 12 children to her husband but only three survived into adulthood (Plutarch, *Tiberius Gracchus* 1). In the Principate, Augustus's daughter Julia bore five children to Agrippa, and one of them (Agrippina senior) bore nine children to Germanicus, of whom six survived. The fertility (or political fortunes) of this branch of the imperial family declined, however, and the one child of Agrippina junior, the emperor Nero, died without leaving an heir. Most of the emperors of the first two centuries of the Principate urged on the Romans the virtues of large families, but none of them set a personal example until Marcus Aurelius, who fathered at least 12 children for his wife Faustina, although few of these survived to adulthood. The one surviving son, Commodus, was the first 'natural' heir in the imperial house for nearly a century. Epitaphs of lower-class families seldom record more than two children.

That one of the purposes of marriage, indeed the primary purpose, was to produce children is frequently attested in the ancient sources. The phrase *'liberorum quaerendum gratia'* ('for the purpose of producing children') recurs often enough, with minor variations, to suggest that it was a legal or ritual formula. From an early period of the Republic, the phrase appears to have been part of a citizen's declaration to the censors, i.e. that he would marry to produce children.[9] In the first century BC, Sulla divorced his third wife (Cloelia) for infertility (Plutarch, *Sulla* 6.11). It was an 'honourable discharge' for Cloelia, who left Sulla's house with praise and gifts; but no one suggested that Sulla was behaving dishonourably in making childbirth a condition of marriage.[10] (Some were sceptical, however, as to whether this was his genuine motive for the divorce, for he married another woman, Metella, very soon afterwards.) A whole range of rewards and penalties was intended by various regimes to encourage child-rearing and to discourage celibacy. For instance, Julius Caesar's laws of 59 BC made land available to fathers of three or more children as well as to Pompey's veterans. Cicero felt that in a well-run state the censors should forbid celibacy, and in 46 BC he urged Caesar to use his autocratic powers to encourage larger families.[11] In the latter context, Cicero seems to have seen a falling birth rate as one of many social ills of the late Republic that lawcourts should turn their attention to.[12]

Augustus carried through legislation in 18 BC and again in AD 9 (the *lex Iulia de maritandis ordinibus* and the *lex Papia Poppaea*) to give political preference to fathers of three or more children, and to impose political and financial liabilities on childless couples and unmarried persons over the age of 20 (for women) or 25 (for men).[13] When a case was referred to him in which a woman's sons claimed that to spite them she had remarried in advanced age (beyond childbearing age) and had then died leaving all her property to her new husband, Augustus had ruled that her will should be cancelled. The sons could claim her estate, and the husband could not keep her dowry 'because the marriage had not taken place for the purpose of producing children'.[14] Emperors after Augustus, for at least a century, felt it desirable to keep his legislation in effect, and Pliny the Younger's gratitude for being exempted from the requirements by the Emperor Trajan suggests that such exemptions were not lightly given.[15] The legislation seems not to have been successful, in that there is no evidence of an increased birth rate in the upper classes — on the contrary, many families are known to have died out.[16] Equestrians had made a public protest to Augustus in AD 9; and in AD 20 Tiberius had found it necessary to relax the laws to some extent,[17] but they were nevertheless taken seriously (i.e. they were not a dead letter). They inspired all kinds of ingenuity to circumvent them.[18]

Trajan extended his concern for the rearing of families to humbler members of society than those aimed at by Augustus's laws.[19] In Rome, he allowed all children from birth to be registered on the lists for free and subsidised grain distributions (Pliny, *Panegyricus* 26.3, 27.1); in Italian country towns, he organised an 'alimentary' (child endowment) scheme which used the interest paid by farmers on state loans for the support of local children. Again, it is doubtful if this scheme achieved its aims — either to rehabilitate agriculture or to encourage larger families — but it continued to operate for many years (see references in Chapter 2). Antoninus Pius created a special fund for girls of poor families to honour his wife Faustina senior: the beneficiaries were the *puellae Faustinianae*. This institution was expanded by Marcus Aurelius in honour of his wife, Faustina junior, when she died.[20] Roman coinage of the second century AD was used to advertise widely the alimentary programme and the ideals of Roman motherhood often in association with women of the imperial family.[21]

This concern on the part of Roman governments to encourage larger families, through at least two centuries, especially in the upper classes, is consistent with other evidence that families were in fact small and that many did not perpetuate themselves. Many reasons have been suggested for this. One theme that recurs in Latin literature is that wives are difficult and therefore men do not care much for marriage. This was referred to by a censor as early as the second century BC. He urged the senate to make marriage compulsory in order to increase the birth rate,[22] conceding that if men could live without marriage they would gladly be free of the troubles it brought:

> Since, however, nature has ordained that we cannot have a really harmonious life with our wives but that we cannot have any sort of life at all without them, we ought to consider our long-term welfare rather than brief pleasure.

Some felt that this was too frank an admission of the difficulties of marriage, but others felt that this established the censor's credibility better than a rosy picture would have. Augustus was impressed enough with this speech, which had been preserved, to read it out to the senate as support for his own legislation to encourage marriage. Its recommendation appears to have enjoyed no less chilly a reception at its second delivery. Augustus was also subjected to a noisy demonstration by husbands pressing him to reveal his claimed secret of keeping his own wife in control. One is tempted to reject these expressions of hostility to marriage or wives as a time-worn cliché,[23] but we shall see later that there was some tension between the ideals (set by men?) for marriage and the actual practice and expectations of women. Women's protests against their social conditions had already begun by the beginning of the second century BC: they organised a successful demonstration for the repeal of anti-luxury legislation (the Oppian law) in 195 BC. They may also have begun to rebel against motherhood as their only role.

Other reasons suggested for a low birth rate have included biological weaknesses, lead poisoning, poor medical standards, political repression, financial greed, poverty and the liberation of women.[24] Most of these presuppose that Romans had the knowledge and means to limit the size of their families if they wished, although there must have been a considerable degree of involuntary childlessness. A textbook by Soranus (*Gynaecology*) which survives from the second century AD gives advice on contraception as well as on conception and the care of infants. Recent studies (see Bibliography under 'Medicine') have shown in detail that various methods of contraception were known at Rome; and Chapter 9 below also discusses this. In addition infant mortality was probably high,[25] and the practice of 'exposing', or abandoning, newborn babies never disappeared — there was no general legal sanction against it. (Some abandoned children were rescued and raised by foster-parents. Chapters 7 and 8 discuss some of the implications of this.)

Men who had no children or whose children failed to live to adulthood sometimes compensated for this by adopting a son from another family to continue the family and to observe the various family rites when the father had died. Most of the adoptive sons of whom we know were already adult at the time of adoption: by then, chances of survival were greater and the adopting father could see what he was getting as a son and heir. Most of the emperors of the first two centuries AD had to rely on adoption to secure themselves an heir: in the period AD 14–200, only Claudius, Vespasian and Marcus Aurelius were survived by natural sons (and Claudius's son Britannicus was soon murdered by Claudius's adoptive son, Nero).

By contrast with the generally small number of descendants in a household, the number of slaves could be very large. As the Principate developed, the imperial household (the *familia Caesaris*) became probably the biggest in Rome, providing a great diversity of services to the state and to the emperor and his family personally. Other wealthy Romans might own hundreds of slaves.[26] (These large households were not usually housed under one roof but were scattered over a number of properties, engaged in labouring or small industrial work as well as in domestic or clerical service.) If a man were exiled he could often take up to 20 slaves with him (e.g. Dio 56.27.3), in addition to any members of his immediate family who chose to go with him:[27] men important enough to be exiled were often conceded the right to a certain standard of living, and this involved a not negligible *familia*. Most modest households might have only one or two slaves (Westermann 1955:88–9). It is striking, however, how often epitaphs attest slaves belonging to humble people, often ex-slaves themselves.

Slaves in most households could have good hopes of winning their freedom and becoming Roman citizens. The law set a minimum age of 30 for full manumission, but special circumstances could lead to an exemption, and there are many very young freedmen attested. Some of these had probably been *vernae*, home-bred slaves who were often raised with the master's child(ren) and had a privileged position (see Chapter 7 below). Freedmen still had certain obligations to their ex-master (now their patron) (Duff 1928:ch.3; Treggiari 1969:68–81). Some continued to live in their patron's house, as did Tiro, Cicero's secretary, after receiving free status.[28] Others presumably established separate households, but the bond with their patron's house continued — more or less close depending on the personal and economic relations between patron and freedman. An outward sign of this bond was the family name (the *nomen*) which the freedman derived from his or her ex-master: Tiro, the slave of Marcus Tullius Cicero, became Marcus Tullius Tiro on manumission. The family name was public evidence of freedom and Roman citizenship, and freed persons and their descendants would help to pass on that name to future generations. Sometimes freedmen were the only members of a family who survived to perpetuate the family name. The privilege often accorded them of being buried in the family tomb was also a responsibility — they and their descendants were expected to maintain the commemorative rites due at the tomb at regular intervals.

The name which an ex-slave took on achieving freedom indicated in another way, too, the relationship with ex-master. To use Tiro once again as our example, he became Marcus Tullius Marci libertus Tiro (usually abbreviated to M. Tullius M. lib. Tiro), i.e. Marcus Tullius Tiro, freedman of Marcus (Cicero). The formal name of Cicero's son was Marcus Tullius Marci filius Marci nepos Cornelia (tribu) Cicero (usually abbreviated to M. Tullius M. f. M. n. Cor. Cicero), i.e. Marcus Tullius Cicero, son of Marcus, grandson of Marcus, of the Cornelian tribe.[29] A slave had no father in the eyes of the law, so his patron's name took the place of a father's when he became a citizen. That the patron–freedman relationship was similar to that of father and child is revealed in many ways: their responsibilities to each other (e.g. Ulpian in D.37.15.9), the terms of epitaphs dedicated by one to the other, and the explicit use of *parens* to apply to a patron (Wilkinson 1964). The relationship was not always one of warmth and trust, of course — nor was it for fathers and sons or daughters.

In addition to the conjugal family, slaves and some freedmen, there were sometimes other dependent members of a *familia*. The role of 'foster-children', in particular of *alumni* and *vernae*, is discussed in Chapter 7 below. Some instances are known of several conjugal families living under the one roof, but they seem to have been rare. Cicero saw the family unit as married couple, children, a single household (*De officiis* 1.53). There were also, he said, bonds between other relatives (e.g. brothers and cousins), but as these could not be accommodated in a single house they would form households of their own, 'like colonies'. The Roman concept of family could sometimes include such an extended family, and this network could serve useful political and social purposes.[30] But it was not the normal household, in the city at least.[31] The examples of Crassus's family[32] and the Aelii[33] seem to have had short-term financial implications. Caesar's father died when Caesar was 16, but his mother seems to have been living in his house 20 years later, long after he was married.[34] The fate of widows and elderly and other relatives should be further investigated. Grandparents, who have often played an important role in the later European family, seem not to be prominent in the Roman family. Was this due only to an early death for most grandparents? The rarity of joint or extended families in Roman society may help to explain the apparent ease with which the powers of the formal head of the family continued to operate. If adult sons or daughters and their children had lived in the same household as the *paterfamilias*, they may well have found the constant awareness of his powers and position a great strain. With separate households, however, this kind of role conflict did not exist: the father and the mother had virtually complete authority in their own establishment.

Roman marriage was monogamous, so there was only one woman in the household whose role was wife to the head and mother to his children. A husband might well take what pleasures he could get from his female slaves, but he could not set a woman up in the rather special role of concubine in his house while he had a wife living. A concubine's position, though inferior to that of a legal wife, was considered comparable to it in many ways.[35] After Augustus's marriage legislation,[36] members of senatorial families could not marry persons of freed status. Thus the women with whom the Emperors Vespasian, Antoninus Pius and Marcus Aurelius formed enduring relationships after their wives' deaths were concubines and not wives.[37] These relationships were public and the women enjoyed considerable prestige, even honour. (The fact that Domitian resented his father's concubine (Suetonius, *Domitian* 12) need not be related to her status. She was in the place of a stepmother to him and such relationships were often strained — see below.)

Concubines are frequently attested in lower classes of society, and we cannot always be sure why the couple lived in this relationship rather than marriage, especially when the most common form of marriage involved no essential ceremonial and was based on enduring cohabitation. The slave status of at least one partner when the relationship began must, however, account for most of these unions. At least there is no incontrovertible evidence of two free citizens choosing concubinage rather than marriage when there was no legal impediment to their marrying.[38] Concubinage, a *de facto* marriage, seems to have followed the monogamous nature of marriage. The concept of adultery could be applied to it (although a man did not have a husband's rights of prosecution of his guilty partner, but could bring a suit in another capacity: Ulpian in D.48.5.14 pr.), and many such relationships were of long duration. There are a few instances recorded at Rome of a *ménage à trois*, but these are rare.[39]

Thus the Roman household was usually quite small, providing an opportunity for close relations between its members. The prime public purpose of marriage continued to be the procreation of children, but many families did not produce sufficient children to perpetuate themselves. This enabled the membership of the more numerous slaves and freedmen to assume a special importance. The small number of children and the monogamous nature of marriage must also have heightened the conjugal couple's consciousness of themselves as spouses rather than parents.

Relationships between Members

The various relationships within the Roman family (husband–wife, father–son, father–daughter, mother–son, mother–daughter, between brothers and sisters and between all of these and other dependants) have received unequal attention from Roman historians, and we need to know much more about all of them. The account below will show that the aspects which have been most treated have been those of husband–wife relations and of the male head's role.

The wide powers of the family head (i.e. the oldest surviving male ascendant) have provoked surprise, even disbelief, in modern readers. But there is no denying the formal situation.[40] We must therefore look at what this formal position was and then see what limitations operated against this in actual practice. The virtually absolute power of the head (the *paterfamilias*) over the rest of his household may have been necessary or desirable in early days when the state had no regular courts or police force and did not much involve itself in private morality. The head's power of life and death over his dependants may have continued, at least in theory, into the Principate.[41] A Republican *cause célèbre* (Livy 39.18) was the execution of many people involved in the Bacchanalian excesses of 186 BC. Women who were found guilty of involvement were handed over to family councils for infliction of the death penalty; only those women who were not legal dependants of anyone were executed by the state. The household head almost always consulted a family council before deciding how to use his powers, and the state was often glad to leave responsibility for women, minors and slaves to such a body. Even after Augustus had made adultery a public offence, the next emperor, Tiberius, allowed family councils in some circumstances[42] to take the necessary action against their immoral women members ('matronas prostratas pudicitiae'), in accordance with ancestral custom, and there is evidence that such councils continued to operate later.[43]

The extent of the power of the *paterfamilias* is further illustrated by the fact that Tiberius himself was in his mid-40s and the father of an adult son when he was adopted by Augustus. In becoming a member of Augustus's family, Tiberius not only gave up his Claudian name for the Julian one but passed absolutely under Augustus's authority (his *patria potestas*). This involved his surrender of all financial independence (Suetonius, *Tiberius* 15). There were particular political reasons operative here because of the importance of having the prospective heir to imperial power formally and absolutely in the Julian family. But in all families the head retained full powers over the family property and, irrespective of age, his children could own nothing in their own right (unless positive, complicated legal action had been taken to alter this for a particular individual, and there is no evidence that this was normally done). Moreover, in property matters there is no evidence that the head was expected to consult a family council before making decisions.

This state of dependence did not impede a man's political career. He could rise to the highest office in Rome even if he was not technically the head of his own family. Clearly, practice must have been much more liberal than the letter of the law. We certainly know of adult young men living apparently free and affluent lives. Caelius, defended by Cicero in 56 BC on a charge of attempted murder, was a well-known, perhaps notorious man-about-town.[44] He lived away from his father's home in an expensive apartment on the Palatine hill. Although Caelius must have been at least 32 years old at the time of his trial, Cicero felt obliged to explain Caelius's bachelor apartment on the grounds that Caelius's family home was too far from the forum for political convenience (*Pro Caelio* 17). Probably Caelius received an annual allowance from his father,[45] as aristocratic young men in Europe often did before it became more acceptable to take paid employment. In the early Principate, a young man was receiving such an allowance.[46] The word for this allowance — *peculium* — was also applied to the 'pocket-money' which slaves were allowed to acquire: in both cases, the money technically belonged to the *paterfamilias*, but the son, daughter or slave had considerable freedom in administering it.[47] The financial role of the *paterfamilias* may have contributed greatly to a cohesiveness of father–son public views: a generation gap is hardly possible in such circumstances. From the political point of view, as Daube has observed, it must have affected campaigns for public office, especially in Republican times: if the *paterfamilias* held the purse-strings, 'It is difficult to conceive of a more powerful brake on any deviation from traditional family politics' (1969:83). When a son prosecuted his father in AD 24 it made a deep and shocking impression ('exemplum atrox': Tacitus, *Annals* 4.28), even though the charge was treason and the son could claim to be doing his public duty.

It should be obvious that most of the above concerns only the propertied classes. The situations where members of the lower classes were affected by such legal powers must have been fairly rare (e.g. choice of a spouse). Moreover, before we attach too much importance to the wide religious, financial and disciplinary powers which a family head had over his descendants until the day he died, we should remember that many men did not live long into their children's adulthood.[48] We need to examine systematically the age of death of Roman fathers, and how many fathers are known surviving when their sons are mature adults. Moreover, in the lower classes there were many fatherless families, where the mother had the real responsibility for raising her children and thus acquired the *de facto* power, prestige and worries of a head of household.[49]

A father's relationship with his daughter[50] was similar in many ways to that with his son (but see below for differences from the time of the coming of age ceremony). Although the birth of a son probably gave many fathers especial pride and joy, as it does many fathers in many societies today, and although sons could follow in their father's footsteps in public life more closely than could girls, there seems to have been parity of esteem for sons and daughters in most respects. Perhaps at the humblest levels of society, if a parent had doubts about being able to raise a newborn child, a daughter was more likely to be abandoned than a son, but it is difficult to know how often this actually happened; there is no clear evidence of a serious imbalance of the sexes in the Roman population.[51]

Daughters could not pass on the family name to their offspring (although in the imperial period there was a growing tendency for children to incorporate their mother's name as well as their father's into their own name or to adopt simply the maternal name),[52] but they retained their own family name for life. Women did not change their family name on marriage, and in the so-called 'free', or informal, marriage (which was the most common in our period) women remained members of their own *familia* in a very real sense (see below). Daughters had always had equal rights with sons to a share of the family property if the father died intestate. In the second century BC legislation was introduced (e.g. the Voconian law of 169 BC) to limit women's rights of inheritance. It was aimed at comparatively wealthy families, and presumably sprang from a fear that too much property was passing into women's hands. This fear may have been motivated partly by the recurrent charge that extravagance was getting out of hand and that women were the leaders in that trend; but it was probably also motivated by concern that any family property that went to women would probably be passed on to another family name. But well-loved daughters and only daughters were frequent enough for Romans to find a number of ways of circumventing the law. Legacies, dowries and other forms of transmitting property resulted in some very wealthy women in the late Republic and in the Principate, and by then they were also able to bequeath their wealth fairly freely. This made older women, especially if they were widowed and childless, very vulnerable to 'legacy-hunters', those fawning, self-seeking opportunists recorded so frequently in imperial literature.[53]

Wives were not completely dependent financially on their husbands, especially when their marriage was of the most common form, 'sine manu' (i.e. the wife did not come under her husband's complete authority — his *manus*). He was accountable for the money or property which she brought as dowry, and this was usually reclaimable by the wife if the marriage was dissolved. She might also have other property put at her disposal by her father, and even if she remained technically under her father's authority this was probably not very effective — financially or otherwise — when she lived in a different household. Moreover, there were various means by which a woman could free herself from the financial supervision of any man. One of the most important of these was the *ius liberorum*: a freeborn woman got her financial independence by bearing three children, and a freedwoman if she bore four.

As noted above, the form of marriage most common in the late Republic and in imperial times was the so-called 'free' marriage in which the woman remained under the authority of her original *paterfamilias* (if he was still alive), or remained independent and did not come under her husband's formal authority. This meant that in some sense she did not belong to her husband's *familia*. She certainly did not become an agnatic member of his family, and thus was (at least formally) excluded from the group that included their joint children and her husband's father and other agnates.[54] One might expect this to mean that she could not fully share in the family religious rites of her conjugal home. We know too little of the detailed practice of these rites to assess what importance this would have had, but it seems unlikely that the Roman woman, if she was closely associated with her husband's and children's lives in other respects, should have been excluded in any real sense from family 'worship' (whatever this entailed).[55] Her links with her husband's

family were probably strengthened once she had borne children
to the family, and if her marriage endured till her death and her
husband survived her he probably buried her in his family tomb.
(There are, however, examples of women buried in their father's
family's tomb, and the legal responsibility for burial seems to
have depended on whether the woman's father or husband had
rights to the dowry. It may be fruitful to examine systematically
the place of burial of wives to see if there is enough evidence to
allow a generalisation on this matter.[56])

There were three forms of marriage which could bring the wife
under her husband's full authority — *confarreatio, coemptio* and
usus.[57] These were comparatively rare during our period, but
confarreatio, which involved an elaborate ritual, continued to be
the required form of marriage for holders of certain religious
offices — they must be born of such a marriage and any marriage
of their own must be of this type (Gaius *Inst.* 1.112; cf. Corbett
1930:76). Since men continued to be found (though with
difficulty) to fill these offices, some couples must have continued
to marry in this way, perhaps for the specific purpose of making
their sons eligible for these priesthoods. In some families there
seems to have been a tradition of holding such office in successive
generations. A close examination of all the known holders of
such office may tell us more about this kind of family and this
form of marriage. It would be interesting to know if those
members of the imperial family who were patricians contracted
confarreatio marriages, or if all imperial marriages were at least
of the kind that brought the wife under her husband's *manus*.
Augustus might have been expected to favour such a form, with
its overtones of ancient tradition and wifely obedience. The
emperor's role was, moreover, partly that of religious leader of
his people (he regularly held the office of *pontifex maximus*), and
it may have been considered important that his wife, who
assumed an increasingly important public role, belong fully to the
imperial family. It has been suggested that the form of wives'
names, as recorded especially in inscriptions, can indicate *manus*
marriages.[58] This requires further investigation.

No marriage relied basically on any particular ceremony for its
validity. Cohabitation of eligible partners, accompanied by
'marital intention and regard', constituted marriage. 'If you lived
together "as" man and wife, man and wife you were' (Crook
1967b:101). But traditional ceremonies of betrothal and wedding

helped to establish marital intention and were frequently observed.

First marriages, at least, were normally arranged by the parents of the couple. Although these marriages must often have been intended to suit the interests or ambitions of the parents rather than the inclinations of the couple, the law required that when betrothal and marriage took place both partners should be old enough to understand the vows and both should consent. Since boys were normally older than girls at marriage (a five-year difference was probably most common[59]) and would already have begun some of the activities of a citizen, a son's wishes may have been taken more seriously than a daughter's. The grounds on which a daughter could withhold her consent were severely restricted: she had to claim (and prove?) that the proposed husband was of bad moral character. One suspects that sometimes the young rakes were more attractive potential partners to young women than were sounder, duller men, and that they would not necessarily withhold their consent from such matches. Cicero's daughter Tullia and her mother chose the dissolute Dolabella for Tullia's third husband when Cicero was safely out of the way in his province in 51 BC. Cicero probably disapproved, and foresaw the unhappiness that this marriage would bring his daughter, but he was a fond enough father to hope that the women's judgement would be justified.[60] Tullia had had two previous marriages arranged for her by her father, and they may have given her no reason to associate soundness of character with the ability to make a wife happy.

Moreover, at a girl's first betrothal she was probably very young and not in a strong position to press her preferences against those of her parents. The legal minimum age of marriage was 12 for girls and 14 for boys, and betrothal could take place some time before that: Augustus fixed the minimum age for betrothal at 10. In exceptional circumstances, such as the need to make dynastic arrangements in the imperial family, betrothal did sometimes take place in infancy. Claudius's daughter Octavia was only one or two-years-old when her engagement to Lucius Iunius Silanus was announced in AD 41 (the boy was probably in his early teens). But there was no question of contracting any sort of marriage until Octavia reached an age probably associated with puberty. In fact, several years later the engagement was broken because Claudius, a loving father, was persuaded that Silanus was morally corrupt (Tacitus, *Annals* 12.4). A new engagement was arranged (with the future emperor Nero), and the marriage took place four years later in AD 53, when Octavia was 13 or 14 years old.[61]

Whether or not such early marriages were common is a vexed question. Hopkins (1965a) believes that in the upper classes a girl's first marriage usually took place in the age range 11 to 17. Examples of considerably later marriages are easy to find, but it is still hard to establish what was normal. It is worth noting, however, that Augustus's laws did not begin to penalise young people for non-marriage until a girl was 20 and a man 25. Moreover, it is hard to accept Hopkins' argument that pre-pubertal marriages occurred and were acceptable.[62] The motivation (financial, social, political) for early marriage in the upper classes was no doubt strong. This was not necessarily true of poorer, less distinguished families. The child-endowment scheme which operated under Trajan in the early second century AD (the *alimenta*) provided state support for girls to the age of 14 and for boys to the age of 18, which suggests that children in needy families in Italian towns would not normally be married before those ages. The humblest epitaphs set up in Rome (the *sepulcrales*, in *CIL* 6), many of them for slaves or ex-slaves, reveal a wide age range for 'marriage',[63] but the biggest groups whose age of marriage is indicated belong to the range of 12 to 18 for women and 19 to 21 for men. Even if such unions were urged or fostered by a master solely for the purpose of producing more slave children for his household,[64] the partners often remained together for many years, not uncommonly after one or both had won their freedom; for instance, the names on the epitaph of Munatius Felicianus (*CIL* 6.22657) suggest that he and his wife, Munatia Aphrodite, and perhaps their son, Munatius Felicianus, were all ex-slaves of the one household. This appears to have been Munatia's first 'marriage': she had lived with her husband for 34 years, from girlhood ('a virginitate'), when he died at the age of 66. It seems that sometimes slave girls were taken into the care of older male slaves or freedmen in the same household with a view to marriage when the girls were old enough. (See Chapter 7 on Aurelia L. 1. Philematio (9499).)

Apart from the legal requirement (sometimes evaded) that two people could not marry before reaching a minimum age, there were other factors which could disqualify people from contracting a legal Roman marriage. Those affecting people in Rome were, in brief, non-citizenship; too close a degree of blood-relationship; social class, if one partner was of senatorial family and the other an ex-slave;[65] and guardianship of a ward (but only from the second century AD: Cicero married his young ward Publilia). In some of these situations, a *de facto* marriage was formed which borrowed many of its ideals and trappings from legal marriage. Any children born, however, were illegitimate and took their status (and *nomen* if the mother was a citizen) from their mother; the father had no legal rights over them. Such unions were often enduring and might continue into a time when the partners had obtained the right to marry legally. We have most evidence of this for slaves and ex-slaves. Slaves were continually passing into the ranks of citizens, and inter-'marriage' between slave and freed, freed and freeborn, was frequent. This great class mobility must have made for a continual exchange of social values. Emphasis has usually been placed on the influence which 'slave morality' had on other levels of Roman society;[66] but there are many signs that slaves and immigrants (often synonymous terms) were anxious to assimilate to Roman forms and practices as quickly as possible. They applied to their own unions much of the terminology of Roman family relations.[67] The personal names which they gave their children tended to be Roman rather than Greek or barbarian; they proudly advertised the Roman family name if they had the good fortune to acquire one; they proclaimed the standard Roman attributes on their tombstones (e.g. *piissimus, sanctissimus, bene merens, optimus*); and if they could afford sculpture for their tomb it often represented them in the pose and toga which were the mark of the great Romans whom they saw at public ceremonies or in representations on public monuments.[68]

Where both partners were slaves when a union began one might win freedom before the other; he or she might then be able to buy the freedom of the others. Or, if they belonged to the same household, the master might be disposed to make freedom a gift for one or both of them. Freedom normally brought with it automatic Roman citizenship, so that any children born of ex-slave parents after their manumission would be freeborn Roman citizens. Sometimes mixed marriages show several stages in the parents' changing status, and successive children could have different status from one another (and from their parents). In a regular Roman marriage, children took their status from that of their father at the time of their conception, otherwise they took their status from that of their mother at the time of their birth. Thus two slave parents would produce a slave child; if one partner were freed, there could still be no proper marriage, and a further child would be a slave if the mother had remained a slave, but freeborn (and illegitimate) if only the father were now a slave; if both parents finally won their freedom, any later children would be freeborn and legitimate. The possibility of such different status among parents, brothers and sisters must have encouraged much freedom of movement between different classes.

Imperial slaves and freedmen had a rather special status, and free women would not find unions or marriages with them beneath their dignity. (See Weaver, Chapter 6 below.) When Terentia Helpis (*CIL* 6.13025) 'married' Ariston, he was a slave and she either a slave or a freedwoman. By the time their first child was born, the mother was probably already free, and she was able to give her 'family' name (taken from her ex-master) to her daughter Terentia Ariste (commemorating the father in the girl's personal name). But then Ariston won his freedom from the emperor Marcus Aurelius and was able not only to call himself Marcus Aurelius Aug(usti) lib(ertus) Ariston but was able to confer the Aurelian name on his next two children, who were legitimate freeborn Roman citizens, Aurelia M(arci) f(ilia) Egloge and Marcus Aurelius M(arci) f(ilius) Ariston.

Mixed marriages were not always able to endure, especially if the partners belonged to different households. The children of such unions were often sold into another house at an early age — e.g. when Antestia Glycera (*CIL* 6.11924) died at the age of three she had already been separated from her natural parents, Alius Potitus and Munatia Paulina, neither of whom had had the status to give her a family name at her birth. By the time the child died, all three had obtained their freedom, but in different households. This illustrates the obstacles in the way of 'normal' family life for people who belonged to, or were just moving out of, the slave class.

Although we know a good deal of the ceremonies and legal status of marriage, it is difficult to assess what the Roman couple's expectations of married life would have been. From literature and epitaphs, we know something of the standard virtues attributed to ideal husbands and wives (e.g. Lattimore 1942; Williams 1958), and from imperial propaganda (e.g. coins) and the law code we can deduce what virtues the state hoped to inculcate in their married citizens; but it is hard to know how much more than clichés or wishful thinking these usually were. We have seen the public importance attached to child-bearing, but also the private unwillingness (or inability) to have many children. Moreover, there is a tension between the ideal of fecundity on the one hand and the status of the Vestal Virgins on the other.[69] Some women of the imperial family were identified with the Vestal Virgins even when they were already mothers, or their husbands hoped very much that they would bear children.[70] Vestal Virgins had an important public role in Roman society — not only religious, but also political and probably economic.[71] They came from distinguished families, their persons were sacrosanct, they were freed from their father's power, and they enjoyed front seats at public entertainment, high precedence in public processions, liberal property rights, and they were free to marry, if they wished, after their term of service (when they would be nearly 40 years of age).[72] The qualities of Castitas and Pudicitia which are often advertised are especially appropriate to vestal virgins, but apply not only to the chastity of a virgin but also to marital fidelity.[73] Yet laws against adultery were felt necessary, and divorce was frequent.[74] Domestic virtues were often praised by upper-class writers, but upper-class women had plentiful slave labour and were more likely frequently out of their homes to visit friends, to attend festivals or poetry readings, or to buy at expensive shops.[75] Was the gap between ideal and practice so great and, if so, were spouses disillusioned or is this what they knew to expect and accept? They surely did not expect marriage to be a life-long union (their own observations would contradict this), but did they regret this? It is arguable (though not a popular view) that easy divorce is a sign of a healthy society: intolerable bonds can be severed and personal freedom protected. In a Christian society, there are religious factors which induce guilt about divorce. Were there any such factors for the Romans?[76]

It may, of course, be the fragmentary nature of our evidence that gives such a picture of inconsistencies between ideal and practice. As has nearly always been true of historical writing and literature until recent times, the notorious, the flamboyant and the upper class dominate our records. Moreover, the women of Rome have themselves written almost nothing that remains for posterity: our evidence, already distorted for so many other reasons, has the further limitation that it almost all derives from men (Finley 1968). We know what qualities Pliny thought desirable in a husband for his friend Junius Mauricus's niece;[77] we know nothing of the girl's reaction to these. Did she have another set of priorities (which perhaps would find fulfilment in adultery later)? If so, through what conditioning did she acquire these? Through education, through the example of parents and friends, through public entertainment, through private works of art?[78]

Analogies are frequently made today between women's position in our society and that of deprived minorities. In one respect at least the analogy holds for Rome: for both women and the lower classes, it is only through their epitaphs that we have any record composed by themselves. Women who predeceased their husbands were probably not the authors of epitaphs about themselves, and the virtues listed for them tell us more about husbands' ideals than about wives' practice. But there are a great many epitaphs which have clearly been set up, paid for and, I believe, composed by women who had lost husbands, children or other close ones. The sentiments expressed are usually as commonplace, even trite, as those in other epitaphs, e.g. 'to my well-deserving husband', 'to my sweet, well-deserving husband', 'to my dear husband', 'to my well-deserving husband with whom I lived without a quarrel', and 'to my dutiful and well-deserving son' (*CIL* 6.17657, 17745, 17848, 17856, 17850), and cannot tell us much about wives' real expectations in marriage. The very fact, however, of a woman's responsibility for such a duty, and her role often as the single parent, tell us something of her status in the family.

The apparent conflict between ideal and practice in married life ought to be more closely examined. Writers on modern marriage often blame unrealistic ideals for difficulties which spouses, especially wives, experience. Both men and women seem responsible for fostering 'the romantic ideal' of marriage, but it is apparently wives who have suffered most disappointment when everyday marriage has failed to conform to that ideal. In Rome, it may have been the husbands who were disappointed when their wives declined to assume the limited, domestic role that they were told had been that of their ancestors. This concept of a wife's role may have been transmitted and fostered by the men, for the same reasons of self-interest and self-protection which have often made modern western men resist women's attempts to break out of the mould. This could help to explain the note of hostility to women and marriage that is expressed by men in Latin literature from time to time. Moreover, Roman men's commitment to a supposed older ideal which women found unsatisfactory could have resulted in spouses' sexual dissatisfaction with each other. In their search for a different kind of relationship some women resorted not only to adultery but also to unions or marriages with men of inferior social status, despite the fact that the law (made by men) frowned on some of these relationships. We cannot say how frequent they were, but there is evidence that they occurred and that women thus refused to accept 'traditional' standards of propriety.[79] The hypothesis of such tensions between male and female ideals and aspirations might be profitably explored, for, apart from its obvious influence on marital relations, such a situation could also affect many other areas of society (e.g. children's experience, men's public actions and attitudes, and literature). But the paucity of evidence from the female side may make it impossible to test the hypothesis thoroughly.

Records of specific actions can yield some evidence — if only indirectly — about the relationship and attitudes between husbands and wives. In AD 21 there was a debate in the senate as to whether wives should be banned from accompanying husbands during their terms as provincial governors (Tacitus, *Annals* 3.33-4). The men were overwhelmingly against the motion for banning.[80] The presence of wives had been rare in Republican times when tours of duty were normally no more than a year long, but from the early Principate longer terms became the norm and husbands felt the benefit of their wives' companionship. As one of the senators in the debate expressed it,

It is a good thing, a cause for rejoicing, that much of the ancient harshness [towards women] has changed. . . . Wives share most aspects of life with their husbands, and that is no impediment to peace [in the provinces]. Certainly, war must be waged by soldiers without encumbrance; but when they come home after their efforts what more honourable comforts can they enjoy than those provided by a wife? . . . Surely it would be a mistake, because of the weak character of a few husbands [who cannot control their wives], to deprive husbands in general of their wives, their partners in prosperity and adversity — and at the same time to have them leave behind the weaker sex, exposed to its own extravagance and others' desires.

He argued that broken marriages were less likely to occur if husbands kept their wives near them rather than left them on their own for years at a time.

There were probably reasons of official convenience in having the governors' wives with them as hostesses.[81] But the sentiments expressed in Tacitus's account of the senatorial debate above, and the known instances of devoted wives of governors or military commanders,[82] suggest that the concept of 'togetherness' was not altogether hollow or absent. It is not easy to discover how often children accompanied such parents out of Italy. We know that Agrippina senior and Germanicus often had some of their young children with them abroad; but others of their children remained at Rome, presumably with relatives. The children of a middle-aged governor or commander might well be married before his appointment. As for husband–wife relations in the lower classes, we have seen that there are many examples of a couple beginning a liaison in slave days, when marriage was impossible, but remaining together, or rejoining each other, after they had both won freedom: they needed quite strong motivation to see to it that they spent the rest of their lives together. In the special — but quite frequent — situation of a freedwoman freed by her patron for the purpose of their marrying, the woman could not leave him for another union unless he gave his consent. This must have imposed strains on some marriages and made this class of wife particularly disadvantaged in a time of easily-dissolved unions.[83]

Roman upper-class men were reasonably cultivated: they had well-developed literary interests (many were amateur writers themselves); they put considerable effort into polishing and shaping the speeches which they were frequently called on to make; they liked to be surrounded by what they considered fine sculpture, paintings, *objets d'art*, architecture and gardens, and many of them enjoyed good musical performances. There is an intellectual content to much of this, which is enhanced by sharing and exchanging views on it with others of similar interests. There was no class of educated courtesans at Rome corresponding to the Athenian *hetairai*, but we know that upper-class women of good family could be well and widely educated (see below) and that they could attend most of the social functions attended by their husbands.[84] This domestic, bourgeois intellectual life was no doubt not always on a high level, and it may have had varying effects on different areas of Rome's artistic production. One could hypothesise that talking to one's wife about the best (i.e. the most beautiful and most functional) architecture can lead a man to commission an excellent building; but talking to her about poetry may not inspire him to write great love poems. In fact, Rome's great love poetry was all written in the late Republic and very early Principate, when women were already literate and cultivated but when most upper-class men were still preoccupied with politics and public affairs and were frequently absent in the provinces. The love poetry written then was probably almost all inspired by adulterous affairs with temporarily deserted, upper-class wives. Later, husbands were less fully committed to public affairs, or took their wives to the provinces with them, and love poetry at Rome died.

Husbands may not write good love poetry — not to their wives, anyway — but an expression of conjugal love that might well be called 'poetical' has been preserved on a long epitaph inscribed about 8–2 BC to a woman who has come to be called Turia. (In fact, the top of the stone has been broken off, and we do not know who the wife actually was: she has become a kind of symbolic unknown wife.[85]) It cannot be dismissed as merely a conventional tribute to the dead. It deserves to be read in full to make its impact felt. It is full of circumstantial detail about the trials and fortitude of a woman caught up in the civil wars at the end of the Republican period. Her husband tells of her devotion to his cause during these difficult times and then of her further consideration of his interests in peace: blaming herself for their failure to have children, she offered to make way for another woman. The idea of such a divorce almost drove the husband to distraction. For him, to retain a beloved wife was infinitely preferable to the chance of having children: 'What desire or need of children could have been great enough to shake my devotion to you, to make me exchange the certain for the doubtful?', he asks. It is strongly implied that he will not marry again: his wife is irreplaceable. We cannot tell how typical these sentiments were, but they add to the other evidence already referred to which indicates that many couples saw marriage as a close relationship between husband and wife: the role of spouse was at least as important as — perhaps more important than — that of father or mother.

The mother's influence on her children's upbringing has often been stressed, and there are famous mothers who are usually cited in this context. They are almost always cited as mothers of famous *sons*;[86] but it might be useful to look also at mothers' influence on daughters (especially the daughters who grew up to be notable mothers). It is usually assumed that the mother was almost fully responsible for her daughter's education. This assumption rests partly on the belief that girls learnt only domestic skills; but we know that many upper-class mothers were hardly expert at these themselves (see above) and that girls could have a much wider curriculum and that some went to public schools (see below). By the end of the first century AD most upper-class mothers had given up breast-feeding their babies: wet-nurses were hired for this purpose.[87] Moreover, as we have already seen and will again see (with reference to custody after divorce), children were very much members of their father's family. Thus mothers may have become less deeply involved in, or committed to, their children's lives. This could have had a liberating effect or a dislocating one. At the moment, our image of the Roman mother and of her relationship to sons and daughters is a fragmentary one, based on sporadic and sometimes conflicting evidence.

We have seen, then, that the father's role has tended to dominate the picture of the Roman family. His role in real life was potentially dominating, but there is evidence of considerable independence on the part of sons, daughters and wives. In Roman women we have glimpsed stirrings of discontent with current social values, and we need to look further to the roles (mother, wife, mistress) available to them. Relationships between siblings and between kin members and other members of the household have scarcely been touched on here but are surely important to an understanding of how the family functioned. In looking further at the role of parents in the Roman family, we might also take account of what activities families undertook together. We know, for instance, that from Augustus's time separate sections of the theatre or amphitheatre were set aside for different groups. For the watching of plays, gladiatorial contests, animal shows and other games, married men, women and schoolboys all sat in different places, (the schoolboys' slave attendants — the *paedagogi* — who were responsible for their conduct sitting in a section adjoining the boys'). At the Circus, families could sit together to watch the horse racing (Suetonius, *Augustus* 44-5). Children apparently attended their parents' dinner-parties, at least for some of the time (Quintilian 1.2.8). Children seem to have been exposed to many influences besides that of their parents. If this was conscious policy, it reflects a view of the family's place in the broader social context that is of considerable interest.

Broken Families

(i) Widowhood

When a husband died, a widow was expected to go into mourning and not remarry for a period of 10 months.[88] The reason for this particular length must have been to prevent any doubt about a child's paternity. No such period of mourning was required of men. (Widowers did, however, often observe mourning.[89]) In early days, it was considered more admirable for a widow not to remarry.[90] But Augustus, anxious that a woman's child-bearing years should not be wasted, required widows up to the age of 50 to remarry within a period of two years.[91] There was probably never an attempt to enforce this in the lower classes, with whose birth rate Augustus was not especially concerned. Even in the upper classes there were some notable cases of non-enforcement. When Antonia (daughter of Mark Antony and wife of Tiberius's brother, Drusus) lost her husband, she was about 27 years of age and in the full flower of her beauty, but she refused to marry again in spite of pressure from the emperor Augustus.[92] She was a strong-minded woman,[93] but the fact that she had already borne three children may well have strengthened her position.[94] Her devotion to her husband's memory seems to have won her a high reputation. Continued widowhood was imposed on Agrippina senior, whom Tiberius refused permission to remarry after her husband's death. It is not clear whether Tiberius's powers in this matter were those of a *paterfamilias*[95] or simply those of an autocratic ruler, but his motivation was fairly clearly to prevent Agrippina, who was the grand-daughter of Augustus, remarrying outside the imperial family, and thus producing potential rivals for imperial power. Could this have been Agrippina's purpose in seeking remarriage? She had been a devoted wife to Germanicus, and had mourned him magnificently. But she burned with resentment at the injustices surrounding his death (which she believed was murder), and she turned much of this resentment against Tiberius. She may have seen her remarriage as a threat to Tiberius and as a new means of fulfilling her own ambitions. Of course, she may simply have fallen in love again. But the model of her mother-in-law Antonia on the one hand, and her own political activities on the other, suggest that she would have had more powerful motives for 'deserting' the memory of Germanicus.

The woman who had only one husband (*univira*) continued to win praise in literature and on tombstones.[96] This may cause surprise in the light of Augustus's legislation to enforce remarriage after widowhood or divorce, but it may show the strength of traditional attitudes even in the face of (unpopular) moral legislation. It may also have been a form of congratulation for the good luck of those women who had not needed to remarry in a period of high mortality as well as of easy divorce.[97]

(ii) Divorce: Procedure, Causes, Effects

Divorce procedure was probably as informal as that of marriage could be. The decision to separate could be unilateral — either partner or, sometimes, a partner's *paterfamilias*, could bring about the end of a marriage. A simple notification of intent to divorce was sufficient, and no cause need be given: on the whole, the concept of 'the guilty party' was not important.[98] The causes for divorce which we can reconstruct are varied. We have seen that one reason for divorce could be a couple's failure to have children. (It seems to have been assumed that this was the woman's 'fault', or deficiency, but such divorces seem to have taken place without public recrimination or unpleasantness. The psychological effect on women, however, cannot be assessed. For some it was no doubt a painful and humiliating experience, but others may have welcomed the new freedom it brought, especially as they would have their dowry returned to them and probably gifts from their husband as well.[99]) Political reasons could dictate divorce as they could marriage alliances. In the field of morals, a wife's continuous adulterous behaviour seems to have been the reason for some Republican men divorcing their wives (e.g. Lucullus's wife, Claudia, Pompey's wife, Metella). Wives (or their fathers) presumably took the initiative in obtaining a divorce in those cases recorded where the purpose was obviously a new marriage for the woman. The marriage of Sulla's step-daughter, Aemilia, for instance, was dissolved so that she could marry Pompey and thus give a family basis to the political alliance between these two men. (She was already pregnant by her first husband, and died in childbirth within months of marrying Pompey.) Octavian (the later Augustus) was so anxious to marry Livia that she obtained her divorce while she was still pregnant by her first husband. Although Octavian no doubt put whatever pressure he could on Livia's husband, he had no legal standing in her divorce: she must have taken the initiative, formally or informally.[100]

It is often claimed that there was a double standard for men and women at Rome with respect to adultery and that, because we have few specific references to wives divorcing their husbands on these grounds, wives must have accepted their husbands' adultery as a matter of course. This is possible. But we should remember in the first place that public reasons for divorce were not usually given, and that we do not always know who initiated the divorce.[101] In the second place, it is possible that not many husbands gave their wives cause for complaint on this score — either they were uxorious husbands or discreet ones. It is at least worth noting that, except for Julius Caesar and some of the emperors, adulterous behaviour is not a common accusation hurled at prominent Roman men (even in a period when almost every conceivable kind of abuse was freely used), nor is there evidence of extra-marital affairs being carried on flagrantly in public.

Whatever the causes of divorce, they were normally the private business of the family concerned during the Republican period.[102] Until Augustus, the state normally took no interest in divorce and the relations between married partners, except to recognise a husband's right to kill a wife and her lover if they were caught *in flagranti delicto*. Augustus's moral legislation in 18 BC severely restricted this right but made adultery a criminal offence, and a special court was established to hear prosecutions. If a husband had caught a wife in the act of adultery he was required to divorce her and then bring her to trial for adultery. This was his public duty. If he failed to do so, he made himself liable, with the guilty couple, to prosecution by any outsider. In other situations of adultery a husband could, if he chose, merely divorce and leave prosecution to others; or he could take no public action at all and this would protect his wife from outside prosecution. A woman could divorce her husband for extra-marital activities, and could on this count make more rigorous demands for restoration of dowry (Ulpian *Reg.* 6.13), but she could not initiate a criminal charge against him. The absolute obligation to divorce a partner caught in the act seems not to have applied to the wife of a guilty husband; but the realities of everyday life probably made such discovery most unlikely. Adultery was more likely to take place at the woman's home than at the man's.[103]

Adultery (*adulterium*) strictly applied only to affairs with married women. There was another crime (for which the more general word *stuprum* came to be reserved) which covered fornication between unmarried 'respectable' women and married or unmarried men. (It also applied to male homosexuality.) The penalty for both crimes was usually exile. There was, then, some discrimination against women in these laws — they could be punished for affairs with slaves and low-class persons while men could not be. But the area of discrimination was much narrower than is sometimes suggested. Augustus's concern was not essentially to ensure the moral purity of marriages. If it had been, he could not have allowed a husband to continue living with a guilty wife. Nor is it clear to me that he particularly wanted to limit divorces (i.e. to strengthen the stability or duration of marriage). In some situations he now made divorce obligatory. His concern seems to have been rather to protect the 'purity', or official legitimacy, of upper-class family descent. He aimed, first, to guard against married women bearing illegitimate children who would inherit an unsuspecting husband's name and property. (If the husband chose to acknowledge an illegitimate child as his own, that was all right, it kept the situation tidy in the state's eyes.) Second, he aimed to prevent women of good family producing children outside the conjugal family unit — such children could not inherit a father's name or rank, they were under no *paterfamilias*, and would not fit naturally into the career structure of equestrian or senatorial families (the ones in whom Augustus surely was interested). In matters of legitimacy, it is the woman's situation that must first be legislated for: but Augustus's laws seldom let the male accomplice go unpunished. Augustus's concern for the orderly workings of public life, which led him to intrude the state into citizens' private lives, opened the way to informers and prosecutors, many of whom probably had political motivation to ruin a rival rather than moral aims of saving society.[104]

Some emperors enforced the adultery law more strictly than others.[105] There seems to have been strong public opinion (at least in the upper classes) against all of Augustus's moral legislation, and a number of women made their own protest in Tiberius's time by registering themselves officially as prostitutes so that the law would not apply to them (the crime of adultery did not apply to slave women or to women of ill repute such as prostitutes and actresses). The motive for this extraordinary action by women (apparently of rank) was surely women's liberation (to free women's private lives from intolerable interference by the state, and perhaps to claim for themselves the freedom granted to men to have 'disrespectable' liaisons without fear of punishment) rather than depraved lust.[106] This seems not to have been an isolated example, because various lawyers recorded action taking account of this situation.[107]

The independence of Roman wives — but also their separateness from their husband's family — is highlighted by the absence of any concept of alimony (beyond restitution of dowry). As we shall see below, the husband almost certainly retained the children of the marriage, so the divorced wife was very much 'on her own'. The effects of this on female attitudes and behaviour should be studied more closely. If a divorced woman found that she was pregnant soon after the divorce, her ex-husband had some rights and obligations towards her; but these were in the direction of his relationship to the child to be born, rather than assisting his former wife financially or otherwise. Certain rules of procedure were laid down,[108] and the father seems to have had the right — and probably the duty — to recognise the newborn child as an heir. As there is no reference to the cause of a divorce in this part of the legal code, and as the idea of 'the guilty party' does not play an important part in Roman divorce, the question of the 'most fit' parent was probably irrelevant to the matter of custody. In fact, a passage in Cicero suggests that a guilty husband would nevertheless keep the children: he would simply have no claims on his wife's dowry for their financial support.[109] Children already born or conceived at the time of divorce belonged to the father in the eyes of the law; they were members of his family rather than of their mother's,[110] they bore his name, and in most circumstances he could retain part of his wife's dowry for the children's maintenance.[111] The father's rights have continued to be strong in western society, until in the twentieth century there developed a belief in the mother's greater fitness to rear a child and in the child's greater need of the female parent. The psychology behind this is changing again, but there was a period when the mother's biological and nurturing functions seemed to give her greater claims to custody. For the Romans, mother and father were equally parents in the natural sense (but Blayney, in Chapter 9 below, refers to some belief in the father's greater role in conception). The Roman family, however, was far more than a biological unit: it was a social and sometimes political unit, and it was important for society (and probably for the individual) to know to whose family the child 'belonged'. The *nomen* (i.e. the inherited family name) determined this. (Illegitimate children belonged to the mother's family on this criterion.)

Perhaps the apparently greater number of references to stepmothers than to stepfathers also reflects the fact that children of a dissolved marriage usually lived with their father (and thus the step-parent, if any, was a stepmother). The stepmother in most periods of history has suffered a bad reputation, and this was true in Rome too,[112] though not uniformly.[113] There were no doubt tensions also between stepfathers and their wives' children. Although widows probably normally raised their own children, they did not inherit the father's role in any legal sense: they had no *potestas* (legal power) over their children.[114] It would be useful to have a thorough examination of all the broken marriages of which we have a record to determine if there is a pattern in the destination of the children of these marriages.[115]

As divorce procedure was so simple in Rome, and did not involve the expensive services of lawyers, the poor might have divorced one another as easily as the rich. In this, Roman society was different from most modern societies, where divorce has been a middle- and upper-class luxury. But even at Rome there may have been financial restrictions on poor couples' freedom to separate. If there were children, it may have required the earnings of both parents living together to support them. On the other hand, many members of the lower-class population who are attested were ex-slaves, and of these many had specialised skills: women of this kind were not dependent on their husbands for financial support and were thus more free to leave them than most wives have been until the twentieth-century phenomenon of the wage-earning wife. But if divorce was frequent in the lower classes we have no record of it (Kajanto 1969:99). Moreover, as explained above, many of the couples in this sector of the population were probably living in *de facto* rather than legal marriages, because of the slave status of at least one partner at the time the union began. Thus divorce did not technically apply.

(iii) Slave Conditions

Broken families amongst the lower classes were, however, very common, for three reasons: (1) high mortality; (2) continued slave status of at least one partner; and (3) a slave trade in children. What is striking in the epitaphs of such families is not so much the fragility of family life but the tenacity with which many people without ample means[116] clung to the belief that it was a family's duty to come together to commemorate the death of one of its members. This manifestation of family feeling is not so evident on Greek tombstones, and especially not on those of the lower classes (cf. Lattimore 1942:266, 275). It seems to be a particularly Roman characteristic, and one adopted readily by many people of foreign birth or foreign extraction. It is one aspect of the assimilation of 'outsiders' to Roman values, rather than vice versa.

Extra-Family Groups and Influences

In the conditions described above, however, the family unit could not always survive, and various other units developed to fulfil the support role of the natural family. There are epitaphs set up by fellow slaves, fellow freedmen and patrons (all of whom were fellow members of a *familia*, of course, in its wider sense); there are foster-parents and their *alumni* (see Chapter 7); and there are the funeral clubs whose prime purpose was that of a mutual provident society to ensure a decent burial for its members, but which may also have served a social purpose. The imported religions which won so many followers at this time must also have provided their members with many of the things traditionally associated with the family — togetherness, a feeling of belonging, spiritual comfort, the opportunity to 'be one's self'.

Many of the extra-family activities of Roman society affected families through their impact on the individual. In particular, the religions noted above attracted many women of all classes and thus merit study from the point of view of their influence on wives, mothers and daughters. Cults such as that of Dionysus, with its emphasis on initiation and the mysteries, must have heightened the awareness of many women and given them a new emotional and perhaps intellectual freedom. When a woman returned home after one of these sessions, were her attitudes and behaviour affected as she took her children through their lessons, or played games with them, or as she presided with her husband at a dinner-party? Similarly, what influence did the many festivals and public entertainment have on members of the family? Discussion of these questions is beyond the limits of this chapter, but they should be considered if we are to understand the many factors shaping and influencing a family and its interrelationships.

Education .

One activity, education, is usually considered to have been very much a concern of the family. (See Bibliography for references; on the mother's influence, see above.) It not only must have influenced Romans' attitudes but its content was in turn much influenced by the family itself (by parents, by parents' friends and associates, and by slaves and freedmen associated with the family). Education can have its effect in several ways, e.g. through the curriculum, through the individuals associated with it (especially teachers), and through the physical environment in which it takes place. Classroom facilities at Rome were primitive. There was none of the sophisticated equipment that we have come to think important in teaching and learning — usually there were merely the basics for reading and writing. In public schools, the space available was noisy and crowded; at home it would probably be any room or corner vacant. Teachers, dependent on fees from parents, were poorly paid, of low social status, and enjoyed little prestige. (Some emperors, however, allocated funds to particular teachers, e.g. Vespasian gave Quintilian a subsidised professorship in the latter part of the first century AD. Earlier, Julius Caesar had tried to attract teachers to Rome by offering them Roman citizenship: Suetonius, *Iulius* 42.1.) I know of no Roman who remembered a teacher with admiration and attributed to him any great influence on his development.[117] There were, however, some teachers in the eastern Mediterranean who enjoyed a great reputation, and it is interesting to note the willingness of upper-class families in Republican times to let their teenage sons go abroad for quite long periods to study under these men. Slaves whose job it was to accompany children to and from school and generally supervise them were often well educated, and probably contributed to the formation of a child's ideas. Their potential moral influence, for good and bad, was recognised by parents who therefore took some care in choosing a man for this role of *paedagogus*.

In most respects, the Roman state took little responsibility for the quantity or quality of what children learnt: education was neither compulsory, free, nor state-directed. The state did, however, intervene on occasions to discourage or ban teachers who departed from the traditional curriculum.[118] This presumably reflects the collective wish of upper-class fathers that their children should not be confronted with new ideas — or indeed with ideas at all. The traditional curriculum was almost entirely based on texts of Greek and Latin literature (usually poetry). The pupil's knowledge of history, geography, science, and almost anything else, derived from the teacher's commentary on these texts. There was a canon of approved texts which was seldom changed, and the method of dealing with them changed little over a long period. At the elementary level, at least, the 'three R's' were drummed in by rote learning and the discipline of the stick. Even at higher levels, education depended a great deal on dictating, memorising and reciting, for literary manuscripts were expensive. This in itself gave much emphasis to the spoken word, and this aspect was consciously developed since almost all public life[119] depended on the ability to speak well.

There is little evidence of 'the joy of learning' in formal Roman education; little attempt to make the curriculum open new horizons; little concern with relevance to real life. For the last, children depended very much on their parents and their parents' contacts. In the lower classes, where little or no formal education could be afforded, children must have picked up as much education in the streets as at home; but some of them probably learnt a trade from their parents — there was no formal, public technical education at Rome. Some imperial slave boys got a systematic training at a special imperial school, and in the other wealthier households slave children may have got some tutoring from their parents (if they lived in the same household) or from some of their older, well-educated fellow slaves. If they were *vernae* (i.e. home-born slaves) they often had a privileged position in the household, being raised and sometimes educated with the master's children.[120]

In families that had the leisure and ambition to give serious attention to their children's education, it was the mother who was traditionally responsible for the earliest years. If tutors were employed at home, the mother's influence could extend well beyond infancy.[121] There can be no doubt that upper-class Roman women could be well educated: there are many direct references to well-educated mothers;[122] we know of specific women noted for their literary or intellectual gifts;[123] there are many other references which indicate a good education for girls;[124] and their significant role in the family councils or when their husbands were absent often called for more than native good sense.[125] But we know very little of the details of girls' education. It would appear from the above that it may not have differed significantly from boys' education in the elementary or secondary stages: some girls went to public schools, at least at the primary stage. Girls as well as boys participated in public religious ritual (e.g. they both helped perform Horace's Secular Hymn at the centennial games celebrated by Augustus in 17 BC). But from a boy's coming-of-age ceremony he became a citizen in a sense that his sister never would be: he would have a vote and could have a public career ahead. It was at this point that the father's influence must have been decisive, and the unequal political roles of men and women thus differentiated the father–son relationship from the father–daughter.

By the time that their sons reached the age of 14 or so, many fathers had already taken them with them into the city, introduced them to their friends, let them observe life in the forum — public meetings, the law courts, business deals and, if they were a senatorial family, the boy could catch something of senate debates from outside the chamber.[126] When the father decided that his son was ready for the responsibilities of adulthood (and it is interesting that the state did not fix a uniform age for this: although the usual age was between 14 and 16, known examples range from 12 to 18[127]) he took his son, with a party of male friends (probably the most senior and prestigious of the father's friends: Pliny, *Letters* 1.9.1), to be inscribed on the roll of citizens. Since the son was inscribed in the same voting district (*tribus*) as his father, and would need to depend (either as a candidate or as a 'client', i.e. a semi-dependent voter) on the same network of contacts as his father, the pressure on an adolescent boy to vote the same way as his father must have been great. It was probably these circumstances — the early age of admission to voting rights, the ceremonial surrounding the coming of age, the political inexperience of the boy, and the basis of electoral support — rather than the effect of *patria potestas* that strengthened a boy's natural inclination to adopt his father's political attitudes. It is now known, thanks to the survey techniques of political science, that (in some countries, at least) at their first vote modern voters (even at the age of 21) are likely to vote the way their parents vote, and that that first vote tends to set the pattern for most of their future voting behaviour.[128] How much more likely this was to happen at Rome, where other elements in a boy's education were conservative, cultivating a respect for tradition, and where there was no well-developed system of political philosophy to give birth to party politics rather than family politics.

One element especially in children's education must have strengthened the tendencies of the family environment to encourage respect for age, authority and the ways of one's ancestors.[129] This was the emphasis on examples, or precedents, from previous Roman history as models of behaviour. Moreover, the upper-class child's view of history was often moulded by family records. The busts and death masks of notable ancestors decorated the walls of the *tablinum*, an important room in the house, and were paraded on important family occasions such as funerals.[130] Private archives contained accounts of Roman history which focused on the contribution made by members of that family.[131] This stimulated a child's pride in being a member not only of the Roman nation but of a particular family, and provided a double reason for advertising his or her Roman name. The *tria nomina* (the three elements as in Gaius Iulius Caesar) showed Roman citizenship, and the central part, the *nomen* ('Iulius' in the preceding example), indicated the family.[132]

The Family Name

There are many indications of the importance of the *nomen* and hence membership of a particular family (in the broadest sense). Reference has been made above to the role of the *nomen* in indicating the bond between patron and ex-slave. One of the other two elements of the *tria nomina*, the *praenomen* or the *cognomen*, is sometimes missing from a person's name, but in general the *nomen* continued to be used until the fourth or fifth century of the Christian era. Women in Republican times bore only the *nomen* (it is a puzzle how several daughters were distinguished from one another), but many added a *cognomen* in imperial times.

Tombs were often set aside for the exclusive use of bearers of a particular family name, and penalties invoked against those who did not respect this (Crook 1967b:133-8). For instance, the inscription on the tomb of the Racilius family (*CIL* 6.7788) reserved the tomb for members of that family, their freedmen and freedwomen and the descendants of those freedmen and freedwomen; 'and if anyone wishes to act against this monument after my time, or to take it away from the family name, he shall pay a fine of 5000 sesterces to the Roman treasury'. Sometimes the abbreviation 'h.m.h.n.s.' is found on tombs: it stands for 'hoc monumentum heredem non sequetur', i.e. (literally) 'this monument will not follow the heir'. It was always possible that the property containing the family tomb would be bequeathed to an extraneous heir who would not feel any obligation to attend to the tomb; thus people might go to some pains to see that the tomb itself and access to it were retained by the family.

To be excluded from the family tomb was a serious matter and would be specifically stipulated only for gross ingratitude or disloyalty to the family name. Augustus's will excluded his daughter and granddaughter, both named Julia, from his family tomb (Suetonius, *Augustus* 101): they had sinned against his marriage legislation and had already suffered severe penalties;

now they were to be disowned by their family in death as well as in life. Augustus's tomb, the large circular structure still visible in Rome,[133] acquired special significance as the burial place of many members of the Julio-Claudian line and came to be considered the imperial family's tomb. It is probable that the emperors Vespasian and Nerva, both looking for legitimacy at the beginning of new dynasties, chose to be buried in this tomb.[134] Nero, however, was not buried here. Having been declared a public enemy he probably had no right, but he may have preferred to dissociate himself from this tomb anyway. He was a rebel against his maternal background (the Julian line) in many ways, and had tried to raise his family of origin (the Domitii) and his adoptive family (the Claudii) to the same level of prestige as that of the Julians.[135] Perhaps his faithful mistress, Acte, knew his wishes: at any rate, after his death she and two of his former nurses buried his ashes in the Domitian family tomb (Suetonius, *Nero* 50).

The very frequent formula on tombstones, 'libertis libertabusque meis posterisque eorum', i.e. 'for my freedmen and freedwomen and their descendants', although it came to mean very little in the later part of our period, did reflect the concept of a family based on a common name. It would not automatically occur to us today to share our burial place with dependants who were not blood relations (just as it would not occur to us, and did not to the Greeks, to give slaves freedom, a family and citizenship simultaneously); but for the Romans a freedman, bearing the family name, *was* a member of the family and he and his posterity could help continue that name to future generations. The widespread setting-up of stone monuments — handsome or modest — to record the family name reflects a strong sense of family and the wish of great and small members of society to have something of themselves continue beyond their own brief life span.

It is from the names recorded on tombstones that we have in recent times been able to reconstruct something of the family life of the lower classes at Rome, and it is from this source that further new work might derive. Our predecessors have bequeathed to us a reasonably sound knowledge of Roman political and social institutions: can we now discover more about personal interrelationships within those institutions, at all social and economic levels and in all areas of human activity?

44   *The Roman Family*

Notes

1. The hardest questions to resolve are the 'counting' ones, e.g. how many people lived in Rome at any particular time, what proportion of those were of a particular social class, or age, or sex, etc. See, however, the impressive results and discussion of such matters in Brunt (1971a). See also under 'Demography' in Bibliography.

2. See Thirsk (1964) for the French family, and Herlihy (1972) for Italy. Cf. Laslett (1971b) for pre-industrial England and the wider-ranging volume edited by him (1972), and its successor, Wall (1983).

3. None of these terms has a satisfactory single-word English translation. For good discussions of them, see Adcock (1959:13-17) and Earl (1967:20-43). Approximate equivalents for them are:

virtus — may sometimes be translated as 'virtue', at other times as 'courage', 'manliness', or 'character'.

dignitas — 'prestige', 'worthiness', 'the respect that is associated with (senatorial) rank'.

auctoritas — 'prestige', 'authority'.

gloria — 'fame', 'high reputation'.

pietas — 'dutifulness (to gods, country, family)'.

gravitas — 'seriousness', 'dignity', 'weightiness'.

4. e.g. Meyer (1895) and Plassard (1921) on concubinage, a practice which they have misunderstood and from which invalid moral conclusions have been drawn (see n. 38 below). See also on the older social histories of Rome, Bibliography. There are more than 23,000 Latin inscriptions now available for people in Rome who did not belong to the upper (senatorial and equestrian) classes of society. The publication of these was begun by Theodor Mommsen and has continued since his death, in the many parts of volume 6 of the *Corpus Inscriptionum Latinarum* (hereafter abbreviated as *CIL*); and *Année Epigraphique* continues to give a yearly publication of new inscriptions. Inscriptions of this kind have sometimes been dismissed as insignificant, or isolated examples have been selected to illustrate a point. It is necessary to be familiar with the whole collection in order to say anything worthwhile about them. Greek inscriptions relevant to the Roman world are collected in *Inscriptiones Graecae ad res Romanas pertinentes*.

5. Weaver's book (1972) brought to a wider readership the results of his specialised work of the previous ten years or so. It has an important section entitled 'The Family Circle'. Other important names in the specialised studies referred to (which are not specifically concerned with the family) are H. Chantraine (in German) and the Swede H. Thylander (in French). A number of Finnish scholars, led by I. Kajanto, are also very much concerned with studies of this kind. For work specifically related to family matters, Keith Hopkins' contributions have probably been the most significant (1965a, 1965b, 1966).

6. In the juridical sense, status was clearly defined for members of Rome's population. The broadest division was between Roman citizens and non-citizens. For most purposes, this division can be taken as synonymous with that between free and non-free. All Roman citizens were, by definition, free. Some free foreign residents at Rome (*peregrini*) were without Roman citizenship, but they figure very little in our records: most of the non-citizens of whom we know were slaves. The non-free were slaves (*servi*). The free were either freeborn (*ingenui*) or freed (*liberti*). Freedmen were ex-slaves who had obtained freedom (i.e. been 'manumitted') by one of a number of methods (formal or informal; during a

master's lifetime or by means of his will; by paying the master a sum of money from the savings which slaves were often permitted to accumulate; or as a free gift). The freedman's ex-master was known as his patron, and from his patron the freedman took his formal name and citizenship. Thus at Rome almost all ex-slaves obtained freedom and Roman citizenship simultaneously. Within the freeborn section of the population the highest class, on almost any criteria, was that of the senators, who had to satisfy a high financial requirement and who had an important political role — the most important in the state in Republican times. Usually ranked next below the senatorial class — also with a financial qualification, but whose political role was usually an indirect one until the second century AD. Below the equestrians were the ordinary plebeians, many of them very poor. The freeborn element at this level of society seems to have declined from the first century BC onwards, but the proportions of freeborn and freed here are still a matter of some controversy. In general, 'the lower classes' can be taken to include this third, lowest level of the freeborn population as well as freedmen and slaves. But some slaves and freedmen, especially those belonging to the imperial household, became very wealthy and powerful and on many criteria would have more in common with the upper than with the lower classes. Their ex-slave status, however, is often relevant for their family relationships.

7. The greatest part of the available evidence falls within this period. No society, however, is likely to be static over three centuries, and future studies of the Roman family should aim to document changes and developments.

8. There are also essential differences between Rome and the provinces — which spread from Britain, the Rhine and Romania to North Africa, and from Spain almost to the Euphrates, at the peak of Rome's power. It is a weakness of some writings on Roman society that evidence is drawn arbitrarily from a wide geographical area — the area of Rome's political power — without account being taken of possible local differences.

9. Aulus Gellius 4.3.2 (and cf. 17.21.44). To remain loyal to this oath, Spurius Carvilius Ruga divorced a beloved wife because of her sterility. (The date is probably 231 BC, but see Corbett (1930:218, 227). Festus (p. 312 Lindsay, s.v. *quaeso*) gives two examples of the phrase from the second century BC plays of Ennius. Plautus's *Captivi* (line 889), earlier in that century, uses the phrase, and in another of Plautus's plays (*Aulularia*, line 148) Eunomia advises her brother to take action which will do him everlasting good — marry 'to produce children' ('liberis procreandis'). The phrase recurs in Suetonius, *Iulius* 52, where it is claimed that 'liberorum quaerendorum causa' Caesar planned legislation to allow him to marry whatever and however many wives he wished. Caesar did not produce a natural heir (although his concern to have a son is unlikely to have led him to legislation as wild as Suetonius's claim suggests), and his heir was finally his grandnephew Octavian, whom he adopted in his will as his own son.

10. Sulla passed 'marriage laws' (Plutarch, *Comparison of Lysander and Sulla* 3.2), but we do not know their details. They seem to have been associated with anti-luxury legislation. There is a long history of such legislation at Rome, all apparently futile; cf. Julius Caesar in 46 BC.

11. On Caesar, see Suetonius, *Iulius* 20.3; Appian, *Civil War* 2.10; Dio 38.7.3. For Cicero, see his *De legibus* 3.7 and *Pro Marcello* 23 ('propaganda suboles').

12. There is no reason to doubt that this was Cicero's real analysis of his society, although his disapproval of Caesar's powers may have made him insincere in other parts of the *Pro Marcello* speech. It has more conviction, as a commentary on his fellows, than the bland philosophical generalisation in *De officiis* 1.53: 'It is natural to all animals to desire to procreate.'

13. For a good concise account of Augustus's legislation, see Sherwin-White

(1966:558). For further references see Bibliography under 'Marriage'.

14. Valerius Maximus 7.7.4. Cf., for Augustus's period, Horace, *Epistles* 1.2.44-5, where a man's hope is that he will have a beautiful wife with whom to conceive children: 'quaeritur argentum puerisque beata creandis/uxor . . .'

15. *Letters* 10.2. Cf. 2.13.8, 10.95. Claudius granted exemptions from the Papian law to citizens who would build merchant ships; if women did this they got the 'ius quattuor liberorum', i.e. the privileges associated with having four children. These exemptions were still in force in the early part of the second century AD (Suetonius, *Claudius* 19). Livia was given an honorary place on the lists of mothers of three children by way of consolation when one of her two sons died in 9 BC (Dio 55.2.6).

16. See, for example, Syme (vol. 2, 1958:574, 612). Cf. *Cambridge Ancient History*, vol. 11 (1936:10) (Charlesworth), 308 (Weber), 746 (Duff). See also n. 17 below. But Hopkins (1983:chapter 3) argues that some families opted out of politics rather than died out.

17. Dio 56.1.2 for AD 9; cf. Suetonius, *Augustus* 34.2. See Tacitus, *Annals* 3.25, for AD 20: the Papian law was moderated, as it had not resulted in more marriages or children ('praevalida orbitate'), but informers had become a menace. The interpretation of Suetonius, *Claudius* 23.1, is difficult, but it seems to indicate Claudius's willingness to tolerate what had seemed a fraudulent ploy to Tiberius. Cf. Suetonius, *Nero* 10: Nero reduced the rewards paid to informers under the Papian law.

18. e.g. Augustus found that men were contracting engagements to girls who were well below the age of marriage (because betrothal conferred the benefits of marriage in this context) and that they were changing partners frequently, in order to escape the penalties of celibacy and the responsibilities of marriage; so he shortened the length of betrothals and imposed restraints on divorces (Suetonius, *Augustus* 34; cf. Dio 54.16.7). In Tiberius's time, a man was punished who had married the day before lots were drawn for allocation of quaestors' duties and then divorced his wife the day after (Suetonius, *Tiberius* 35). (Similarly fraudulent marriages have been known in modern times, e.g. Australian women have gone through a ceremony of marriage (with immediate separation and then divorce promised them by their grooms) with foreign men who wished to obtain Australian citizenship in this way.) Informers were encouraged by rewards to bring such fraudulence to court — see n. 17 above. In AD 48 Claudius had a list of unmarried (*caelebs*) and childless (*orbus*) men prepared, in order to place the censor's black mark against them; but his agents' investigation had been sloppy and the men were able to prove that they were indeed husbands and fathers (Suetonius, *Claudius* 16.3). In AD 62 there were complaints from genuine fathers about the fraudulent adoptions performed by men who wished to obtain the benefits of fatherhood (Tacitus, *Annals* 15.19). Juvenal (6.602-9) suggests that suppositious children were not uncommon; cf. 9.70-90, where a miser is glad to recognise his wife's illegitimate children in order to get the financial benefits of fatherhood.

19. Augustus, had, however, allotted special seats at public entertainment to lower-class married men (Suetonius, *Augustus* 44); and had included younger boys than usual in his distributions of largesse (*congiaria*) (Suetonius, *Augustus* 41.2).

20. For Antoninus, see Scriptores Historiae Augustae, *Antoninus Pius* 8, and Mattingly and Sydenham, vol. 3 (1930:165). For Marcus, see Scriptores Historiae Augustae, *Marcus* 26.

21. See Mattingly and Sydenham vol. 2 (1926:250, 261, 277-8, 286-7), for *alimenta*; vols. 2 and 3 *passim* for Fecunditas and the goddesses Venus Genetrix and Juno Licina (both associated with procreation). The concepts Pudicitia and Pietas also laud the ideal Roman wife. Cf. Pliny's wishful thinking in *Panegyricus*

22.3: at Trajan's entry to Rome women had a great desire to bear children, seeing for what an emperor they would be producing citizens, and for what a general they would be producing soldiers ('feminas etiam tunc fecunditatis suae maxima voluptas subiit, cum cernerent cui principi cives, cui imperatori milites peperissent').

22. Livy, *Periochae* 59. Cf. Aulus Gellius 1.6.1-6, probably referring to the same speech by the same censor, Quintus Caecilius Metellus Macedonicus, in 131 BC. The extract quoted in the text is from Gellius.

23. After all, the censor Macedonicus was himself remembered as a man singularly fortunate in his family life: his wife was noted for her *pudicitia* ('modesty, fidelity') and *fecunditas* ('fertility') and his children all fulfilled his hopes (Valerius Maximus 7.1.1). Perhaps the bearing of seven children kept Macedonicus's wife sufficiently repressed. (Pliny the Elder, *Natural History* 7.59, says that there were six children.)

24. For the effects of political repression, see Pliny, *Panegyricus* 27. See Suetonius, *Tiberius* 47, and Tacitus, *Annals* 2.37, for imperial subsidies for needy senatorial fathers. On women's liberation, see Balsdon (1962:195-7, 1969:82-5). The lead-poisoning theory has been discounted by Hodge (1981) and Phillips (1984).

25. Cf. on Cornelia, Agrippina senior and Faustina above. See also Balsdon (1969:88).

26. Pedanius Secundus in AD 61 had 400 slaves, apparently under the one roof (Tacitus, *Annals* 14.42-3). Pliny the Younger, a wealthy senator of the late first and early second centuries AD, probably owned at least 500 slaves. He provided for 100 in his will (*CIL* 5.5262), and his general attitude to his slaves suggests that this was probably the 20 per cent of his household which was the legal maximum that could be freed by will (Gaius *Inst.* 1.42-3).

27. Various women won praise by accompanying members of their families into exile, e.g. after the Pisonian conspiracy of AD 65 (Tacitus, *Annals* 15.71); under the Flavians (Pliny, *Letters* 7.19, 9.13; Tacitus, *Histories* 1.3); but not Terentia, wife of Cicero.

28. There were freedmen living in the large household of Pedanius Secundus; see n. 26 above.

29. The tribe was the electoral division to which a citizen belonged. A freedman was allocated to one of the four city tribes when he obtained citizenship (there were 35 tribes altogether, so freedmen's votes had a restricted value by being confined to only four of the tribes) but he did not normally use the tribe in the official form of his name (Taylor 1960:147 and n. 55). A name that includes a tribe is a good sign of a freeborn — rather than freed — Roman citizen.

30. See above on Gelzer and Münzer. The Romans had a great variety of terms for extended family relationships, e.g. *amita* for paternal aunt, *matertera* for maternal aunt, *patruus* for paternal uncle, *avunculus* for maternal uncle, *amitinus* for a cousin who was a father's sister's child, *sobrinus* or *consobrinus* for a cousin who was a mother's sister's child (though sometimes used of cousins generally). But Latin occasionally used the same word for both a collateral and a stem relationship. Thus one of Mark Antony's wives, Antonia, who was also his cousin (his father's brother's daughter), could be referred to as his *soror*, literally 'sister' (Cicero, *Philippica* 2.99; cf. Plutarch, *Antony* 9, for the relationship). (Ovid, *Metamorphoses* 1.351, has a similar usage of *soror*.) Two paternal cousins are called *fratres patrueles* ('brothers through the father') by Cicero (*Pro Plancio* 27), and a cousin is sometimes simply *frater*, 'brother' (Cicero, *Ad Atticum* 1.5.1, *In Verrem* 2.3.170, and *Post reditum in senatu* 25; Catullus 66.22; Ovid, *Heroides* 8.28 and *Metamorphoses* 13.31). More surprisingly, Latin had no single word at all for nephew or niece: *filius/filia fratris* ('brother's son/daughter') sufficed. The

third century AD lawyer Paulus found this worthy of comment (D.38.10.10.14), and gradually *nepos* ('grandchild') came to do duty also for 'grandnephew' and 'nephew', until the meaning of 'nephew' became predominant, as in the Italian word *nipote* and in the original use of 'nepotism'.

The relationships set down by law as preventing marriage included not only blood relationships but also those of stepmother–stepson and some in-laws (Paulus *Sent.* 2.19.3-5). The implications of all of this for the Roman concept of family relations bear further investigation. Cf. Talcott Parsons on the possible connection between distinctive terminology for different relations and the actual institutional structure of kinship, in Anshen (1959:245-8).

31. Cf. Herlihy (1972:9-10) for the differences between city and country in mediaeval Florence with regard to the frequency of joint families and of multi-generational families.

32. Plutarch, *Crassus* 1. Cf. *Cato the Elder* 24.2.

33. Valerius Maximus 4.4.8.

34. Suetonius, *Iulius* 1, 13; Plutarch, *Caesar* 7.2. Cf. Plutarch, *Caesar* 9.2: Aurelia (Caesar's mother) was in a position to try to guard the virtue of Caesar's wife (Pompeia).

35. D.32.49.4 (Ulpian): 'sane enim nisi dignitate nihil interest'. Paulus *Sent.* 2.20.1: 'eo tempore, quo quis uxorem habet, concubinam habere non potest. concubina igitur ab uxore solo dilectu separatur'. Cf. D.25.7.4; C.5.26.1; and C.7.15.3.2: 'omnibus etenim uxores habentibus concubinas vel liberas vel ancillas habere nec antiqua iura nec nostra concedunt'. Watson (1967:9-10) believes that this concept was not yet so formalised in the Republic. But we know of no Republican married man having a relationship with a woman which could be called concubinage. The case quoted by Cicero (*De oratore* 1.183) is rather bigamy — the public intention was that the second union should be seen as marriage.

36. See above and D.23.2.44 (Paulus) and Ulpian *Reg.* 13.

37. Vespasian had had some difficulty 'regularising' his wife's status (Suetonius, *Vespasian* 3), but there was no hope of doing this for his concubine Caenis, who had been a prominent slave and then freedwoman in the imperial household for a long time. Crook (1967b:101) writes that Marcus's concubine was 'almost certainly freeborn', but this is far from certain. Her father had been a procurator of Marcus's wife and may well have been slave-born. In that case, his daughter would at best be the daughter of a freedman and perhaps therefore too humble for an imperial marriage; or she may have been a freedwoman herself. If her father did not become free till the age of 30 (the normal age for imperial freedmen), she may well have been born before that. In the absence of information about her mother, we cannot be sure. Marcia seems to have had the position of concubine to Commodus, but her status is uncertain.

38. In spite of claims to the contrary by Meyer (1895) and Plassard (1921). Their evidence is faulty for many reasons, e.g. they confuse the terms 'free', 'freeborn', and 'freed'; and they assume to be freeborn a great many people who have the Roman name but whose status is not formally indicated — such people are of doubtful status, but often the probability is that they are freed rather than freeborn. Thus it is always possible that the reason for the concubinage is that at least one of the partners was a slave at the time the union was begun. See Rawson (1974).

39. *CIL* 6.36456. The term used of the woman here is *contubernalis*, not *concubina*, presumably because of the slave status of at least one member. Cf. *CIL* 6.22425: two men, apparently slaves, dedicate to a slave woman as their wife, 'coniugi'. Treggiari (1981c) is unconvinced. See Durry (1961:14-15) for a possible example from Pompeii.

40. See Bibliography under '*Patria potestas*' for references, of which Crook

(1967c) has been most useful for this section. That the power of a father over his children was still important to him is shown by the reluctance of fathers in the early Empire to nominate their sons for the priesthood of Jupiter or to let their daughters marry into that priesthood (Tacitus, *Annals* 4.16). In both of these cases the father lost his *patria potestas*. The same factor may have contributed to fathers' reluctance to nominate their daughters as Vestal Virgins.

41. Seneca, *De clementia* 1.15, tells of a Roman equestrian who had flogged his son to death and was rescued by Augustus from lynching by an angry mob. There is no suggestion that he was brought to trial for any crime. A Republican example of a father's execution of his son is in Sallust, *Catilinae coniuratio* 39.

42. Suetonius, *Tiberius* 35 — if a member of the public did not come forward as prosecutor. Cf. Tacitus, *Annals* 2.50, where the woman was related to Tiberius. Cf. Dio 58.11.7 re Livilla and Sejanus — in AD 31, Tiberius had Livilla put to death: 'I have heard that Tiberius spared Livilla out of regard for her mother Antonia and that Antonia herself of her own accord killed her daughter by starvation.'

43. e.g. under Nero: Tacitus, *Annals* 13.32, where the charge against a distinguished woman was *superstitio externa* — Judaism? an Egyptian cult? Christianity? Cf. Seneca, *De clementia* 1.15.2-7: Tarius called a *consilium* to try his son for attempted murder of himself; Augustus attended as a private citizen and friend of the family.

44. He probably followed Catullus as Clodia's lover. The attempted murder of Clodia was part of the charge against him.

45. Cicero claims that Caelius incurred no debts in his own name; but in this context Cicero may simply be taking evasive action to protect his client from presenting detailed accounts.

46. Seneca, *De clementia* 1.15.2-7: his generous father continued the allowance when the son was in exile in Marseilles after attempting to murder his father.

47. Cf. Crook (1967b:110). In the special context of stipend and booty won in military service (*peculium castrense*), the law came to recognise the son's absolute ownership: see Daube (1969:76 ff).

48. The law in fact realised that a father might die and leave as heir a teenage boy who was technically a citizen but who was not mature enough to administer a large estate. It therefore imposed some form of financial guardianship on young men until they were aged 25. Crook comments (1967b:117), 'The Romans, having ended their guardianship too early, now take minority and its protection up to too late an age.'

49. Cf. similar situations in poorer minority families in the United States today. See, for example, Burgess, Locke and Thomas (1963:88-9) on the matricentric black family. They point out that in the 1960 census there was a larger proportion of families with women heads among blacks than among whites.

50. See now Hallett (1984), not available to me at the time of writing.

51. Dio (54.16) states that in Augustus's time 'there were far more males than females in the upper classes'; but this may be his own guess to support his interpretation of Augustus' marriage laws. Dio thinks that the permission for marriage between freed and freeborn (except senators) was a widening of opportunity, rather than a confirmation of existing custom (see n. 65 below), and he sees it as affecting only upper-class men, whereas it also affected women. Interpretation of epitaph statistics to determine sex distribution is difficult: see Hopkins (1966, esp. p. 260).

52. e.g. two of the sons of Calpurnia and Nonius Asprenas were called Nonius Asprenas Calpurnius Serranus and Nonius Asprenas Calpurnius Torquatus (see *PIR*[2], stemma opp.p. 54; and *PIR*[1], under N98 and N99). Again, Ummidius Quadratus bore the family name of his grandmother, Ummidia Quadratilla, who

raised him (Pliny, *Letters* 7.24). Corellius Pansa, consul in AD 122, may be the son of Corellia Hispulla, the boy who Pliny hoped would live up to the distinction of his maternal descent (Pliny, *Letters* 3.3; Sherwin-White 1966:212). Nero's wife Poppaea took her mother's family name because her maternal grandfather was more distinguished than her father (Tacitus, *Annals* 13.45). Cf. the practice of some of the older families of the United States, e.g. the nineteenth-century ancestor of the present Cabot Lodges, Henry Cabot Lodge, was the son of John Ellerton Lodge and Anna Cabot. See other examples in the genealogies of Hess (1966).

53. e.g. Pliny, *Letters* 2.20; Juvenal 12; Tacitus, *Histories* 1.73.

54. D.50.16.195.2 (Ulpian): 'communi iure familiam dicimus omnium adgnatorum'. Cf. Gaius *Inst.* 1.156.

55. Prudentius, a fourth-century Christian writer, gives a few details of pagan family ritual, and he represents the mother praying before the stone cult objects: *Contra orationem Symmachi* 1. 199-214.

56. Cf. what Freedman writes (1958:30-2) of rural Chinese families during the last 150 years of the pre-communist period: a wife's assimilation to her husband's group was never complete during her lifetime; she retained her own surname through life and was ritually a part of her original family, at least to the extent of mourning for her parents. Her place in her new home was strengthened first by her bearing children and second by her death (when she might obtain a place in the ancestral hall with an ancestral tablet). For Roman law on burial of a wife, see D.11.7.21 (Paulus); 11.7.16, 22, 27 (Ulpian); and 11.7.28 (Pomponius on Sabinus).

57. No agreement has ever been reached on the history and chronology of these forms. Dumézil (1979) related them to the tripartite and trifunctional ideology of the Indo-Europeans.

58. Marquardt (1886:17); Plassard (1921:109). They claim that in *manus* marriages the wife's name was followed by her husband's name in the genitive, e.g. 'Iulia Drusi Caesaris' (*CIL* 6.5198) for Julia, wife of Drusus Caesar. This form is comparatively rare in inscriptions and literature of our period, but it is used frequently for women in the imperial family. If the claim were tested and seemed a good criterion, we would have further information on family traditions, the image families had of themselves, and the legal relationship between specific husbands and wives.

59. The ages at which Augustus's marriage laws became operative were 20 for women and 25 for men. The actual gap may often have been greater.

60. 'The ladies are evidently quite charmed with the young man's attentiveness and engaging manners': Cicero, *Ad Atticum* 6.6.1, trans. Shackleton Bailey vol. 3 (1968).

61. The date of Octavia's birth is not certain, but it was not later than early AD 40: Gallivan (1974) *contra* Hopkins (1965a).

62. Hopkins' interpretation of the historians' evidence (pp. 315-16) is highly subjective: I do not find in them 'surprise' that pre-pubertal marriages were not consummated. Cf. Laslett (1971a:221), 'In most societies known to me — certainly in all societies belonging to the Christian tradition, and perhaps in almost every other, too — sexual maturation is an essential preliminary to marriage for both sexes.' Hopkins says otherwise for India.

63. i.e. the beginning of a lasting union. Many of these unions began in a couple's slave days and continued after one or both had won their freedom. There is no way of telling whether any of these were second or later 'marriages'.

64. That fertility was important in female slaves is indicated in various sources. Lawyers from the late Republic onwards discussed the question of whether a female slave who proved to be sterile could be returned to the seller

and the price reclaimed (Aulus Gellius 4.2.9-10). Columella rewarded his slave women who produced children: four children earned them their freedom (*De re rustica* 1.8.19). Varro (*De re rustica* 1.17.5; cf. 2.10.6) recommended fostering a family life for slaves on country estates, especially those in responsible positions, to make them more reliable and more committed to the estate.

65. This ban was formalised by Augustus's legislation. Some scholars believe that before Augustus the ban applied to all freed–freeborn unions, and that Augustus narrowed the scope of this ban; but I prefer to follow Corbett (1930: 31-4), who argues convincingly that there was no formal ban on such mixed marriages until Augustus introduced it for senatorial families.

66. See e.g. Last (1923), quoted early in this chapter. Cf. Friedländer, vol. I (1908:243), 'Further, slavery, as everywhere, left its track of immorality very visible in Roman conjugal life'; and Carcopino (1940:101), 'Other causes contributed to hasten this decadence or rather to determine this reversal of family values. . . . Some were social, and had their origin in the poisonous virus which slavery injects into a free population.'

67. e.g. even for unions not recognised as Roman marriages: *uxor*, 'wife', *maritus*, 'husband', *coniunx*, 'spouse', as well as the specifically *de facto* terms such as *contubernalis*, 'partner', and *concubina*, 'concubine'.

68. As Taylor remarked of their portraits (1961:132), 'Even though a *cognomen* like Apollodorus or Irenaeus betrays their foreign origin, they look grim and stern as they thought old Romans ought to look. And, carefully draped on their shoulders, they wear the toga to confirm the proud declaration of the *tria nomina*, "civis Romanus sum".'

69. This is not to be explained away simply by the notion of 'sacrifice' on the part of the Vestal Virgins. Where that notion is present, e.g. with Christian nuns, there has usually been also the idea of withdrawal from many aspects of life, retaining purity by avoiding contact with corrupting influences. But — see text further — the Vestal Virgins were often involved in central issues of public life and had front seats at theatrical performances which were considered too shocking for most ordinary women.

70. The emperor Gaius conferred the privileges of the Vestal Virgins on his grandmother Antonia and on his three sisters (Dio 59.3.4). All of his sisters were married, and Agrippina must have been pregnant with Nero at the time (AD 37). The honours conferred on Messalina in AD 43 seem to be those of the Vestal Virgins (Dio 60.22.2). Tiberius's purpose in having his mother Livia sit with the Vestal Virgins at the theatre (Tacitus, *Annals* 4.16.6: AD 23) was rather to enhance the prestige of the vestals, for whom recruitment was becoming difficult, than to honour Livia; but the identification of the Augusta with the chaste vestals began the creation of an image fostered by other emperors. Cf. the identification of second-century empresses with Vesta as well as with fertility symbols (e.g. Mattingly and Sydenham, vols 2 and 3).

71. e.g. their intercessions — political rather than religious — on behalf of important citizens: Suetonius, *Iulius* 1; Tacitus, *Annals* 11.32; Tacitus, *Histories* 3.81.3. Their interpretation of an 'omen' during the Catilinarian affair in 63 BC, and their subsequent action, were essentially political (Plutarch, *Cicero* 20.1-2). See also Cicero, *Pro Murena* 73.

72. No record of specific Vestal Virgins marrying is known for our period. It would have been difficult for most men to match the status and wealth of a retired virgin, apart from any feelings of taboo that may have continued to attach to her person. Vestal Virgins could remain in office for life if they wished.

73. Valerius Maximus 7.1: the wife of Metellus Macedonicus was 'uxor pudicitia et fecunditate conspicua'.

74. An epitaph of the early imperial period (the *Laudatio Turiae* — see n. 85 below) comments on the rarity of such a long marriage (41 years) unbroken by

52   The Roman Family

divorce: 'rara sunt tam diuturna matrimonia, finita morte, non divortio in[terrupta]' (1.27). Cf. Seneca, *De beneficiis* 3.16.2, on how commonplace divorce has become in high society. These are amongst the more unsensational witnesses to this trend.

75. Columella, writing in the first century AD (*De re rustica* 12 pr.), claimed that until 'the memory of our fathers' wives had been responsible for almost all the domestic work. But in his own time, he said, many women were led by indolence and luxury to despise even spinning and weaving; so home-made garments had gone out of fashion and expensive bought ones were preferred. Moreover, Roman women found country life a bore, so the Roman couple left their estates in the care of a steward and his wife who thus took on the old citizen roles and duties. Cf. Tacitus, *Agricola* 4 and *Dialogus* 28; and Plutarch, *Cato the Elder* 20.

76. Cf. Riesman (1950:331): 'These uneasinesses among the newly liberated are one source of the current attempts to reprivatise women by redefining their role in some comfortably domestic and traditional way. Many people, both men and women, are troubled by the so-called disintegration of the family and look longingly back to the family structure of societies at an early point on the curve of population. They usually fail to see that the current divorce rate is, in part, an index of the new demands for sociability and leisure freedom of sensitive middle-class couples. . .'

77. *Letters* 1.14: from a respectable, sound part of Italy, good family, senatorial rank, energy, diligence, a sense of propriety and respectfulness, good looks and senatorial bearing, plus wealth.

78. Quintilian (1.2.8) complains of the bad example which parents and their dinner-party guests set for children, in their own extra-marital behaviour and in the kind of entertainment provided. Propertius (2.6.27-34) implies that some of the paintings in private homes are 'suggestive'.

79. Julius Caesar took extreme action against one of his freedmen who had had intercourse with the wife of an equestrian. It apparently offended his sense of social propriety and rank (Suetonius, *Iulius* 48). The emperor Claudius in AD 52 tried to inhibit relationships between free women and other people's slaves, but early in the second century Hadrian repealed the harsher aspects of this decree (Gaius *Inst.* 1.84, 160; Tacitus, *Annals* 12.53): see Weaver in Chapter 6 below. At the end of the second century Septimius Severus expressed strong opposition to a freedman marrying either his own patroness or a female member of his patron's family (C.5.4.3). In such situations there could be a conflict between the rights of a patroness and those of a husband.

80. Note, however, the evidence of D.1.16.4.2 that it was made quite clear that husbands were personally responsible for their wives' financial or other actions in the province. (Cf. Tacitus, *Annals* 4.20, for AD 33.) By the third century it was still permissible for a governor to take his wife with him, but the central government preferred that he did not.

81. In fact, early in the third century the emperor Severus Alexander provided various necessities for his governors, including a concubine for unmarried governors (Scriptores Historiae Augustae, *Severus Alexander* 42). Marriage to a woman in a governor's province was not permitted to him, although it seems that he could choose a concubine there (Paulus *Sent.* 2.20.2).

82. e.g. Plancina, Agrippina senior, Arria senior, Pliny's wife, Calpurnia, as well as the imperial women referred to in Tacitus's account.

83. For a bitter testimonial of an abandoned patron-husband, see *CIL* 6.20905. It should be noted, however, that freedwomen-wives did obtain freedom and citizenship through such marriages and were relieved of some of the normal obligations to a patron.

84. Pliny's wife was probably unusually modest in sitting behind a curtain to

listen to her husband's public reading of his works (Pliny, *Letters* 4.19). At some forms of public entertainment, e.g. the theatre and (after Augustus) gladiatorial games, women had to sit apart from the men, in higher rows; but the only ban on their actual attendance was Augustus's exclusion of women from athletic contests (Suetonius, *Augustus* 44).

85. See Bibliography under 'Women' for references.

86. Agrippina senior, however, is probably better remembered as the mother of Agrippina junior than of the emperor Gaius.

87. Varro, *De re rustica* 2.10.8; Tacitus, *Dialogus* 28.4. Cf. Quintilian 1.1.4, where the *nutrices* are probably wet-nurses: they should speak well and be of good character, since a child's first impressions are lasting. Soranus, *Gynaecology*, discusses what are desirable qualities in a wet-nurse. See Bradley, in Chapter 8 below.

88. In the fourth century this was extended to a year (C.5.9.2).

89. See Pliny, *Letters* 9.13; cf. 8.5; and Paulus *Sent.* 1.21.13.

90. Some religious rites were confined to once-married women, and the *pronuba*, the bride's matron-of-honour, was supposed to be a woman who had not had more than one husband: Livy 10.23; Servius's commentary on *Aeneid* 4.19; Festus (ed. Lindsay) pp. 282, 283; Valerius Maximus 2.1.3; Plutarch, *Roman Questions* 105.

91. Ulpian *Reg.* 14. 16; Suetonius, *Augustus* 34. At first, Augustus's *lex Iulia* had made the period one year, but his later legislation, the Papian law, gave widows an extra year in which to find a new husband.

92. Valerius Maximus 4.3.3; Josephus, *Jewish Antiquities* 18.180.

93. Antonia's daughter, Livilla, was accused of involvement in Sejanus's treason against Tiberius and of murdering her own husband. For this she was put to death. One source (Dio 58.11.7) says that Tiberius gave Livilla over to Antonia's authority for execution. Cf. n. 42 above.

94. Although I can find no evidence in the law code or elsewhere to support this, I feel that it is likely that women who had borne three or more children would not have been forced to remarry or penalised for refusing. It is almost inconceivable that all widows were able to find new husbands within a short space of time, even if they wished to. But until we can find out more about mortality rates for men and women at different ages we cannot be sure what was the state of the remarriage market.

95. If Agrippina's marriage with Germanicus had been a *manus* marriage, as I suggested above may have been true for all members of the imperial family, she would have come under the power of her husband's *paterfamilias*, who was Tiberius after Germanicus's adoption (which took place probably a year before Germanicus's marriage).

96. e.g. *CIL* 6.3604, 732, 12405 (all of whom died young), 14404; Valerius Maximus 4.3.3 (Antonia); Horace, *Odes* 3.14.4 (Livia, who had however been married already before she married Augustus: the phrase here is 'unico gaudens mulier marito'). In Propertius 4.11.36 Cornelia takes pride in having been 'uni nupta'. See also Williams (1958).

97. As suggested by Hopkins (1965a:324 n.56). Cf. Tacitus, *Annals* 2.86: Tiberius gave preference, in choosing a new vestal virgin, to the girl whose mother was still married to the girl's father. The other candidate's household had lost some dignity when the mother was divorced.

98. But see Corbett (1930:130) on *retentio propter mores*.

99. Cf. D.24.1.60: gifts occur often when divorce takes place because of sterility or because of the demands of a priesthood.

100. In Hadrian's time, a man who met a woman — apparently casually during a journey — and took her home with him sent notice of divorce to her

husband. This was presumably on behalf of the woman. He was exiled for three years — apparently for inspiring a frivolous divorce (D.24.2.8).

101. Cicero, *Topica* 19, envisaged the theoretical situation of a wife initiating divorce against a guilty husband. And the law provided stricter rules for restoration of dowry when a husband's morals were open to blame (Ulpian *Reg.* 6.13). Moreover, it came to be the case (and may have been from the beginning of Augustus's legislation) that if a husband prosecuted his wife for adultery he could be penalised himself if his own behaviour had been no better; 'for it is most unjust that a husband should demand from his wife a standard of morality which he himself does not live up to': D.48.5.14(13).5 (Ulpian).

102. But in 295 BC, when Rome was involved in a war against the Samnites, some women were tried publicly for improper sexual behaviour (*stuprum*) and fined (Livy 10.31.9). The magistrate who imposed the fine used the money for the building of a temple to — ironically — Venus! (probably Venus Obsequens, who had helped him in battle, rather than specifically the goddess of love: Servius's commentary on *Aeneid* 1.720).

103. Apart from obvious reasons for convenience, Quintilian 7.3.10 suggests this ('domi' seems to indicate the woman's home rather than the man's).

104. It is not easy to tell how frequent such prosecutions were. We know that prosecutions under Augustus's other moral legislation were frequent (see n. 17 above), and that adultery trials continued for at least two centuries, though probably not in the courts established by Augustus for that purpose (see Garnsey 1967:56-60).

105. Domitian was one of the strictest enforcers, in spite of his own *stuprum*, over a long period, with his niece Julia. See Martial 6.2 and 4 (and 5.75 and 6.7 for pressure to marry); Juvenal 2.29-33; Suetonius, *Domitian* 8; Dio 67.12.1.

106. Suetonius, *Tiberius* 35: the context seems to refer to senatorial and equestrian ranks; the women chose to give up their 'ius ac dignitas matronalis' ('women's rights and dignity'). Tiberius made this sort of action punishable by exile. Cf. Tacitus, *Annals* 2.85, for AD 19: the senate passed severe decrees to control the licence of women ('libido feminarum'), and forbade prostitution for women whose grandfather, father or husband had been a Roman equestrian. Vistilia, a woman of praetorian family, had registered with the aediles for prostitution; her husband Titidius Labeo was arraigned for not bringing his obviously guilty wife to trial; he escaped punishment but Vistilia was exiled.

107. D.23.2.41; 48.5.11.2; 48.5.14.2 (Marcellus, Papinian, Ulpian respectively). Quintilian (7.3.10) conceives of at least the theoretical situation that adultery with another man's wife may take place in a brothel.

108. Paulus *Sent.* 2.24; cf. D.25.3. The woman was required to report her pregnancy to her ex-husband or his father within 30 days of a divorce. If she tried to suppress this evidence (presumably to deny her ex-husband his child), the ex-husband could, if he suspected pregnancy, require her to submit to a physical examination. Julius Caesar annulled the marriage of a senator who married a woman within two days of her divorce (Suetonius, *Iulius* 43.1) — so swift a remarriage would cloud the question of paternity of any child born within the next nine months or so.

109. *Topica* 19. (But in the second century AD a father's scandalous conduct could result in the mother being granted custody: D.43.30.3.5.) Cf. Tacitus, *Annals* 2.86, for AD 19 — a candidate for a Vestal Virgin's position is clearly in the custody of her father, who is divorced from her mother. Livia's sons were in the custody of her first husband until he died and they came to live with her and Augustus (Dio 48.44.5). On Roman law's lack of provision for 'dividing a child' between parents, see Daube (1966).

110. D.50.16.196 (Gaius): 'feminarum liberos in familia earum non esse palam est, quia qui nascuntur patris familiam sequuntur'.

111. Cicero, *Topica* 19; Ulpian *Reg.* 6.10, 6.12-13.

112. e.g. Plutarch, *Cato the Elder* 24.4; *Comparison of Aristides and Cato* 6.1; Scriptores Historiae Augustae, *Marcus* 29; as well as the sinister nature of the stepmother's role in Tacitus's treatment of Livia and Agrippina junior.

113. Sulla's stepmother (Plutarch, *Sulla* 2.4); Octavia reared with her own children Antony's children by two other wives (Plutarch, *Antony* 87); Fannia (Pliny, *Letters* 7.19, 9.13.3).

114. A legal guardian (a *tutor*) had to be provided for a widow's daughter. If one had not been named in her husband's will and there were no agnatic relations to be consulted, the widow asked the consuls to choose a suitable *tutor*, as Anteia did soon after her remarriage (Pliny, *Letters* 9.13.16). Cf. Claudius's provisions (Suetonius, *Claudius* 23.2). See Schulz (1936:162-97) on guardianship.

115. Two imperial examples are of interest. The emperor Gaius was raised by women until he was 18 (Suetonius, *Gaius* 10). Nero's mother, Agrippina junior, was exiled when he was two years old: when his father died a year later Nero was raised by a paternal aunt until his mother returned from exile a year or so after that. Agrippina remarried, but this stepfather of Nero died not long after, leaving Nero a generous inheritance. When Agrippina then married Claudius, Nero accompanied her to the imperial household and was not long afterwards adopted by Claudius as his own son (partly for dynastic reasons) (Suetonius, *Nero* 6.3).

116. Hopkins (1966:247) believes that the mass of Roman tombstones belong to the 'respectable classes', i.e. the relatively well-to-do (cf. 1965a:322). Although it is very likely that the poorest inhabitants of Rome could afford no individual burial place or monument at all, and that therefore all record of them has disappeared, nevertheless the many modest memorials in the *sepulcrales* of *CIL* 6 are, by definition, the record of people who had almost nothing to tell of themselves except their name and a few personal details. There are approximately 23,000 of these inscriptions, which exclude almost all the senators, equestrians, soldiers, important imperial officials, skilled tradesmen and anyone else who had a special niche, however humble, in Roman society. Moreover, Hopkins' evidence on the cost of tombstones comes largely from Africa. If it can be applied to Rome (which is doubtful) it still represents a sum which a comparatively humble slave or citizen might hope to be able to save in a not unreasonable period of time.

117. The closest to this is the freedman Cornelius Epicadus, who enjoyed the affection and confidence of Sulla and Sulla's son. He completed Sulla's autobiography (Suetonius, *De grammaticis* 12). Adult Romans often cultivated the company of philosophers and literary men, but these relationships were not the same as that between an immature pupil and a professional teacher.

118. Suetonius, *De rhetoribus* 1 re action in 161 BC and 92 BC. The censors' edict of 92 BC is very revealing: it includes the statement, 'Our ancestors established what they wished their children to learn and what schools they wanted them to attend. The present innovations, which go against the custom and tradition of our ancestors, do not meet with our approval.'

119. Politics, the law courts, military commands. The imperial bureaucracy depended less on oral communication. It was originally composed mainly of freedmen and slaves, but from the second century AD it began to draw substantially on men of equestrian rank. But equestrians seem to have continued to receive the traditional rhetorical education.

120. One of the best-known teachers in Rome in the first century AD, Quintus Remmius Palaemon, had been a *verna* (Suetonius, *De grammaticis* 23). He was trained first in weaving, but when he took over responsibility for accompanying to school the son of the mistress of the household he acquired an academic education for himself. On being manumitted he went to Rome (from northern Italy) to teach.

121. Examples of this are Corellia Hispulla, who educated her son in association with tutors until he was about 14 years of age (Pliny, *Letters* 3.3); and Iulia Procilla, mother of Tacitus' father-in-law Agricola, who supervised Agricola's education until his early manhood (Tacitus, *Agricola* 4).

122. e.g. Agricola's mother (see preceding note), who not only guided him through a broad liberal arts curriculum but who knew when to divert him from such 'impractical' concerns and set him on a path more appropriate for a Roman and a senator; Cornelia, the mother of the Gracchi brothers (Plutarch, *Tiberius Gracchus* 1; cf. Cicero, *Brutus* 104; Quintilian 1.1.6; Tacitus, *Dialogus* 28); Caesar's mother Aurelia and Augustus's mother Atia (Tacitus, *Dialogus* 28).

123. e.g. the poetess of Augustan times, Sulpicia; Hortensia, daughter of the famous Republican speaker Hortensius, herself an accomplished speaker (Quintilian 1.1.6); Clodia, a literary patroness as well as mistress of talented young men; Pliny's wife Calpurnia, who surely needed an education as well as wifely devotion to take the interest she did in Pliny's writings and career.

124. e.g. Cicero, *Brutus* 211; Juvenal 6.185-193, 242-5, 398-412, 434-456, who did not like the educated woman who was fluent in Greek and could rival men in her knowledge of the law, current affairs, literature, and rhetoric; Pliny, *Letters* 5.16 and note thereon by Sherwin-White (1966:347). Quintilian (1.1.6) recommended that both fathers and mothers should be as well educated as possible.

125. Political influence — Brutus's womenfolk, especially his mother Servilia: Cicero, *Ad Atticum* 15.11; cf. Servilia's social influence: *Ad Atticum* 5.4.1. Marriage of a daughter, which would almost certainly involve dowry arrangements: Cicero, *Ad Atticum* 6.6.1; Valerius Maximus 4.4.10.

126. See Pliny, *Letters* 8.14.4-6, on the importance of practical example from fathers and senior citizens. When he says this used to happen 'antiquitus', i.e. in former times, he means that Domitian's reign interrupted a long tradition. For senatorial sons at the door of the chamber, see Taylor and Scott (1969:533).

127. Examples below 14 are very rare, applying only to Nero, Commodus and Caracalla (Marquardt 1886:128-30). There is some difficulty about Gaius's coming-of-age, but it was probably in his 19th year, i.e. between his 18th and 19th birthdays.

128. See Campbell *et al.* (1960:146-9) for the US; Butler and Stokes (1970:55-64) for Britain; and Aitkin (1982:chapter 6) for Australia.

129. True, Livy (26.22.15) commented that in his day — the Augustan period — elders and even parents could not command much respect for their opinions from their children ('parentium quoque hoc saeculo vilis levisque apud liberos auctoritas'), but this is a timeless criticism of the younger generation.

130. The importance of such occasions in displaying a family's history and traditions is reflected in an incident of AD 16: Scribonius Libo Drusus was convicted of treason, and a motion was put to the senate that Libo's mask should be excluded from future funeral processions of his family (Tacitus, *Annals* 2.32).

131. As these family archives were often the source of Republican history writing, they have had a distorting influence on Roman historiography, which has worried both ancient and modern scholars. See, for instance, Cicero, *Brutus* 62.

132. Claudius made it a capital offence for foreign citizens to assume a Roman family name (Suetonius, *Claudius* 25.3).

133. For illustrations, see Nash (1961:vol. 2, 38-43).

134. The evidence for Vespasian is the inscription *CIL* 6.893. I do not know the evidence for Nerva, which is referred to (without source) by Toynbee (1971:154).

135. Tacitus, *Annals* 15.23. Nero's mother, Agrippina junior, was a Claudian through her father; but it was the Julian line, going back through the women to

Augustus, that was important to both Agrippina junior and senior in their ambitions and claims to a share in imperial power.

2 WOMEN IN ROMAN SUCCESSION[1]

J.A. Crook

Succession to property, which is what this paper is about, may, or it may not, be importantly relevant to the position in family or society of the person who succeeds.[2] If the assets are large they will at least provide the beneficiary with an income capable of commanding an abundance of goods and services and purchasing standing in the community in so far as purchase will do that; but what mainly gives people power derived from property is the power to dispose of the capital; that is, alienate the property and determine the next succession to it.[3] In feudal systems it is almost as if the property had power over the owners. There was nothing of that kind in Rome, so that the possibilities of power derived from property were great; nevertheless, it must be understood that not only are 'property' and 'ownership' English terms with a different semantic range from *dominium* but also both they and *dominium* are totally abstract and quite empty until they are given the practical content allowed to them by the positive law and custom of the particular community.[4]

We shall begin with an exposition of the legal rules that were relevant to the succession of women to property in the classical period of Roman law, and after that look, all too sketchily and impressionistically, at some of the evidence for what actually went on and was expected to go on. There are several reasons for beginning with an exposition of the rules. The first is that, of course, they did not stand entirely still from the Twelve Tables to Caracalla, and out of their chronological changes it is customary to derive accounts of the advance of women's rights. The accounts are not always the same, though they are always a story of movement from *agnatio* to *cognatio*. A second reason is that statements of the rules — in such accounts as the above, and elsewhere — are not always altogether accurate. The rules are, indeed, in some cases imperfectly known anyway, and it may be salutary to draw attention to some of the doubts and problems. Finally, seeing what people actually did makes sense only in the context of the rules by which they were supposed to be operating.

58

A last prolegomenon concerns 'primitive' Rome and the chronological story. Rome of the Twelve Tables — behind which, except by conjecture, we cannot get — already possessed sophisticated legal institutions (see Watson 1975). If there was once a 'patriarchal joint family', exclusion of females by males, *manus* marriage only, and so on, they had gone, and if there was a road leading from *agnatio* to *cognatio* an important fraction of it had already been trodden, by the time we begin to perceive the rules and the practice clearly. This chapter will not concern itself much with *Urgeschichte*.

I

The rules of Roman law that are relevant to women's succession to property need to be looked at reasonably broadly. Nevertheless we should begin at the obvious place, with the rules of intestate succession as given in the Twelve Tables, for overwhelmingly most scholars now agree (though it is not obvious) that automatic family succession preceded testament at Rome. The principle is that of agnatic descent: heirs to a person will be (if there are any) the *sui heredes*, i.e. all the people, irrespective of sex, who, being in his *potestas*, do not at his decease fall under any other *potestas*. (Notice the asymmetry at the very beginning in that word 'his': for only males have *potestas*.) Agnation is an artificial concept: adoption and *manus* bring people under *potestas*, adoption, *manus* and *emancipatio* take people out of *potestas*. *Sui heredes* become heirs to equal portions (*per stirpes*) irrespective of sex. So far as women are concerned it is to be noted that if they are married with *manus* (and it is probable — not more — that at any rate down to the Punic Wars most women were) they have simply changed the descent group in which they will be among the *sui heredes*.

Parenthetically it may be added here that dowry is of the utmost importance in all these matters. It is a transfer of family property with the woman, perhaps in the case of early *manus* marriage an irreversible transfer; but unless you believe that the ceremony of *coemptio* points back to primitive 'bride-price' you do not really have grounds for conjecturing an original two-way transfer of family property. More will need to be said about dowry later; at this point it should be noted that though dowry was substantial (not just trousseau) there is no trace of a rule that it had to be the woman's intestate portion, nor any trace of a rule that dowry was legally obligatory.

Scholars have been very reluctant to believe in the equal inheritance of women as among *sui heredes*, at least for the 'primitive' period, mainly because they have wanted to find a *potestas* head for the family, which a woman could never be.[5] (Actually, partibility itself does not square well with the 'patriarchal joint family' that people have been keen to posit.[6])

If there are no *sui heredes* the inheritance passes to *proximus agnatus*, that is to say the agnate person, irrespective of sex, in the nearest degree,[7] or persons, if there are more than one in that degree. Brothers and sisters are the most likely case. Inheritance here is *per capita*; more important, it does not pass any further down: if *proximus agnatus* refuses the inheritance no other agnate as such gets it: it goes to the *gentiles*. That succession was real enough, and can be found in Cicero, but it was thought of as hardly being a real succession at all but a kind of caducity.[8] Here we have to record the first change in the civil law rules after the Twelve Tables (presumably on the basis of legislation, for it was not merely *iure honorario*): at some date *proximus agnatus* on the female side was held not to count at all beyond *consanguineae*, sisters. Taking that modification into account Voci (1960:389) describes the intestate right of women thus: women have equal rights with men when they are succeeding to father (as *sua heres*), brothers or sisters (as *prox. ag.*), but outside those limits succession went only to men. The date of the modification cannot be ascertained. Gaius (*Inst.* 3.23) treats it as part of the Twelve Tables system, whereas Paulus *Sent.* 4.8.20 is categorical that it was not and speaks of it as arising *iure civili* but 'Voconiana ratione' ('on Voconian principles'). That presumably implies that it was known not to have been part of the actual *lex Voconia* of 169 BC but was seen as an analogous anti-feminist move. I do not think it is likely to have been much later: perhaps it arose by juristic interpretation of intestacies resulting from the operation of the *lex Voconia*.[9]

Nothing in these rules excludes or makes anomalous succession to (i.e. inheritance from) women. Indeed, it is very important to know what will happen in the end to the property that has descended to a *sua heres*. When a woman dies she has no one in her *potestas*, and therefore no *sui heredes*, so her inheritance goes straight to *proximus agnatus*: that will be (if there are any) her brothers and sisters by the same father, unless she is married with *manus*, in which case she is *filiae loco* to her husband and her nearest agnates are likely to be her children.

Manus, it is perhaps almost superfluous to say, affects the intestate succession of women because a woman who goes into *manus* leaves her original agnatic descent group and enters that of her husband. Any property she takes with her simply merges with that of her new *paterfamilias*. That was perhaps originally irrevocable whatever happened to the marriage, but in the classical period it could apparently all be counted as dowry and might, like any other dowry, fail to be repaid.[10]

By a process that, though gradual, was pretty complete between the Twelve Tables and the end of the Republic the praetors modified the rules of intestate succession in practice by granting *bonorum possessio ab intestato* to a wider range of people than the Twelve Tables envisaged. They brought in, first, people who would have been *sui heredes* but for the formal rule that adoption, emancipation and *manus* took them out; and if there was still no successor they brought in, after *proximus agnatus*, any other agnates (though in the case of women still not beyond *consanguineae*); and if there was still nobody they went on downwards (or outwards) to *cognati*, in which category even the women who had been barred as non-consanguineous agnates could have their chance;[11] and at the bitter end came the sole case of intestate succession between affines, viz. husband and wife. One consequence of all that was that a woman *in manu* had the possibility of intestate succession in both lineages. On the other hand, if an emancipated woman had a dowry and expected to be called in by the praetor to *bonorum possessio* against *sui heredes* and *prox.ag.cum re* (that is, so to speak, shouldering her way in and diminishing their shares) she was made to put the dowry back into the total fund, for she had had, if not her full intestate portion, a big slice of the cake already.[12] 'Emancipated' here probably included married with *manus*;[13] in the case of non-*manus* marriage there may be an implication in this rule that when your daughter married without *manus* and you gave her her dowry you normally emancipated her, so that she was no longer in your *potestas*. It is a pity that one does not really know whether it was normal to emancipate sons when they married.

The modifications introduced by *ius honorarium* into the intestate system seem to imply a very strong feeling for partibility, a feeling that a man's children ought all to have their share. It is sometimes supposed that the emancipation of children from *potestas* (sons as well as daughters) was used as a device for defeating partibility and leaving a single heir, and that this somehow ceased to be thought right. Such a change does not ring very plausibly, and the evidence is very conflicting, for emancipation seems sometimes sought after, sometimes a penalty. What should perhaps be remembered is that by the time the praetorian rules came into existence it was normal for a *paterfamilias* to make a will, so that the intestate rules would be regulating the residual cases.

That said, it is important not to downgrade the intestate rules: they never became obsolete or unimportant. For, notwithstanding the strong social and psychological pressure on people to make wills, if a will failed — as it might do for many reasons — the rules of intestacy came into play. That is why they were still being modified right down to the *senatusconsulta Tertullianum* and *Orfitianum* of the second century AD.

Before going on to testation we should consider certain other aspects of the property-owning woman in relation to the family. We have seen women acquiring ownership by inheritance, but we ought not to forget that women were perfectly entitled to receive gifts. In the case of a woman *in potestate*, exactly as in that of a man *in potestate* or for that matter a slave, anything she acquires accrues automatically to her *paterfamilias*, who can if he chooses treat it as *peculium* in her hands (though we do not actually hear very much about *peculium* of *filiafamilias*). But when, for whatever reason, a woman is *sui iuris* (i.e. in no one's *potestas*), gifts to her are straighforwardly hers.[14] Women may, then, have more property than they have got through the family. Can they, however, use it, and, particularly, dispose of it?

That question obliges us to consider briefly *tutela*. Until the end of the Republic every woman who was not in someone's *potestas* was, all her life, in someone's *tutela*. Again there was an asymmetry of males and females, because *tutela*, like *potestas*, was a power belonging only to males, and also because *sui iuris* males were in *tutela* not for life but only till puberty. The old automatic rule was exactly parallel to the rules of succession: the *tutela* over a woman was held by her (male) agnates[15] precisely because succession to her would go to them (though also, it is true, to *consanguineae*) and they could prevent anything serious being done with the property of which they disapproved. An *impubes* could not carry out legal acts; a woman could: the acts were hers, but were only valid if they had the authorisation of her guardian(s). And that applied with particular force to alienating property and taking herself into *manus* (and so out of their agnatic control).[16] A woman in *legitima* (that is, agnate or patronal) *tutela* therefore only had fully independent disposal of income; the capital would in the end go where it would have gone if she had never been there. On the other hand, there might not be any agnates; and in the *testamentum per aes et libram* a *paterfamilias* could cut the agnates out of *tutela* just as he could cut them out of succession, and choose a guardian for his daughter or let her choose one, as could a husband for a wife *in manu*. Such a guardian, having no automatic expectations about the property, had no personal motive for refusing authorisations to alienate.

All the emphasis so far has been on agnation. It should, parenthetically, be said about women's place in the family in general that some recent writers share the view expounded by Professor K. Lipstein in a brilliant seminar many years ago, that agnation is something of a mirage. In the certainly very important sphere of *potestas* and automatic succession and *cura* of *furiosi* and *prodigi* agnation prevails, but in the rest of Roman life the tie of people with their mothers and their maternal kin seems to have been taken into account just as much as agnation.[17]

Testation 'took over' in Rome.[18] The earliest will, *calatis comitiis*, which is probably the sort implied in the Twelve Tables, is likely to have been an adoption will, and it is virtually certain that women could neither make such a will nor be instituted under one. But there developed as a kind of 'dodge' based on the Twelve Tables the will *per aes et libram*, which remained for a very long time the normal, proper Roman will;[19] and it was a purely private act, and under it there was very little a testator could not do. In particular, under such a will women could be instituted as *heredes*; they could also be given legacies, including *legatum partitionis*, legacy of a fraction of everything (just like *hereditas* except that it did not burden you with debts); and they could, too, make such a will themselves.

For the latter purpose, however, a woman had not only to

have the authorisation of her guardian(s) but, down to Hadrian, to go through a rigmarole, the 'so-called *coemptio*'.[20] Being a *capitis deminutio* the ceremony broke (with their consent) the power of the existing guardians. It was a kind of fictitious going into *manus* and coming out again, and is thought to reflect an early time when the only situation in which a woman's agnates ceased to have a residual interest in her property was when she went into *manus* (because they ceased to be her agnates); whether she went into *manus* depended on their authorisation anyway. In this matter of testation also other sorts of guardian than agnates, having no expectations about the property, had no motives other than general care and prudence for forbidding a woman to go through the procedure and make her will.

One of the principal freedoms given by the power of testation is the opportunity to disinherit people who would otherwise have automatically come into the whole or a part of the inheritance. They could still be given just as much of the assets as a legacy, but they would not be *heredes*, with the duty to uphold the *sacra familiae*, responsibility for debts, and so on. There is a tendency to want to believe that Roman *patresfamiliarum* preferred to make males their *heredes*, since they could transmit the *potestas* side of things; they would leave plenty to their daughters, but disinherit them and leave it in other ways. We certainly cannot get a quantitative picture of this, but some evidence does point in that general direction.

There is an asymmetry between the sexes in the rules about disherison, though its implications are not easy to fathom. Disherison was entirely valid if carried out in due form; but *filii sui*, sons who were *sui heredes* (i.e. *in potestate*) must be disinherited by name, otherwise the will was void, whereas *filiae* could be disinherited effectively in a general clause ('let all others be *exheredes*'), and if that was not done the will was not void but — *iure civili*, not merely by praetorian intervention — the *filia* could *accrescere in partem* (i.e. shoulder her way into her intestate share). A *lex Iunia Vellaea* of AD 26 extended the rule to grandsons and granddaughters. The praetor did modify the rules by granting *bonorum possessio contra tabulas* on much the same principles as he used in granting *b.p. ab intestato*: to *filii sui* who had to be disinherited *nominatim* if the will was not to be void he added emancipated *filii*, and both males and females who had been passed over without due form he would allow to eliminate extraneous heirs altogether. But that last privilege was clawed back from females by Antoninus Pius.[21]

What is at the back of all this? Well, it looks as if sweeping away all the male heirs (perhaps all but one, to achieve primogeniture by the backdoor and defeat partibility and splitting-up) was not thought very nice; you could do it but must come clean about it.[22] Sweeping away the females is, perhaps, not minded so much: you can leave them legacy of their dowry, and so on. But notice also that the failure to disinherit *filii sui* in proper form makes the will void, so there will ensue an intestacy, and all the *sui heredes*, male and female, will get their share: ignore a son and all come in. Failure to disinherit *filiae suae* in proper form will not produce an intestacy, it will just bring *them* in, while expressly disinherited sons will still remain out. Ignore a daughter and only she comes in: she will, indeed, have to bring her dowry into contribution as usual. The praetor, doubtless reflecting prevailing conceptions of what was right and proper, did not like children being cut out of heirship altogether by strangers to the family: what induced Antoninus Pius to mind that less when the children were female, I do not know.

From at least the late Republic onwards even people who had been quite correctly disinherited had a potential remedy: the *querela inofficiosi testamenti*. You had to prove that the omission was unfair. Only those could sue who had an intestate claim (however remote), so not just old friends or mistresses, and you could not sue if you had received from the testator, by any means, a quarter of your intestate entitlement; but if successful you shouldered your way in to your whole intestate entitlement. Women could sue under these rules just as much as men.

The most famous change in the rules relating to the testamentary succession of women was, however, of course produced by the *lex Voconia* of 169 BC. It is a much-discussed statute,[23] but much about it remains obscure: its detailed provisions, its purpose and its ultimate fate are all subject to controversy. It laid down, first, that persons in the highest census class could not validly institute women as *heredes* and, second, that no person might take either by legacy or by *donatio mortis causa* more than the *heredes* took.

That it did not touch the intestate rights of women seems certain because if it had done so the sources on the intestate rules would have been bound to refer to it. It proves, of course — if proof were needed — that by its date women were being instituted *heredes*, and apart from financial considerations it was a blow to the status of the women of the top class that they could not be made testamentary *heredes* any more. In terms of property one can work out that the effect of the statute was to confine the women of the top class to their intestate portion if they were up against males. That is what the woman would get if you simply left yourself intestate; if you decided to make a will you could make the males your *heredes* and leave any female a *legatum partitionis*; if you made a will and just ignored the women they would *accrescere in partem*. But the statute was hard on women where there was no male in the family, for example on only-daughters, whose *paterfamilias*, to comply with the statute, would have to institute an extraneous male, who would get half, in order to give his daughter half as legacy, or else go intestate, which people hated doing and deprived him of the chance to do all the other things wills were for. The dodges by which the Voconian was circumvented are well known,[24] especially *fideicommissum hereditatis* and it is plain from Cicero's account (*De finibus* 2.55) of a man who took advantage of sanctimonious adherence to the letter of the Voconian to keep an inheritance he had been asked to transfer that the radical youth of Cicero's younger days rebelled, in such a case, against the spirit of the statute.

The *lex Voconia* is usually seen in a 'Catonian' context as part of a wave of anti-feminist sentiment, or at any rate of male dislike of the relatively new phenomenon of flaunted female luxury. That is probably right, however much we may think that they might have chosen more effective methods to reach the result. The law was, in fact, part of the story of Roman sumptuary laws. A different suggestion has recently been made as to its purpose. We tend to focus our attention on *filiaefamilias*; but Pomeroy (1976:222f) pointed out that widows and orphans were exempt from *tributum*, and suggested that the main motive for the legislation was to prevent large fortunes escaping tax. (It was passed, as it happens, just before *tributum* was in effect abolished.) But if the purpose was to prevent widows and orphans escaping *tributum*, why did the Roman people not simply subject them to *tributum*? The Voconian would be an absurdly tangential way of going about that: it was not confined to widows and had nothing to say about orphans.

What happened to the Voconian law? By the late Republic all

sorts of things were being done — and not only by *fidei-commissum* — that suggest that it was being ignored, and one might have supposed it already dead if we were not told that Augustus exempted certain women from its provisions — perhaps *iure liberorum*.[25] Gaius treats it as still in force, while Gellius says that it has withered away.[26] A puzzle. I think it is reasonable to guess that after Augustus it did not inconvenience anybody much.

The Augustan legislation affected women's property and succession position in various ways on which we need not linger. Women were freed from *tutela* by virtue of having a certain number of children, *iure liberorum*.[27] On the other hand, *caelibes* and *orbi*, female as well as male, were subjected to some limits in the matter of inheritance. What was the extent of those limits? First, if the *Gnomon of the Idios Logos* can be treated as giving a general rule, this set of rules applied only to the top property class (sect. 32). In that class unmarried persons could not take inheritances or legacies at all, and childless persons could take only half,[28] except under a 'military will'[29] (so there were some wealthy soldiers about!). What thus fell vacant swelled the shares of those who *were* entitled to take. The prohibition could be circumvented by *fideicommissum* until that loophole was closed. Nothing prevented *caelibes* and *orbi* from making wills. All modern scholars take it as incontrovertible that these rules concerned only testamentary succession;[30] and although Gaius and the *Gnomon* speak as if all *caelibes* and *orbi* (of the first class, anyhow) were caught, modern scholars also tend to accept from *Frag. Vat.* 216 and Ulpian *Tit.* 18 that there was a long list of exceptions,[31] such that almost anybody who was a relative was exempt from the ban and it would only really have hit extraneous persons. It is not easy to see why, in that case, there was such a fuss over the legislation.[32] Under the Augustan rules rather strict limits were also placed on the testamentary capacity of husband and wife as between one another,[33] but *iure liberorum* they could have full capacity.

Claudius abolished the agnatic *tutela* over women.

In the second century were passed the two *senatusconsulta*, the *Tertullianum* under Hadrian[34] and the *Orfitianum* of AD 178, which further modified the intestate rules as between a mother and her children. By the *Tertullianum* a woman, *iure liberorum*, was given *bonorum possessio* in the class *unde legitimi* (i.e. as if she were an agnate instead of merely a cognate) to the property of her children. By the *Orfitianum* children, whether legitimate or not and irrespective of *ius liberorum*, were given *bonorum possessio* in the class *unde liberi* (i.e. as if they were *sui*), to the property of their mother. It is striking that succession of mother to children was dealt with earlier than that of children to mother.

A comprehensive survey of the relation of women to property would give careful attention to the rules about invalidity of gifts *inter vivos* between husband and wife. The principle was said to be *moribus*, eventually rationalised as being '*ne mutuo amore invicem spoliarentur*': 'lest they should be despoiled by one another through mutual affection'. It lasted all through the classical period, being modified in AD 206 to the extent that such gifts, instead of being *ipso iure* totally void, were henceforward merely voidable if the donor so chose. A great deal of detailed law grew up, but here we can do no more than refer to the standard treatments.[35]

Proper consideration ought really also to be given to the complex Roman rules about dowry, for they relate in a fundamental way to women's position in property, succession and the family. *Pacta dotalia* were probably an almost universal concomitant of marriage. The purpose of dowry is plainly expressed at D.17.2.81: 'ut ea [the dowry] vel alii marito dari possit'; that is, its primary function is in relation to what happens when the marriage comes to an end. The husband had, during the marriage, full ownership (not just usufruct) of whatever was given in dowry, though by an Augustan rule he was not permitted to alienate *dotale praedium*, not at least if it was *solum Italicum*, except with his wife's consent;[36] but he would, under most circumstances, have to return or account for every penny of the dowry when the marriage ended. *Dos profecticia* was that contributed by the wife's *paterfamilias*; *dos adventicia* was that from any other source — the wife herself, other relatives, or friends of the family. One meets *dos* contributed by friends quite a lot in both the legal and the lay literature;[37] it was evidently a regular *officium* of the well-to-do. Both the rules and the dotal pacts were basically concerned with return or retention of dowry at the end of marriage: the pacts could enshrine almost any arrangement the parties cared to make, and so depended on their relative social and financial bargaining position. In the absence of a pact the rules were (stated very crudely) these:

If the marriage ended with death or *capitis deminutio* of the wife, *dos adventicia* was kept — it represented a profit — but *dos profecticia* went back to the *paterfamilias*, less certain retentions for children (a fifth per child). If the marriage ended from any other cause, which included, of course, death or *cap.dem.* of the husband and also divorce, all *dos* had to go back, less certain retentions for children if divorce had been at the will of the wife's side, a third per child up to three, and as penalty for adultery. A small but significant point is that the *iudicium rei uxoriae*, the suit by which a woman could sue for return of her dowry, was not 'actively transmissible'; that is, it did not pass to her heirs. In other words, the dowry was not for anybody's sake or purposes but hers. Dowry does, however, come into succession: we have seen some rules requiring *collatio dotis*, but we should also note that it seems to have been common for a husband to leave his wife a legacy of her dowry. It might be wondered why that was necessary, since she was entitled to get it back anyway, but the advantage of legacy was that she was at once owner and could vindicate it, and so, now, could her heirs.

II

If we turn to consider what kind of things happened in practice there are still two rather different categories of evidence to consider. First, from passages in the *Digest* and the *Code* one can see what particular questions arose when the rules were applied to individual cases — and of course we have to confess that there are the usual difficulties, that of knowing whether cases were real or imaginary, and that of knowing whether the case is atypical precisely because it is problematic. And then, secondly, there is what we can learn from historical sources — letters, anecdotes and surviving wills and other documents of practice. In what follows these categories will be taken in reverse order.

The earliest point at which we meet reasonably hard evidence is the debate in Livy on the repeal of the Oppian law,[38] which belongs precisely to the age of what one might call 'Voconiana ratio'. Cato in his speech[39] stresses how women in the 'good old times' were either *in manu*, or else could carry out no act *sine tutore auctore*; his opponent recalls how the wealth of the widows kept the government going during the war, and speaks of '*manus* and

tutela but not *servitium'*. Presently,[40] we come to Fecenia
Hispala, the freedwoman who gave information that led to the
suppression of the Bacchanalian conspiracy. What Livy tells us
about her may be to some extent a 'doublet'. First, before the
event, we are told that, her *patronus* having died, she was 'in
nullius manu' (i.e. in no one's *tutela*); she correctly applied to the
authorities for a *tutor* and, presumably with his authority, did a
coemptio (this is not mentioned by Livy) and made a will. Later,
we are told that the privileges she was given by the senate for her
services (they are notoriously obscure[41]) included the right to
mancipate and alienate, which one would have thought she already
had. She was permitted to count as if she were a freeborn widow,
with free choice of *tutor* as if granted by a deceased husband's
will. But the most striking part of the story is its implication that
the tribunes and the praetor had not thought a freedwoman (and
known prostitute) too humble for them to give a guardian to
upon properly submitted application.

The family and testamentary affairs of the Scipios have been
excellently illuminated by Boyer (1950). First — the evidence is
virtually all in a few pages of Polybius (31.22 and 26-8) — we
hear of the conspicuous expenditure of Aemilia the wife of
Africanus — just the kind of flaunting of material wealth that led
to 'Voconiana ratio'. Then we are told that Aemilianus, being
heir to his adoptive father the son of Africanus, but also to
Aemilia,[42] paid the remaining half of the enormous dowries of
the Cornelias, the sisters of his adoptive father and daughters of
Africanus, the first half having been paid by Aemilia. Boyer
infers from all this that Africanus must have instituted his wife
Aemilia as his *heres* and disinherited the daughters but given
them legacy of their dowries. He is worried that nothing is said
about the sons of Africanus being made *heredes*, but it would not
have been relevant to discuss the sons; they probably were made
heredes but the dowry legacies were charged on Aemilia's share
alone. Pomeroy (1976) makes the suggestion that these huge
dowries were yet another dodge to circumvent the Voconia: as a
general point that is worth considering, but in this case I do not
think it can be right, because the original dotal promise had been
made by Africanus, and that is too early.

When Aemilius Paullus, the brother of Aemilia and the
natural father of Scipio Aemilianus, died in 160, leaving 60
talents, Aemilianus and his brother were Paullus's heirs. The *lex*

Voconia being by then in force, Paullus could not institute his daughters, even if he wished to. Aemilianus's natural mother, Papiria, the divorced first wife of Paullus, was, we are told, in straits after her divorce and was helped financially by her son: when she died she made him her *heres*, with a lot of the jewels and plate and so on of Aemilia that had come to him and he had made over to her (and, as Boyer says, she made him her *heres* of course by will, for he had no intestate claim). That inheritance he handed over to his natural sisters, Paullus's daughters, who, not being agnates of Papiria, had no intestate claim either and (presumably) could not be instituted by her. Notwithstanding the 60 talents, Paullus's heirs could not repay the dowry of his widow (that is, his second, unknown wife) without selling real estate.

Boyer suggests that since even before the *lex Voconia* the Cornelias were not made *heredes* any more than the Aemilias were after the *lex Voconia*, that statute was only enshrining in law an existing social custom, to emancipate your daughters, disinherit them and leave them their portion of the assets as legacy. And that might not necessarily be out of less regard for them and their status: it had one great advantage, that they did not have to concern themselves about debts or about administration of the estate.

Cicero's accounts of the dodges used to get round the Voconian we can take more or less as read.[43] In the *Verrines* we hear of a man with an only daughter who did 'quod eum natura hortabatur' and instituted his daughter, on the view that he was not caught by the Voconian because he was not on the census roll. Verres as praetor gave *bonorum possessio* to the *secundus heres*, quite rightly one would think, *pace* Cicero's fuss, though in the midst of that story we are regaled with another, in which a 'pecuniosa mulier' called Anneia ('recently') instituted her daughter, being not on the census, and got away with it. In the *De finibus* we hear of the other dodge, *fideicommissum hereditatis*, in one case for the benefit of an only daughter and in another for a widow.[44] On the Voconian Cicero gives us one more passage. In *De re publica* 3.17, Furius Philus is made to say that the *lex Voconia* is unfair to women, for why can a woman be heir to a Vestal Virgin and not to her own mother? The Vestals could presumably institute women notwithstanding the *lex Voconia* (because *ex hypothesi* they had no intestate heirs?): but what is significant is the implication that a woman would particularly expect to be heir to her mother.[45]

The affairs of that very Ivy Compton-Burnett family in the *Pro Cluentio* yield some points of interest (33f. and 45f.). Cn. Magius had as his heirs, in the first grade a hoped-for posthumous son, with, in that event, a large legacy to his wife, and in the second grade — as substitutes in case of need, as he was nervous that the son might not be born and the wife be unfaithful, which is what happened — a nephew, the young Oppianicus, with a *legatum partitionis* not to his wife but to his mother Dinaea. Dinaea presently made this same Oppianicus her heir, with a legacy to a surviving son at the time in the captivity of the enemy, conditional upon his return. Further on we come to Cicero's client, Cluentius. He had not yet made a will, because on the one hand he did not want to leave a legacy to his mother Sassia, whom he hated and who hated him, but on the other he could not write a will leaving out the name of a parent entirely.[46] It was known that if he died intestate Sassia would scoop the lot: Watson (1971:178, n.3) corroborates my inference that she must have been married with *manus* to Cluentius's father but not to any other of her numerous husbands, so that she was Cluentius's nearest agnate. Otherwise one would have to think of the class *unde cognati*, but it is doubtful whether that yet existed.

In *Ad familiares* 7.21 we meet a lady called Turpilia who has made a will that is said to be void because she lacks *testamenti factio*. Watson (1971:78f), followed by Shackleton Bailey,[47] assumes that her lack of *t.f.* was because she had failed to make a *coemptio*: it is equally possible that she had simply acted *sine tutore auctore*.

In the *Pro Flacco* (84, 86) one of the charges on which Cicero has to defend his client relates to the intestate inheritance of one Valeria, the wife of Sextilius Andro. Flaccus had taken it over: on what claim? He was a Valerius, she was a Valeria: was she his sister, aunt or niece and he *proximus agnatus*? It is difficult to see what could have been objected to, and the text leaves one with a feeling that she was not out of the same drawer as the proconsul. Watson (1971:181) treats this as a case of gentile *tutela* and succession, not observing that Cicero implies that Flaccus is one of the *legitimi tutores* of Valeria. If not agnate, then perhaps patron of a freedwoman,[48] for that *tutela* and succession counted as *legitima*; but there remains a difficulty because Flaccus is one of a plurality of *tutores legitimi*. Anyhow, it was claimed that

Flaccus was unentitled to the inheritance because she was *ingenua*, to which Cicero replies that there is nothing the matter with *legitima hereditas* to *ingenuae*. (If Flaccus was claiming *legitima hereditas* as patron and she was really *ingenua* he would not have the same claim to *legitima hereditas*, and Cicero in that case is sliding past an awkwardness.) It was also claimed that Flaccus was unentitled because Valeria was *in manu*. Rubbish, says Cicero: she can't have been, because a woman can only go into *manus* if all the guardians agree, and Flaccus was one of the guardians and would obviously not have agreed. It was also claimed that she had declared her entire fortune to be dowry: well, if she did, says Cicero, it was of no effect, because that too would have needed the consent of all her guardians, of whom Flaccus was one.

Another little family tale can be extracted from Cicero, *Pro Caecina* (11-12, 17). Fulcinius made his son his *heres* with a usufruct of the entire estate to his wife Caesennia 'ut frueretur una cum filio' (that she should make over half the income?). When this son died he made a certain P. Caesennius (who sounds like his mother's brother) his *heres*, with a big pecuniary legacy to his wife and a legacy of the major part of the estate to his mother Caesennia, 'itaque in partem mulieres vocatae sunt' (which means, I suppose, that the two women between them in fact took all the assets, Caesennius just being a trustee). Later still Caesennia married Cicero's client, Caecina, and when she died she left the bulk of her fortune to Caecina.

Catullus 68.119f. goes as follows:[49]

> Your love [Laodamia] is even greater than that of a man bent with age for a grandson born at long last to an only daughter, born at last to take his grandfather's wealth and add his name to the witnessed tablets, driving the unholy smile off the face of the members of the *gens*. . .

'Witnessed tablets' is the key to this: such a grandson would have no intestate claim to succeed, for he is in his father's agnatic line, not his mother's; but of course he can be made *heres* by will. His mother cannot, presumably because of the *lex Voconia*; so but for that lucky late grandson the estate would have gone as an intestacy to the *gens*, of which some member was waiting, alert in the background. Why, one asks, not to the daughter as *sua heres*?

The old man is evidently not intending to institute an outsider; or perhaps he would do that as a *very* last resort. But the daughter may have been married with *manus* or (otherwise) emancipated.

A certain lady, Murdia, according to the funeral oration spoken about her by a son, of which part survives in an inscription,[50] make all her sons her *heredes* to equal shares, '*partitione filiae data*' (i.e. with legacy of her intestate share to her daughter). In addition to her dowry, which was *profecticia* but would stay with her widowed husband (presumably because her *paterfamilias* was dead), she left him a pecuniary legacy. This was all evidently very praiseworthy. It does, however, turn out that the shares were not quite so equal: one of her sons of her first marriage got a *praelegatum* which represented the payment to him of what his father had left to her with the request that it should come to the son in the end.

We cannot try to solve all the complications and mysteries of the *laudatio [Turiae]*.[51] Roughly, I think, the relevant portion can be paraphrased thus:

The two of you [sisters] were pressed to let the will of your father, in which we [or I, or you and I, or you and I and your sister, or I and your sister's husband?] were heir[s], be declared void. . . . And thus, being sole *sua heres* because your sister was married with *manus*, you would be in the *tutela* of those people who said they were agnates. You said 'no, it's not void, but even if it is I shall carry out what my father wanted and share all with my sister — and they're not even *gentiles* let alone agnates, so they can't stop me.'

The main question is: what price the *lex Voconia*, if these women were *scriptae heredes*?

Valerius Maximus has stories of wills that were regarded as dotty. Aebutia, who had been wife of L. Menenius Agrippa, had a large fortune and two daughters. She instituted only one of them as *heres*, and left nothing to the other, only a legacy to her sons. The second daughter could have challenged the will but did not (Val.Max. 7.8.2). There is an oddity about this tale: the Menenii Agrippae were a distinguished family in early Roman history, but they drop out of sight from about 350 BC; but this story must relate to the late Republic or early principate and, if so, one notices that the *lex Voconia* does not seem to matter any more. Another silly will was nullified by Augustus (Val.Max. 7.7.4): Septicia of Rimini, having remarried, cut her sons out and instituted her husband.[52]

These cases take us once more in the direction of the *querela inofficiosi*, and so we should note that Quintilian (9.2.34) refers to a speech by Asinius Pollio on behalf of a woman called Liburnia who had been omitted from her son's will. That naturally leads to the letter of Pliny (5.1) about a son instituting a *querela* for being left out of his mother's will. In both cases, unless there was *manus*, the intestate claims must have been quite remote, in the class *unde cognati*.

Other items in Pliny's correspondence claim brief reference: 2.4, the problems for a woman of entering upon an inheritance burdened with debts; 4.2, succession to a mother on condition of emancipation (and the purpose in this instance was to prevent the father from embezzling); 4.10, the will of a woman incorrectly drawn; 6.32, *dos adventicia* from a family friend; 7.24, a 'sensible' will by a woman, instituting her grandson to two-thirds and her granddaughter to one third; 8.18, the will of the immensely rich Domitius Tullus: all to his daughter, but with big legacies. The troublesome will of Matidia, the great-aunt of Marcus Aurelius,[53] has notable features, particularly a crazily extravagant alimentary foundation; and the matrimonial affairs of the widow, Pudentilla, also shed useful light on practice (Apuleius, *Apologia* 68, 71, 91-2, 100). Julius Caesar did not institute his wife *heres* to any fraction, however small; Augustus made Livia his *heres* to a third; the poet Persius[54] divided his substantial fortune between his mother and his sister, with a codicil to his mother containing a *fideicommissum* of money and books to Cornutus. Cornutus later left the money back to the women.

The testamentary documents in *FIRA* III yield the following: the soldier Antonius Silvanus (no. 47) institutes his son as *heres*, failing whom his brother, with a legacy to his wife; Dasumius in his vast will (no. 48) institutes his daughter perhaps to half, with a lot of co-heirs;[55] another soldier, Longinus Castor, manumits two female slaves and makes them heirs (no. 50); Aurelius Hermogenes (no. 51) institutes his five children, two of whom are daughters; Aurelius Colluthus (no. 52) institutes his wife; 55(a) and (d) exhibit alimentary funds created by women; 59 and 60 are *cretiones* by daughters, the latter as heir to her mother; in 61 there is *bonorum possessio unde legitimi* of a mother; and in 65 a woman petitions for a legacy.

It remains to put the *Digest* and the Justinian *Code* to some use. That the independent, property-owning woman is there to be found in abundance is now a commonplace. Huchthausen made a good study (1974) of the *Code*, from which it emerges that down to the time of Diocletian just under 19 per cent of all rescripts are to women. They perhaps found — or professed to find, or were expected by the men to find — the complexities of the law rather tiresome: it is amusing to see a group of Severan rescripts explaining relatively elementary legal points to baffled ladies.[56]

D.25.4 and 5 and 6 and D.37.9 are about *possessio ventris nomine*. A woman pregnant at her husband's death must be guarded and inspected to ensure that no suppositious child is foisted on the lineage, but under those safeguards the mother will be able to claim *missio in possessionem* on behalf of the child to come. Whether Roman society, with frequent remarriages and partible inheritance, found the problem of *turbatio sanguinis* more disturbing than did feudal aristocracies with primogeniture I do not know: Humbert suggests that the prescribed period of mourning for widows, whatever its original function, came to provide a safeguard against such *turbatio*.[57]

A well-known and striking rule of Roman law is that the *paterfamilias* who is *prodigus* (a concept never defined!) can be subjected to the control of his agnates, as can the *furiosus*. A text in the *Digest* applies this rule to a *luxuriosa mulier*,[58] but in the case of women the rule may not have mattered as much while they were in *tutela* (especially agnatic) anyway.

Under legacy the most interesting aspect is what we hear about conditions, for example legacies to *filiae familiarum* on condition that they marry (or do not marry) so-and-so, or legacies to come into effect only if children are born (this also to widows). Legacy, however, to either sex on condition that they refrain altogether from marrying was void. Needless to say, there is a lot about legacy of *penus* and *supellex* to widows.[59]

Reference has already been made to mothers instituting sons on condition of their emancipation; the *Digest* has this for both sons and daughters (see n. 14). This was not necessarily (though it was so in the case of Regulus) because the mother believed the father would embezzle, but because she wanted her children to have the *bona materna* as soon as possible. The feeling certainly seems to have grown in the classical age that *bona paterna* and *materna* were, and should be kept, special and separate:[60] by Papinian's time a man is instituting one *heres* to his *bona materna* and another to his *paterna* and being told still that technically this is incorrect and the two *heredes* are joint heirs to all — but of course it can be sorted out by the action for division.[61] The culmination, under Constantine, is C.6.60.1.

One is struck sometimes by the absence or scarcity of discussion of matters that might have been expected to have importance. We are accustomed, for example, on the basis of such texts as Cicero, *Topica* 17, to think that *ususfructus omnium bonorum* was originally and especially an arrangement for widows, rather than instituting them *heredes*;[62] there is in fact very little reference to women in the titles on usufruct:[63] *habitatio*, the right to remain in the house, seems to come in rather more often.[64] Similarly, there is surprisingly little in the titles in Book 33 about legacy of annuities.[65] Also scarcer than one would expect is mention of women under the rules of the *senatusconsultum Macedonianum*,[66] and in the titles relating to *peculium*; and so far as the *Digest* goes you would scarcely suppose that women ever sued for *bonorum possessio contra tabulas*. It would, of course, be rash to draw much in the way of conclusions from these absences.

On the other hand I think we can see enough cases of people instituting their sons as *heredes* and cutting out their daughters[67] to feel that there is some corroboration for the idea that this may have been a frequent or even regular practice. That does not cut the women out of succession to property, which they can have in the form of legacy; its main motive may have been to save them responsibility and anxiety, as suggested earlier.

Very interesting aspects are raised by Humbert in his study of remarriage (1972), principally in the part devoted to the patrimonial effects. He notes, historically and sociologically, the frequency of second and later marriages of both men and women, and focuses attention (perhaps excessively, but it does no harm for it to be brought out) on the situation where there are children of more than one marriage. What follows, by its brevity and its concentration on doubts and disagreements, does not do justice to the work's importance.

The passages in the *Digest* about legacy by husband to wife on condition that she has children are difficult to get a *rationale* out of: certainly some of them mean *his* children, but not all or necessarily so.[68] Humbert suggests that the unfavourable rules of succession of married persons to each other were for the protection of children (they were, be it remembered, an Augustan creation), and also that the (or a) main purpose of the *querela inofficiosi* was to protect children against the surviving spouse scooping the lot. Not much can be shown, in fact, by way of examples of one spouse leaving all to the survivor to the detriment of children; but there is some evidence to bear out Humbert's inference that when people *remarried* they sometimes undutifully cut out the children of their first marriage, 'novercalibus delenimentis . . . corrupti' (D.5.2.4): we have seen such a case referred to by Valerius Maximus, and there is another in Pliny's letters.[69] *Donationes mortis causa* were also used to the same effect: that was stopped by the *senatusconsultum* of AD 206 (D.24.1.32 pr.-2), imposing the *Falcidia* where appropriate.

Humbert sees a development in the purpose of usufruct, beginning in favour of the widow to enable her to maintain her status and ending as an annuity with survivorship for children; he sees the *praelegatum* to a *filiusfamilias* of his *peculium* as designed to ensure that his *bona materna* (which will be part of it) are not dissipated; and he sees wives as trying to secure their *dos* to the children of their first marriages. And 'sans affirmer que les pratiques relevées constituent . . . un système de protection organisé' he nevertheless concludes (pp. 293f.) that the protection of children of first marriages was the principal tendency of the practice — practice only, because not till the post-classical period was it thought right to interfere by legislation with the freedom of property-owners to dispose of their property as they thought fit. But the practice produced a kind of 'vulgar law' — not a decadent kind, but on the contrary progressive and meeting the real desires of society. There seems to me to be some exaggeration in this thesis, but nevertheless much truth.

III

Whether, and in what sense, conclusions can be properly drawn from this kind of survey will be a matter for argument. However, a few points, even if only further questions, may be worth putting forward: they are about tendencies or attitudes.

There were women of great wealth already within a few years of the Punic Wars. Their real power over — and from — that wealth depended on the workings of *tutela* and *manus*: agnatic *tutela* frequently seems to be the really determinant factor. Yet we find women disposing of property often in surprising or idiosyncratic ways, and wonder in such cases where their agnate *tutores* had got to: did they mostly, quite early, no longer have them?

Women make wills in favour of sons, daughters, husbands, nephews; women are instituted *heredes*, and if the Voconian stands in the way it is bypassed — and this not only for daughters, but for wives and mothers. On the other hand, if there are sons, people have a tendency to institute them and cut their womenfolk out with a legacy.

By and large the Roman will looks a very 'family' thing: the sentiment is that something should be done for everyone. Mothers institute daughters, or leave them a *partitio*: men institute mothers. And all this gives, so to speak, a much more 'cognatic' than 'agnatic' impression. In my view agnation gave way to cognation as a testamentary principle (and this represents the real substratum of Roman family sentiment) quite early, and the trend just got stronger and stronger. Intestacy, remaining important, was a bastion of the old agnatic lineage principle and took longer to shift: *unde cognati* may not emerge till the late Republic and the struggle is still going on in the second century AD with the *Tertullianum* and *Orfitianum*.

In a cognatic arrangement property goes, not down straight vertical lineage lines, but to the children of marriages. Would it be correct to see this as helping to spread property across the community (within the propertied class, of course)? And — which is to me the abiding mystery, for Rome as for Aristotle's Sparta — how *does* property accumulate and finish up in the hands of women?

Notes

1. As a contribution to the seminar in 1981 this chapter has not, and was not intended to have, any originality. Its sole function was as a background statement of legal rules, for reference and for the elimination of some recurrent misunderstandings. Matters of succession perhaps always have some relation to family life, but they are not necessarily very simply so related; much of what

follows may appear as no more than tangential to most of the contributions in this volume.

2. Consider, for example, the cases of the Athenian ἐπίκληρος, the heir to a feudal entail, or the son of a wealthy Roman freedman.

3. Recent work on the position of Athenian women tends to stress that although they could under some circumstances, over and above the ἐπίκληρος rules, inherit property and receive it by gift their power to do anything with what they owned was limited almost to nothing by various sets of rules. See Wolff (1944), de Ste Croix (1970) and Schaps (1979), more or less *passim*.

4. For some relevant comments in relation to *patria potestas*, see Crook (1967c; esp. 119-22).

5. Neither can an *impubes*, so it has been urged that 'originally' *impuberes* were not *sui heredes* either, and that has been invoked to explain the anomaly of *substitutio pupillaris* in the rules of testamentary succession.

6. Hence attempts to smuggle back primogeniture by one side-door or another. See Crook (1967c:114-18). The introduction of Laslett and the essay of Goody in Laslett (1972) make salutary reading. Voci (1960:17-20) argues from the *testamentum calatis comitiis* — which was an adoption testament — for a preferential status of male *sui*.

7. Which is just calculated by counting in steps up and down to and from the common agnatic ascendant.

8. Watson (1975:67-8) discusses how gentile succession may have worked. But when the praetor granted *bonorum possessio ab intestato* on a less restricted list than *sui* plus *prox.ag.* he did so '*ne quis sine successore moriatur*' (Gaius *Inst.* 3.33). Watson thinks that even *prox.ag.* was a liberalising extension by the decemvirs.

9. That suggestion is entirely mine; but for discussion see Watson (1971:177-8).

10. Cicero, *Topica* 23; *Pro Flacco* 86.

11. *Cognatio*, though we speak of 'blood relationship', was in fact an artificial term: all agnates counted also as cognates, so that, for example, my adopted brother would be not only my agnate but also my cognate, D.1.7.23.

12. The title on *collatio dotis* is D.37.7.

13. Cf. '*emancupata . . . Cluvio*' in the *Laudatio Turiae*, *FIRA* III, no. 69, pag. 1, 1.16.

14. There are numerous cases in the *Digest* of mothers leaving inheritances or legacies to sons or daughters on condition of their being emancipated, e.g. D.5.3.58; 35.1.70 and 77 (to sons); 39.5.28 (to a daughter). This is not necessarily because the mother has quarrelled with the father, but because it is the only way the children can come into the *bona materna* straight away upon her death.

15. It went by degrees, I think.

16. The plural depends on Cicero, *Pro Flacco* 84: if Cicero is not there grinding an axe, authorisation has to be *nem.con.*

17. See, for example, Watson (1975: 34-8), and similar material used by Pomeroy (1976). There is much besides.

18. I treat it in this chapter as a fact of Roman life. This is not the place to wrestle with the question whether there was a time when no testation was possible at Rome or when no conception of private ownership of property existed, nor to raise problems of chronology. For the strength of the sentiment in favour of testation at Rome, see Crook (1973).

19. An important paper is Magdelain (1983).

20. *Gnomon of the Idios Logos* 33: τὴν καλουμένην κουηεμπτίωνα.

21. Gaius *Inst.* 2.125-6.

22. I do not think the rule is merely coextensive with the rule that *postumi sui* make a will void. See Roby (1902:I.191-2).

23. Most recently by Astin (1978:113-18).
24. See Crook (1967c:122).
25. Dio 56.10.2; and for a special dispensation to enable the Empress Livia to inherit from Augustus, Dio 56.32.1.
26. Gaius *Inst.* 2.274; Gellius, *Noctes Atticae* 20.1.23.
27. See for example *P. Oxy.* 2777 (lines 10-11) of AD 212, a woman selling a slave: she is χωρὶς κυρίου χρηματιζούσης κατὰ τὰ 'Ρωμαίων ἔ θη τέκνων δικαίῳ.
28. Gaius *Inst.* 2.286-286a.
29. Ibid. 2.111.
30. See Thomas (1976:488-9); older, very full, Roby (1902:I.379-82).
31. Very like the list of persons who would take on intestacy.
32. For a convenient summary of the issues, see Wallace-Hadrill (1981:73ff).
33. Details in Roby (1902: I.379-82).
34. Probably in AD 133, see Degrassi (1952; *ad loc.*).
35. D.24.1, and Roby (1902:I.159-66).
36. Gaius *Inst.* 2.63.
37. e.g. Pliny, *Letters* 2.4.2 and 6.32.2; Apuleius, *Apologia* 23.
38. Livy 34. 2f. See now Briscoe (1981; *ad loc.*).
39. On the unauthenticity of the speech, see Briscoe (1981:39-42).
40. Livy 39.9.7 and 19.5. See Watson (1974:331ff).
41. 'datio deminutio gentis enuptio tutoris optio . . . quasi ei vir testamento dedisset'.
42. Whether testamentary or intestate we do not know; Aemilia may well have been *in manu*.
43. *II In Verrem* 1.104; *De finibus* 2.55 and 58.
44. According to Plutarch, *Cicero* 41.5, Cicero himself was in just this position in relation to the young Publilia, viz. legatee of a vast estate under a trust to convey it to her: so he married her. We do not, alas, know more.
45. There is another 'pecuniosa mulier' making a will in Cicero, *Ad Atticum* 7.8.3, a certain Livia; and it was a complex one, since Dolabella and two other people were joint heirs to a third of the inheritance.
46. That is, presumably, he could not bring himself to do so. There cannot have been a legal compulsion; the nearest Sassia could be to him was an agnate through *manus*. Would such an omission have grounded *a querela*?
47. Vol. II of his edition of the *Ad familiares*, at p. 472.
48. So *Schol.Bob.*, Stangl p. 106.
49. Watson (1971:180), mistranslated, thinking the birth was of a daughter.
50. Conveniently, *quoad* this bit: *FIRA* III, no. 70.
51. *FIRA* III, no. 69.
52. I do not include 7.8.1 because the text is uncertain.
53. Fronto, ed. Haines, II, pp. 94, 98. Some account of this is given in Champlin (1980:69-72, 75). For Matidia herself, see *AE* 1975, no. 515.
54. Suetonius, *De poetis:Persius* (ed. Rostagni 1956:173-4).
55. But perhaps not Dasumius and query as to the relationship of the other persons: see the new fragment of this famous inscription, *AE* 1976, no. 77, with Eck (1978).
56. C.2.30.1; 3.34.1; 4.29.2;4.49.1, and *Apokrimata* (*P.Col.* 123, ed. Westermann and Schiller 1954) no. V, with the excellent commentary of the late A.A. Schiller at pp. 63-6.
57. D.3.2.11.1; Humbert (1972:119).
58. D.27.10.15 pr. For a *furiosa*, see D.27.10.4: she is to be in the care of her son.
59. D.33.9 and 10.
60. See Pliny being sentimental about his *praedia materna* in *Letters* 2.15, and Apuleius, *Apologia* 68, where a grandfather is keeping for his grandsons, their

father having died, the *paterna bona*.

61. D.28.5.79 pr.

62. So, confidently, Thomas (1976:202), with the surprising statement that 'until the time of Hadrian, women in general could not themselves make a will'.

63. See, however, D.33.2.37.

64. e.g. D.7.8.4.1.

65. One, to a widowed daughter, at D.33.1.22. In legacy of *alimenta*, 34.1, the discussion is virtually all about *libertini*.

66. The legislation prohibiting loans of money to persons *in potestate*, D.14.6.

67. e.g. D.28.6.47; 30.108.13; 32.41.7.

68. See e.g. D.35.1.61 and 62 pr. These texts are from commentaries on the *leges Iulia et Papia Poppaea*: were they just related to *ius liberorum*?

69. Val. Max. 7.7.4; Pliny, *Letters* 6.33.2.

3 FEMININE INADEQUACY AND THE SENATUSCONSULTUM VELLEIANUM

J.A. Crook

The *senatusconsultum Velleianum* of the first century AD was a piece of legal discrimination as between women and men. Whatever its comparative obscurity amongst historians nowadays — though it is much discussed by jurists[1] — the *Velleianum* has had a longer life than most Roman institutions: remodelled by Justinian, enshrined in the legal systems of all Europe save England, its rules were only finally abolished in South Africa a few years ago. A fine nineteenth-century work of scholarship was called by its author, Paul Gide (the father of André Gide), *Étude sur la condition privée de la femme dans le droit ancien et moderne et en particulier sur le senatus-consulte Velléien*, and was, over and above its erudition, an eloquent plea for women's emancipation.[2]

The present paper takes up two themes. First, historians ought to be more surprised than they have been that such a measure was passed at such a time, for it might be supposed that in the age of Messallina and Lollia Paulina Roman women had reached a high plateau of emancipation, property-owning and participation in every sphere of social life.[3] How should we place the *senatusconsultum* in the history of subjection and liberation of women in Rome? The second theme concerns the motives, real or alleged, of the male Romans who excogitated the *senatus-consultum*. Two opposite motives have been alleged:[4] either the Roman males felt (justifiably or not) the need to protect their women from a specific danger, or else they simply wanted to exclude them from a field of activity in which they did not think it seemly for women to appear. It is the intention of this chapter to offer a small suggestion not hitherto made, which, if thought cogent, would have a bearing on the answers to these questions. The author is at the same time aware of at least one important objection against what he proposes. Nevertheless, he thinks the argument and the objection are worth a run for their money, and it is in that spirit that he offers them.

Certain facts must first be recalled. All persons were in the *potestas* of their eldest male ascendant[5] until the last such ascendant died or suffered *capitis deminutio*. That meant that they owned nothing and could dispose of nothing. But when the last ascendant had gone there arose an asymmetry: sons had to have a guardian until they reached puberty, females had to have one all their lives. Women out of *potestas* could own and succeed to property just like males, but property only gives social power in so far as it can be alienated or given in inheritance. The original, and perhaps to the very end the primary, purpose of the Roman institution of guardianship was to keep control of family property in the hands of those next entitled to succeed to it, during any time when it was vested in someone who might alienate it to their detriment. Women under guardianship could only alienate their property upon authorisation by their guardians. The original Roman guardianship, of males and females alike, was in the hands of their male *agnati* (in practice, brothers or uncles), because those were the automatic residuary beneficiaries of the estate of which their ward was owner, so that it was in their interest to see that the property stayed intact. They could refuse authorisation to any alienation by a female ward, or any change in her status, of which they disapproved. Quite early in Roman history — as soon, indeed, as it became possible to make a will — a *paterfamilias* could in his will appoint for his daughter or his wife *in manu* any guardian he liked, or give her the right to choose her own. Such a guardian, not being necessarily an agnate, had no automatic residual interest in the woman's property, for he was not an automatic next heir; so he had no motive for refusing to authorise the woman's disposal of her property as she liked, beyond any desire he might have to help her in prudent management. And so by the end of the Republic guardianship, except agnatic guardianship — in which many women still were — had become a formality. If a woman did not like her guardian she could have him replaced, she could force him to authorise, and so on. But a woman in the guardianship of her agnates could not shake that off. The point comes out very well in Cicero's *Pro Flacco*.[6] His client, Flaccus, was one of several guardians of a certain Valeria, and had succeeded to her property. His succession was challenged, first on the ground that Valeria had married with *manus* (so taking her into a different family, who acquired the right to be her automatic intestate successors), and further that Valeria had declared her entire fortune as dowry. For Cicero's dismissal of these arguments see Chapter 2 (pp. 72-3 above); it is clear that agnatic guardianship still had teeth in Cicero's day.

A second preliminary must be to review briefly some famous texts containing the view of women as the weaker sex, impulsive and unstable of judgement, easily swayed, easily discouraged, subject to passions and follies from the consequences of which they needed protection. Some scholars maintain that all that was only rationalisation; at least by the late Republic, it is urged, no intelligent Roman, in the presence of the Terentias and Servilias and Clodias and Fulvias, could seriously have believed that women were in greater need of protection than men. It was all a cover-up for the simple unreasoning determination of Roman males to exclude women from some spheres of activity, the *virilia officia*. Others are still content to suppose that the Roman males genuinely believed that women's capacities, as well as roles, differed, by and large, from those of men, and that means *were* needed, by and large, to protect women. Yet another school of thought holds that the apparent evidence of Romans believing in the need for protection of the 'weaker sex' is either a projection of Greek notions of the sexes, mediated through Hellenistic rhetoric, or a late interpolation in texts that originally said nothing of the sort.[7]

The 'weaker sex' philosophy is expressed classically by Cicero at *Pro Murena* 27: '*mulieres omnes propter infirmitatem consilii maiores in tutorum potestate esse voluerunt*' (he adds that the lawyers have corrupted it all: '*hi invenerunt genera tutorum quae potestate mulierum continerentur*').[8] The same philosophy is exhibited in Pliny's letter to a lady who was heiress to an old friend of his: 'but for my willingness to buy off your father's creditors you might have hesitated to accept an inheritance that might be *etiam viro gravem*' (*Letters* 2.4.1). Paulus in the *Digest* is found stating that women, like minors, are allowed in certain cases to plead ignorance of law as well as fact, *propter sexus infirmitatem*.[9] Best known of all is Gaius in the *Institutes* saying, first: '*veteres voluerunt feminas, etiamsi perfectae aetatis sint, propter animi levitatem in tutela esse*' (1.144), and then a bit later on.

feminas vero perfectae aetatis in tutela esse fere nulla pretiosa ratio suasisse videtur. nam quae vulgo creditur, quia levitate animi plerumque decipiuntur, . . . magis speciosa videtur quam vera [. . . 'is plausible rather than true'] (1.190)

For, says Gaius, women do in fact run their own affairs.[10] So to him, certainly, the thought had occurred that the belief in the helpless little woman was only a rationalisation. Finally, Paulus again:[11] 'moribus feminae et servi (sc. impediuntur ne iudices sint), non quod non habent iudicium sed quia receptum est ut civilibus officiis non fungantur.'

After those preliminaries we can turn to the *senatusconsultum*. Its date remains irritatingly impossible to state exactly on present evidence:[12] enough to say that the limits are AD 41 and 65 (i.e. it is Claudian or Neronian). It laid down one rule, *ne pro ullo feminae intercederent. Intercedere* is to intervene, interpose oneself between a debtor and a creditor, that is to undertake a debt on someone's behalf (i.e. in the commonest case to guarantee someone's debt, to be a guarantor or surety). That is what women were to be prevented from doing. Ulpian quotes the *senatusconsultum* verbatim and, presumably, in extenso (D.16.1.2.1):

> Marcus Silanus and Velleus Tutor, consuls, having raised the question of the obligations of women who become liable on behalf of others, as to action to be taken the senate decided as follows. With respect to the undertakings of suretyship and the loans[13] by which women intervene for others, although already hitherto the practice of the courts has been to forbid suit against women on such undertakings, in as much as it is not equitable that women should undertake the duties of men and become bound by obligations of such a kind, the senate is of opinion that those who are applied to in legal authority will do well and properly to see to it that in this regard the senate's wish is upheld.

Surety was the commonest and most important form of Roman security for loans of money, and therefore important commercially; but it is necessary to stress that there were many other commercial activities, for example moneylending, from which women were not at all debarred. Why then, from this activity? A reason may appear when one notices something that was not brought under the umbrella of the *senatusconsultum*: there was nothing to stop a woman from giving her money to pay someone's debt, for that was not the assumption of an obligation (D.16.1.4.1). A gift may be just as big a favour, so wherein lies the difference? It lies in the fact that suretyship is more perilous. If you make a gift you know what you are spending, and when it is done it is done; but even nowadays people do not always realise what they are letting themselves in for when they agree to be sureties or guarantors.[14]

As to the mechanism of the protection afforded, the *senatusconsultum* itself speaks only of *denegatio actionis*, i.e. refusal by the praetor to allow a creditor to sue a woman at all on a suretyship; but the mode that became standard was an *exceptio*, which is to say that the woman could be sued, but if the praetor thought her case warranted it he would grant a plea of estoppel.

That raises the question of the purpose of the *senatus-consultum*: protection of the weaker sex, or protection of a male preserve? The text of the *senatusconsultum* speaks of *virilia officia*, which some scholars think smacks more of exclusion that protection. So does the language of Paulus in the fragment with which the *Digest* title on this *senatusconsultum* begins (D.16.1.1.1):

> For just as by tradition civil duties are taken out of the sphere of women and are mostly null and void by operation of law, all the more was it proper to remove from them a duty in which not only their participation and simply their assistance are involved but actual peril to their family fortunes.

In the commentary under the name of Ulpian that immediately follows the text of the *senatusconsultum* we are given '*sexus imbecillitas*' as the reason for the rule (D.16.1.2.2):

> Let us express approval of the sagacity of the exalted order, for bringing aid to women who are a prey to many cases of this kind by the weakness of their sex.

But there are fairly strong reasons for suspecting that those words were written much later than Ulpian.[15] Vogt goes so far as to maintain that there was no motive of protection of women in the first century AD, and passages that suggest it are all interpolated.

That will surely not do in the face of Pliny's letter, or of Gaius's statement, in the second century, that *vulgo creditur*, it is the 'plain man's view', that women do need protection because of *levitas animi* (not, of course, protection for their personal sakes but for the sake of the property they may cause to be lost). Vogt does, however, make points that deserve attention, some of them going back to much earlier discussions. For example, the alleged text of the *senatusconsultum*[16] seems curiously vague: 'jurisdictional magistrates are asked to see to it that the senate's wish is upheld.' How? By *denegare actionem*. The other procedure, by *exceptio* (not in the *senatusconsultum*) differs significantly because the praetor has discretion, the woman having been sued, not to grant the *exceptio* and so to make her pay up on her suretyship after all — if, for example, she was not doing it under any error or misunderstanding but knew quite well what she was doing. The *exceptio* procedure sounds much more like a device for the protection of women. Vogt agrees, and suggests that it was not what the senate originally envisaged but a later development, when opinion was shifting towards a 'protection of women' philosophy, and when a lot of exceptions to the rule were devised. It came, for example, to be the case that a woman was debarred from having the *exceptio* if she had done her *intercedere* in full knowledge of what she was doing (D.16.1.2.3);[17] or if there had been just cause for her to *intercedere*, such as a family crisis (D.16.1.21.1); or if the *intercedere* had been wholly or partly for the woman's own financial benefit (D.16.1.13 pr.). All those exceptions make the rule itself sound as if it was for the protection of women when they had taken on themselves, for someone else's sake, something the consequences of which they did not at first appreciate; if they did, they lost the benefit of the *exceptio*. But Vogt maintains that those exceptions were not part of the original intention: they were the way in which the lawyers, on behalf of their clients, defeated the senate's intention.

Be that, for the moment, as it may, it is a striking historical fact to find, in the middle of the first century AD, a new statutory restriction being placed on the field of activity of women — an item, as it were, of de-emancipation. Immediately before his quotation of the *senatusconsultum* Ulpian informs us that the initial steps were taken earlier (D.16.1.2 pr.): 'Originally, in fact, in the time of Augustus and then of Claudius, by edicts of those emperors it was forbidden to women to *intercedere* on behalf of their husbands.' And it emerges from the wording of the *senatusconsultum* that the courts had been refusing actions on suretyships by women before the senate passed that measure. Why? Schulz, who stated in *Principles of Roman Law* the reasons for not overestimating the degree of emancipation of Roman women in any part of the classical period,[18] has in *Classical Roman Law* a characteristic outburst:[19]

> This [sc. the *senatusconsultum Velleianum*] was an outspokenly reactionary enactment in conformity with the general attitude of the senate which at that period was the centre of reaction. Once more the senate proclaimed the old Roman principle *mulieribus virilibus officiis fungi non est aequum*, and for that reason (not on account of the *imbecillitas sexus*) prohibited legal acts whereby women rendered themselves liable for the debts of other persons. . . . It marks the beginning of a reaction against the emancipation of women which had been achieved at the end of the Republic.

Some say that the reaction against women's emancipation had already begun with Augustus, with his *lex de adulteriis* and his attempt to recall women to a more old-fashioned role. None of this, however, is altogether satisfactory. First of all, Schulz was the last major representative of the interpolationist school, prepared to dismiss all pieces of evidence for the belief of Roman men in the *imbecillitas* of women as post-classical on grounds that are no longer accepted as valid. Secondly, the *senatusconsultum Velleianum* has a specific legal context, beginning with edicts of Augustus and Claudius. Why those two emperors? And why both of them? And why was the problem first seen as one of women going surety for the debts of their husbands? Nothing else is known about those edicts; but there is something else that Augustus and Claudius (just those two emperors) are known to have done: between them, they abolished the agnatic guardianship over women. Gaius tells us, first, that by the *lex Iulia et Papia Poppaea* women were wholly released from all forms of guardianship *iure liberorum* (i.e. if they had the appropriate number of children): that release included release from agnatic guardianship, but women without the requisite family would still be subject to it. Gaius then also tells us that a *lex Claudia* abolished agnatic guardianship (though not other sorts) altogether, for all women.[20]

By the time of Augustus agnatic guardianship of women was, as has been said, the only sort that had any 'teeth' left, because the agnatic guardian could not be forced to authorise and could not be removed. As to husband and wife, there were several mechanisms by which a wife was prevented from lavishing her family property on her husband: gifts between husband and wife *inter vivos* were null and void, and Augustus limited sharply the power of testamentary disposition between spouses. But there was nothing to stop a wife undertaking her husband's debts, except the power over her of agnate guardians.

That perhaps justifies a suggestion: that when Augustus freed some women, *iure liberorum*, from all (including agnatic) guardianship it began soon to be perceived that a dangerous aspect of their new freedom was that they could be coaxed or bullied into going surety for the debts of their husbands. Augustus therefore passed an edict protecting women by making the praetor refuse an action against the wife to a creditor of the husband. And when Claudius freed all women from agnatic guardianship yet more women were thought to be in like peril, and the Emperor reinforced Augustus's edict in some way with one of his own. And then, because the male Romans thought the principle to be salutary, the courts began to apply it generally, and finally the senate extended it formally to all cases of *intercedere* by women.

If that suggestion is right it constitutes some support for the view that the *Velleianum* was a measure — not isolated but based on a whole train of thinking — based primarily upon the perceived or supposed need of women for protection in a potentially dangerous field of activity when agnatic guardianship no longer provided the safeguard. It did not, after all, exclude women from business; it did not even exclude them from the business of moneylending. Seen in that light the exclusions from its protection that we hear about were entirely in the spirit of the original *senatusconsultum* and not a reaction against it; and the measure itself can be seen as part of a continuous and uninterrupted line of Roman male attitudes about the *infirmitas sexus muliebris* that resulted in the continuous and conspicuous lack of emancipation of Roman women.

The thesis, however, that the abolition of agnatic guardianship is the clue to understanding the *Velleianum* has to face at least one strong objection.[21] Evidence can be brought to bear[22] that people were keen to escape from having to be agnatic guardians, just as they certainly were from having to be other sorts of guardian; such people must have seen the job as a burden and not as a protection for their property expectations, and so not been interested in the control it afforded. Therefore, it can be argued, Claudius when he abolished agnatic guardianship was only acknowledging a *status quo*, not making a significant attack on a still relevant institution; and therefore there cannot have resulted from his and Augustus's edicts a new class of vulnerable women creating a new need for their protection. The point is quite strong; but if it is valid we must ask what, in that case, the purpose of the *senatusconsultum* was. It cannot properly be denied that it was some kind of extension of Augustan and Claudian edicts preventing women from being sureties for their husbands: in such a context the idea that its purpose was to exclude women from *virilia officia* does not seem plausible. And if the purpose was something to do with maintaining the separation of marital property, why were not husbands equally debarred from being sureties for their wives?

Notes

1. Two well-known treatises will serve as bibliography enough: Vogt (1952) and Medicus (1957). They purvey opposite points of view; see Vogt's critique (1967) of Medicus.

2. Thus, at p. 466: 'l'égalisation graduelle des deux sexes dans l'ordre civil est l'une des grandes lois du progrès social.'

3. In Roman public life, though, even in public religion (except for the Vestal Virgins, on whom see Beard 1980), women played virtually no part; it is worth emphasising that that never ceased to be so. Not even in the first century AD were there women officials, women voters, women jurors, women civil servants, women barristers or jurisprudents. The concept of *virilia officia* was very strong.

4. Medicus is at pains to insist that there should not be a total either/or.

5. Or, in the case of a woman married with *manus*, her husband or his eldest male ascendant.

6. *Pro Flacco* 84, 86. Perhaps the case is one of *tutela legitima* over a freedwoman, but the effect is the same.

7. Schulz (1951:180-4), 'Irrationality of the Classical *tutela mulierum*'; but cf. Beaucamp (1976:485).

8. Schulz maintains that this passage is an echo of Aristotle, and so not a truly Roman sentiment at all.

9. D.22.6.9 pr. — almost universally held, however, to be post-classical.

10. 'quae volgo creditur' shows that in Gaius's day the ordinary man did believe that women suffered from *levitas animi*; and 'magis speciosa' shows that

Gaius recognised that most men so believed. Schulz has no refuge but to maintain that the whole of 1.190 is a late interpolation in Gaius.

11. D.5.1.12.2. One can certainly hear the echo, and refutation, of Aristotle here.

12. See W. Eck in *RE* Supplbd. XIV. 828, quoting Syme (1956:210).

13. These loans, *mutui dationes*, of the *senatusconsultum* are a mystery, not least because, according to a rescript of Septimius Severus (Westermann and Schiller, *Apokrimata*, p. 63), 'women are not forbidden to borrow money and pay on behalf of others.'

14. Chief Justice Appleton in 1870 (quoted by Megarry, *A Second Miscellany-at-Law*, 332-3): 'Almost all who sign as surety have occasion to remember the proverb of Solomon "he that is surety for a stranger shall smart for it and he that hateth suretyship is sure".'

15. See, however, Beaucamp (1976:498-9).

16. Vogt thinks it is a mere travesty of what the real *senatusconsultum* must have contained.

17. Under Justinian's development of the *senatusconsultum* a woman could sign away her right to the *exceptio*, and that was the form in which the rule reached modern jurisdictions.

18. 1936:208-9.

19. 1951:569, 571.

20. *Inst.* 1.145 (cf. 1.194, 3.44) and 1.171, respectively.

21. It is stated by Dixon 1984, esp. pp. 363ff.

22. For example, Gaius *Inst.* 1.168:

agnatis et patronis et liberorum capitum manumissoribus permissum est feminarum tutelam alii in iure cedere; pupillorum autem tutelam non est permissum cedere, quia non videtur onerosa, cum tempore pubertatis finitur.

4 FAMILY FINANCES: TERENTIA AND TULLIA

Suzanne Dixon

I

This is a study of dotal arrangements and the disposition of matrimonial property as they are represented in Cicero's correspondence.[1] From Cicero's explanations, suggestions and worries about his daughter's third marriage and his own fortunes, I have tried to piece together a picture of the extent and function of a wife's contribution to the economy of a senatorial marriage, and to gauge the scope of her material obligations to the children. For this purpose, the letters are of particular value: Cicero wrote to and about his wife Terentia during his exile, and later during a period of civil conflict, when he was not only absent from Rome, but in fear of confiscation. His situation obliged him to commit to writing those financial concerns which would otherwise have left no record. The correspondence exposes not only the arrangements actually made for the use of property within marriage, but the conventions which determined them.

The material of this study is intended as a supplement — and at times a counter — to the more formal account of the division of property within marriage afforded by the imperial compilations of the law. In plotting the history of matrimonial property at Rome, it is important to keep in mind the limitations of the material which has come down to us. As in other areas of law, the concentration of the sources has been on the problem cases. Law necessarily intervenes where problems have arisen. Dowry was, however, for long a private affair with no need of external regulation. The apparent omission from the Twelve Tables of any reference to *dos* is a result of the general agreement as to its function rather than to its absence from Roman society in the fifth century BC (see Corbett 1930:147-8).

The sources first refer to this ancient institution in relation to the famous case of c. 230 BC, when Carvilius Ruga divorced his wife on the ground of her sterility and was apparently prosecuted by her family for the return of the dowry. This raised new

93

questions about the conditions of return of the dowry on divorce. The result was the development of a distinct legal action — the *actio rei uxoriae* — for the recovery of dowry on the dissolution of marriage and the institution of the custom of stipulating, at the time of settling the dowry, the conditions of its whole or partial return.[2]

Until Augustus's law preventing husbands from mortgaging or alienating dotal land without the consent of the wife,[3] there was no legislative restriction on the husband's ownership and use of property which he acquired as dowry. The rules formulated for the payment of dowry on marriage and any deductions made before its return to the woman (or her father) on its dissolution were derived from custom or from the decisions made in particular cases *de re uxoria*. Such decisions formed a conglomerate of praetorian law (*ius honorarium*) which was sufficiently large and coherent by Cicero's day for his acquaintance, Servius Sulpicius Rufus, to compose a book on the subject, which has not survived.[4]

It should therefore be borne in mind that we have neither of the chief sources of information on the Republican dowry — extensive records of the disputed cases, from the praetorian courts, or the *pacta dotalia*, the private agreements reached between the parties before marriage, determining the amount and payment of the dowry and the conditions of its return on the dissolution of marriage. What we do have are anecdotal *memorabilia* of the more sensational cases, highly selective references in the imperial codes to the opinions of Republican jurists and some references by Republican authors (notably Plautus and Cicero) to contemporary practice. These authors, differing in so many respects, were alike in their assumption that their audiences were familiar with the workings of the institution they alluded to, and therefore provide little information of a very basic character. It does, however, emerge that there was broad agreement on how dowry should be paid and re-paid, and it is likely that the *pacta dotalia* in general tended, like wills, to follow a certain pattern, which presumably formed the basis for praetorian decision and subsequent law as the standard to be applied in cases where there was a point of dispute.

The law of the classical jurists and the Justinianic compilations on the distribution of property within marriage present much the same picture, in more ordered form, which we derive from the

Republican literary sources. Law, however, necessarily reduces issues to a lowest common denominator of agreed principles. The greater detail of Cicero's letters fills out the legal evidence, demonstrating, for example, the greater leeway provided by private compacts as against the more restricted possibilities covered by the rules governing dotal retentions which the jurists record. Even the financial side of Roman marriage had its human element, and the letters reveal notions of obligation which sometimes transcend a legalistic interpretation of family relationships.

II *Fidissima atque Optima Uxor:* The Exile 58–57 BC

Cicero left Rome in March 58 BC in anticipation of his expulsion. As *tribunus plebis*, his enemy Clodius Pulcher pushed through successively harsher bills which gave Cicero ample ground for the fears he expressed in abandoned letters to Atticus and Terentia throughout his banishment. Friend and wife alike played an important role in canvassing support for his recall and attempting to soften the effect of the confiscation of his property. Inevitably, questions discussed in the correspondence throw light on the organisation of property within Cicero's marriage.

On 30 April, Cicero, who had sailed from Italy, replied to a letter in which Terentia had expressed concern about his manumission of slaves. Here, as elsewhere, we can only infer Terentia's remarks from Cicero's answer, since we have none of her letters. Cicero explained that the measure was a device to evade the consequences of the confiscation of his property, and need not entail an outright loss: 'de familia liberata, nihil est quod te moveat. primum tuis promissum est, te facturam esse ut quisque esset meritus' (*Ad Familiares* 14.4.4). There is an apparent contradiction: to effect a manumission, however informally,[5] Cicero must have been owner of the slaves, yet he distinguished in his explanation between Terentia's (*tui*) and his own (*nos, nostri*). Terentia could determine the fate of her slaves, regardless of the precautionary manumission, but Cicero's own might have to be awarded the status of *liberti*, although he hoped not.

It would seem that the manumission enabled sympathisers to hold the slaves for Cicero on the understanding that they would be returned on his restoration. If the manumission preceded the confiscation, the freed slaves ought not to be included in an inventory of Cicero's property for auction. The slaves Cicero termed *tui* were, I believe, part of Terentia's *dos*. According to the law, a Roman husband (or his *paterfamilias*) became outright owner of his wife's *dos* on its receipt,[6] and it could have been included in an official list of his holdings, but since it was in essence returnable, it was customary to refer to it, loosely, as 'the wife's'.[7] It is not clear whether Cicero was speaking here of a *fait accompli* or of a prospect he was contemplating: the expression *de familia liberata* could be conditional or mean simply 'about the business of emancipating the slaves'.[8] It would in any case be possible for Cicero to emancipate 'Terentia's slaves' in his capacity as owner only if they were part of her dowry. He would be unable to take or consider such a step if they belonged to her in the legal sense, and the text as it stands would be baffling.

Does this mean that the wife could lose 'her' dowry if her husband's property were confiscated? It is a vexed question. Controversy has settled on the issue of Gaius Gracchus's wife, Licinnia, who, according to Plutarch, lost her dowry when his goods were sold at public auction after his death. The *Digest* quotes Javolenus,[9] who cites the opinion of Publius Mucius, that Gaius Gracchus was liable (posthumously) for monetary compensation for the damage done in the riots which he had incited. Various scholars have proposed solutions over the centuries[10], some arguing that the dowry was usually excluded from confiscation, others that it was usually included. It cannot have been a clear-cut issue. For Cicero, the point would have been that the confiscation of Terentia's dowry was a possibility. He was a constitutional worrier, and knew that Clodius was vindictive and powerful. He wished to reassure Terentia on the matter of her dotal slaves, and to make it clear that the property was not lost. He clearly felt he owed her some explanation. In more usual circumstances, he would be liable to Terentia for the return of the dowry or its monetary value on the dissolution of the marriage.

His concern was not, however, entirely material, that is, it was not occasioned purely by fear that Terentia might take him to court for its return if she divorced him. This is suggested by a parallel in the case of Milo, who was condemned *in absentia* in 52 BC for the murder of Clodius. His property was accordingly put up for public auction in 51 BC. On hearing that Cicero's agent

Philotimus was a buyer, Milo had expressed his concern to a mutual friend. Cicero explained to Atticus that it had been his intention to hold the property in safekeeping for Milo against the possibility of his return from Massilia. The similarity of the device to the false sale of slaves to sympathisers is evident. Of additional interest is Cicero's further claim that he had been anxious to preserve the property of Milo's wife Fausta which he knew to be Milo's particular wish: 'consilium . . . hoc fuerat, . . . deinde ut Faustae, cui cautum ille esse voluisset, ratum esset' (*Ad Atticum* 5.8.2).

I suspect that this was also a matter of dotal property, legally classified as Milo's but distinguishable as Fausta's. Confiscation extinguished the claims of creditors against the individual in imperial times;[11] the Republican situation might not have been the same, but the individual in question, stripped of all property, was incapable of making good any claims, and it was not until later that the state could be treated as the heir of the confiscate estate with transferred liability. If this property, or amount, which *cautum ille esse voluisset* for her was not her dowry, Milo was at least showing a husbandly concern for Fausta's interests which had nothing to do with legal obligation. It is interesting that both Cicero and Milo should have spared a thought for their wives' predicament when they themselves were in far worse straits.

If all went well, then, Cicero hoped to preserve Terentia's *dos* even in the event of confiscation. In his more despairing moments he feared that her own property might also be at risk (*Fam.* 14.4.4), but in general he assumed that it would be safe, since it was legally distinct from his own. One incident which caused Cicero great distress is recounted in frustratingly allusive terms in *Fam.* 14.2: according to Cicero's dramatic depiction, Terentia was hauled from the temple of Vesta[12] to the Tabula Valeria.[13] The incident has been variously interpreted, Shackleton Bailey maintaining that Terentia was brought before the tribunes, who met near a painting known as the *tabula Valeria*, while Tyrrell and Purser held to the more obvious view that a bank was indicated.[14] In either case, Terentia was subjected to some form of public humiliation possibly connected with her dealings on behalf of her absent husband. Subsequent references to her own holdings certify that her fortune, if at risk, survived the event.

If Terentia did not share the exile, or its financial consequences, Cicero felt that she shared his disgrace. He reproached himself bitterly because he, who should have brought honour to Terentia and their children, had degraded them (e.g. *Fam.* 14.4.3, 14.3.2). The *tabula Valeria* incident brought on a bout of self-laceration:

> hem, mea lux, meum desiderium, unde omnes opem petere solebant, te nunc, mea Terentia, sic vexari, sic iacere in lacrimis et sordibus, idque fieri mea culpa, qui ceteros servavi ut nos periremus. (*Fam.* 14.2.2)

Lacrimae there surely were, but the *sordes* were relative. In November, Cicero spoke in similar vein of Terentia's *squalor* and misery (*Fam* 14.3.2) which were, in essence, a loss of status: any reflection on her reduced circumstances, if intended, was misplaced. Her dowry, classified as Cicero's property, might have been at risk — though partially secured by the means described — and Cicero's home was lost, but Terentia's personal fortune was intact. Cicero, resolved that it should remain so, took exception to Terentia's own inroads into it. On learning that she was spending her income in his cause, Cicero wrote in October to remonstrate with her: 'illud doleo, quae impensa facienda est, in eius partem te miseram et despoliatam venire' (*Fam.* 14.2.3). He begged her to let their friends bear any such expense, for if the worst should come they would need her property to ensure the future. When Terentia disregarded his plea and informed him that she had sold some houses (*vicus*), his tone became frantic: 'quid, obsecro te (me miserum!), quid futurm est?' (*Fam.* 14.1.5). He resorted to emotional blackmail, suggesting that reckless spending now could endanger young Marcus Cicero's future: 'per fortunas miseras nostras, vide ne puerum perditum perdamus.'

This is revealing: Terentia's status was tied to that of her husband, and his ruin might reduce her standing, but they were so far from being viewed as an economic unit that Cicero's confiscation scarcely threatened Terentia's personal holdings. So sharply was their property divided that Cicero had no power to control her financial transactions. His insistence that she leave the expenses to others had been disregarded; in lieu of any sanctions, he adopted the nagging tone of the powerless. The passage highlights Terentia's independence: there are many contemporary societies in which a husband's financial veto would carry far greater moral force, regardless of its legal value.

The separation of property did not entail a separation of interest. Terentia shared Cicero's assumption of her devotion to his cause and the availability of her fortune to their children in case of need. His presumption of loyalty is notable: he worried intermittently that Tullia's husband, C. Calpurnius Piso Frugi, might *not* continue to stand by an exiled father-in-law.[15] Cicero expressed no such fears to Atticus about Terentia, nor did he suggest, however insincerely, to her that she would be better off if she divorced him. Presumably a sham divorce, like the sham sale liberation of slaves, would have been a possibility, but no such scheme was mooted.

We may safely assume that Terentia's father was dead and that she was *sui iuris* and therefore technically subject to the limitations of *tutela mulierum*. The function of the *tutor* (or *tutores*) was to safeguard the property of the person in his *tutela*. The institution had been designed originally to protect the interests of the family.[16] Women and children had no *sui heredes* and, at the time of the Twelve Tables, no capacity to make a will. The *tutor agnatus* was the nearest intestate heir of the woman or *impuberis* in his *tutela*,[17] and it was in his interest to see that the estate was not diminished. His *auctoritas* was requisite for the validity of a number of acts, specified by law,[18] which might have this effect.

The introduction of the *testamentum per aes at libram*,[19] which was open to women *sui iuris*, provided they followed the proper procedure,[20] created a difference in the situation of the two groups (that is, women and *impuberes*) covered by *tutela*, and in time the once parallel institutions operated and were viewed differently. The developing law and popular morality increasingly emphasised the protection of the *pupillus/pupilla* by the *tutor impuberis*, and his function came to be viewed as a duty rather than an act of self-interest.[21] *Tutela mulierum*, on the other hand, was gradually weakened by imperial legislation and by custom. A *tutor impuberis* actually administered the affairs of his *pupillus/ pupilla*, but the *tutor mulieris* — at least by Ulpian's day — simply gave his assent to certain actions as specified by earlier law.[22] Augustan legislation released free women absolutely from all forms of *tutela* if they produced sufficient children,[23] and the agnatic *tutela* of women was abolished entirely by Claudius (Gaius *Inst.* 1.147, 171), presumably in recognition of the general reluctance of agnatic relations to undertake the task: *tutela* might be accepted as a tiresome (but finite) necessity in the case of young children clearly incapable of managing their own affairs, but seemed simply onerous in the case of women.[24] A woman could, if she wished, take any intractable *tutor* other than a *tutor legitimus* (that is, a patron, emancipating *pater*, or agnatic *tutor*) to court to force his unwilling consent to a particular action.[25] Thus, by early imperial times, only the *tutor legitimus* had any real power over the woman *in tutela* — which meant in practice that most *ingenuae* who were *sui iuris* had no effective curb on their financial activities, and even *libertae* could gain release by dint of fertility.

The general outline is clear, but it is more difficult to fill in the details of the historical process by which the apparently restrictive *tutela mulierum* of the Decemviral period declined into a mere shadow of its former self by the second century AD. It is, therefore, worth noting that Terentia's transactions were evidently made on the assumption that her *tutor's* sanction could be taken for granted. The sale of the property, like the decision as to how to use her income, was very much her own affair (*Fam.* 14.2.2.3; *Fam.* 14.1.5). Cicero's argument, that her fortune might be needed for their children in the future (*Fam.* 14.1.5), suggests the persistence of the notion that property was in some sense a family trust to be handed on through the generations, but the 'family' he invokes is not the agnatic network which underpinned the institution of *tutela* at its foundation.[26] Whether Terentia's *tutor* was a close relation — a *tutor agnatus*[27] — or a family friend or dependant (*tutor extraneus*), her fortune was seen as hers to disburse and as destined for her children rather than her agnates. A woman *sui iuris* such as Terentia evidently had free access to her own goods in this period, if she wished to exercise it. They were not in male ownership — as they were in the case of a woman *in manu mariti*[28] — nor under effective masculine supervision. She owned and administered her holdings in her own right.

In British law, husband and wife have traditionally been treated as a unit, juridically and economically.[29] The Roman view was more complicated, since early law defined the partners in terms of wider family membership. A wife in her husband's *manus* retained little legal relationship with her own family, while a wife *not* in her husband's *manus* was, at law, a relatively distant connection — that is, cognate — of her husband and of their common children, who were in his *potestas*.[30] The chief effect would have been in the determination of the line of succession into which the woman would fall in the case of the intestate death of a member of either family. Her feelings of identification and obligation would be less straightforward. In the case of a mature woman *sui iuris*, such as Terentia, her contribution to the joint matrimonial household and to the children's upkeep ended with the final payment of her *dos*. Yet she and Cicero saw it as natural that she should assume responsibility for young Marcus's future, if this proved necessary.

Quintus Tullius Cicero supported his brother Marcus with material aid, as well as political help, in his exile. Although Cicero deplored the necessity of taking money from Quintus and was painfully sensible of the hardship it might be causing, he accepted the sacrifice and seemed to regard it as fitting. His remonstrance was based on the fact that he had enough for the present (*Ad Quintum fratrem* 1.3.7) not, as in Terentia's case, on the irresponsibility and impropriety of expenditure on his behalf.

The case of the children was rather different. Cicero 'commended' his family to Quintus and said that he knew his children could never truly be orphans so long as their paternal uncle was safe (*Q.fratr.* 1.3.10). This *commendatio* was of a general kind: men commended their wives and children to the care of friends when they were about to risk danger or leave Rome on a routine journey. It need not entail full financial support for the people commended.[31] The general import of Cicero's letters is that if he were stripped of his property he would expect to be maintained by his brother, while his children could look to their mother. Brother and wife alike were required to work hard for his return as, to a lesser extent, his friend Atticus and son-in-law Piso were expected to do. This variegated chain of family obligation does not quite coincide with the legal framework whereby the children had only the distant claim of *cognati* on their mother's estate in the event of her intestate death. Yet Cicero repeatedly spoke as if Terentia rather than their paternal uncle Quintus (a close agnatic relation) would be their obvious recourse if the worst came to the worst. Thus, even in an emergency, when all family elements rallied around, the financial separateness of the spouses was maintained much as the law required, but the maternal–child links apparently exceeded any legal definition of obligation.

In sum, then, the correspondence of the period of exile points up the *de facto* assumption of the wife's eventual right to the return of the dowry. Even if Terentia's dowry might be confiscated with his possessions, Cicero considered himself accountable to Terentia for *his* disposal of it. Terentia, on the other hand, did not consider herself accountable to Cicero for her use of her private holdings, although she shared his assumption that, in an emergency, she would provide from them for her son, though apparently not for the elder Cicero himself, who would be more likely to look to his brother for such support. As a wife and mother, Terentia was prepared to exert herself for her matrimonial family, and to use her personal fortune if necessary but not to relinquish her right to decide how best to display her loyalty. She was apparently unhampered by the restrictions of *tutela mulierum* in her commercial transactions and proceeded on the assumption that her activities would be routinely authorised.

III Death, Divorce, Disaster: 50–44 BC

In 50 BC, while Cicero was proconsul of Cilicia, Tullia was betrothed to Cn. Cornelius Dolabella.[32] The match was arranged by Terentia and Tullia. Cicero, who had some reservations, none the less sanctioned it (*Att.* 5.6.1). We do not know who discussed the dotal terms with Dolabella or his representatives in Cicero's absence but, once agreed to, it became Cicero's debt at law. It was settled that the sum should be paid in three equal, annual instalments, beginning 1 July 49 BC. This was probably a stock arrangement — it accords with that characterised by Polybius (31.27.5) in the previous century as κατὰ τοὺς τῶν Ῥωμαίων νόμους.

Cicero's return from his governorship[33] was soon followed by Caesar's historic crossing of the Rubicon in January 49 BC and, later, by Pompey's departure from Italy. In June Cicero, his brother and their sons left the country to join Pompey. Their departure was not excessively hasty, and Cicero imagined that he had left his finances in good order. Among his dispositions were arrangements for the payment of Tullia's *dos*. Tullia and Terentia remained in Rome.

The years which followed were tragic for Cicero: the Republic collapsed, his wife and brother in turn betrayed him and his daughter died. The effect of the civil war was to separate him from his friend Atticus for a protracted period: though Cicero returned to Italy after Pharsalus, he spent a trying time in Brundisium from October 48 BC until September 47 BC awaiting Caesar's forgiveness and permission to travel to Rome. Cicero uncovered Terentia's dishonest interference in his affairs by early 48 BC, and ceased to write intimately to her; but he continued to confide in Atticus, so we are well supplied with details of his concerns.

The matter of Tullia's dotal payments was a source of recurrent anxiety. Civil disturbance did not itself disrupt routine financial transactions to the degree one might have expected, but problems arose for Cicero none the less. Five letters written to Atticus from Greece between January and July 48 BC (*Att.* 11.1, 2, 3, 4, 4a) reveal serious financial worries. The sudden disappearance from Rome of his agent had left Cicero ignorant of the precise state of his affairs, though conscious of some irregularity. It is highly probable that he suspected Terentia (*Att.* 11.1.2). A timely inheritance ensured Cicero's credit, but Atticus's probings revealed other grounds for concern. He reported that HS 60,000 had been deducted from the amount set aside for the remaining payments of Tullia's *dos*, and that Tullia herself was in sore straits financially. Cicero, shocked and despairing at this confirmation of a wilful erosion of his resources and particularly distressed by Tullia's predicament, insisted that all of this had been done without his authorisation or knowledge: he had thought his daughter well provided for. He asked Atticus to take care of her needs:

> de dote quod scribis, per omnis deos te obtestor ut totam rem suscipias et illam miseram mea culpa et neglegentia tueare, meis opibus, si quae sunt, tuis, quibus tibi molestum non erit, [facultatibus]. . . . sed haec minima est ex iis iniuriis quas accepi. (*Att.* 11.2.2)

The wrong which could overshadow Tullia's plight must have been terrible indeed. It was too early for Quintus's attack, and seems to be related to Cicero's financial rather than political worries. Again, I think the reference is to Terentia's fraudulence.

The passage appears to distinguish between the question of
dos and Tullia's own situation.[34] Cicero's provision for his
daughter had consisted not only of the agreed instalments, but,
apparently, of a separate, regular payment for her everyday
expenses, which Atticus was now to dispense on her father's
behalf. It may have been these difficulties which moved Cicero to
doubt the wisdom of making the second dotal payment at all, but
he hesitated to dissolve the marriage when the outcome of the
civil conflict was so uncertain. He passed the decision on to
Atticus and Tullia herself (*Att.* 11.3.1; 11.4a). They must have
decided to continue the marriage, for the payment was made
(*Att.* 11.25.3; 11.23.3).

To Terentia, who had informed him that the designated
property could not be sold in time to make the payment, Cicero
said nothing of his doubts. In July, he dispatched to his erstwhile
optatissima coniux the first of a series of short, formal missives
quite different from those she had been wont to receive from
him. With uncharacteristic firmness, he insisted coldly that the
obligation be discharged somehow:

> ex tuis litteris quas proxime accepi cognovi praedium nullum
> venire potuisse. qua re videatis velim quo modo satis fiat ei cui
> scitis me satis fieri velle.

In a formal expression of thanks, he then acknowledged
Terentia's part in the whole business of Tullia's financial
embarrassment: 'quod nostra tibi gratias agit, id ego non miror te
mereri ut ea tibi merito tuo gratias agere possit' (*Fam.* 14.6). This
seems to refer to assistance given Tullia by her mother in paying
the debts she owed and thus relieving her immediate plight,
although it could be held to concern a contribution by Terentia
from her own funds to the second payment of Tullia's *dos*.[35]

It is evident that separation of property was more than a
guiding principle in these marriages. Once the dotal payments
had been made over according to the contract, the *dos* —
referred to, as we have seen, as 'the wife's' — could be used by
the husband as he saw fit. All things being equal, he was liable
for its return if the marriage were dissolved, but there seems to
have been no expectation that he would spend its income on the
wife or even devote it in part to the running expenses of their
common household. It is particularly important to consider this

point. It has at times been taken too much for granted that this was the original purpose of *dos* and its primary function.[36]

Perhaps I should stress that, since neither Terentia nor Tullia was in her husband's *manus*, we are not dealing here with the wife whose property necessarily merged with her husband's on marriage. As a *filiafamilias*, Tullia could not own property in her own right, and seems to have looked to her father to maintain her as much after marriage as before. It was to this end that Cicero settled some property on her, presumably in 49 BC: the *fructus praediorum* ought to have seen to her needs. It was an arrangement similar to that he made for Marcus in 45 BC.[37] When she found herself in an awkward position, she applied to her mother rather than to her husband. Dolabella was probably out of Rome, but Tullia could have applied to his agents if she had regarded him as the obvious person to turn to. There is, however, no trace in Roman law of any idea that a husband was liable for his wife's debts if she was not in his *manus*. Even the obligation to feed her was very late, very slight and linked to her *dos*.[38] It did not exist in the law of the late Republic.

The application to her mother itself seems to have been an extraordinary step, justified only by severe difficulties. Normally, Terentia's assistance would have extended no further than the *dos* she brought to her marriage, as administered by Cicero partly for the children's benefit. Cicero spoke of Terentia's aid on this occasion almost as if it were the work of a family friend, who was duly thanked by Tullia, then Cicero, for the favour. Once Cicero understood his daughter's position, he was able to restore affairs to their proper order by having *his* friend undertake to discharge Tullia's debts.

This strictly compartmentalised view of family obligation and matrimonial property is very different from our own — both that expressed in the legal code and our less precise, popular version. We tend to take the vague, rather messy view that spouses share most of their property, except where otherwise specified, until death or divorce forces a greater clarification. In the case particularly of divorce, the legal basis of 'clarification' can be a shock to the lay mind. Roman language and custom left no room for surprises — everything was 'his' or 'hers', save the *dos*, which was 'hers', but 'his to use for the time being'. Terentia, a hitherto trusted partner of some 30 years' standing, had sufficient access to her husband's concerns to abuse her position, but she had acted as an agent or helper of Cicero in enjoying this access, not as a joint owner. There was no fundamental difference between her own and Atticus's position when she intervened in Cicero's affairs.

Even when he feared dispossession, Cicero looked to his wife to secure the children's fortune, but not to provide for him as well. Similarly, Tullia saw no reason to call on her husband when she was in difficulty, although she appears to have lived in his house in Rome and he had received the agreed first payment of her dowry. Presumably Dolabella, like Cicero, made arrangements for the maintenance of his town house in his own absence and Tullia's expenses arose from her personal requirements. In the case of maternal obligation, I have emphasised that social demands exceeded the requirements of law: I shall point out further aspects of this, in relation to the size of *retentiones* for children and expectations of a fitting maternal testament. I must, however, stress that between husband and wife the firm boundaries for determining ownership, use and payment within the family οἰκονομία were not lightly overstepped.

As the time drew near for the final payment of Tullia's *dos* (July, 47 BC), Cicero worried again whether he should make it. He lamented that he had not seized the opportunity to end the marriage the year before,[39] but again in the end he paid.[40] For all his complaints to Atticus, it must have been of some use to a man in Cicero's anomalous position to look to a son-in-law so busily and conspicuously in Caesar's service. It was not in any case until 46 BC, within a year or so of his restoration to Rome, that Cicero brought an end to his own and his daughter's marriage, although he had found both unsatisfactory for two years before that. It might simply have been more convenient to arrange matters from a position of greater stability. By the end of 46 BC Tullia was divorced and awaiting the birth of Dolabella's child: Cicero was divorced and awaiting Dolabella's first repayment of Tullia's *dos* while desultorily considering candidates for his own second marriage,[41] which he contracted some time between November 46 and March 45 BC.[42]

The arrangements for the return of Terentia's dowry were not settled at this time, or perhaps the birth of Lentulus[43] and Tullia's death necessitated some change. Whatever the reason, there was some difficulty between Terentia and Cicero at this time apparently connected with the property to be settled on young

Marcus, and the new will which Cicero made in March 45 BC (*Att.* 12.18a). At the same time, property was assigned to the infant Lentulus: both this and the negotiations with Terentia were conducted by Atticus.

It was not that grief rendered Cicero incapable of attending to business — he made out his will, recognised the need to make arrangements for his grandson Lentulus, and attended to Marcus's provisions — so much as that he wished to devote his energies to acquiring land for a shrine to Tullia's memory. He could not be bothered with either of his wives at this time — Publilia, whom he had acquired almost carelessly in his need for *novarum necessitudinum fidelitas*[44] and her sizeable dowry, he now discarded. He instructed Atticus with mounting irritation to attend to Terentia's complaints without troubling him.[45]

Relations with Dolabella continued to be good long after the divorce and Tullia's death. The first repayment had evidently been made in January, the second and third were expected in July 45 BC and January 44 BC. The birth of a child required an adjustment in the terms, and Cicero authorised Atticus to make the necessary settlement for him on any reasonable basis (*Att.* 12.28.3, 30.1). The settlement involved slaves, though other forms of property may have been included. That Cicero acknowledged some duty beyond this settlement is shown in his offended defence of his will, which Terentia had criticised behind his back: 'dabo meum testamentum legendum cui voluerit; intelleget non potuisse honorificentius a me fieri de nepote quam fecerim' (*Att.* 12.18a.2). This suggests that both he and Terentia felt that he ought to include his grandson in his will, although a daughter's child had a very distant claim by the rules of intestate succession.[46]

In spite of Cicero's misery, many financial matters were settled or put in motion. Atticus's arrangements for Lentulus were carried out smoothly, and he saw to the problems which Terentia had raised. Where Dolabella had begun repaying Tullia's dowry in January 45 BC[47] and paid the second instalment six months later,[48] the negotiations for the repayment of Terentia's *dos* were a little more prolonged and vexatious. The settlement to be made on Marcus, now aged 20, was the focus of the discussions. It is important for us – to whom the expression 'child support' suggests a very basic, enforced payment usually from the father to his children up to the age of 16 or so — to note that the

Roman equivalent was very different in conception. A senatorial youth like Marcus Cicero was dependent on his father for his livelihood: as a *filiusfamilias*, he could not, strictly speaking, own or alienate property on his own account. Cicero was liable for Marcus's debts as he had been liable for Tullia's.

We never learn the precise nature of the difficulties Terentia made in relation to the property to be assigned to Marcus from her dowry: what the law would term a *retentio propter liberos*. Its extent — which proved considerable — was determined at meetings between Atticus and Terentia, or her agents. Presumably the original dotal pact of c. 79 BC[49] had allowed for such deductions, but when the time came the matter was discussed in a way that suggests there was some room for manoeuvre. The differences were none the less ironed out with a speed which would dismay modern lawyers — which may show the advantages of pre-marital pacts, the pragmatic capabilities of the Roman character, or the strength of general agreement on the appropriate income level of a young noble and the mother's obligation to contribute to it.

The resolution of Terentia's 'difficulty' (whatever it was) apparently enabled Cicero to arrange for the payment of Marcus's allowance for a forthcoming sojourn in Athens. On 19 March, Cicero approved a suggestion of Atticus's for closing with Terentia (*Att.* 12.23.2); on 24 March he intimated that it might be in Marcus's interest to accompany Atticus to a meeting with her, and on 28 March he proceeded to detailed suggestions about the means of instituting the allowance (*Att.* 12.28, 24). Here, as elsewhere, Cicero expressed his anxiety to provide liberally for Marcus and to ensure that his funds were equal to those of other young nobles. It was partly affection which prompted the wish, but also a matter of Cicero's own standing.[50] He felt that the rents from properties on the Argiletum and the Aventine should amply fulfil Marcus's needs in Athens — they were what Cicero would have assigned him if Marcus had remained in Rome and set up his own establishment.

These properties were almost certainly part of Terentia's *dos*, retained for the express purpose of providing Marcus's living expenses. This becomes clear in letters of the following year (44 BC), when the dishonesty of Cicero's agent Eros caused Marcus financial embarrassment. Investigation and settlement of the affair led to correspondence which yields more information about the settlement made in March 45 BC. In relation to the suspect account, Cicero spoke of income from 'dotal properties'. Marcus had written to Atticus that he had received no payment since 1 April, when the first annual sum, transferred to Athens, had been exhausted. Atticus advanced Marcus HS 100,000 and informed Cicero, whereupon Cicero suggested Atticus retrieve the sum from Eros, who received the rents in question: 'quod scribis tibi deesse HS Č, quae Ciceroni curata sint, velim ab Erote quaeras, ubi sit merces insularum' (*Att.* 15.17).

It was all reminiscent of Tullia's difficulties in 48 BC. As on that occasion, Atticus agreed to cover Marcus's expenses and await reimbursement from Cicero senior. Cicero announced his intention of quizzing Eros about the accounts in general, and in particular about the rents from the dotal properties, which ought in themselves to have been sufficient to supply Marcus's needs, not only in Athens, but permanently:

> reliqua diligentius ex hoc ipso exquiram, in his de mercedibus dotalium praediorum; quae si fideliter Ciceroni curabuntur, quamquam volo laxius, tamen ei prope modum nihil deerit. (*Att.* 15.20.4)

This 'basic' income — to be supplemented from time to time by Cicero for special expenses and to bring the allowance up to a more lavish standard — must have been substantial. The HS 100,000 advanced to Marcus by Atticus appears to have been in lieu of the second annual payment which the agent Eros has failed to transfer. Calculations are made difficult by the number of unknown factors, such as the extent to which Cicero regularly supplemented the dotal rents. Plutarch tells us that Terentia had brought a dowry of HS 400,000 to her marriage,[51] which could scarcely yield HS 100,000 annually.[52] Assuming that Plutarch's figure is accurate, we are still ignorant of the size of the *retentio* finally agreed to. The amount given for the total dowry is presumably based on the valuation made at the time when the property was promised or handed over to Cicero and his father some 30 years earlier. Property values had changed since then: rents might therefore have been greater than the old estimates would lead one to expect. A further possibility is that Cicero chose to repay Terentia the cash value, based on the original *aestimatio*, of the properties termed *praedia dotalia* and that these were, therefore, Cicero's own contribution to Marcus's income; but I doubt it. All the references suggest that Terentia accepted the responsibility — probably imposed on her by the dotal pact — of helping maintain her son regardless of whether she remained married to his father, and even that she might have agreed after some resistance to donate more than the *pactum* had allowed for.

Marcus was able to lead a gentleman's existence in Athens substantially on the income from the properties.[53] Very likely, the properties in question would have been diverted to the same purpose if the marriage had continued. Cicero was legally responsible for Marcus's debts, and saw to the direction of the dotal income. He also took credit for keeping Marcus in noble style, but in practice the retention from the *dos* meant that Marcus was maintained by the joint contributions of mother and father.

That Terentia possessed other property is apparent. She may well have used the remainder of her *dos* for her subsequent marriages, but Cicero expected her will to favour her children. In 47 BC, while still at Brundisium, beset by worries about his own restoration, Quintus's malevolence and Tullia's marriage, he had been outraged at the terms of Terentia's new will which he heard of from Camillus and Philotimus, the freedmen agents. Cicero had all but resigned himself to her dishonesty by this time,[54] but the provisions of the will provoked an outburst: 'auditum ex Philotimo est eam scelerate quaedam facere. credibile vix est' (*Att.* 11.16.5). We never learn precisely what brought on these rather extravagant expostulations. It seems to have been linked in Cicero's mind with Tullia's plight. He asked Atticus to remonstrate with Terentia, to see if it was too late to change the will. Already worried about Tullia's situation, he seemed to feel that the will made it worse: 'de hac misera cogites, et illud de quo ad te proxime scripsi, ut aliquid conficiatur ad inopiam propulsandam, et etiam de ipso testamento.'[55]

When Terentia attacked Cicero's own will in March 45 BC, he was stung to counter that she had been more secretive and less dutiful than he. It is difficult to deduce much from these references, but the suggestion is there that a mother, like a father, was expected to make a 'dutiful will' in which her children at least figured prominently. As it happened, all this worry about wills was misplacd, but Cicero could not know that Terentia

would outlive them all and attain the impressive age of 103.[56] His
expectations show that the common view of the maternal bond
and its financial implications was not determined solely by the
place a woman occupied in the line of intestate succession. Cicero
had himself felt an obligation to 'do the right thing' by his
grandson in forming his will, although the relationship was
remote in law.[57]

To sum up the yield of the letters of 49–44 BC: matrimonial
property as we conceive it was not at issue in a Roman marriage
where the wife was not *in manu mariti*. If her father was living,
she looked to him to supply her expenses and pay her debts;
there is no discernible difference in Cicero's responsibility for his
bachelor son and his married daughter.[58] A wife *sui iuris*, such as
Terentia, transacted her own business through agents. The
husband-father conducted his affairs separately, administering
the wife's *dos* according to his own judgement for the duration of
the marriage. The domicile was usually the husband's property,
but a wealthy senatorial married couple would generally own a
number of country estates between them. They could spend
lengthy periods in the husband's or wife's estates. There must
have been some mingling of slaves — the husband's, the wife's,
and dotal slaves — but this did not seriously impair the principle
of the separation of property.

The *dos* — assigned to the husband and paid within a few
years of marriage — appears to have been used in part at least
for the benefit of children during the marriage, although the
husband may have exercised his discretion on this point. There is
no evidence of any obligation at this period to spend it on a
common household: indeed, the very notion of a common
household scarcely applied. Rather, the wife was deemed to
occupy her husband's home. She might supervise his slaves, and
even arrange matters of business for him in his absence, but it
remained his and not their home, just as the dowry, which he
used, remained in essence 'hers'.

IV Divorce and the Rules

The treatment of property and marriage at Rome — or merely of
the matrimonial dispositions of Tullia and Terentia — would be
incomplete without some discussion of the restitution of dowry

following divorce. Thus far, we have dealt with the question of practical arrangements, whereby *dos* was paid in annual instalments at the beginning of a marriage and re-paid somewhat more rapidly at its demise. In this final section, I shall deal rather sketchily with the basis on which such repayment was made, comparing the picture presented in Cicero's correspondence with that of the non-literary legal sources.

This chapter is in essence a 'case study' of the economics of Roman marriage, and space does not permit a detailed discussion here of theories about the origin of the Roman *dos* or the degree of formality required of divorce in the late Republic. Rather, I shall present a bare summary of the regulations which have come down to us concerning the restitution of *dos*, and check this against the information we have of historical transactions. The differences which emerge suggest that caution should be exercised in arguing from the law directly to practice on the question of dotal settlements consequent on divorce or of the function of the *dos* within marriage, particularly in this period before imperial legislation. I suggest that *dos* was essentially a private matter, to be settled wherever possible outside the courts, by means of social institutions such as the family or friends, on reasonably clear lines laid down by convention, though with room for manoeuvre. Neither the conventional rules nor the flexibility were necessarily to be found in contemporary law, which took longer to absorb changes and crystallised the baseline regulations underpinning the usual agreements.

The legal formulae eventually devised were essentially straightforward: deductions, or *retentiones*, could be made from the wife's *dos* either as a punishment for misconduct (*retentio propter mores*) or to provide for children of the union (*retentio propter liberos*): adultery was deemed a more serious form of misconduct, and one-sixth of the total *dos* could be deducted for it. Less serious offences (all others, as Ulpian put it)[59] entailed a deduction of one-eighth the total. Deductions of one-sixth could be made for each child, up to one half.[60] Thus the woman (or her father) regained the greater part of the *dos*, unless there was some reason why she should not.

Another factor which could affect the final property settlement was *culpa*: there was always a certain feeling at Rome that divorce was a step which required justification, and that the initiator ought to be able to demonstrate this.[61] Failure to do so could leave the initiating party open to criticism and economic penalty. This appears to have been what Cicero had in mind when, in July 47 BC, he regretted having paid the second instalment of Tullia's *dos* in the previous year when he could have justified divorce, whereas the move to divorce in 47 BC might lead Dolabella to insist on the third payment in any case according to the original compact:

> melius quidem in pessimis nihil fuit discidio. aliquid fecissemus ut viri, vel tabularum novarum nomine vel nocturnarum expugnationum vel Metellae vel omnium malorum; nec res perisset . . . placet mihi igitur (et idem tibi) nuntium remitti. petet fortasse tertiam pensionem. considera igitur tumne cum ab ipso nascetur an prius (*Att.* 11.23.3)

To judge from this, a veritable smorgasbord of causes might reasonably be cited — Dolabella's adultery and political reckless-ness between them would, Cicero implies, have enabled him to demand the return of the sum already paid and to retain the rest. On the face of it, his assumption that unjustified initiation of divorce carried material penalties fits in with the rule he himself cited in his *Topica*, 19(IV): 'si viri culpa factum est divortium, etsi mulier nuntium remisit, tamen pro liberis manere nihil oportet.' That is, if the woman could demonstrate good reason for ending the union, she need not lose deductions for the maintenance of the children.

Later sources took a similar line: 'sextas liberorum nomine ita demum retineri posse, si culpa mulieris divortium intercessit.'[62] Ulpian also ruled that such *retentiones* should be made if the wife or her father were at fault: 'propter liberos retentio fit, si culpa mulicris aut patris cuius in potestate est divortium factum sit' (*Tit.* 6.10).

The obvious conclusion would be that 'culpa' played a significant part in the determination of dotal return, at least from Cicero's time, and that a woman who initiated a divorce without clear cause could expect a financial sanction. This conclusion is not, however, supported by the facts as Cicero presents them in his own case. Tullia's divorce from Dolabella had been amicably decided by late 45 BC, when Cicero awaited the first repayment of the dowry. On the birth of a child to Tullia, Cicero speedily settled property on him. There may have been talk of injuries, but there is no suggestion that it visibly affected the financial arrangement, and relations between Cicero and Dolabella remained good until late 44 BC.

Terentia's case was otherwise: the settlement was not made amicably, though it was not inordinately protracted. There was talk of Marcus's interest (*Att.* 12.19.4; 12.28.1) and of some obligation on Cicero's part, which he accepted, if only to maintain moral ascendancy (*Att.* 12.21.3). Yet Cicero's letters reveal that he had good reason to doubt Terentia's honesty. Contemporary and subsequent speculation about the reason for the divorce[63] suggest that no specific reason was known to their friends. Cicero none the less retained substantial property from which Marcus could be maintained — it does not seem to have been one-sixth, necessarily, nor to have been awarded on the basis of Terentia's 'fault'.

This is by no means conclusive, but it gives one pause. I suggest that we are best advised to keep in abeyance any notion of hard-and-fast rules for this period. The constitution of *dos*, with accompanying *pacta dotalia*, the institution of divorce and the full or partial repayment of *dos* were all, at bottom, matters for private settlement. The process of negotiation allowed a certain flexibility not possible at law, where sanctions would have to be applied according to formula. Convention would furnish ample rules for private discussion, but there would always be a little more leeway, and any changes in moral attitudes would more readily be accommodated. Even adultery, that classic ground for divorce, was not always cited by Cicero's contemporaries in cases where it was commonly known or rumoured.[64] Cicero clearly saw the courts as an extreme means of recovering the final payment of Tullia's dowry. Even then, he had waited almost a year for it and was moved to take the step by outrage at Dolabella's political activities. He could, moreover, rely on Atticus to soften his own vindictive intentions: it was clearly not the usual, and not the preferred way of settling such an issue (*Att.* 16.15.2).

The evidence is meagre and none of this is conclusive. Perhaps Cicero did cite Terentia's dishonesty in the negotiations but it remained a well-kept secret; perhaps Tiro, when treating with Dolabella for Tullia's divorce, listed his faults to his face without impairing Dolabella's relations with Cicero. Neither seems likely, but they are possible. Nor do we know enough of the volume of *actiones rei uxoriae* to come before the praetor, when divorced husbands failed to repay the *dos* as agreed or the parties could not come to terms in the first place. Cicero's letters cannot give us any notion of the function of *dos* in a simpler household, where one or two slaves or a small parcel of land would make a vital difference to life. And, whatever the force of convention, there are those who defy it — which is why it is sometimes promoted to the status of law. Augustus was later to find that the number of husbands who violated the generally understood rule that a husband should not diminish his wife's dowry warranted legislative intervention.[65] *Dos* might not, after all, have become a distinct category at law, nor would the *actio rei uxoriae* have developed if it had been possible to settle all disagreements privately. There is, none the less, just enough information in the letters we have examined to cast doubt on any presumption of strict cause and effect in the matter of divorce and the consequent return of dowry, and to suggest that private negotiation was the preferred mode of settlement.

V

I have concentrated in this chapter on the financial aspects of marriage and family obligation as they appear in a single literary source. The limitations of such a study are evident: even if all the conclusions I have drawn from the material were unarguable (which is far from being the case), it could always be countered that Cicero's family, or particular members of it, were eccentric and a poor basis for generalisation. It is, indeed, a sad fact that we can never have enough detailed information of the dynamics of Roman Republican families to enable us to determine 'typicality' in any statistical sense but, while this should urge us to caution, it need not inhibit us altogether from forming reasoned judgements from the evidence we have.

The proper allocation and transmission of property within the family is a subject related at length by the legal sources. These consist in the main of imperial citations. As I have attempted to demonstrate, the bare-bones view they project of any given situation may need at times to be tempered by examination of 'real-life' examples and not only of the more fantastic instances beloved of the classical jurists. Reconstruction of Republican

legal relations is a difficult and painstaking business. Some
elements may safely be retrojected from the later compilations of
the law, but they must be measured where possible against
contemporary sources to test their applicability. The specialised
sample I have presented here provides considerable food for
thought. It suggests that late Republican notions of family
obligation in the senatorial class did not always, or not quite,
coincide with the priorities implicit in the long-standing rules of
intestate succession. In particular, the financial manifestations of
the maternal–child bond appear to have been stronger than a
study of the laws alone would suggest. The separation of the
property of husband and wife, on the other hand, seems to have
been observed quite as strictly as the written law would lead us to
expect, in cases where the wife was not *in manu mariti*.

The two types of evidence — legal and literary — are
complementary: the concentration of this chapter on a single
literary sample is not intended as a substitute for study of the
laws, but as a supplementary technique to be employed in the
larger process of reconstructing the historical development of
property relations within the Roman family and, where possible,
uncovering the sentiments which determined them.

Notes

1. This chapter is a slightly abridged version of the article in *Antichthon* 18
(1984), 78-101.
2. The story of Sp. Carvilius Ruga is told, with varying dates and details, by
Valerius Maximus 2.1.4; Aulus Gellius 4.3.2, 17.21.44; Dionysius of
Halicarnassus 2.25.7; Plutarch, *Comparison of Theseus & Romulus* 6.6, *Lycurgus
& Numa* 3.11.
   The original character of the *actio rei uxoriae* and the significance of the case
of Carvilius Ruga have been much discussed by modern scholars. A few of the
key works are: Esmein (1893), Leonhard (1905), Watson (1965) and Yaron (1964).
3. Probably part of the *lex Iulia de adulteriis coercendis* of 18 BC: Gaius *Inst.*
2.63, Paulus *Sent.* 2.21b. See Weiss (1925) on the question of which law is meant
by the *lex Iulia de fundo dotali*.
4. Aulus Gellius 4.3.1-2; D.1.2.2.43; and see e.g. Jolowicz (1965:91).
5. Possibly by manumission *inter amicos*, as Shackleton Bailey suggests (1977,
ad loc). On this form of manumission, see Buckland (1908: ch.XIX) or Schulz
(1936:83-4). *Ad familiares* is hereafter abbreviated as *Fam*.
6. This was the case even after Augustan limitations on the husband's right to
alienate or mortgage dotal land: Gaius *Inst.*2.63.
7. Cf. Polybius 31.27.4 on the remaining dowry payable for Scipio's adoptive
aunts, which, as the subsequent account shows, was certainly given to their
husbands. Consider, too, the many references in section III below to *Tulliae dos*,

though her father paid it and Dolabella received it.

Ulpian, as quoted in D.11.7.16, referred to the traditional view of *dos* as a quasi-patrimony, as evidenced by its possible use for funereal purposes.

In post-classical law, there were other statements acknowledging the equivocal character of *dos*: Tryphonius in D.23.3.75; C.5.12.30 pr. and 1; Boethius on *Top.*17.65. These had little effect on the formal law. Like everyday speech, they were commonsense recognition of the fact that dowry was in some sense the wife's, even though the husband was, for the duration of the marriage, the undoubted owner at law.

8. Again, see Shackleton Bailey (1977, *ad loc*).

9. Plutarch, *C. Gracchus* 17.5; Javolenus is cited at D.24.3.66.

10. There is no agreement on the subject. See Mommsen (1899:1010), and the more recent articles by Daube (1965) and Wieacker (1970:211-14). Waldstein's thorough and, to my mind, convincing treatment (1972) dissents from the conclusions of Daube and Wieacker: he thinks there can be 'no doubt' that Licinnia did receive her dowry and that this line of reasoning prevailed in all subsequent rulings.

11. On this, see M. Fuhrmann under *'publicatio'* in *RE* 23.2, esp. 2491-508; and, for the later ruling, D.46.1.47; 58.23.3.

12. Of which her half-sister Fabia was a priestess — Asconius 91.19.

13. Cf. Cicero, *Pro Sestio* 145: 'eversa domus est, fortunae vexatae, dissipati liberi, raptata coniux'.

14. Shackleton Bailey (1977), Tyrrell and Purser (1894), *ad loc.*

15. e.g. *Fam.*14.4.3.4: he need not have worried — Piso worked energetically for his return.

16. On this, see e.g. Sachers (1943) and Thomas (1975:44-5) on Justinian *Inst.*1.13.

17. That is, it followed the same sequence as the determination of intestate hereditary succession — Gaius *Inst.*1.155ff. Consider also the reasoning recorded by Gaius 1.165 on the extension of the classification of *tutela legitima* to that of the *tutela* of a patron or his descendants over freedwomen, which was based on the Twelve Tables ruling on the succession of patrons to the estates of *liberti/libertae* dying intestate: 'crediderunt veteres voluisse legem etiam tutelas ad eos pertinere, quia et agnatos, quod ad hereditatem vocavit, eosdem et tutores esse iusserat.'

18. Ulpian *Reg.*11.27 — and see Gaius *Inst.*1.192 on the survival of the right of *tutores legitimi* to determine whether the woman might make a will, alienate *res mancipi* or undertake obligations.

19. Gaius *Inst.*2.102 ff.; and see Jolowicz (1965:253ff).

20. Cicero, *Topica* 18; Gaius *Inst.*1.115a, 2.112.

21. Cicero, *De officiis* 1.25.85 and Aulus Gellius 5.13.2 and 5.19.10 testify to the development of the attitude which culminated in (e.g.) *Inst.*1.25. Again, see Sachers (1943, esp. 1499-500), as well as Thomas (1976:454ff.) on the development of actions against fraudulent *tutores impuberum*. Cf. Gaius *Inst.*1.191.

22. Ulpian *Tit.*11.25: 'pupillorum pupillarumque tutores et negotia gerunt et auctoritatem interponunt: mulierum autem tutores auctoritatem dumtaxat interponunt.' Gaius *Inst.*1.190 (n. 25 below) is also relevant.

23. Three in the case of *ingenuae*, four for *libertae* by the provision of the *lex Iulia* of 18 BC and the *lex Papia Poppaea* of AD 9 — Gaius *Inst.*1.145.

24. This is the implication of Gaius *Inst.*1.168.

25. Gaius *Inst.*1.190: 'mulieres enim quae perfectae aetatis sunt, ipsae sibi negotia tractant, et in quibusdam causis dicis gratia tutor interponit auctoritatem suam, saepe etiam invitus auctor fieri a praetore cogitur.'

26. See, again, Gaius *Inst.*1.155ff., and 165, and notes 16 to 18 above.

27. The P. Terentius Hispo with whom Cicero was on close terms (*Fam*.13.65) and whom he described in *Att*.11.10 as *meus necessarius* might have been a relation of Terentia, but it need not follow that he was her *tutor agnatus*. *Tutores* could also be appointed by testament of the *paterfamilias*: Gaius *Inst*.1.144.

28. Cicero, *Topica* 4.23; Gaius *Inst*.2.96, 139.

29. See e.g. Blackstone (1821-2: I.ch.15): 'By marriage the husband and wife are one person in law.' The principle has been eroded by successive twentieth-century statutes, but remains an important common-law precept, and lingers in many lay assumptions about marriage partners.

30. See Gaius's summary, *Inst*.1.156; for the effect of the change of status 1.158. The Twelve Tables principle and its implications for hereditary succession are cited in *Inst*.3.4.pr:

> lex duodecim tabularum ita stricto iure utebatur et praeponebat masculorum progeniem . . . ut ne quidem inter matrem et filium filiamve ultro citroque hereditatis capiendae ius daret, nisi quod praetores ex proximitate cognatorum eas personas ad successionem bonorum possessione unde cognati accommodata vocabant.

31. Consider e.g. Catiline's letter to Catulus — Sallust, *Catilinae coniuratio* 35; and compare Cicero's *commendatio* of Tullia to Atticus in January 47 BC:

> alium enim cui illam commendem habeo neminem, quoniam matri quoque eadem intellexi esse parata quae mihi. sed si me non offendes, satis tamen habeto commendatam patruumque in eam quantum poteris mitigato.

There are numerous instances of men about to die commending their loved ones (including wives not *in manu*) to friends e.g. Caesar, *Civil War* 2.41; Terence, *Adelphi* 457. It can amount to a general request to look out for their interests. It is *not* synonymous with *tutela* or with a request to finance the children, wives or aged parents named, or to take them into one's household.

32. Piso Frugi had died in 57 BC. Tullia's subsequent marriage to one Furius Crassipes took place probably in 55 BC, and had been severed by the time Cicero went to Cilicia.

33. He reached Brundisium in November 50 BC, but delayed his entry into Rome in hopes of a triumph.

34. Cf. 'videbis ergo ut sustentetur per te': *Att*.11.4.

35. The second interpretation would relate the 'favour' to the sale of property and the due payment alluded to in the preceding sentences of the letter. I am obliged to Professor J.A. Crook for this suggestion that Terentia might have supplied a promised portion of Tullia's *dos*.

36. e.g. Corbett (1930:146): 'In its essential character and purpose dowry is a contribution from the wife's side to the expenses of the household.' This is made as a general observation, and has a plausible ring, but its particular application to the Roman case must be carefully examined. Certainly the wife was not only not expected, but not *permitted*, to contribute to the common household from her personal holdings — see D.24.1 for later exceptions to this rule. The exceptions show that the rule had held in the late Republican period.

37. Cicero assigned the rents of certain properties to Marcus from 45 BC: *Att*.12.32.2; 15.20.4, and see the discussion below.

38. e.g. D.24.1.15; 24.3.22, 8 (both Ulpian) see Koschaker (1930).

39. *Att*.11.25.3; 11.23.3 — both from July 47 BC.

40. In *Fam*.14.13, Cicero revoked an earlier instruction to Terentia to send Dolabella a notice of divorce — also in July 47 BC.

41. In *Att*.12.8, which alludes to Dolabella's imminent departure (for Spain)

and dates to October 46 BC, Cicero's reference to the expected first payment indicated that the divorce terms had by then been negotiated. The discussion — or dismissal — of candidates for his own marriage (*Att*.12.11) probably belongs to late November. In *Fam*.6.18, written just after his grandson's birth, he said that he was remaining in Rome in expectation of the first payment.

42. That is to say, between *Att*.12.11 and *Att*.12.32, written after Tullia's death (when Cicero was avoiding his new wife).

43. Dolabella was apparently adopted in 48 BC, probably by Cn. Lentulus Vatia, and acquired the *cognomen* Lentulus, which passed to his son. See Vogt (1905) and Shackleton Bailey (1960:258-9, n.3).

44. 'contra veterum perfidiam': *Fam*.4.14. His ungracious treatment of his wife's family must have strained these new relations considerably (*Att*.12.32.1; 12.34; 13.47a.2) and sits oddly with his continued cultivation of Dolabella (e.g. *Fam*,.9.11, 12; *Att*.14.17, 17a), and of Furius Crassipes.

45. e.g. *Att*.12.19.4, 12.1, 21.3 and, especially, 22.1.

46. *Inst*.3.4. pr. (quoted above in n.30) recalls the principle.

47. In January 45 BC, Cicero wrote to Q. Lepta that he had remained in Rome for Tullia's confinement, and was now there still in expectation of Dolabella's agents, for the first payment: *Fam*.6.18.

48. In May 45 BC, Cicero was confidently looking forward to a cash payment, which he planned to use for a land purchase: 'Dolabellae nomen iam expeditum videtur': *Att*.13.29.

Cicero was absorbed in these financial details at the time; it is difficult to believe he would not have mentioned any failure to pay.

49. See e.g. Weinstock (1934) and Schmidt (1893:I.175) for discussion of the precise date of the marriage, which must have taken place by 77 BC at the latest.

50. *Att*.12.7 and consider *Att*.15.15: 'tibi pro tua natura semper placuisse teque existimasse scio, id etiam ad dignitatem meam pertinere eum non modo liberaliter a nobis, sed etiam ornate cumulateque tractari.'

51. = 10,000 denavii: Plutarch, *Cicero* 8.2.

52. Although Cicero's inheritance from Cluvius, which he accepted February/ March 48 BC (*Att*.11.2.2) apparently brought him HS 80,000 per annum by April 44 BC (*Att*.14.10.3), and he and Atticus hoped the yield would increase to HS 100,000. If this is the inheritance Plutarch alludes to in *Cic*.8.2, it was valued at HS 360,000.

53. Cf. the example Cicero uses in the *Paradoxa Stoicorum* 49 of the man who manages to make do with an annual income of HS 100,000 by living frugally though still genteelly.

54. Consider the weary, almost sardonic tone of *Att*.11.24.3 (August, 47 BC):

de Terentia autem (mitto cetera quae sunt innumerabilia) quid ad hoc addi potest? scripseras ut HS $\overline{\text{XII}}$ permutaret; tantum esse reliquum de argento. misit illa CCIƆƆ mihi et adscripsit tantum esse reliquum. cum hoc tam parvum de parvo detraxerit, perspicis quid in maxima re fecerit.

55. *Att*.11.23.3 and consider 11.25, although a textual uncertainty makes this less conclusive in its connection of the will and Tullia's current situation.

56. Pliny, *Natural History* 7 (48) 158; Valerius Maximus 8.13.6.

57. See again n.30 on *Inst*.3.4.pr.

58. Compare the similar predicaments of Marcus and Tullia at different periods, both dealt with by Cicero through Atticus, as noted above.

59. 'graviores mores sunt adulteria tantum, leniores omnes reliqui': *Tit*.6.12.

60. These provisions are summarised by Ulpian *Tit*.6.9-10; *Frag.Vat*. 105-7 (= Pauli *resp*. lib.8).

61. Consider, for example, the expulsion from the senate of L. Annius in 307

BC, for repudiating his young bride without summoning a council of friends to explain his action: Valerius Maximus 2.9.2.

62. *Frag.Vat.* 107 (= Pauli *resp.* lib.8).

63. Antonius jeered at him for ending such a long-standing union; Tiro felt bound to reply in writing to Terentia's version, and Plutarch was still speculating about the divorce after a century and a half: *Cicero* 41.

64. Consider, for example, Pompeius's divorce of Mucia or Caesar's of Pompeia (*Att.*1.12; Suetonius, *Iulius* 50), not to mention Tullia's of Dolabella. In each case, adultery was talked of, but not cited as a cause of divorce.

65. D.23.5.3; Gaius *Inst.*2.63; Paulus *Sent.*2.21b.2 and, above all, *Inst.*2.8.pr.

5   *PATRIA POTESTAS*[1]

W.K. Lacey

When I was writing *The Family in Classical Greece* (*Family* hereafter) some 15 years ago, I argued that the *oikos* was the institution through which one could reach an understanding of Greek society and the Greeks. It was a concept both social and egalitarian — or at least it very quickly became egalitarian with the advent of hoplite warfare and the city's need for men for its phalanx.

In the historical period society was concerned to maintain at a high level the number of *oikoi* in the state (*Family*, ch.VI) and the Greek *poleis* evolved institutions with that object in view: Sparta had the system whereby the elders of the tribe allocated a *klaros* to the infant Spartan whether as its *kyrios* (as some commentators appear to have supposed) or as its successor-designate (which is the view I myself put forward, *Family*, 196-7; *Family*, ch.IV, esp. 90ff.); Athens had the system whereby after the Cleisthenic reorganisation (and possibly also before it, though the sources are hardly good enough for certainty) the whole settled land area of the state was divided into *demes* and the *demes* were subdivided into *oikoi*, and the citizens were registered at their *dokimasia* as being in the *oikos* of so-and-so (*Family*, p. 278, n.49) — it being uncertain whether so-and-so was the ancestor at the time of Cleisthenes' reorganisation or the oldest living agnate. Whence presumably came the habit of naming the oldest son after his paternal grandfather. We also know from *Ath. Pol.* (by inference) 56.2 (*Family* 55 and p. 258, n.30) that concern for the *oikoi* was the responsibility of the eponymous archon in early times, a responsibility which was very much enlarged under Solon — it is indeed my view that the enlargement of the numbers available for the army, and the defence of their *oikoi* against the rich and the noble, was the object of Solon's reorganisation. In the democratic period (*Family*, 73ff.) we can be much more confident, from the evidence of the same source (43.4, 56.6), with some support from Aristophanes and the orators, that any κλῆρος which became ἔρημος through the death of its κύριος without leaving sons was proclaimed ἔημος publicly at the next κυρία ἐκκλησία (or its ἐπίκληρος was proclaimed ἐπίδικος if there was one, *Family*, 139-40), and that the democratically-selected jurors of the law courts determined the validity of the claims of applicants (*Wasps*, 578)[2] and that the orators had a habit of stressing (presumably because jurors were influenced by the argument) that their claimant was the one who would best maintain the *oikos* in the interest of the state (*Family*, 147-8 and notes).

When we turn to Rome, the concept of the *oikos* defended by the state, or indeed the state as having a magistrate like the archon or jury courts whose purpose was to defend the *oikoi* of the state to ensure an adequate supply of soldiers, simply does not exist.[3] A number of reasons might be suggested: there is the fact that the Romans knew they were not autochthonous (Livy 2.1, for example), hence they had roots in the soil much less deeply implanted than the Athenians' (cf. *Family*, 16-19); there is the fact that they expanded their citizen numbers by expanding the size of the city, forcibly incorporating new peoples in early times,[4] and thereafter gaining new reserves of manpower by settling citizens on captured lands[5] and by *foedera*, whether *aequum*[6] or *iniquum*,[7] and alliances of various sorts which obliged the 'ally' to provide troops; there is the fact that the wider family links were weak, for instance the *gentiles'* functions were so weak that they are hardly traceable at all in the historical period, and are described by Gaius as defunct;[8] the case of Turia (so-called) as presented on her memorial (*FIRA* III, no. 69), however, shows that such claims could be countenanced in the revolutionary period, since she defeated her relatives' claims on the grounds that they were not of the same *gens* (lines 23-4), not that as *gentiles* they had no claims. Much more significantly, however, even the Twelve Tables did not institute *agnatus* or *gentiles* as *heredes*; they are only to have the *familia* — they did not, in other words, preserve the *oikos*, they absorbed it.[9] Similarly with children's inheritance from a mother; in Athens a woman's dowry was destined for her children along with her husband's *oikos*; if she had none her dowry returned to her own family at her death.[10] In Rome this never occurred, since, if she was married *cum manu* she owned nothing, hence her children succeeded to her property only if her husband (if *paterfamilias* and *sui iuris*) died intestate or disposed of his property to them in his will; if she was married *sine manu*, her children had no civil law right of succession to her, they were only cognates under the praetorian law, not even having first priority as cognates till the *s.c. Orfitianum* of AD 178.[11] The law again here shows a clear orientation towards *patria potestas* and not towards the *oikos* and its wider socio-religious groups, and a structure of society in which wide discretionary powers are put in the hands of individuals, and society is seen as a nexus of *patres* and their dependents rather than as a nexus of equals linked together in groups based on kinship real or imaginary.

Similarly with fully public activities; Rome's ways of doing things are sometimes attributed to the fact that there had been kings, so that, for example, the consuls were kings in committee[12] and so on; but I think we should ask why in that case Rome developed differently from Athens, which also had an early kingship and moreover one that was hereditary and not an elective one as the Romans thought theirs had been.[13] On the other hand, the Romans' ways of doing things seem to be closely analogous to their family structures, based as they were on the hereditary formula of *patria potestas* under which the continuity of the line was so fundamental that at least till the late Republic Roman names were hardly personal names at all, but the name of the *familia* with son following father exactly, without any alteration whatsoever. So I would like to explore the idea that it was *patria potestas* which was the fundamental institution underlying Roman institutions,[14] and that, in consequence, public life followed the assumptions of private life, and not vice versa.

I would like to discuss this under four headings:

1. The idea that the Roman state was a family, and that the gods of the state were the gods of a family and were worshipped in the same way.
2. The idea that the state did not need many magistrates; it needed only a sort of *paterfamilias* with very wide discretionary powers exercised in turn by those with the knowledge and experience, each magistrate moderated by a colleague and assistants, who also had wide spheres of action and discretionary power. Along with this went the idea of individual responsibility and individual discretion over a very much wider field than is found in Greek societies.

3. The idea that citizens were not equal; some were *patres familiarum*, some were not, but the fact of not being a *paterfamilias* in no way diminished a man's status as citizen, nor was his freedom compromised by the fact that he could be punished arbitrarily by his *paterfamilias* for actions in public life as well as in private. In this state of unequals, differing rights could be held by different individuals depending on age, knowledge of the law (human and religious), the position of their family in the state and the individual's position in the family. An acceptance of this idea lies at the root of the patron/client relationship, since this relationship also illustrates the Romans' acceptance of inequalities between free men, and relationships in which one man has a claim on another inherited from a *paterfamilias* by his *heres* or *heredes*. This hereditability of the relationship, based though it was on *fides*, and not on the total subservience in property matters of those in *potestas*, nevertheless shows the Roman notion that inequality was acceptable, and the proper management of a man's relationships with those of higher and lower status was a measure of his *fides*[15] (see further below).
4. The idea that the magistrate, like the *paterfamilias*, should exercise his power in consultation with his peers who formed his *consilium*; this *consilium* comprised a mixture of those who had a right to attend[16] and those whom the *paterfamilias* invited because he respected their knowledge and judgement; in the case of the *publicum consilium*, men were added to it by the judgement of the kings,[17] then the magistrates[18] (censors after they were instituted till the time of Sulla). Neither magistrate nor *paterfamilias* was obliged to take the advice of his *consilium*, but if he did, he acted with their support, and if he did not, his judgement was suspect, he lost *dignitas*. And for the member of the *consilium* the weight his *sententia* carried — as in the senate — was a measure of his *dignitas*.

I am not claiming that all these things were built into, or established by, *patria potestas*, just that it was the world view stemming from the assumptions of *patria potestas* which resulted in the Romans developing their institutions the way they did, and creating their most dearly prized values, for what was a Roman worth without *dignitas*[19] and without *fides*?

1. The State as a Family

The Romans saw themselves as a family. The clearest evidence of this lies in the cult of Vesta, the hearth. We note that within the public shrine of Vesta itself there was no anthropomorphic representation of the goddess (Ovid, *Fasti* 6.295-8); she *was* the living fire (*id*.291) on the hearth of the home; there were anthropomorphic renderings of her person which seem to have stood in the vestibule of her shrine[20] and perhaps in a small shrine outside the Atrium Vestae (where the Vestals lived) from at least the time of Hadrian,[21] and among the gilded statues of the *Di Consentes* in the Forum and later in the *porticus Divorum* on the Capitol was included a statue of Vesta.[22] These statues may all be of the period after Greek influence had penetrated Rome and have been made because by then the Romans recognised only versions of the human figure as visibly representing deities — a flame would simply have looked wrong — out of place for example, among the *di consentes*. I don't believe that thoughtful Romans ever seriously thought of the city's Vesta as a woman but as the flame of the home hearth. Her hearth was most truly the site of Roma (a feminine deity we note); and that this was so is confirmed perhaps by the fact that it was Numa to whom the first temple on the site was attributed,[23] and it was Numa who incorporated the village of Romulus on the Palatine and the community off the Quirinal into the city of Rome with its hearth at his palace.[24] (Here I should stress I do not suppose I am talking history as we would recognise it, but history as that which the Romans thought were the origins of their city and its most special deity.)

'Vesta and the earth are the same thing; beneath each lies a perpetual fire, the earth and the hearth stand for one's own *sedes*.' So wrote Ovid (*Fasti* 6.267-8). *Sedes* is hard to translate; 'home' (Frazer's translation) is much too weak, since in modern society 'homes' are freely bought and sold; it is the place where a person belongs by right especially of descent or long-time occupation; the Maori concept of one's own Turangawaewae expresses it precisely — it is the place where you stand proudly because that is where you belong.[25] By definition you cannot move the earth where your home is; equally you cannot move your Vesta; you can take the flame from one place to another, as the Vestal fire of Rome was traditionally brought from Alba Longa to which it had been brought in one tradition — but not Virgil's — from Troy. But it did not become Rome's Vesta till it achieved its *sedes* in Rome.[26]

So Vesta was the most basic of the city's gods, immovable, because, if moved, she would cease to be the Vesta of Rome. In part of her temple, or as Frazer points out (1929:vol. 4, 181), in her shrine (for it was an *aedes* not a *templum*), possibly indeed within its inmost sanctum, the city's *Penates* were housed, the gods of the king's, hence the city's, store-cupboard. *Penates* were of the utmost importance to all communities who do not have the idea of a welfare state, and whose members starve if they do not have enough food.

Vesta, then, was the goddess of the place, the spirit of the inmost sanctuary of the *domus*, the inside, female principle of the family (as Gould has put it for Greece, 1980:49f.), which does not, despite the Marxists, argue for primitive matriarchy, and because Vesta's was the most central shrine, this goddess alone among Roman goddesses had her permanent staff of priestesses dedicated to the task of keeping alive the flame which was the proof of her enduring presence.

The persons of the Vestal Virgins came under the *potestas* of the *Pontifex Maximus* at the time they entered their office, since they passed out of parental *potestas* at that moment (Gaius *Inst.*1.130; Gellius 1.12.9);[27] whether they were thought of as wives or daughters is disputed;[28] in historical times at least their property was not in his *potestas*. By that I mean that the Virgins were really possessed of their property — which was a fortune by imperial times (2 million *sestertii*: Tacitus, *Annals* 4.16.6) — with which the state endowed them when they were taken as Vestal Virgins (Livy 1.20.3), and they could dispose of it by will to anyone they wished (Gellius 1.12.9); they could indeed dispose of it only by will, since their becoming Vestals destroyed their agnation, and if they died intestate the *aerarium* got their wealth back (Gellius 1.12.18).

The distinction between the civil rights and the property — the fact that *pontifex maximus* had their persons in his *potestas*, but not their property — is of great interest since it is a reflection, albeit in mirror image, of the Romans' ability to treat the persons and the property of its citizens in totally different ways, simultaneously. A *filiusfamilias* in respect of his property, inherited or acquired, with a few exceptions which will be dealt with below, was virtually in the same condition as a slave; that is, he could acquire only for his *paterfamilias* and have the use and power to expend only a *peculium* liable to be recalled by his *paterfamilias*. But in public life a *filiusfamilias* was classed as if he were a property owner (senators' sons, that is, were enrolled in the centuries of *equites* and not among the *capiti censi* as having no property), and exercised a public career, that is, served in the army as *eques, praefectus* and *tribunus* and progressed into and through the *cursus honorum* in exactly the same way as a coeval whose father had died, thus making him *sui iuris* and in due course *paterfamilias*. The well-known story of the consular *filiusfamilias* and his *paterfamilias* demonstrates that, as far as *iura publica* were concerned, a man's status as *paterfamilias* or *filiusfamilias* made no difference at all. And so far as we know a *filiusfamilias* was perfectly competent to perform public duties of a civil sort, act as witness, *familiae emptor* or *libripens* at the making of a will, unless he was in the *potestas* of one of the parties, or act as guardian, *curator furiosi* and similar functions.

The same contrasts apply in reverse to Vestal Virgins; in respect of their property they were *sui iuris* and *pontifex maximus* had no control over their power to use it, acquire additions to it or dispose of it, but in respect of their public life they were under the control of the *pontifex maximus*; they could not refuse to do their *munera*, they had to spend their lives where they were told, doing what they were told, and they lacked the power to dispose of their persons in marriage, or indeed in any form of sexual activity. And yet, despite the differences, both *filiusfamilias* and Vestal Virgins were subject to discipline, the *filiusfamilias* of his *paterfamilias*, the Virgin fo the *pontifex maximus*.

In historical times the *pontifex maximus* exercised his responsibility for them, with the college of *pontifices* as his *consilium*; whether he always acted with this *consilium* or whether he had a right in the earliest days of the city to act like a *paterfamilias* without one is unknown. My own view, for what it is worth, is that it is likely that he always did act with a *consilium*, since in early days the girls were all patrician, and even if they no longer belonged legally to their own family they retained links with it — of which the most familiar example is the Claudia who prevented the tribunes from stopping her father's triumph (143 BC) (Cicero, *Pro Caelio* 34). So, even when *patria potestas* was at its strongest, the *pontifex maximus* might be wary of punishing a

Vestal without the support of his *consilium*. He was apparently personally responsible for thrashing them if they let the fire go out,[29] as he was for beating to death a man found guilty of sexual relations with one of them (Livy 22.57) in 216 BC, but we are not told in either text whether he acted of his own volition or following the advice of a *consilium*.

But the Vestal Virgins kept the official hearth for the *pontifex maximus*, and it is notable that even in the mid-first century BC the feeling perhaps existed that the *pontifex maximus* should be an older and not a younger man (Suetonius, *Iulius* 13), though we should not press the text in this sense despite the fact that Suetonius certainly used original documents for his *Iulius* and the story about Caesar's words to his mother shows that the post of *pontifex maximus* was salaried. Nor is there any example known to me of a *pontifex maximus* who was not a *paterfamilias* — though this too is a very weak argument since we know so little about earlier *pontifices maximi* and their family situations. But Caesar certainly was *suo iure* in 63 BC, and he had a wife and a child, even if he had no son. Though he was the youngest, he was the only patrician candidate. Did that fact help him? Our sources do not in fact say so.

Vesta was also the individual's home-goddess. We mostly concentrate on the other aspects of family religion: the *imagines* of the ancestors brought out from storage for funerals, the *Lares* and *Penates* of whose daily worship we know a little;[30] but I would suggest that the Vesta, the home, the place that cannot physically be moved, was at least as important, as she was worshipped every day in the sacrifice of incense on the flame in the family altar and the libation — because libations are made to gods below, within the earth, who are *ex hypothesi* not movable. And we notice that the worship at the family's altar was one of the actions of the bride the morning after her wedding night (Balsdon 1962:185). This incorporated her into the worship of the family regardless of whether she was married *cum manu* or *sine manu* (i.e. whether she had or had not, in a property sense, joined the *familia* of her husband or his *paterfamilias*). She was within the *domus* of her husband; she would, it was hoped, become the mother of the children who would be in her husband's *potestas* (or that of his *paterfamilias*), so she worshipped. To say that because she and her property had not been transferred to her husband's *familia* she had not become a member of her husband's *domus* is to deny that the words *ubi tu Gaius ego Gaia* have any meaning at all; it is to say that she was a chattel on whom her husband had the *usufruct* and the progeny. On the contrary there is a parallel with the Vestal Virgins who lived in the *domus* of the Vestals under the control of the *pontifex maximus*. Like the bride married *sinu manu*, they were not in his *familia*, they had not added their property to his, but they were in his *domus*, and while in it subject to his discipline.

The cult of Vesta, then, is very clearly a reflection of Rome as a family under a *paterfamilias*, originally the king, but with the religious functions of the kingship split up amongst a number of people under the Republic, and the titular *rex sacrorum* in fact the second in rank in the religious hierarchy.

Outside this religious sphere, as the Romans were an agricultural people, they conceived the world in terms of farms; Roman territory was the *ager Romanus*; within that territory there was the homestead itself, the *domus*, the part in which the Roman people was *domi*. Round it lay the lands of the urban tribes, beyond that the country. Within the *domus* no arms were carried save for the purpose of getting to the place of assembly for war, and for training for war (the Campus Martius). The area in which the Romans were *domi* was of course the *pomerium*,[31] and the feeling that the Roman people was at home, under the protection of the family gods, when it was inside the *pomerium* is the obvious explanation both for the fact that, amongst other things, prorogued *imperium* lapsed when the holder crossed the *pomerium*,[32] at all times in the Republic and even under the Empire except for the Emperors and those (generally only members of their immediate family) given an *imperium* equal to theirs, and for the unhappiness which prevailed in the late Republic when the senatorial request to the consul (or whoever) 'to see to it that the Republic came to no harm' was interpreted as an invitation to garrison the public buildings with troops even within the *pomerium*.[33] The *pomerium*, in fact, divided the world into the two domains of '*domi*' and '*foris*' precisely because it was felt that the Roman state was a family with a home.[34]

If Vesta was the inmost sanctum of the house, the door (*ianua*) was its outermost limit. It was the precinct of the god of beginnings, Janus, who looked both ways from the realm within the *domus* to the world outside and from the world outside to the interior of the *domus*. The place of Janus is often underrated, but the god of beginnings and entrances was in fact very important indeed; for example, girls entering a house as brides performed their first ritual acts at the door;[35] in literature, as Charinus bids farewell to his home (Plautus, *Mercator* 830), he starts with the door (lintel and threshold), before mentioning his parents' *Penates* and the *Lar* of the *familia* (Rose 1948:33). Moreover, in family religion Janus and Juno are coupled in invocations at the beginning of each month,[36] and Janus Curiatus and Juno Sororia are the deities of puberty for males and females.[37] In formal invocations, Janus sometimes preceded even Jupiter (Livy 8.9.6, for example).

The ceremonial doorway of the city too was at the Temple of Janus, though it appears it was never a gate either on the walls or on the *pomerium* (Ogilvie, *Comm.* 93-4). It was the site for the ceremonial beginnings of war and peace,[38] though it appears that the closing of the temple doors to mark a time of peace was an Augustan resuscitation of an ancient practice (Ogilvie, *l.c.*). The gate concept, however, even if only ritual and purificatory, provides an analogy with the doorway of the home through which, as has been noted, the bride passed ceremonially on her wedding day to become a member of the *familia* from being an outsider.

2. *Paterfamilias*

Political power, like political standing, was separable from property-owning power and property-owning standing (as has been noted). Roman tradition believed that they originally had a king, who was got rid of because he behaved tyrannically, and to prevent a recurrence of this kind of behaviour they chose a succession of *patres* to hold the chief magistracy in turn. Is this a denial of the concept of *patria potestas*? In a sense it is, because *paterfamilias* was single, and there for life without being chosen, but the Roman treatment of their dual magistracy was such as to suggest that what they were trying to do was to have a kingship with checks on the arbitrary competence of the king, the two checks being the presence of a colleague with equal power, and a term of office limited to one year at a time. A third check, though one of only moral importance, was the expectation that the magistrate would consult with his *consilium*, the *publicum consilium*, the senate — *patres conscripti*, a phrase whose meaning the Romans themselves had forgotten by the time of Cicero at least.

While it is possible to emphasise the differences between *paterfamilias* and consul, it is possible to see resemblances too. In the first place, *imperium* was a power like *patria potestas*; it was infinitely far-reaching, and was limited only by statutory enactment and custom; there was no codified list of what a consul could or could not do. In the second place, the consul had the *auspicia*, the same right to determine the will of the gods for the *res publica*, as *paterfamilias* did for his *familia*. In the third place, the collegiate character of the consuls can easily be exaggerated; they did not work in tandem; they had the *fasces* in alternate months — that is, they had charge of public business, and stepped down from it alternately, so that there was always only one active consul at a time, his colleague being active only in the sense that he had the right to intervene and check his colleague by the exercise of his *par potestas*. This was the significance of the *fasces*, of which there was only one set in the traditional accounts of the early Republic,[39] and one active and one dummy set in the later Republic, though both appear to have preceded the consul until Caesar's consulship, when, according to Suetonius,[40] he revived ancient tradition and was preceded only by an orderly (*accensus*), the *fasces* following behind him.

In a sense the Roman *res publica* only had these two magistrates; the others were no more than the consuls' assistants, of whom only the praetors among the regular magistrates had any share of the consular power, *imperium*. But it was at all times recognised that the praetors' *imperium* was inferior to that of the consuls — for example, praetors never convened the senate when the consuls were in Rome, nor could the praetors' *imperium* impede the consuls in the exercise of theirs. Even when the consuls were away from the city and not available (or willing) to return, the praetors had not the right to arrange for the election of consuls to succeed those in office or even their own successors: Cicero, *Ad Atticum* 9.9.3, confirmed by Gellius 13.15.4 (from Messalla, *De auspiciis*). Though the praetors were in a sense the consuls' colleagues, they were thus agreed to be junior colleagues, and their *imperium* was in fact limited in normal circumstances to what they needed to carry out their function of compelling people to appear for legal hearings and executing their judgements.

The same is true of the temporary magistrates, the censors, though they appear to have had *imperium*, as is shown by their share in the *auspicia maxima* (Gellius, *l.c.*)[41] and though it is true that the censors acquired immense summary authority, and that by the first century BC it was a pinnacle of achievement to have been censor — though not to have completed the *lustrum* probably diminished the honour. Livy, however, is clear (4.8) that the office was initiated as a clerical task — *rem minime consularem* — and relates that on this, the first occasion censors took office, the aristocratic patricians did not want the job.

In successive reforms in the late Republic the numbers of the lower magistracies increased enormously. The number of consuls, however, remained untouched at two, from the earliest times of the Republic until the crazier emperors. Why was this? It seems to me probable that the only sensible explanation is that the Romans simply did not believe in boards or committees; they believed in a single executive officer, controlled by an equal colleague, whose powers extended over all areas except those in which executive action was forbidden. He was a sort of *paterfamilias* for the state, who held the *auspicia* for the *patres* during his period of office, and was responsible for the *pax deorum*.

In *De legibus* (3.1.2f.) Cicero saw a very close assimilation between the magistrates, the laws and *imperium*, and spoke of *imperium* as being the thing without which no *domus* or *civitas* or *gens* or anything else could maintain its standing. Plautus (*Menaechmi* 1030 [over a slave], *Bacchides* 450 [over a son]) also uses the word *imperium* as applicable within the family, and in this context calls *paterfamilias magister*. *Magister populi* was the ancient word for the dictator (Varro, *De lingua Latina* 5.82; Cicero, *De legibus* 3.9); his deputy was *magister equitum*[42] and a censor is called *magister morum* (Cicero, *Ad familiares* 3.13.2). The word *magistratus*, magistrate, derives from *magister* (D.50.16.47).[43] The association of ideas between public and private authority seems very close.

In this discussion I have ignored the tribunate on purpose; there can be no serious doubt that, as an institution, the tribunate was intended to frustrate magisterial actions contrary to the interests of the plebeians rather than to promote long-term policies or even short-term political initiatives.[44] It has thus, as an institution, no connections with *patria potestas*, nor is there any instance known in which tribunes intervened to prevent a *paterfamilias* from taking actions by his *patria potestas* against members of his family. To this extent indeed the *paterfamilias* was in a more autocratic position than the consul — not that this is surprising, since the *paterfamilias* was expected to be checked by the affection which he felt for his family, a sentiment which a consul could hardly be expected to feel for the whole citizen body.

3. Inequality of Citizens

It was also perhaps because of *patria potestas* that the Romans acknowledged the fact that all citizens were not equal. It can be said that neither in Athens nor Sparta, despite the label *homoioi*, was it true that all citizens were equal. Certainly, in both communities a man had to achieve the age of 30 before being allowed, in Sparta, to attend the assembly, in Athens to serve as a juror or a member of the *boulē*, but this was a distinction possibly based on the view that young men aged 20–30 had military service to do as their chief contribution to the state; it was their part to bear the brunt of the fighting, and hence it was more important to maintain a peak of physical fitness than to undertake the sedentary occupations of council chamber and law courts.[45] Yet these disabilities were purely of age and were overcome by all who were tough enough to reach the age of 30.

By contrast, Rome was always a society of unequals, both in respect of age, in that the centuries of *seniores* in the *comitia centuriata* must always have contained fewer potential voters than those of the *iuniores*, simply because of the constant death rate (if the estimate of Jones[46] is correct, as I think it is), and in that admission to the senate, certainly when access to it was established through holding the quaestorship,[47] was restricted to those aged 30 and above (though there were breaches of the quaestorship-at-30 rule and a reduction to 27).

Roman society was divided between those who were *sui iuris* and those who were in the *patria potestas* of another; only the former enjoyed the *ius commercii*, since those not *sui iuris* did not have the right to incur financial obligations without the consent of their *paterfamilias*.[48] True, they might have a *peculium* and a *libera administratio* of the *peculium*, that is, they might own property *de facto* and be able to incur obligations up to the extent of their *peculium*, but no further, and the Roman law had harsh things to say about those who lent money to *filiusfamilias* in anticipation of his father's death (i.e. in anticipation of his ability to repay the debt when he became *sui iuris*).[49] Consequently, it always remained true that those who were in the *patria potestas* of another lacked a full *ius commercii*.

Plainly, the Romans themselves found this situation awkward and tried to solve it by various expedients, such as the *libera administratio* of a *peculium*[50] mentioned above, or the emancipation of the *filiusfamilias*, which made him *sui iuris* in his father's lifetime, and thus able to exercise *ius commercii* to the full. But, especially in the early period, emancipated sons remained in an inferior position in regard to inheritance, both to estates and to property.[51] Originally, too, emancipated sons could be disinherited as easily as all other *extranei*, though here again by the classical period the praetors' rulings restored their position as far as getting possession of the property was concerned (Gaius *Inst.* 3.123-9).

Whether indeed it was this need which caused the Romans to breach the Greek principle (which may never in fact have existed in Rome, though it is likely that it did) of a son's absolute right to an equal share in the property of his *paterfamilias* is a matter open to discussion; personally I think that the need to restore the son emancipated because he wanted to and was capable of managing his own property was the probable source of the elaboration of the rules about wills; the right to make a will itself certainly preceded the Twelve Tables.[52] In other words, it seems to me probable that the development of the will was to allow the *paterfamilias* to emancipate a son so that the son could enjoy the *ius commercii* in his father's lifetime without losing his succession rights to *paterfamilias* when he became *sui iuris*, rather than that the will was developed in order to enable the *paterfamilias* to disinherit, wholly or partially, one or more of his children, and I think that the feeling against those who wanted to disinherit is reflected by the legal rulings which kept making it more and more difficult to do it effectually, while the ill effects of emancipation were more and more eroded by (praetorian) legal rulings, which shows that there was little or no feeling against emancipation — perhaps, as I said, a recognition that it was a sensible way of allowing a *filiusfamilias* to exercise the *ius commercii* fully.[53]

But it never occurred to the Romans to abolish the power of *paterfamilias* in respect of property, and say that once a Roman was enrolled as an adult member of his tribe he had full rights over any property he owned. It was only soldiers in imperial times with *castrense peculium* who had full power to dispose of their property even if they were *filiusfamilias*,[54] a dispensation which the civil servants were eventually able to convert to their own advantage.[55] This shows the abiding power of *patria potestas*.

Further, Roman society was divided between those who were patrician and those who were plebeian; plebeians were never the equals of patricians. This again goes back to the origins of Roman society, and there is a great deal of uncertainty, though I am myself on the whole in agreement with Ogilvie[56] who believes that in regal Rome the leaders of the patrician Latin *gentes* were compelled by the Etruscan kings to accept non-patrician (i.e. plebeian because Etruscan or immigrant) families into the governing class, and certainly into the senate, and that the coming of the Republic resulted in the patrician leaders, the *patres* of the Latin *gentes*, trying — and gradually succeeding — in getting rid of these Etruscan, non-patrician families from the privileges of governing the state, if not from the state altogether.

Even in the last years of the Republic, the *patres* consisted only of patricians, and it was still the case that in the lack of consuls the *patres* held the *auspicia* and one of them became *interrex* for five days at a time.

Some priesthoods remained patrician preserves: the *rex sacrorum* was not necessarily a patrician, but the three major *flamines* were all patricians exclusively: they ranked after the *pontifex maximus* and *rex sacrorum*. In historical times there is no example of *rex sacrorum* being important politically,[57] but the importance of *flamen Dialis* was strikingly demonstrated in 87 BC when Cornelius Merula was appointed *consul suffectus*. The situation was one of acute political strife; the patrician, L. Cornelius Cinna, had been driven out, and had taken refuge with the army of another patrician, Ap. Claudius Pulcher. At this moment Merula, the *flamen Dialis* (whose taboos included not entering the presence of an army or even riding a horse[58]), was chosen to succeed Cinna. From a military point of view nobody could have been a less appropriate choice. Merula must have been chosen because he was holding a post of supreme religious importance, to counter patrician claims with higher patrician claims to respect. It did not work, of course, but the attempt is a warning against looking at everything in purely political terms. Merula was succeeded by Julius Caesar who was stripped of his position by Sulla (Suetonius, *Iulius* 1) and punished — another proof of its importance? — and the post remained vacant till the principate. Why? The usual explanation is that nobody wanted to undertake a *confarreatio* marriage, but if this were so Augustus would not have been able to find candidates at the start of the principate, and he did find candidates for this and for the other posts of *rex sacrorum* and the other *flamines*.[59] So the reason for the non-filling must be different. Perhaps it was the same sort of envy of those in prominent positions which caused the withering of colonisation in the same period — much though it was needed — because, presumably, it created substantial pockets of organised *clientes*.[60]

How far back into history we have to go before the plebeians suffered real political disadvantages, and how serious these disadvantages were, are of course matters of scholarly dispute; did, for example, the disability to hold the consulate outlast the disability to intermarry with the patricians? What is clear is that a period of agitation by the plebeians came immediately following the publication of the Twelve Tables — the moment in fact at which the patrician legislators let the plebeian members of the citizenry know exactly what the law (hitherto a patrician preserve) actually was, and hence the exact nature of the disadvantages from which they were suffering. This was the moment when the monopoly of knowledge of the law by the *patres* came to an end, so it was in fact important in the development of the position of the *patres*.[61]

When we go back before the Twelve Tables, we are on even shakier ground, but I think that there can be little doubt that the founders of the *res publica* constituted their state as a group of *patres* sharing (as was necessary if they were to live in a community together without a king) the political offices but remaining fiercely independent of one another in respect of their private property. And they treated their dual magistracy,[62] which raised their families to the status of noble, as much like a single magistracy as they could, as has been argued above.

In administering the civil law, the Romans also used methods appropriate to those of a *paterfamilias* (again subject to the political necessity of taking turns). The praetor had to appoint a day for litigation (*diem dixit*), or the parties could not litigate at all; he then determined the correct formula under which the case could proceed and either gave judgement himself[63] or appointed a *iudex* by agreement of the parties, or on his own authority — or assessors — who decided the case.

In early Rome the *patres* delivered judgement (*ius dixerunt*) for their own *clientes* in as authoritarian a manner as they did for their own families,[64] with the exception, perhaps, that they gave grounds for their judgements to their *clientes*, who perhaps did not have to accept them. Otherwise, where did the Roman habit of explaining their rulings arise? It was certainly not out of any jury court system, either Roman (with ballots into a basket) or any common-law British system with a jury discussion in private at the end of the case, or appeal judgements by higher courts composed of trained and experienced professional judges. When their own *clientes* (or they themselves represented by a procurator) were in dispute with the *clientes* of another *paterfamilias*, then the two *patres* discussed things either between themselves or with advisers in a *consilium*.

4. The *Consilium*

This brings me to the next characteristically Roman feature which seems to me to show holders of *patria potestas* and *imperium* behaving in the same, typically Roman way. This concerns the *consilium*. As is well enough known, neither in public life was the magistrate obliged to consult the *consilium publicum* (the *patres conscripti*, the senate) before taking the actions he had in mind, nor was he compelled to put a matter to a vote nor, if he did put it to a vote, was he bound to accept the result of the vote as having any binding power on him.[65] Equally, *paterfamilias* was under no obligation to convene a *consilium* — a family one that is, a *privatum consilium*, if he had an important matter to decide, but both consul and *paterfamilias* were expected to seek advice[66] and to take the advice of a clear majority if such was evident, or at least of the best and most respected advisers. And both, if they did convene a *consilium* and act in accordance with the advice of that *consilium*, had a body of influential opinion to back them up: people who were expected to support the action decided upon.

The earliest recorded evidence for a *paterfamilias* convening a *consilium* is the story of Valerius Maximus (5.8.2), where it is reported that the father of Sp. Cassius, who sat in judgement on his son when he laid down the tribunate, convened a *consilium* of kinsmen and friends (*propinquorum et amicorum*) to try him — Livy's date is 481![67]

By contrast, the father of Horatius (who murdered his sister for sympathising with the enemy in the regal period) is said by Livy to have asserted that he would have exercised his *patria potestas* over his son without any mention of a council had he not acquitted him (Livy 1.26.9). The tradition here is particularly interesting in that *patria potestas* is said to have entitled a father to condemn without the intervention of the state, but (presumably because the case involved blood-guilt) when he acquitted him the state was also concerned, and was not obliged to accept the *paterfamilias'* acquittal of his son. When it did so, the community laid on *paterfamilias* the obligation to see to the necessary purifications (Livy 1.26.12), though the community itself bore the cost.

In the case of L. Iunius Brutus, listed by Valerius Maximus (*l.c.*) as another example of parental *severitas*, it is hinted by Valerius himself and made explicit by Livy (2.5.) that Brutus's action in punishing his sons was as consul not as *paterfamilias*.[68]

Some 350 years later (140 or 139 perhaps) T. Manlius Torquatus is said to have been a man of such *dignitas* that it was accepted by the senate and the Macedonian complainants against his son, that he did not need a *consilium* even of his *necessarii* (closer relatives) to hear a case against him. This case is not strictly an example of the use of *patria potestas* because the son had been given in adoption to D. Iunius Silanus, and Torquatus did not in fact condemn his son, but caused him to commit suicide. But the story shows that by this date at least a *consilium* was expected. Almost a century later (after 70 BC), L. Gellius, by then ex-censor, convened almost the whole senate to act as his *consilium* (Valerius Maximus 5.9.1).

So, the usages of the *paterfamilias* and of the state developed on parallel lines. Which influenced which? It is easy to suppose that the use of the *consilium* in public life came first, not least because it is attested first, but I think we should hesitate because, if things had developed that way round, it would have been more natural for a law requiring a *paterfamilias* to use a *consilium* to have been passed, whereas no such law in fact was passed; it was never more than *mos* for a *consilium* to be convened, either in public or private affairs before the imperial period.[69]

Augustus's use of the senate as a *consilium* is also of great interest.[70] Naturally, the restoration of a *res publica* form (or façade) of government after the civil wars restored the senate nominally to its important role as the *publicum consilium*; Augustus also organised, some time before the fifth Cyrene edict,[71] another *consilium*, the committee of senators chosen partly by office, partly by lot, whose membership changed, either in whole or in part, every six months. He also had, like *principes* of the Republican era and Hellenistic monarchs, another *consilium* of men chosen by himself, who really did the business of the state — his *amici*.[72] Yet when he punished his errant daughter, Julia, he wrote to the senate (Suetonius, *Augustus* 65.2). True he was not asking their advice as to what to do with her, nor did he tell them the whole truth,[73] but he had by then become *pater patriae* so that his actions taken as *paterfamilias* could be seen as being of concern to the senate, the *publicum consilium* of the *res publica*.[74] Augustus had earlier introduced his adopted sons, Gaius and Lucius Caesar, to the *publicum consilium* from the time they were given the *toga virilis* and became *principes iuventutis*, consuls designate and priests, in the same way that noble youths were as a matter of course introduced to their father's *consilium* on being given their *toga virilis*. Was this anticipating (in 5 BC) and reflecting (in 2 BC) the title *pater patriae*? We cannot say, but by 2 BC Augustus's programme of associating his family's gods with those of the state when he became *pontifex maximus* (from 12 BC), and of associating the successes of the Julian house with those of the Roman state,[75] had clearly identified his roles as *paterfamilias* and as *pater patriae*. The development was a wholly natural one for the Romans.

This is not an attempt to say that he had become a universal *paterfamilias* in a property sense. Plainly he had not. The relationship belonged more to the area of *clientela*.[76] The institution of *clientela* itself was an aspect of *patria potestas*; the *potestas* of the *patronus* who had manumitted a slave 'was at all times wide, and originally almost unlimited'; it had 'a coercive power of the same nature as *patria potestas* — and probably one aspect of it — and originally equally independent of the State'.[77]

Though the *potestas* of the *patronus* and his *heredes* over the descendants of the original *clientes* naturally waned — there was, for example, never any question of re-enslaving a citizen who was *ingenuus*,[78] the institution was founded on the ideas inherent in *patria potestas* — 'for the patron . . . stood to his clients in the position of a father, and they were expected to ask his advice as a son would ask a father's before taking decisions of particular importance' (Badian *FC* 163-4).

It thus seems evident that, in the Romans' most characteristic institutions, *paterfamilias'* power of governing his family through *patria potestas* was reflected in the patron's management of his independent *clientes*, relations with whom were based originally on *potestas* but later on *fides*, and in the citizen's management of the *res publica* where he acted as a magistrate through *imperium*. And in all these spheres the Romans saw a separation between governmental power and property-owning rights, as the latter were total in respect of those in *patria potestas*, partial in respect of those in a relationship of *fides* as clients,[79] and non-existent in the magisterial sphere. Consequently I offer the suggestion that for government *patria potestas* was the fundamental institution of the Romans which shaped and directed their world-view or *Weltanschauung*.

Notes

1. This chapter is considerably modified from the paper originally presented at the Canberra seminar. I have to thank participants in the discussion for pointing out some invalid arguments and errors, and of these particularly Professor John Crook and Dr Robert Develin. Neither, however, should be held in any way responsible for what appears here. In these notes I have abbreviated two works frequently cited: Ogilvie 1965 as *Comm.*; Badian 1958 as *FC*.

2. See D.M. MacDowell's note (Oxford, 1971, edn) *ad loc*.

3. Cicero's *Pro Roscio Amerino* should certainly contain such arguments had they been acceptable to Roman jurors.

4. Livy 1.28-9, for Alba; the tradition was clearly much older: Ogilvie, *Comm. ad loc.* cf. 1.33 for Politorium, Telleuae, Ficana and Latins generally.

5. Livy 1.46.1 (locality unstated); Signia and Circeii in the regal period, Livy 1.56.3.

6. Like the treaties with Gabii and Crustumerium, Dionysius of Halicarnassus 4.58.4, 3.49.6 (Sherwin-White 1939:18-19) and the *foedus Cassianum*, Livy 2.33.4, Dionysius of Halicarnassus 6.95; see *Comm.* 317-18 for further bibliography.

7. For the denial that there was any real difference, Badian, *FC* 25-6.

8. The only known reference is in the Twelve Tables (5.5), but the rule was obsolete before the classical period; it prescribed that *gentiles* were to have the *familia* if an intestate person had neither *heres suus* nor *agnatus proximus* —

Gaius *Inst.* 3.17, though Gaius says *nullus agnatus.*

9. This in fact is controversial; Zulueta 1953:II, 123, though even he does not consider the *sacra* of the *familia.*

10. Isaeus 3.36; Lacey (1968:138-9); Harrison (1968:I, 56).

11. Buckland (1963:373). Cf. Crook, Chapter 2 above.

12. Ogilvie, *Comm.* 235 doubts this view, however: 'the whole doctrine that regal *potestas* was of the same quality as consular *imperium* was an invention of Roman legalists', and references cited by him. See Versnel (1970), however, for a more recent discussion, upholding the view in the text with evidence from the rules about the triumph, esp. chs. 5, 8.

13. Livy 1.17.9, 22.1, 32.1, 46.1; contrast 4.9.3; whatever the truth, this was the tradition. The fact that the interval between consuls in the Republic, when it occurred, was called *interregnum* must show that this provision went back to the regal period, and thus an automatic hereditary transmission was not the tradition.

14. In the Romans' own belief, *patria potestas* was an institution peculiar to their own society: C.1.9.2.

15. Badian, *FC*, esp. 1-10 and texts there cited. Note the attribution to Romulus: Cicero, *De re publica* 2.16.

16. Note the failure to consult the senate was a sign of Tarquin's tyranny, Livy 1.49.4.

17. Livy 1.35.6; again it is the tradition not the true historicity of the facts that matters. Cf. Dionysius of Halicarnassus 2.47, O'Brien Moore, *RE* Suppl. 6 s.v. Senatus.

18. Initially by Brutus: Livy 2.1.10.

19. Lucretius 2.11ff. mentions *ingenium, nobilitas* and *labor,* but not *dignitas,* perhaps for no better reason than that it will not fit into a hexameter line (in any case); but it was for his *dignitas* that Caesar started the civil war (or so he said according to Cicero, *Ad Atticum* 7.11.1, a contemporary document).

20. Cicero, *De natura deorum* 3.32.8; *De oratore* 3.3.10; and Livy, *Per.* 86.

21. Frazer (1929:192-3; note on Ovid, *Fasti* 6.263).

22. Varro, *De re rustica* 1.1.4; Frazer (1929:219-20, note on Ovid, *Fasti* 6.295) for the view that Vesta had a characteristic attitude, shielding her eyes.

23. Livy 1.20.2; Gellius 1.12.10; Ovid, *Fasti* 6.259; Ogilvie, *Comm.* 97-8, for criticism of the Alban origin and further references. Cf. Ovid, *Fasti* 2.69 where the shrine is known as Numa's sanctuary; 'the view that the hearth of Vesta was originally the hearth of the king's house is probably correct': Frazer (1929) *ad loc.* (2.301).

24. Ovid, *Fasti,* 6.257-64.

25. For the idea that *sacra* are immovably attached to places rather than people, cf. the speech of Camillus in Livy 5.51ff. esp. 51.2, 'ut in sua sede maneret patria'; 5.2, 'sacrificiis sollemnibus non dies magis stati quam loca sunt in quibus fiant'; 5.25ff., and note that the *sedes* of Jupiter Opitmus Maximus is on the Capitol, 51.9. Note also the gods named which cannot be moved — Jupiter, Vesta, Mars, Quirinus — Vesta, that is, plus the three deities who are so peculiarly Roman that they have a *flamen.* For the value of the speech as evidence of the views of Livy and his contemporaries, Ogilvie, *Comm.* 741ff.

26. A new residence is a new Vesta, not the Vesta of your ancestors.

27. So did a young man taken as *flamen Dialis* if he was not already *suo iure,* and without *capitis deminutio,* Gaius *Inst.*1.130, 3.114; Festus 198 (Lindsay) on Rex Sacrorum.

28. Frazer initially suggested wives, then changed his mind to support the view that they were daughters (1929 on Ovid, *Fasti* 4.182-3), as does Rose (1926; 1948:53). The idea that they were daughters is supported by their duty of ceremonially waking the Rex Sacrorum (Servius on *Aeneid* 10.228): Rose (1948:56), and may suggest that they were originally in his *potestas* rather than in

that of Pontifex Maximus who at some time after c.275 BC superseded Rex Sacrorum (Ogilvie, *Comm.* 237, in Livy 2.1.11).

29. Festus, s.v. *ignis*; Frazer (1929:38) n.5 on Ovid, *Fasti* 3.143.

30. A truly pious girl offered prayer with incense and wine every day and garlands: Plautus, *Aulularia* 23-5; cf. *id.* 383 for incense and garlands as a cheap offering; Horace, *Odes* 3.23.1-4 prayers at the new moon; Juvenal 10.137-8.

31. In Livy's belief (1.44) the sacred area on which the walls stood, and hence the *sedes* of the Roman people. For criticism of this, and the view that it was really a line marking off the space inside as hallowed, Ogilvie, *Comm.* 179-80.

32. This lapsing was only one aspect: Develin (1977: esp. 54ff). 'The *pomerium* of Rome marked the limits of domestic *imperium*, and, in reverse, of military *imperium*. The city was also the point of definition for *auspicium* or *auspicia*. The *curiae* made up a religious assembly confined solely to the city of Rome as a non military body' (58-9).

33. The so-called '*senatus consultum ultimum*'. Bringing in troops is the one common element in the actions of all those whose actions we know in detail, from L. Opimius in 121 BC to the civil wars which began in 49 BC.

34. For the contrast *domi/foris*, Livy 1.43.2 (the Servian organisation), 3.31.1, 6.11.1; Cicero, *De officiis* 1.76; Suetonius, *Iulius* 9.3, *Claudius* 22.1. The better-known contrast *domi/militiae* often appears when military actions are actually in progress, outside the *ager Romanus*. The fact that the tribunes of the people had the right to act outside the *pomerium* shows that not all the world outside it was '*militiae*' all the time. In imperial times the prefect of the city's jurisdiction extended 100 miles beyond it.

35. They were actually her first real acts; she had been a more or less passive participant in the ceremonies up to this point. See Fowler (1908:ch. 5); Balsdon (1962:181ff.), esp. 185 for the ancient sources.

36. Macrobius 1.9.16, 1.15.18-9, who declares that they preside over the beginnings of every month, hence the Kalends is sacred to them.

37. Ogilvie, *Comm.*117.

38. 'War magic' as Rose describes it (1948:56); thought by Ogilvie (*Comm.* 93) to be an elaboration of the sacred archway of purification (*tigillum*) by which returning soldiers were purified from blood-guilt at the end of a campaign (*Comm.* 17).

39. Cicero, *De re publica* 2.55; Livy 2.1.8.

40. Suetonius, *Iulius* 20; Mommsen (1887-8:(3) 1, 37ff.) — who points out that the idea of an *accensus* preceding a consul appears in the account of the *decemviri* of the first year (Livy 3.33.8).

41. Versnel (1970:338f.), quoting Cancelli (1957), and cf. Cancelli (1960).

42. 'quod summa potestas huius in equites et accensos' (Varro, *De lingua Latina* 5.82).

43. I have to thank Dr R. Develin for these references.

44. Livy 6.37.4; cf. Mommsen (1887-8:2.281, 285, etc.).

45. Age was also thought to bring greater distinction, but the marrying age and therewith often the assumption of *kyreia* of the *oikos* seems to me more likely to be the crucial point.

46. (1957:82), based on Burn's figures for Africa in the period AD 1-250 (1953:31).

47. That is, under Sulla's arrangements; he claimed (of course) to be merely establishing by law what was *mos maiorum*.

48. Buckland (1963:277); cf. for acquisition by *filiusfamilias*, Gaius *Inst.* 2.87.

49. First known for certain under Claudius: Tacitus, *Annals* 11.13; it is usually assumed that Claudius's law was the first establishment of this rule (which was subsequently strengthened by the *s.c. Macedonianum* passed under Vespasian: Suetonius, *Vespasian* 11), but Tacitus's language (he says 'saevitiam creditorum

coercuit') may suggest that it was an attack not on the practice but on the money-lenders' relentless execution of the agreements.

50. Well enough established for slaves — e.g. Buckland (1963:65), and *Digest* references there cited.

51. Originally they were not *sui heredes* at all and had no rights to an intestate inheritance, and though the praetor later allowed them to share even with (unemancipated) *sui heredes*, they were disadvantages in two respects:

(1) They had to claim, and establish, their right; and
(2) they had to bring their own property into the estate to claim a share.

This latter rule was of course analogous to the position of a wife; if she was married *cum manu*, she was *sua*, if not, she was *extranea*. Even then she got *bonorum possessio* — i.e. ownership of the property — not the honour of being *heres* (for what that was thought worth in the more sophisticated age). See Crook (1967b:118-19) for a very clear summary.

52. Obviously it originated in the need of soldiers to make provision for their families in case they failed to return from campaign, hence the original forms, Gaius *Inst.* 2.101.

53. Note especially the rules under which wills can be voided by the birth of children (Gaius *Inst.* 2.130ff.), even to descendants in *potestas*, and by those who become *sui heredes* by the process known as quasi-agnation (*id.* 133ff.).

54. Crook (1967b:110-11) with references: that to Juvenal 16.51ff. is a particularly revealing one as it shows this fact was not an arcane secret of the lawyers.

55. By *quasi-castrense peculium*; but this was Constantinian: Justinian *Inst.* 2.11.6.

56. *Comm.* 236-7, 293-4, 451ff.

57. The one known in the first century BC was L. Claudius who is so obscure that his *praenomen* has been doubted — because the politically active Claudii never used it; obviously this priestly family simply had a different *praenomen*. Broughton (1952:1, 187). For his ranking after *pontifex maximus*, Festus 198.30.

58. Gellius 10.15 for the fullest account. Many other references.

59. Of the *flamines* in the first century BC, Cornelius Lentulus (Niger) rose as far as the praetorship; he was *flamen Martialis* in 56; a *flamen Quirinalis* was Sex. Iulius Caesar who was quaestor in 48 and governor of Syria thereafter, where he was killed (Broughton 1952:1, 206, 289, 297, 554, 575; but the identification has been challenged, *id.* 304).

60. Badian, *FC* 162-3 for the principle involved.

61. Ogilvie, *Comm.* 451ff., esp. 452.

62. Whether called *praetor* or *consul* at the time hardly matters: Ogilvie, *Comm.* 230, for a summary of earlier views including that which holds that Rome originally had a senior and a junior chief magistrate (whether the senior was called *magister populi*, *dictator* or *praetor maximus*).

63. As is implied by Cicero, *De legibus* 3.8 and Livy 3.55.11 to have been the norm in early times.

64. Three examples at least of punishing *clientes* are recorded in the sources; two concern Julius Caesar (Suetonius, *Iulius* 48); one of these records the infliction of the death penalty, as does the other (Valerius Maximus 6.1.4). These *clientes* were all *liberti*, which is probably a significant fact.

65. But not to do so showed an arrogant attitude, like that of Tarquinius Superbus (Livy 1.49.4).

66. Note the case in Valerius Maximus 2.9.2, dated 307 BC, in which the censors expelled L. Annius from the senate for having put away his wife without

consulting his *consilium* of *amici* ('nullo amicorum consilio').

67. 486 in the Varronian *fasti*.

68. The comment shows that the powers of consul and *paterfamilias* were thought to be analogous. Though Livy's account contains no explicit record of a reference to the senate of the question of the punishment of the traitors, the securing of the evidence is a hint that the consuls determined that their action would stand public scrutiny by the *patres*. Livy's contemporaries would of course recognise the parallel with 63 BC, which clearly influenced Livy's account, as Ogilvie makes clear: *Comm.* 243.

69. Even the imperial rulings such as D.48.8.2 (from Ulpian, *On Adultery*), D.9.15.pr. (a ruling of Constantine), C.8.46.3 (a ruling of Severus Alexander) seem to demand a public hearing, not that a private *consilium* hear the case.

70. Lacey (1974:176ff., esp. 183-4).

71. *FIRA* 1.68.5.

72. Crook (1955: chs 2, 3).

73. Lacey (1980:136ff).

74. Compare the reports made periodically to the senate by proconsuls and propraetors — or at least the more conscientious of them — when they were governing provinces and fighting wars: e.g. Cicero, *Ad familiares* 15.1 and 2, 3.3.2; Caesar, *Gallic War* 2.35.4; 3.38.5. They were informing the *publicum consilium* rather than asking advice on every occasion.

75. In the symbolism and layout of the forum Augustum and the temple of Mars Ultor: Lacey (1980:133-6).

76. The Caesars claimed the whole *plebs Romana* — perhaps the whole *populus Romanus* — for their *clientela*: Yavetz (1969:96, 152); note also the evidence provided by the legacies left in turn by Caesar, Augustus and Tiberius.

77. Badian, *FC* 2-4 and references. Badian also (rightly) stresses that the right of *coercitio* which a *patronus* could exercise over *clientes* must also include the moral obligation to hold a hearing — and hence to seek the *auctoritas* of a *consilium* in serious cases.

78. In so far as a descendant of a slave was ever *ingenuus*: the point is discussed by Mommsen (1887-8:3.422-3).

79. A client had obligations to his patron in respect of property rights which prevailed against the claims of *extranei*; was this the origin and explanation of the well-established custom of the imperial period which recognised that the emperor had at least an expectation of receiving something under the wills of prominent men? Tacitus, *Agricola* 43.4 provides an example: see Ogilvie's notes (Oxford, 1967 edn) *ad loc.*

6 THE STATUS OF CHILDREN IN MIXED MARRIAGES

P.R.C. Weaver

I What is a 'Mixed Marriage'?

We are not here concerned with marriages between persons of different racial, social or religious groups, but with persons of different *legal* status.

A 'mixed marriage' may be defined as a stable union of a couple where one partner is a Roman citizen (or a privileged non-Roman (*peregrinus*) who had the *ius conubii*) and the other does not have *ius conubii* at the time when the union began. That is, all 'marriages' in Roman society that could not be *iustae nuptiae* or a *iustum matrimonium*. The non-citizen partner could be either an alien (*peregrinus/a*) or a slave (*servus/a*). The citizen partner could be either freeborn (*ingenuus/a*) or freed (*libertus/a*)[1] i.e. manumitted in the proper manner by a Roman citizen who was legally entitled to do so. In this sense a partner can be free (*liber*) whether he or she was originally born free or born as a slave of a Roman citizen or acquired after birth as a slave by a Roman citizen and subsequently freed according to the formal requirements of Roman law on manumission.

In this chapter I am not concerned with 'marriages' where the non-citizen partner was an alien, or a Junian Latin, or a *dediticius*, but primarily where he or she was of slave status when the union began, and when the children were born.[2] Either father or mother can be of slave status, but not both; the other must be a Roman citizen at the relevant time.

There is no ancient term to describe such a union. The fact itself was recognised but penalised by legislation from the *senatusconsultum Claudianum* of AD 52 onwards till Justinian, but discussion has remained spasmodic until comparatively recently. As with such modernisms as 'familia Caesaris' and, I believe, 'consilium principis', it would be useful to have a succinct term of reference for mixed marriages. The nearest is '*contubernium*'. *Contubernium* and *contubernales* in the legal sources refer to 'marriages' where both partners are slaves or one partner is slave and the other is free (Paulus *Sent.* 2.19.6: 'inter servos et liberos matrimonium contrahi non potest, contubernium potest'). In the funerary inscriptions also the term *'contubernalis'* is only used when at least one partner had been a slave during the union. It makes no difference whether one or both partners have been subsequently freed, as frequently such partners continue to refer to each other as *contubernales* after their manumission or even after the manumission of the one partner who had been of slave status, when *matrimonium* would have been the appropriate term to describe the relationship made possible by their free status. The term *'contubernalis'* thus can refer to an earlier stage of a relationship begun when at least one partner was a slave.[3]

This, however, is too broad a term to describe a 'marriage' where not only must one partner have been a slave, but one partner must also have been a citizen, freed or freeborn, at the time the union *began*, not just at any point *during* the union. In the latter case marriage could have begun while both partners were slaves and even if one partner were subsequently freed we would still have *contubernium*, not a 'mixed' marriage. The key point about 'mixed' marriages is the citizen status of one partner. It will be important later to distinguish between the origin of that citizen status, that is, whether it derived from free birth (*ingenuitas*), i.e. from a mother with citizen status (*ingenua* or *liberta*) at a time of the child's birth, or from manumission, that is a citizen ex-slave and thus born from a mother who was a slave (*serva*) at the time of the child's birth. Thus while all 'mixed' marriages are *contubernia*, not all *contubernia* are 'mixed' marriages. An adjective or phrase qualifying *contubernium* is required. I propose *'contubernium cum cive'*.

The term *'contubernium cum cive'* (hereafter *c.c.c.*) stresses the two necessary characteristics of a 'mixed' marriage: (1) that one partner was of slave status at some time during the union (*contubernium*); (2) that the other partner was of citizen status at the time the union began (*cum cive*). *'Civis'* has the advantage of leaving the question open whether the citizen partner in these unions was male or female; it embraces both.

Bearing in mind that *'civis'* here has the same meaning as *'liber'*/*'libera'* and that male *'liber'* includes both freeborn (*ingenuus*) and freedman (*libertus*) and that female *'libera'* includes both freeborn (*ingenua*) and freedwoman (*liberta*), we thus have the following classes of unions which may be classified as *c.c.c.*

I   *serva*   = *ingenuus*
II   *serva*   = *libertus*
III *servus* = *ingenua*
IV *servus* = *liberta*

To examine the status of children in *c.c.c.* we need to know the status of the mother at the time of birth of the children as in accordance with the rule of the *ius gentium* it is the status of the mother that will determine the status of the children born 'in contubernio'. We may, therefore, group together classes I and II and classes III and IV, as for this purpose it makes no difference whether the mother was freeborn or a freedwoman at the time of birth of her children. It will become apparent, however, that for women without status indication but with *nomen* (i.e. *incertae*), the distinction between *libertae* and *ingenuae* is difficult and often controversial, and that herein a number of problems lie.

The remaining terminology of family relationships needs cause us less concern. '*Vir*', '*maritus*', '*uxor*', '*coniunx*', etc. are constantly used both in the inscriptions as well as in the legal texts to refer to *contubernium* as well as *matrimonium*. They are of no use in distinguishing between unions of differing legal status,[4] including *c.c.c.* The same goes for '*filius*', '*filia*', '*pater*', '*mater*', '*parens*', etc. These terms denote natural parental relationships whatever the legal status of the father or mother or children, whatever the status of the parental union.

II   What was the Law on '*c.c.c.*'?

On the question of the status of children the rule was that children born 'in conubio' (i.e. of *iustae nuptiae*) inherited the status of their father at the time of conception, according to the *ius civile*, and children of any other union inherited the status of their mother at the time of birth, according to the *ius gentium*.

> semper conubium efficit ut qui nascitur patris condicioni accedat; aliter vero contracto matrimonio eum qui nascitur iure gentium matris condicionem sequi. (Gaius *Inst.* 1.80)

cf. 1.82: 'ex ancilla et libero iure gentium servus nascitur, et contra ex libera et servo liber nascitur.' 'ex cive Romano et Latina Latinus nascitur et ex libero et ancilla servus, quoniam cum his casibus conubia non sint, partus sequitur matrem' (Ulpian, *Reg.* 5.9), and for the difference between conception and birth in relation to status of children, ibid. 10: 'in his qui iure contracto matrimonio nascuntur conceptionis tempus spectatur; in his autem qui non legitime concipiuntur, editionis.'

It would seem straightforward enough then simply to determine whether the mother was *serva* (I, II) or *libera* (III, IV) at the time of birth of a particular child to decide on that child's status: a *serva* would give birth to a *servus/serva*, a mother who was *libera* (i.e. *liberta* or *ingenua*) would give birth to a *liber/libera*, and hence an *ingenuus/ingenua*, and, if the mother was a *civis Romana*, to a child was was also a *civis Romanus/ Romana*.

But Gaius in his next section (1.83) goes on to warn us that the rule of the law of nations (*ius gentium*) may be modified by statute or by what has the force of statute (i.e. the *ius civile*):

> animadvertere tamen debemus ne iuris gentium regulam vel lex aliqua, vel quod legis vicem optinet, aliquo casu commutaverit.

He then gives two examples of such modifications of the rules of the *ius gentium* in relation to the status of children, 1.84: whereby a *civis Romana* could give birth to a child who was a *servus*, and 1.85: whereby a *serva* (*ancilla*) could bear a child who was freeborn (*liber*).[5]

To take the latter case first. It involves classes I and II.

> <item e lege . . .> ex ancilla et libero poterant liberi nasci; nam ea lege cavetur ut si quis cum aliena ancilla *quam credebat* liberam esse coierit, siquidem masculi nascantur, liberi sint, si vero feminae, ad eum pertineant cuius mater ancilla fuerit. (Gaius 1.85)

The anomaly here is twofold: not only does a slave woman (*ancilla*) give birth to a child who is free (*liber*), but this happens only in the case of *male* children (*masculi*), not in the case of female children (*feminae*), who are born slaves of the mother's owner. The anomaly here arises in the first place because of a mistake as to the status of the partner one was marrying. The woman was *thought to be* free. A common enough occurrence, to judge by Gaius's lengthy treatment of the subject, 1.67-75 ('erroris causae probatio'). Relief from the consequences was provided, on condition that a reasonable mistake could be proved to have been made (cf. 1.87).

Gaius goes on to say that the role of the *ius gentium* was restored in these cases by Vespasian, 'inelegantia iuris motus'. It is not certain how long before Vespasian this modification by statute occurred. It could belong to the reign of Claudius, as does the *s.c. Claudianum* (to be discussed below) but it cannot have formed part of that *s.c.* It probably goes back to the Augustan legislation on status, possibly the lex Aelia Sentia of AD 4.[6]

The lex Aelia Sentia contained among its most far-reaching provisions restrictions on the age at which a slave could be formally manumitted. This was set at 30 years under normal circumstances, but among the recognised reasons justifying earlier manumission (*iustae causae manumissionis*) was the freeing of a female slave (*ancilla*) by her *patronus* 'matrimonii causa'.[7] There was a prejudice against freeborn or even freed males 'marrying' female slaves. Hence the provision that *ancillae* (*servae*) could be manumitted early for the purpose of *matrimonium. Contubernium* is thus avoided in these circumstances. Indeed it is assumed by Gaius (1.85 above) that this would only happen when a free man was unaware that his partner was a slave and thought (wrongly) that their relationship was *matrimonium*, not *contubernium*. Hence the variation from the rule of the *ius gentium* for their children. Vespasian's restoration of the rule may have had elegance in its favour but, while removing one source of discrimination (between male and female children) in genuine cases of ignorance of the status of the mother who turned out to be a slave, it discriminated against the children of both sexes.

The correct thing to do, of course, where a free Roman wished to marry a slave woman was either, if she was one of his own slaves, to free her and marry her or make her his concubine[8] or, if he knew her to be someone else's slave, to buy her, free her and then marry her. In neither case would they be *contubernales*. There are many cases in the inscriptions of *patronus* = *liberta*, of dedications such as 'patronus uxori et libertae', etc.[9] so that we must conclude that this was normal social practice among the slave-born classes, including the familia Caesaris. These cannot be considered as cases of *c.c.c.*[10]

The second example whereby the rule of the *ius gentium* in relation to the status of children was modified by statute is more important for *c.c.c.* It covers cases in classes III and IV above. This concerns the *s.c. Claudianum* of AD 52 whereby a *civis Romana* who cohabited with a slave could, under certain conditions, give birth to a child who was a *servus*. Gaius 1.84 runs:

> ecce enim ex senatusconsulto Claudiano poterat civis Romana, quae alieno servo volente domino eius coiit, ipsa ex pactione libera permanere, sed servum procreare; nam quod inter eam et dominum istius servi convenerit ex senatusconsulto ratum esse iubetur. sed postea divus Hadrianus, iniquitate rei et inelegantia iuris motus, restituit iuris gentium regulam, ut, cum ipsa mulier libera permaneat, liberum pariat.

Here we have precise details. The emphasis is on the agreement (*pactio*) that could be reached between a *civis Romana* (who could be either *ingenua* or *liberta*) and the master of another's slave (i.e. anyone else's slave than her own) to the disadvantage of the child. She was to remain *libera* but the child was to be a *servus*. Note that nothing is said about a *civis Romana* cohabiting with her *own servus*.[11] While this may not be taken as a licence to engage in *c.c.c.*, it is in contrast to the prejudice which operated against the reverse situation of a *civis Romanus* cohabiting 'in contubernio' with his own *serva* (mentioned above).

But a different light and emphasis is cast by another important source, Tacitus, *Annals* 12.53:

> inter quae (Claudius) refert ad patres de poena feminarum quae servis coniungerentur; statuiturque ut ignaro domino ad id prolapsae in servitute, sin consensisset, pro libertis haberentur.

No mention is made here of the status of the children or of any unfairness to them. The distinction between the slaves of another master and her own is implied (*ignaro domino*), as is the

reference to the agreement with that master (*sin consensisset*).
But Tacitus says that women who came to that agreement were
to be considered *freed*women (*libertae*), rather than *free* women
(*liberae*) as in Gaius. The two are not conflicting, as *liberae* can
include *libertae*. Tacitus, as indeed do the other sources,[12]
concentrates on the penalty (*poena*) imposed on the *civis
Romana* (*libera*) and it is clear that he is correct and more specific
on this point than Gaius. In other words, the alternatives for a
civis Romana cohabiting with another's slave were either (a) if it
was done with the consent of the master of the slave, to be
reduced to the status of a *liberta*, but to bear children who were
servi, or (b) if done *without* the knowledge and hence without the
consent of the master (a case considered to be more degrading —
'*ad id prolapsae*'), to be reduced to the status of a *serva*, in which
case the children would also be *servi*.

The change introduced by Hadrian was in the interests of the
children when there was agreement between the woman and the
master of the slave, not necessarily in the interests of the woman,
who would be in the same position as before (*libera permaneat*),
whereas the child would henceforth be born *liber* (i.e. *ingenuus*)
and not a *servus*. The provision whereby the woman could be
enslaved, if there was no agreement with the master of the slave,
remained, in which case there was no benefit for the children who
would be born, as before, *servi*. About the same time, or at least
before the time of Gaius (c. AD 160), the conditions for such
enslavement were tightened. Gaius states in 1.91:

> si qua mulier civis Romana praegnas ex senatus consulto
> Claudiano ancilla facta sit ob id quod alieno servo invito et
> denuntiante domino eius ‹coierit› . . .

and in 1.160 cites as a case of *capitis deminutio maxima*

> feminae quae ex senatus consulto Claudiano ancillae fiunt
> eorum dominorum quibus invitis et denuntiantibus cum servis
> eorum coierint.

It is not sufficient for the master of the slave merely to be
unaware of the union, but he must forbid and warn the woman
(*invito et denuntiante domino*), and the woman must persist. Only
then could she be enslaved. Even later, perhaps in the third

century after Gaius, further restrictions were placed on the master of the slave: he must give three warnings (*denuntiationes*), and subsequent enslavement of the woman was only by formal legal process. The implication is clear that Roman citizen women *were able to be enslaved* under the provisions of the *s.c. Claudianum after* Hadrian and throughout the second and third centuries AD, i.e. during the period from which the great bulk of our inscriptional evidence comes. This penalty clause of the *s.c.* was only finally abolished by Justinian.

Support for this interpretation of the effects of the *s.c. Claudianum* comes from further legal texts, especially Paulus *Sent* 4.10.2: 'ad filiam ancillam vel libertam ex senatus consulto Claudiano effectam'. This does not refer to *children* being enslaved under the *s.c..*, as there was no discrimination between the sexes in such an eventuality, as is implied here, and no provision for them to be made *liberti* or *libertae* directly under the *s.c.*, or to be subsequently manumitted, if so enslaved. 'Filia' must refer to adult *cives Romanae* suffering one or other of the penalties imposed by the *s.c.* for persisting in cohabitation with the slave of another master, that is *c.c.c.*

As will become apparent in the next section, this provision of the *s.c. Claudianum* was particularly relevant to wives of the emperor's slaves, who to a far greater extent than for any other group of slaves' wives were not only *liberae* but also *ingenuae*. Another passage from the *Sententiae* of Paulus, referring specifically to *ingenuae* cohabiting with *municipal* slaves, raises the prospect of differential treatment for wives of imperial slaves, not necessarily to their advantage. Paulus *Sent.* 2.21.14: 'mulier ingenua quae se sciens servo municipum iunxerit etiam citra denuntiationem ancilla efficitur.'

Here a freeborn woman does not even have the benefit of a warning, if she is aware of the status of her slave partner. Nothing is said here of the option of her being reduced to the status of *liberta* and of her children being freeborn. The 'dominus' in question would presumably have to be one or more of the municipal magistrates, for whom the exercise of this option would be to the financial disadvantage of the *municipium* and therefore restricted in some way. The passage goes on, however, to mention a '*si nesciat*' provision, which in the event of an *ingenua* being unaware of the status of her partner, and subsequently discovering the truth and desisting from the union, exempts her from the penalties of the law — ibid. 'non item si nesciat; nescisse autem videtur quae comperta condicione contubernio se abstinuit aut libertum putavit.' We have seen an analogous situation above (Gaius 1.85) where, when a free male was unaware that his partner was a *serva*, it is assumed that he will desist or secure her manumission, so making *matrimonium* possible, but not continuing with *contubernium*.

There remains a passage from the Theodosian Code, *Cod. Theod.* 4.12.3: 'cum ius vetus ingenuas fiscalium servorum contubernio coniunctas ad decoctionem natalium cogat, nulla vel ignorantiae venia tributa vel aetati, placet . . .'.

This indicates that until AD 320 *ingenuae* cohabiting with *servi fiscales* (who may be equated with *Caesaris servi* of the early empire for this purpose) were still liable to the penalty of being reduced to the status of *libertae* (*ad decoctionem natalium*), with no allowance made whether they were ignorant of the slave status of their partner or not. In these cases the plea of ignorance would be a likely story! The new rule laid down in AD 320, however, while finally permitting *ingenuae* cohabiting with fiscal slaves to retain their freeborn status, still persists with imposing a penalty, this time on the children, who are not to be *ingenui* but are to be given *Latin* status and classed as illegitimate (*spurii*). Such unions, it declares, are to be avoided, thereby giving continuing expression to the prejudice against *ingenuae* forming unions with *servi*, that is to the general prejudice against *c.c.c.* — ibid.:

> placet coniunctionum quidem talium vincla vitari; sin vero mulier ingenua vel ignora vel etiam volens cum servo fiscale convenerit, nullum eam ingenui status damnum sustinere, *subolem* vero, quae patre servo fiscali, matre nascetur ingenua, *mediam tenere fortunam* ut servorum *liberi* et liberarum *spurii Latini sint*, qui, licet servitutis necessitate solvantur, patroni tamen privilegio tenebuntur.

This is not the place to speculate on the purpose of the *s.c. Claudianum*. As the last words of the passage above suggest, its primary continuing purpose (and no doubt its original purpose) in relation to *servi fiscales* and *Caesaris servi*[13] was undoubtedly financial or fiscal.[14] But in relation to *c.c.c.* the *senatus consultum* with its notion of *poena* expresses the strong prejudice against a freeborn woman forming a lasting union with a slave. Discrimination is shown in the lex Aelia Sentia, where provision is made for the early manumission of a female slave 'matrimonii causa' by a *patronus*, but not for the reverse case of a *patrona* wishing to give early manumission to her *servus* in order to marry him. Where the *patrona* was freeborn the prejudice was strong against even *matrimonium* with her freedman. A constitution of Septimius Severus castigates as 'odiosa' the union of a freedman with his *patrona* or the daughter or wife of his *patronus* and makes such a union grounds of accusation against the impertinent *libertus*. (C.5.4.3.: 'libertum, qui patronam seu patroni filiam vel coniugem . . . uxorem ducere ausus est, apud competentem iudicem accusare poteris moribus temporum meorum congruentem sententiam daturum, quae huiusmodi coniunctiones odiosas esse merito duxerunt'.) Even a *patrona* who was herself a *liberta* was not encouraged by the law to manumit and marry her own slave unless he was her former *fellow* slave (*conservus*) bequeathed to her for this express purpose. D.40.2.14.1: 'sunt qui putant *etiam feminas* posse matrimonii causa manumittere, sed ita si forte conservus suus in hoc ei legatus est.' This prejudice is confirmed by the heavy imbalance in favour of male patrons in the marriage pattern of patrons with their own freedmen/freedwomen, both inside and outside the familia Caesaris. In an analysis of 700 inscriptions recording marriages outside the familia Caesaris, where at least one partner was of slave origin, I found that *patronus* = *liberta* nine times more frequently than *patrona* = *libertus*.[15]

III   *c.c.c.* and the Inscriptions

How far is the situation that appears in the legal texts reflected by the social facts? For this purpose the sepulchral inscriptions are of primary interest, particularly now that a complete word index to the tens of thousands of them from Rome in *CIL* 6 exists at last. It might seem a straightforward matter to sift out the cases of *c.c.c.* and examine whether the rule of the *ius gentium* determines the status of the children or not. If not, should we have recourse to the *s.c. Claudianum* and its modifications?

But major difficulties arise. First, the proportion of such unions in Roman society of the early Empire, given the social prejudices mentioned in the previous section, must have been only a fraction even of marriages classed as *contubernium*; and secondly, the rapid decline in the formal use of status indication as part of Roman personal nomenclature by all classes in society, from at least the middle of the first century AD (with the notable exception of some members of the *familia Caesaris*), makes it increasingly hazardous to determine with certainty the exact status of particular individuals. And status determination is at the heart of this question. The number of persons with *nomen* and *cognomen* only (who must be free, i.e. *ingenui* or *liberti*, but who have no status indication, i.e. filiation [e.g. 'C.f.'], or freed-indication [e.g. 'C.l.'] to indicate which) is enormous. These are the *incerti/ae*.[16] This is one reason why material from the *familia* Caesaris is so prominent — the status of one partner in a union is known to be slave-born. Another reason is that *c.c.c.*, while not a monopoly of imperial slaves, is, I believe, a characteristic of their marriage pattern during the period from the mid-first to the early third century AD. If clear cases are to be found anywhere, they are likely to be here.

From the methodological point of view caution, as usual, is imposed. However, a number of assumptions have to be made, some more easily justifiable than others. One is that a single personal name, in the absence of any evidence to the contrary, is taken to indicate slave status.[17] Another is that *nomen* and *cognomen* (with or without *praenomen*) certainly denotes a *civis Romanus*. It is impossible in this material to sort out the *Latini Iuniani*. And can we be quite sure in all cases that *peregrini* do not lurk among the *incerti* as well? In the basic matter of determining the status of a mother at the time of birth of her child, it is important to know which of the *incertae* are *ingenuae* and which *libertae*, as *ingenuae* do not change their status from birth but *libertae* do, having been born *servae*. Hence the age at which an *ingenua* gave birth makes no difference in itself to the status of her children, but in the case of a *liberta* it all depends on whether she gave birth before or after manumission.

The key question here is to determine which wives are *ingenuae*, as the real anomaly of *c.c.c.* resides in the union of *servus* with *ingenua*, rather than *servus* with *liberta*. To resolve this question for the *familia Caesaris* two further assumptions are necessary: one that, in the absence of evidence of second marriages for wives, the marriage pattern for *servi* and *liberti* is essentially the same. This is because a first marriage for both normally occurred *before* manumission. Thus the pattern for *liberti* represents the same set of facts as the pattern for *servi*, only at a later stage of their married life, assuming there is no marital breakdown. There are, not surprisingly, regional variations in this pattern, especially between slaves in the African provinces and slaves in Rome itself. But one interesting confirmation of this assumption is the close similarity between the proportion of imperial slaves at Rome *and* of all imperial freedmen recorded as married to women with *non-imperial nomina*, i.e. women already free who do not possess *nomina* belonging to the imperial family (e.g. Iulia, Claudia, Flavia, etc.). The proportion is 42 per cent in both cases: 139 of 276 wives of *Caes. servi* and 336 of 758 wives of *Aug. liberti*. This similarity indicates that probably very few wives with these non-imperial *nomina* were earlier slaves (of masters other than an emperor) who had been then manumitted. If a significant proportion of them had been slaves, one would expect a corresponding difference to show between the pattern of *liberti* and *servi*, as the *Caes. servi* should then show a higher proportion of wives who were *servae* from whatever source. On the other hand, for wives with imperial *nomina*, who are therefore much more likely to have been *slaves* (of an emperor) earlier in their lives, a difference does emerge in the marriage pattern of these two groups: 41 per cent for wives of *Caes. servi*, and 53 per cent for wives of *Aug. liberti*, that is, up to 12 per cent of wives of freedmen were most probably slaves (*Caes. servae*) manumitted after their first marriage.[18]

This leads to the second, and perhaps more controversial, assumption that *at least* two-thirds of wives with *nomen* (i.e. who cannot be slaves) with husbands *who were still slaves*, cannot themselves have been slave-born. This is based on (1) the gap between the average age at marriage for women and their average age at manumission; and (2) the gap between the average age at marriage for women and for men from all classes of Roman society.

The normal age at which Roman women could and did marry was very early by our standards: 14 years or earlier. There are some class differences, girls from aristocratic families marrying the youngest.[19] But the early age at which slave girls 'married' is confirmed by the data both for *servae* in general and for *Caesaris servae* in particular: under 20 years — probably well under 20 —

for first marriages, perhaps as young as 15 years for both groups (Weaver 1972:105ff, 182ff). This is to be expected if one of the main roles of *servae* was the economic one of breeding slave children (*vernae*) for their own master's *familia* or for sale. The average age at manumission for slave-born women is less easy to determine. The legal minimum prescribed by the lex Aelia Sentia was 30 years for both males and females, but was evidently more easily reduced in the case of the latter, for whom early manumission 'matrimonii causa' was provided, but not for male slaves. I believe that the provisions of the lex Aelia Sentia were more or less strictly adhered to, in so far as we are here concerned with *cives Romanae libertae* and not *Latinae Iunianae* (who may have been informally manumitted).[20] The average age at manumission for slave women in general was thus likely to have been nearer 30 years than 20, and certainly at least about 10 years after their first marriage.

On the other hand, the average age at marriage for male slaves, including *Caesaris servi*, was older than for female slaves, probably by at least five years, although precise evidence for this is lacking.[21] For *Caesaris servi* manumission came at 30 years, not normally earlier.[22] Thus, while making some allowance for the slightly later average age at manumission for *servi* than for *servae*, we are still left with roughly a ten-year gap between marriage and manumission for both groups, and similarly with at least a five-year age gap between *servae* and *servi* at marriage. The important conclusion follows that for slaves of both sexes, apart from cases of *patronus = liberta*, and a few of *patrona = libertus*, the first ten years of marriage were *contubernium*, and all children born during that period to female slaves before their mother's manumission would have had the status of slaves.

The 'two-thirds' assumption stated above is therefore based itself on the proposition that manumission of the slave-wife would not *regularly precede* that of the slave-husband — indeed, it should coincide or follow — and that the *majority* of children of such a couple would have been born *prior to* the manumission of the mother.

In this context, it is especially impressive that, in the familia Caesaris, of 462 wives of those who are still *Caesaris servi* collected from all parts of the Roman world 357 (i.e. 77 per cent) already had a *nomen* and cannot have been slaves at the time of the inscription and, for Rome only, the figure is even higher 276 of 333 (i.e. 83 per cent).[23] This tends to show (though of course it does not prove) that the large majority of wives in the familia Caesaris were *ingenuae*, not *libertae*, much less still *servae* from whatever source and of whatever master. It also follows that children with *nomen* (i.e. already free) who are recorded on inscriptions as having died early (i.e. under 20 years or earlier, well under the normal age of manumission) are freeborn (*ingenui*), unless there is specific indication to the contrary.[24]

An exhaustive treatment of the epigraphical evidence for *c.c.c.* is not attempted here. The material, given the assumptions mentioned above, is potentially very large and, in individual instances, often controversial. In the remainder of this section I propose to begin with examples of typical and straightforward cases, and then concentrate on a particular group of inscriptions from the familia Caesaris where special difficulties lie.

First children with the filiation 'Sp(urii) f(ilius)', which proclaims freeborn but illegitimate birth e.g.:

(1) 6.18975:   Chrestus = Gellia L.Ɔ.1. Prima (?) + L.
                  Gell(ius) Sp.f. Hes[. . . .].[25]

(2) 29513:   Agrypnus Caes. = Volusena Restit(uta)
                  + L. Volusenus Sp.f. Victor

(3) 15114:   Anthus Caesaris = Claudia Theophila +
                  Ti. Claudius Sp.filius Honoratus (4 years 6
                  months)

In each case the children take the *nomen* of their mother. In (1), from outside the familia Caesaris,[26] the mother is a *liberta*, jointly manumitted by a L. Gellius and a woman, perhaps his wife (who need not have the same *nomen*). In (2) the mother has an unusual non-imperial *nomen*, Volusena, and was probably freeborn. If she were a freedwoman without status indication of a L. Volusenus, her son, Victor, would have to have been born after her manumission. The same applies to (3), where the mother Claudia Theophila could also be freeborn, despite her imperial *nomen*, Claudia. In this case the young age of the child at death (4 years 6 months) makes no difference as we also have filiation; but in other cases without filiation early death indicates the probability of freeborn status for the children, and of freeborn status for the mothers as well, despite the fact that they have imperial *nomina* (and hence might conceivably be former imperial slaves). The children could, of course, have been born after the presumed manumission of the mothers, but there is nothing in the inscriptions (e.g. the occupations of the slave husbands) to indicate why the wives should then all have been manumitted well in advance of their husbands.

(4) 6. 8835: Lydus Caesar.Aug. = Flavia Macaria + T. Flavius Petalus (2 years 10 months 22 days)

(5) 18290=34114: Apollonius Imp. Domitiani Aug. Germ. ser. pec(uliaris) = Flavia Pallas + Flavia Athenais (8 months, 16 days).

(6) 27274: Tertius Augustorum servus = Aelia Nicotyche + Aelius Tertiolus (3 years 9 months 22 days)

(7) *AE* 1932,2: Celadu(s) Caesaris = **** + P. Septimius Getianus (4 years 11 days)

(8) 9. 4782: Daphinis Caes.n.ser. = Aelia Melitine + P. Aelius Karissimus (4 years 51 days)

(9) *IPO* A.251: Trophimus Caes. n. ser. = Claudia Tyche + Claudia Saturnina (15 years)

(10) *AE* 1959,307: (Dacia): Piper(as) Timostrati disp(ensatoris) vik(arius) = Ael(ia) Epicte(sis) + P. Ael(ius) Aelian(us) (3 years)

In (4) and (5) we have the closest chronological fit between the husband and the wife's *nomen*, especially for (5), where one is tempted to invoke 'pathetic' manumission if that were necessary. But wives with imperial *nomina* need not be former imperial slaves e.g.:

(11) 6. 16823: **** = Flavia Cara + M. Flavius Eudaemon, Deuter Caesaris verna,

where the *praenomen* 'M.' of her son shows that Flavia Cara is not an imperial freedwoman unless her unnamed spouse was a 'M. Flavius . . .'. (How, then, can she have another son who is a 'Caesaris *verna*'? See below.) And

(12) 6. 18424: Saturninus Caes. n. = Fl(avia) Successa + Fl(avia) Saturnina fil(ia) (13 years)

where Flavia Successa is probably freeborn as the age of the daughter is too young for her to have been manumitted and too old for her to have been born free after her mother's manumission. On the other hand, in

(13) 6. 28635: Pharnaces = Vestiaria Severa (30 years) + L. Vestiarius Suavis f(ilius) (5 years)

from outside the familia Caesaris the wife Vestiaria Severa is less likely to have been freeborn as she could have borne her son Suavis after her manumission at around 25 years; he survived only five years and may not have predeceased her.

When wives of *Caes. servi* have non-imperial *nomina*, they are even more likely to be freeborn, hence also their children e.g.:

(14) 6. 8444:   Andragathus Caes. ser. arcar(ius) XX
                     her(editatium) = Maia Procula + M.
                     Maius M.f. Orat. Fabianus (9 years)
(15) 33781:   [. . .]s Caesaris [ser]vos ministrator =
                     Caesia Tertia + Caesia C[. . .] = Genialis
                     Caesaris servos victimarius (gener).

(15) is interesting in that it shows the freeborn daughter of a freeborn mother (Caesia Tertia) marrying back into the familia Caesaris in the next generation. She is likely to be freeborn as she has reached the age of marriage, but her father has not yet been set free. If her mother were a *liberta* and gave birth after his manumission, we must suppose an interval of many years between the manumission of her mother and that of her father.

In (14) we have a freeborn but illegitimate son (if the slave Andragathus is presumed to be his father, as I think he must be) who has a tribal indication. I disagree with Boulvert (1974:296, n.182) who claims that illegitimate children were enrolled in the urban tribes, except the *Palatina*, and that it follows that a rural tribal indication of *Palatina* is sufficient proof of legitimate status for children. In particular, this affects the dating and interpretation of inscriptions where the *nomen* of the father who is an *Aug. libertus* is inferred from that of his son. (If the son is legitimate, he must take his father's *nomen*.) I believe this is misleading in several cases e.g.:

(16) 10.6092 =   *ILS* 1500: Tertiolus Aug.lib. proxim(us)
                     rational(ium) et a commentari(i)s
                     provinc(iae) Belgicae = Flavia Irene + T.
                     Flavius Pal(atina) Fuscianus

which seems to me not late first century but late second century at the earliest; and

(17) 6.8470 =   *ILS* 1535: Carpus Aug.lib. Pallantianus
                     adiutor Claudi Athenodori praef(ecti)
                     annonae = Claudia Cale + Ti. Claudius
                     Quir(ina) Antoninus,

which can no longer be considered Neronian but late Flavian at

least.[27] To these may be added
   (18) 10.6666:   Eros Aug.l. Caenid(i)anus = **** + M.
                             Anton(i)us Quir(ina) Candidus,
where the son's *nomen* cannot be normally derived from his
father's.

For children of freedmen the picture is more complicated than
for children of *servi*. In the familia Caesaris, while the marriage
pattern for *Aug. liberti* is essentially the same as for *Caes. servi*, a
freedman, on gaining his manumission, had an option not open
to him while still a slave: he could legitimise his hitherto
illegitimate children (as they must have been while he was still of
slave status) by adopting them when he was capable of
contracting a fully legal marriage with his wife. Legitimisation of
children did not take place simply as a result of parents
converting from *contubernium* to *matrimonium* when they
became capable of doing so. Upon legitimisation the children
would change their *nomen*, if necessary, from that of their
mother to their father's. This explains the fact that a higher
proportion than might be expected of children in the familia
Caesaris who were born of unions that may be classed as *c.c.c.*
bear the *nomen* of their father and not their mother (as would be
regular for illegitimate or 'unlegitimised' children)[28] e.g.:
   (19) 6.10089 =   *ILS* 1766: Ti. Cl(audius) Aug.lib. Philetus
                             = Flavia Procula + Claudia Faustina (16
                             years), Flavius Daphnus, Cl(audius)
                             Martialis
   (20) 14913:   Ti. Claudius Aug.lib. Alexander = Pinnia
                             Septima + Claudia Successa, Claudia
                             Olympias
   (21) 1859-60:   Ti. Claudius Aug.lib. Secundus
                             Philippianus = Flavia Irene + Claudius
                             Secundinus, Claudia Secundina
   (22) 17992:   T. Flavius Aug.lib. Alexander = Iulia
                             Coetonis + T. Flavius Epagathus
   (23) 18305-6:   T. Flavius Aug.lib. Clymenus = Baebia
                             Ianuaria + Flavia Cara qu(a)e et Ianuaria
   (24) 15592-5 =   *ILS* 8063 a-c: M. Ulpius Aug.lib.
                             Crotonensis = Claudia Semne + M.
                             Ulpius M. fil. Pal. Crotonensis (18 years)
   (25) 10935:   P. Aelius Aug.lib. Romanus = Feridia
                             Marciana + Aelia Marcia (16 years)

In most, if not all, of these cases I would prefer to explain the *nomina* of the children as due to legitimisation, rather than birth after the manumission of the father, with the exception of Flavius Daphnus in (19), who for some reason was not so treated. I would assume that the mothers in these cases are probably all *ingenuae* and that the children are not imperial ex-slaves, despite the temptation offered by their imperial *nomina* so to regard them (cf. (24) where a 'M. Ulpius' is expressly freeborn). This is based partly on the ages of the children at death, partly on the personal names (i.e. *cognomina*) of the children, and partly on the *nomina* of the wives. The ages of the children where stated are somewhat too high to have all been born after the father's manumission ((19), (24), (25)) and too young to have been manumitted by the same emperor who manumitted their father. Where wives have imperial *nomina* ((19), (21), (22) and (24)) in two cases ((22) and (24)) they have *nomina* belonging to a dynasty at least two preceding that of their husband, hence are most unlikely to have been themselves imperial ex-slaves. In two cases ((21) and (24)) *both nomen* and *cognomen* of children are derived from the father and not the mother, which could suggest a change from a former name where they originally had the mother's *nomen* and the father's *cognomen*. In (23) the daughter, Flavia Cara quae et Ianuaria, has taken an alternative *cognomen* (Cara) to add to her former one (Ianuaria) derived from her mother, perhaps indicating an alteration of personal name as well. All of these cases, therefore, may legitimately be classed as examples of unions that were originally *c.c.c.*[29]

IV

We come now to cases where neither *nomen* nor the status of children corresponds to that of either parent or is explicable according to the normal rules of the *ius gentium*.

(26) 6.9041:   P. Aelius Aug.lib. Telesphor(us) =
                 Naevia Tyche + P. Aelius Telesphorus,
                 Naevius Telesphorus, Naevius Successus
                 (filiaster)

(27) 14.508 =   *IPO* A.l: T. Aelius Aug.lib. Demetrius =
                 Claudia Marina + T. Aelius Demetrius (4
                 years), C. Cornelius Marinus

In (26), of the three children, Naevius Successus is a stepson born of a previous *contubernium* (?) of Naevia Tyche. But the other two children both have the *cognomen* of their father, Naevius Telesphorus being illegitimate (i.e. born before the father's manumission), P. Aelius Telesphorus (with *praenomen*) legitimate (born after his father's manumission). The alternative is to suppose that both sons were born illegitimate, but only one was subsequently legitimised. (26) points to second marriage as a factor to be considered. This could be particularly relevant for women if the age gap between their first husband and themselves was large. We have no means of estimating the extent of widowhood among these classes, but it would apply just as much to *servae* as to *ingenuae*. (27) also points to a previous marriage, but in this case the son C. Cornelius Marinus took the *nomen* of his father and may be presumed legitimate. The mother Claudia Marina is thus likely to be freeborn as is the son of her second marriage, T. Aelius Demetrius who died young. Note again that a legitimate son takes both *nomen* and *cognomen* of his father.

(28) 3. 1995: Phrygius A(u)gg.nn. = Iulia Valeria + L. Aurel(ius) Castus

(29) 6. 18315: Felix Aug. = Aemilia Chrysauris + Flavia Chrysophorus

(30) 11002: Urbicus Aug. = Mulvia Iucunda + Aelia Urbica

The difficulty here is that none of the wives of these *Caes. servi* can themselves be imperial ex-slaves, yet the children all have an imperial *nomen* that derives from neither parent. They could, of course, all have been manumitted by an emperor, whereas their fathers for some reason had not. But how is the status of their mothers explained? It is just possible that the mothers were slaves of private masters and that after birth as their slaves these children were transferred to the ownership of the emperor; or that the mothers had originally been *Caes. servae* transferred to other owners after the birth of the children and then manumitted by their new owners.[30] Either possibility might suffice to explain

(31) 6. 14452: C. Cartorius Horaeus = Cartoria Elpis + Martialis Aug.l., Elpistus Caesaris[31]

but for (28), (29), (30), one is tempted to look again at the *s.c. Claudianum* and its relevance to *c.c.c.*

More difficult still are cases such as these where the children are imperial slaves with status indication:

(32) 6. 22284:   Ursulus Augg. ser. = Publicia Helpis +
                    Maternus Caes. n.vern. (24 years)
(33) 36507:   Philetianus Augustorum (v)erna =
                    (V)ehilia Horestina + Philetus Aug. n.
(34) 3. 1470 =   Valentinus qui et Potinianus Aug. n. vern.
     7974:   = Cassia Rogata + Valentina Aug. n.
                    vern. (10 years)[32]
(35) 6. 13328:   **** = Aemilia Primitiva + Numida Aug.
                    n. serv., Catulus (26 years)
(36) 8816:   **** = Herria Verecunda + Doryphorus
                    Caesaris a cyato (20 years)

and a further group where the fathers are imperial freedmen:

(37) 6. 38351:   M. Ulpius Aug.lib. Pacatus = Caelia
                    Venusina + Felix Caes. n. ser. vern. (14
                    years)
(38) 8518:   T. Aelius Aug.lib. Aelianus = Folia
                    Chresime (marr. 20 years) + Chresimus
                    Aug.lib., Aphrodisius Caes. n. vern.
(39) 9042:   T. Aelius Theon Aug.lib. = Vetia Verylla
                    + Theon vern. Aug. nostr. (5 years)[33]

In most cases the children here are *vernae*, i.e. born as slaves
within the imperial household, and not acquired from without:
(32), (34), (37), (38), (39) which would tend to rule out one of
the alternative explanations offered above (i.e. that the children
were born slaves of private owners and transferred after birth to
the *familia Caesaris*). The age data where given record several
children in their twenties, that is, they were not favoured with
early manumission. I see no reason to doubt that these mothers
with non-imperial *nomina* are mostly *ingenuae*. Another similar
group of inscriptions[34] where the children have only a single
name, implying slave status, but without the imperial slave
indication contains a mother who actually has filiation, i.e. her
freeborn status is beyond doubt:

(40) 10. 2810:   Amandus Aug.l = Oppia T. fil. Bassilla +
                    Bassus

Finally, a parallel group where the children are *Aug. liberti*
with imperial status indication:

(41) 6. 4228:   P. Aelius Aug.lib. Menophilus = Caminia
                    Fortunata + M. Ulpius Aug.lib.
                    Menophilus adiutor proc(uratoris) ab
                    ornamentis (35 years) = Iulia Passerilla

	(dated to AD 126, from the Monumentum Liviae!)[35] (The son manumitted before the father and married to a freeborn[?] Iulia.)
(42) 10666:	P. Aelius Aug.lib. Cladus = Lucilia Chrysopolis + P. Aelius Aug.lib. Mariensis (20 years 11 months), (P. Aelius Stephanus?)
(43) 10682:	P. Aelius Aug.lib. Erasinus = Aemilia Helene + P.P. Aelii Aug.lib. Musicus et *Helenus*
(44) 13151:	M. Aur(elius) Aug.lib. Eutyches = Valeria Eutychia + M. Aurelius Aug.lib. Marcianus (4 years)[36]

The problem in all these cases is that the status of the children cannot be derived from the mother, whether she is *ingenua* or *liberta* — at least some of these children were born as *vernae* within the imperial household — and it is not compelling to assume that all these mothers were former *Caes. servae* transferred to a private master and freed by him. No trace of such a process has survived and, in any case, these are family inscriptions which, in their affectionate and comfortable wording, at least imply that the family unit survived. Nor can these children derive their status from their father as, if born before his manumission, they would follow the status of their mother, and if born after his manumission they could not be *servi* or *liberti*.

We are pointed in the direction of a solution by one further inscription:

| (45) 6. 15317: | P. Aelius Aug.lib. Ianuarius = Claudia Successa (marr. 31 years) + Ti. Claudius Vitalio (11 years), Ti. Claudius Aug.l. Censorinus. |

The two sons of Claudia Successa (who cannot be an imperial freedwoman) both derive their *nomen* from her. They should be freeborn as she (probably) is. Ti. Claudius Vitalio is the younger son (he died aged 11 years, whereas his brother reached the age of manumission, presumably 30 years. This matches well with the 31-year duration of the marriage between his parents). He was freeborn but his older brother was not. Are we to see in this an application of Hadrian's modification of the *s.c. Claudianum* whereby a free mother would produce a freeborn son? Thus Vitalio was born after Hadrian's modification, but Censorinus was born before, while the *pactio* clause was still in force whereby the mother could remain free but the child be born a slave. This is tempting, and is the solution adopted in this case by Chantraine.[37]

The question, however, goes much further than inscriptions of the reign of Hadrian. We have analogous anomalies after as well as before the time of Hadrian. The solution to all the anomalies in the cases quoted above (no. 31ff.), I suggest, is to be found in the continued operation of the *s.c. Claudianum*, not only in the sense that children of mothers who remain free should be themselves free, and thus freeborn, but in the sense of the other alternative provided for the master of slaves who cohabited with free women, that is that the mother should suffer the full *poena* of the *s.c.* and be reduced to the status of a *serva* (cf. Boulvert 1974:309ff.). It would follow that the status of the children would be the same as that of the mother. But it is clear that, if we are correct in assuming that most wives of *Caes. servi* (and *Aug. liberti*) from the mid-first century AD were already, and continued to be, *ingenuae*, it is precisely this group of wives and children who would have been most affected by the *s.c.* It is also clear, however, from their nomenclature that only a minority of such *children* were born into slavery, whereas no change apparently occurs in the nomenclature of the cohabiting mothers. The emperor, as the owner of slaves covered by the *s.c.*, retained the discretion to enforce its provisions and reduce to slave status those wives who were *liberae*, and especially the *ingenuae*. Such penalisation, it would appear, was applied only selectively, in cases, for instance, when he wished to recruit individual children into his own service in the familia Caesaris. But can we contemplate the corollary, that these mothers who were reduced to slavery still retained their *tria nomina* which they bore as *cives Romanae* and that some of their other children did also? Certain it is that the modification of the *ius gentium* by the *s.c. Claudianum* cannot have left untouched those many examples of *c.c.c.* which are found precisely in the emperor's own household.[38]

Notes

1. In this chapter I use '*libertus/a*' for all references to freedmen and freedwomen, although strictly speaking '*libertinus/a*' is the term denoting freed

status in general, and embraces the three classes of freedmen: *cives Romani liberti*, *Latini* and *dediticii*, Gaius *Inst*. 1.10-12. '*Libertus/a*' strictly expresses the relationship between a particular freedman/freedwoman and his/her patron ('*patronus/a*'). For those of slave status there is no corresponding differentiation in terms and '*servus/a*' serves for both meanings. I believe that little or no confusion is caused by abandoning the term '*libertinus/a*', and some opportunity for confusion is created by retaining it.

Throughout, the symbol = is used to indicate the marriage relationship of husband and wife, whether *matrimonium* or *contubernium*; the symbol + indicates children in the family of a particular couple.

2. The question of what difference is made if one partner (or conceivably both) were manumitted between the conception and the birth of a child, and even subsequently re-enslaved, I leave aside for the moment as both controversial and esoteric, however relevant for the child itself and fascinating for the lawyer.

3. See Rawson (1974:293ff. with n. 50), who effectively disposes of the categories of Meyer and Plassard. Treggiari (1981b) has also documented this case in detail. See also Boulvert (1974:284ff).

4. Buckland (1908:76 n. 15); Weaver (1972:137).

5. Further cases, outside my definition of *c.c.c.*, are given by Gaius at 1.77 and 78. They relate to children of a *civis Romana* and a *peregrinus* between whom *conubium* did not exist; by a *s.c.* of Hadrian, such a child is 'iustus patris filius', and, according to the lex Minucia (AD ?), when a *civis Romana* married a *peregrinus* without *conubium*, the child did not follow the status of the mother, but remained a *peregrinus*. Cf. Gaius 1.79-81 on 'mixed marriages' of Latins, on which see de Zulueta (1946-53:2.32ff).

6. See the discussion by Crook (1967a:8). It was a *lex* and not a *senatusconsultum* and Gaius is careful to distinguish between the two kinds of legislation. Gaius goes on to mention a third case of the modification of the *ius gentium* by statute in regard to the status of children, which occurred under this same *lex* — 1.86: 'sed illa pars eiusdem lex salva est, ut ex libera et servo alieno, quem sciebat servum esse, servi nascantur.' As Crook pointed out, this part of the *lex* cannot be about the same people as those covered by the *s.c. Claudianum*, as it was still in force in Gaius's day (*salva est*) well after Hadrian's modification of the *s.c.* Hadrian restored the rule of the *ius gentium* in regard to children for one group of women (*cives Romanae*) who cohabited with another's slave, whereas this *lex* maintained the opposite for *liberae* apparently in exactly the same position. Crook's suggestion that the *lex* here deals with *Latinae Iunianae* freed under the lex Aelia Sentia or the lex Iunia Norbana is persuasive. Gaius, in previous sections (67-81), discussing mistakes as to status between marriage partners and the status of children in mixed marriages, deals with all the combinations of *civis Romanus/a* = *Latinus/a* = *peregrinus/a*, including the modification of the *ius gentium* by the *lex Minucia* in the case of children of a *civis Romana* and a *peregrinus* (see n. 5 above). In sections 82-6 he discusses for the first time cases arising under these headings (of status of children and mistakes as to status) where one partner is of *slave* status: section 84 deals with *cives Romanae*; section 85 with mistaken status; section 86 with *liberae*, who can only be *Latinae* or *peregrinae*. The former are alone relevant to conflict between the rules of the *ius civile* and those of the *ius gentium*. As Gaius concludes, among those among whom such a *lex* does not exist ('apud quos talis lex non est'), i.e. *peregrini*, the *ius gentium* prevails. In neither case,. however, is *c.c.c.* involved, hence relegation to this footnote.

7. Gaius, *Inst*. 1.19.39; D.40.2.9 and 13.

8. D.25.7.1 pr. (Ulpian): 'quippe cum honestius sit patrono libertam concubinam quam matrem familias habere.' Cf. D.23.2.41; 48.5.14 pr.

9. e.g. *CIL* 6.10321, 10911, 12806, 25090, 38976; cf. Rawson (1974: 291 with

n. 43). For the fam. Caes., 6.9044, 15598, etc.; cf. Weaver (1972: 207ff).

10. There are, however, examples, of dedications by 'patronus et contuber-nalis', e.g. 6.15598: Ti. Claudius Aug.l. Nymphodotus, paronus et contubernalis = Claudia Stepte, who died at 72 after a marriage lasting 46 years. She was therefore married at 26 years. I took this as a case of early manumission 'matrimonii causa' (1972:109). This has been disputed by Treggiari (1981b:48-9), who argues that they were both still slaves when the relationship began. Stepte may have been either a *conserva* or *vicaria* of Nymphodotus while he was still himself a *Caesaris servus* and became his *contubernalis* during that time. She would not then have been freed until *after* the age of 26. Treggiari points out that as the *contubernium* of Nymphodotus and Stepte did not begin till she was 26, Nymphodotus was probably not her first *contubernalis*. This is to insist on the legal definition of *contubernium* whereby one or both partners must be of slave status at the time the relationship began. However, it is curious that the term *contubernalis* is retained when the length of the marriage (46 years!), most of which should have been *matrimonium*, is stressed in the dedication. If one assumes that Stepte was freed at the earliest possible moment after their relationship began (i.e. after Nymphodotus himself had been freed) then either Nymphodotus's own manumission was delayed beyond the usual age of 30 or he was of the same age as or perhaps younger than Stepte. This is reasonable in view of a possible earlier marriage of Stepte and the fact that Nymphodotus survived her.

Another example, however, (not considered by Treggiari, who confines her study to vol. 6 of *CIL*) is not so readily disposed of — 14.524 (Ostia): 'd.m./Aeliae Helpidi/P. Aelius Aug. lib. Symphorus, patro/nus et contu/bernalis bene/merenti. V(ixit) a(nnis) XVI men(sibus) V.' Here we have to assume very early manumission (by the age of 16) and a marriage association that goes back even earlier, if it was begun when Helpis was a slave — perhaps much earlier if the marriage began when *both* Symphorus and Helpis were still slaves, and if Symphorus was freed at the normal age for a *Caesaris servus*.

11. As pointed out by Crook (1967a:7).

12. Gaius *Inst.* 1.91; 160; Ulpian *Reg.* 11.11; Paulus *Sent,* 2.2.1.1; Suetonius, *Vespasian* 11; Tertullian, *Ad uxorem* 2.8.

13. See Weaver (1972: 162ff), where much of the material discussed in this section will be found.

14. Cf. *Frag. de iure fisci* (*FIRA* 2.627 f.) 12: 'libertae Caesar is tam manumissione quam beneficio coniunctionis effectae si testatae decedant dimid-ium, si intestatae totum fisco vindicatur.'

15. For details see Weaver (1972: 179ff).

16. Taylor (1961); Weaver (1972:80ff).

17. Caution is sometimes needed, e.g. 6.9077; 3.4065 (Weaver 1972:143); cf. Rawson (1974:284).

18. For tables and detailed discussion see Weaver (1972:126ff., 133ff).

19. Cf. esp. Hopkins (1965a:316ff); but also Gallivan (1974).

20. Cf. Gaius 1.31. But Ulpian *Reg.* 1.12, dealing with the same law, says:

eadem lege cautum est, ut minor triginta annorum servus vindicta manumissus civis Romanus non fiat, nisi apud consilium causa probata fuerit: *ideo sine consilio manumissum Caesaris servum manere putat.*

The last statement remains a puzzle. *Latini* are mentioned in the next sentence of the *Regulae*, for those informally manumitted by will (*testamento*), so that some distinction is here being made. It seems unlikely that this refers only to *Caesaris servi* and that the lex Aelia Sentia barred them as a special group from informal

manumission, — 'Caesaris servum *manere*' (?).
21. Weaver (1972:182ff).
22. ibid.: 97ff.
23. ibid.: 114ff.
24. Attested cases of very early manumission (under ten years) are often put down, somewhat despairingly, to death-bed or 'pathetic' manumission, in spite of the lex Aelia Sentia.
25. Cf. 6.11206: Herma = Afrania Prote + Sex. Afranius Lautus Sp.f. (10 years 9 months 4 days).
26. Add 6.34321: Ti. Claudius Ialyssus = Aemilia Sp.f. Veneria + Aemilia Sp.f. Pia (16 years)
Aemilia Veneria is freeborn and the union is stated to be 'contubernium' and therefore *c.c.c.* [See Rawson (1966:76; 1974:297); cf. ibid. (303 with n. 72)].
27. For (16) see Weaver (1968:111f.); and for (17) see Weaver (1979:76-9); cf. Bradley (1978b).
28. For comprehensive statistics on such families from *CIL* 6, see Rawson (1974:301ff).
29. On this section, see Weaver (1972:148f.); Boulvert (1974:287f., 290ff).
30. Boulvert (1974:307f.) cf. also 6.29134, the family of an imperial freedman: M. Ulpius Aug. lib. Alexander = Longinia Philippa + Aelia Faustina, Ulpia Calliphania, Aurelius Philippus, Ulpia Alexandria!
31. Rawson (1966:80); who also cites 6.13927:
Caerellius Euodion = Caerellia Capitolina + Aurelia Euodia Aug. lib.
32. Cf. 6.8885, 25033; 9.3640; 10.7819; for details see Weaver (1972:145f.) Note also 6.16823:
**** = Flavia Cara + Deuter Caesaris verna, M. Flavius Eudaemon, where the non-imperial *praenomen* of one of her sons meant that Flavia Cara is unlikely to be an imperial freedwoman.
33. Cf. 6.18824; *AE* 1959, no. 303.
34. 6.6189, 10518, 10712 = 14.4019, 13226; 10.2799; 11.466, 3553. See Weaver (1972:156f.) for details.
35. See, however, Rawson (1974:287 n.23).
36. Cf. 6.8796, 13084, 19710, 27749, 28699; 14.2690, 3393, 4062 = *ILS* 1673 (for details, Weaver 1972:157f.). On 6.8634 = *ILS* 1697, see Weaver (1979:92-5).
37. 1967:77ff., cf. 86f. Rawson (1974:303) invokes the *s.c.* to explain 6.12623: T. Flavius Aug.lib. Eutactus = Salvia M.f. Pisonina + T. Atilius Piso (7m.), but then has to explain away the fact that the son Piso does not bear an imperial *nomen*, assuming that he must have been transferred to another household and been manumitted there before he died at the age of seven months. But given that Piso derives his *cognomen* from his mother and is recorded in the same family unit as she, I would prefer to explain his *nomen* as derived from a freeborn father T. Atilius . . . , who was Pisonina's previous husband: cf. (27) above.
38. This argument was developed by me (1972:145ff., esp. 162ff). I repeat it here not so much in response to criticism as to the profound silence which has ensued.

7   CHILDREN IN THE ROMAN *FAMILIA*

Beryl Rawson

Modern studies have analysed the role of children in various
societies and have thus drawn conclusions about economic
conditions, value systems and levels of sophistication and
sensitivity in those societies. A test often applied is how visible
and how differentiated children are in the source evidence. A
variety of evidence from ancient Rome suggests that children
were far from invisible in private and public life. The role of
children in Roman families and Roman society will be the subject
of a future full-scale study. There is already some knowledge of
the upper-class children who appear in literary sources, and
details of their education are known from Quintilian's extensive
treatise. This chapter attempts to reconstruct something of the
lower-class children who appear only intermittently and anony-
mously in the literary sources, in particular the function of the
familia in providing a family or surrogate family environment for
such children.

Children are recorded not only in literature and sometimes in
art but, more frequently, in funerary inscriptions and in the
Roman law code. They are usually mentioned in the context of
the natural family, especially the nuclear family, but sometimes
they are found as members of the broader *familia*. As we saw in
Chapter 1, the Roman *familia* embraced all those dependent on
the one household head (wife, children, slaves, and sometimes
freedmen and freedwomen). There are few examples of multi-
generational or joint households at Rome. Children normally left
home on marriage (men sometimes left earlier) and established
their own separate households. These households consisted
essentially of the conjugal family, but sometimes resembled
extended families, not so much through the presence of other kin
but through the presence of slaves and ex-slaves.

We saw in Chapter 1 the concern of most governments in the
early Empire to encourage people to bear and rear children. But
this implies a certain reluctance or inability to reproduce. Many
of the incentives offered were aimed at the upper classes. Child

170

endowment schemes such as those of Trajan and Antoninus Pius reached humbler families, but they were far from comprehensive and catered more for legitimate children within the natural family than others.

In the preceding chapter, and in his *Familia Caesaris*, Weaver has discussed the family relationships which existed amongst staff of the imperial household. Treggiari (1981b) has argued that it was especially in the imperial household and the larger households of upper-class families that favourable conditions existed for family life for slaves and ex-slaves. Even beyond these households humble groups have left records which attest a sense of family. A considerable number of the children recorded in the inscriptions of the city of Rome have both natural parents attested (Rawson 1966; 1974).

Kleiner's study of Roman funerary reliefs (1977) has shown that the number of family groups represented, including small children, increased dramatically in Augustus's period, and she associated this with Augustus's emphasis on the family, in his legislation and in the publicity given to his own family, including his young grandsons Gaius and Lucius Caesar. This style was adopted by freedmen, who advertised their new status as citizens not only by the use of the *tria nomina* but also by representing themselves as members of families: slaves had no families, in legal terms, and freedmen had no legitimate ancestors. The conjugal family and the *familia* thus had special importance for this class.

It is clear that in the humbler classes, even amongst slaves, conditions for an enduring and stable family life could exist. At least members of a family group not infrequently combined to commemorate one of their number who had died, even if the group was not co-resident at the time of the death. It was important to them to record their existence as a family. But the conditions of slavery and other economic or social factors must have disrupted or destroyed family life for many others. The frequency of divorce and of the early death of one parent must have led to frequent remarriage, and many step-children must have found themselves in a newly blended family.[1] Inscriptions also reveal many single-parent families — at least, instances where only one parent is recorded along with the name of a child.

In addition to the children who have one or both parents attested, there are those who are defined by a relationship to someone other than a member of the natural family, e.g. *alumni* and *vernae*.² A study of groups such as these helps illuminate social structures which in some ways substituted for the natural family unit in early imperial Rome.³ It helps us discover the fate of children whose natural parents were unwilling or unable to raise them as their own; and an analysis of age, sex and status will help differentiate the members of these groups.

Some such children, of course, did not survive birth. Infanticide was practised, as it has been in most known societies at every cultural level; or it was anticipated by methods of contraception and abortion. Children who survived birth but whose natural parents were unwilling or unable to raise them might be exposed (i.e. put out in a public place — doorsteps, temples, crossroads, rubbish-heaps) either to die or to be claimed by their finder.⁴ Such foundlings could be assumed to be of slave status,⁵ although the law made it possible for freeborn children to recover their free status later if they could provide proof of it.⁶ Roman law also protected the natural parents' rights, even though they had chosen not to exercise rights or responsibilities during the child's early years. They could reclaim the child later, although there was legal controversy as to whether or not the natural parent was obliged to reimburse the foster-parent for costs incurred in raising the child. Exposure was not illegal, but the law was increasingly unsympathetic to it,⁷ and in the sixth century Justinian enacted that exposed children were to be deemed free (C.8.51).⁸

A child's status might well be ambiguous, and evidence of freeborn status difficult to establish, in levels of society where there was considerable residential and class mobility and where key witnesses might die early. An example of this is recorded in documents preserved at Herculaneum by the eruption of Vesuvius in AD 79.⁹ A girl named Iusta had been left by her mother, a former slave, in the care of the mother's patron and his wife. The mother later reclaimed Iusta and reimbursed the foster-parents for the costs of raising her. After the patron and Iusta's mother had died, difficulties arose between Iusta and her former foster-mother. Iusta brought a lawsuit to establish that she was freeborn, i.e. that she had been born *after* her mother's manumission. The foster-mother claimed on the contrary that Iusta had been born while her mother was still a slave and that therefore Iusta was slave-born and that it was only later that she obtained free status by being manumitted (by her foster-father or foster-mother). There was financial interest involved: the foster-mother would have a claim on Iusta's property if Iusta were now her freedwoman rather than a freeborn citizen. The outcome of the case is unknown, but the foster-father's apparent affection for the child is revealed. Although he was reimbursed when the natural mother reclaimed Iusta, he was saddened, one witness claimed, by losing a child whom he had come to think of as a daughter. The thread of parental affection recurs frequently in the evidence on *alumni*.

Alumni

Were *alumni* foundlings? Etymologically, *'alumni'*[10] implies persons nurtured by someone else. By contrast with children explicitly or implicitly identified as *filii*, *alumni* appear to have been nurtured by someone other than their natural parent(s). But were they orphans or illegitimate children or stepchildren who came into the hands of a foster-parent[11] by means other than rescue from exposure? Were they raised as slaves, foster-children, adopted children, or as some form of apprentice (possibilities which are not, of course, all mutually exclusive)? Previous writers have occasionally alluded to the problem of who *alumni* were,[12] but there has not been a systematic study of all the relevant evidence (epigraphical, legal, literary).

In literature the use of *alumnus* is often metaphorical, but something close to 'foster-child' is implied in passages such as Tacitus, *Annals* 2.37, where a senator who had received a subsidy from Augustus and raised four children referred to them as that emperor's *alumni.*

There are 431 usable examples of *alumni* attested in inscriptions of the city of Rome (*CIL* 6 and *AE*). This represents about 1 per cent of the pagan inscriptions surviving largely from the first two centuries AD. The picture that emerges from these inscriptions and from the legal sources is that of usually young persons in a quasi-familial relationship with an older person. They are sometimes of free status, sometimes slave.

The Nature of the Relationship

In the legal sources it is clear that a close bond of affection could be assumed between 'foster-parent' and *alumnus*. The law recognised a group of persons and things so dear or so vital that it was inconceivable that one would use them as a pledge. They could thus not be seized by a creditor. These persons were a concubine, children of one's blood (*liberi naturales*) and *alumni*.[13] There was also a group of persons whose relationship might justify manumission with full Roman citizenship under the legal age of 30. These were natural sons, daughters, brothers and sisters; *alumni*; *paedagogi*; slaves wanted for procuratorial work; or a slave woman whom her master wanted to make his wife.[14]

A number of legal passages refer to or imply parental affection. One man left a legacy to his *alumnus* (who was also his freedman), but put the administration of this in the hands of a friend until the *alumnus* reached the age of 25. He left it to the friend to judge how much should in the meantime be paid to the *alumnus* for expenses; for the friend could be relied on to regard the *alumnus* with the 'affection of a father' (*patris affectus*): D.33.1.21.4 (Scaevola). Another man enjoined his wife to pass on to their joint *alumnus* whatever came to her through the man's will: D.34.2.18.1 (Scaevola). In another case, a testator left some money for the purchase of a farm. The group of persons whom he might have been providing for in this way included a son, a brother or an *alumnus*: D.35.1.71 pr. (Papinian).

An example was put forward, in a legal query, of one man's son being transferred to the care of another man, with the second man promising to treat the boy as his own son, on pain of a financial penalty. The query was whether the second man had broken his promise if he either drove the boy out of his home or left him with nothing in his will; and whether it would make any difference if the boy was the first man's son or *alumnus* or relative. Legal opinion was that there would be a case for requiring the man to show cause why the penalty should not be applied: D.45.1.132 pr. (Paulus).

A man who apparently had no natural children of his own left a property to his freedmen and freedwomen and an *alumna* 'so that it will not pass out of the name of my family': D.31.88.6 (Scaevola). Another testator had displayed parental-type feelings towards his *alumna* by leaving her a legacy in his will, then withdrawing part of it (apparently for her bad behaviour) but leaving the other part of it in the control of her brother, who was to take moral responsibility for his sister and disburse the legacy according to her 'return to a good way of life': D.34.4.30 (Scaevola). (Responsibility for the expenses of the *alumna* was later transferred by the testator to another man, who was asked to prevail on his own heir to see to it that the testator's provisions for the *alumna* should continue.)

The responsibility for an *alumnus* was often passed on to a man's heirs, who might be his own children and thus in some sense the foster-brothers and -sisters of the *alumnus*. In one case where the testator's will was technically defective, legal opinion was that the testator's sons had a moral responsibility to carry out their father's wishes for the *alumna* 'whom he had loved' (thus she was to be manumitted and to receive a legacy): D.40.5.38 (Paulus).

The provisions made by testators for *alumni* often resemble those made for *liberti*; but because of the age of *alumni* legacies have always to be administered by someone else, at least until the *alumni* reach a certain age. Although provisions are usually in the form of a legacy, two legal passages suggest that an *alumnus* could be an heir.[15] *Alumni* are sometimes termed *heredes* on inscriptions, e.g. *CIL* 6.15983:

D M

SOMNO AETERNO

COELIAE PALAESTINE MEM

PHIVS IRENAEVS RENATVS

ALVMNI ET HEREDES COMPARAVER

ET SIBI ET AELIS PROVINCIALI ET VIATORI   *sic*

AVGG LIB EDVCATORIBVS SVIS

LIB LIBQ OMNIVM POSTQ EORVM

H M H N S

('To the spirits of the departed and for the eternal rest of Coelia Palaestina. Set up by Memphius, Irenaeus and Renatus, her *alumni* and heirs, who provided this monument also for themselves and for Aelius Provincialis and Aelius Viator, their educators, freedmen of the joint emperors and for the freedmen and freedwomen of all those named and for their descendants. This monument is not to go with the heir.')

The three male slave *alumni* here had a close connection with the imperial household, having two imperial freedmen as *educatores*. Coelia Palaestine, who raised them, was of free status. If she was an ex-slave she had not been freed by the emperors themselves (her name being non-imperial), but the whole group might well have lived in the imperial household. Coelia could be an example of the relationships discussed by Weaver: a free woman cohabiting (or who had cohabited) with an imperial slave. She had sufficient substance to leave three heirs. It is possible — though to my mind less likely — that the whole group was not co-resident but that the *alumni* attended classes or trade training conducted by the imperial freedmen (see Bibliography under 'Education'). More investigation of the senses of *educatores* is necessary.

Sometimes the testator left to a person a piece of property, the revenue from which was to be used for the support of an *alumnus*.[16] Sometimes the property itself was left to the *alumnus*.[17] Sometimes an amount of money was to come out of the estate, the interest from which was to provide regular payments to an *alumnus*. Often the lump sum was to come to the *alumnus* at a certain age.[18] Sometimes the legacy was to be paid to the *alumnus* only after the death of the testator's spouse. Presumably the spouse was expected to care for the *alumnus* in the meantime.[19] In one case the legacy was explicitly designed to pay for the entry of the *alumnus* into military service when he reached the proper age.[20] In another case the testator added to his money provisions the gift of a slave (*verna*) artisan whose fees would help support the *alumnus*[21]

The parent–child nature of the relationship helps to explain the fear of incest which is clear in the legal disquiet over marriage between a man and his freedwoman-*alumna*. In Justinian's time it was ruled that the legitimacy of such a marriage depended on whether or not the man had raised the girl as a daughter from the beginning (C.5.4.26). Thus the *alumnus* relationship was not necessarily of a filial kind, but there was a strong presumption that it was so.[22] In one situation, however, a distinction was explicitly made between an *alumnus* and a man's own children, i.e. in the application of a senatorial decree about the procedures to be followed if a head of household were murdered. These same procedures were to be followed if a child of the head were murdered, but not if an *alumnus* were.[23]

Sometimes marital intentions must have influenced the raising of (female) children. A slave girl (not explicitly an *alumna*) who was taken into the care of an older male slave or freedman in the same household at an early age was Aurelia L(uci) l(iberta) Philematio. On her epitaph (*CIL* 6.9499), these words are attributed to her about her husband, Lucius Aurelius L(uci) l(ibertus) Hermia, who set up the epitaph for her: 'When I was seven years old he took me into his care' (literally, 'he took me to his bosom'). She then lived with him for 33 years, and was praised as an exemplary wife. She referred to him as her 'parent' as well as her husband. He was also her *collibertus* (i.e. they were freed by the same master), and if she had no other relative in that household when Hermia took her into his care she may well have felt filial as well as conjugal affection for him. Other relationships of this kind, not documented, would be susceptible of more sinister explanation. Sexual exploitation no doubt existed for male and female children. Two emperors within about 50 years legislated to prohibit the castration of slave boys.[24]

One jurist made a distinction between a woman's bond with an *alumnus* and a man's: 'It is more appropriate for a woman to manumit *alumni*; but it is normally acceptable for men also to manumit a person in the nurture of whom they have formed a close attachment' (D.40.2.14: Marcianus). This suggests that a woman's attachment was seen as essentially maternal (and sometimes it was the physical bond of a wet-nurse), whereas the responsibility of the male foster-parent might be more formal, e.g. financial. In the inscriptions, there is no great disparity in the sexes of foster-parents, of whom 55 per cent are male and 43 per cent female (sex being unidentifiable in the remaining 2 per cent). Approximately 40 per cent of the foster-parents occur as couples (one male, one female). Of the foster-parents who occur singly, nearly 60 per cent are male. Even after allowing for men's greater probability of being recorded in almost any situation, it does look as if men were at least as likely as women to be responsible for *alumni*.

Of the small number (35) of *alumni* who are explicitly of freed status, 23 are known to have been freed by their foster-parent. Fifteen of these *alumni* are male, eight female. For three *alumni*, both foster-parents are referred to as *patroni*: thus there are 26 patrons[25] involved: 17 of these patrons are male, 9 female.

The patron–freed bond which was superimposed on the foster relationship was similar and thus reinforcing. The 'genuine concern' (*pietas genuina*) which a father would feel for his son is compared by one jurist with that which a man might feel for his freedman or *alumnus*.[26] As noted above, testamentary provisions for *liberti* and for *alumni* are often similar.

Terms which might indicate wet-nursing are not common in *alumni* inscriptions. There are three instances of *nutrix*, and one each of *mamma* and *mammula*. One *alumnus* has two female *educatores* and another has four *nutricii* (two male and two female). This suggests that wet-nursing is not the fundamental relationship for this group.

Sometimes terms of cognation or agnation are used, e.g. *parens*, *avia*, *vitricus* and *nonna*. But in the great majority of cases no such correlative term is used. In the legal evidence the complete absence of any specific term to relate to *alumnus* is striking. In this chapter I have been forced to find a term ('foster-parent') in order to discuss both sides of this relationship; for the Romans the point of view was one-sided.

As noted above, *alumni* might be seen as similar to *liberi naturales*, a term which included illegitimate children, but were not synonymous with them.[27] Illegitimacy in Roman society seems not to have suffered the same stigma which it has in more recent western societies. It was an inevitable function of the varied status which could be found in any one family at a time of high social mobility. A freeborn illegitimate would normally be considered of higher status than a freedman. There were, however, some legal disadvantages, e.g. their births could not be officially registered during the century and a half following Augustus's introduction of birth certificates (Lemosse 1975:262). But when children obtained the right in AD 178 to succeed to an intestate mother's property, both legitimates and illegitimates enjoyed this benefit (see Crook, Chapter 2, on the *s.c. Orfitianum*), until it was withdrawn from illegitimates in AD 396. It is plausible that illegitimate children would be more likely to be exposed, but there is no hard evidence of that.[28] How often an *alumnus* was really a person's illegitimate child is hard to tell, but there is only one case of this mentioned in the law code. In the early third century AD, a man of senatorial rank, Cocceius Cassianus, had had as concubine a freeborn woman, Rufina, and had made their illegitimate daughter co-heir with his grandson in his will, calling the daughter an *alumna*. There was a dispute as to whether or not the child could inherit, and this seems to have turned on whether or not Rufina's status as a concubine involved immoral conduct (*stuprum*). The child's claim was not automatically ruled out here: but Cocceius had obviously tried to circumvent the possible difficulties by pretending that the child was an *alumna* (who would presumably have had stronger claim to inherit than an illegitimate daughter of an immoral relationship).[29]

In the analysis of name relationships below, it will be seen that 41 *alumni* share a *nomen* with their foster-mother but not with their foster-father. In six of these cases the foster-mother is the manumittor of the *alumnus*, but the other 35 (i.e. 8.1 per cent of all *alumni*) may include illegitimate children whose mother had citizenship at the time of the child's birth. But they will also include other categories, e.g. fellow *liberti*, other kin; so that the number of illegitimates amongst citizen *alumni* does not seem very high.

The legal evidence often refers to testamentary provisions for *alumni* in the plural. It is not clear whether this is just a generalising plural or whether it reflects a common practice of having more than one *alumnus*. Multiple *alumni* are rare in inscriptions.

Age and Sex

For approximately half the *alumni* attested on inscriptions there is no indication of age (see Table 7.1). For those whose age is specified, the age is normally age of death. Of these, almost two-thirds are aged nine years or younger. The median age for all those whose age is known is 6.9 years; the mode (i.e. the age most commonly recorded) is 5 years. The ages summarised in Table 7.1 cannot reflect the real age-structure of any population: the age groups 1-4 years and 5-9 years are over-represented.[30] The concentration of *alumni* in these groups indicates that young children[31] had a better chance than other age-groups of being taken up by 'foster-parents' and of being called *alumni*.

The sex ratio[32] helps us differentiate a little further. The overall sex ratio for *alumni* is 199, i.e. boys outnumber girls almost 2:1. *Alumni* recorded below the age of 5 are much more likely to be boys than girls (sex ratio 170); but between the ages of 5 and 14 girls have almost the same chance as boys (sex ratio 112). This may mean no more than the bare fact that very young girls were less likely than boys to be considered worth a

Table 7.1: *Alumni* by Age and Sex

Age	Male No.	Male %	Female No.	Female %	Sex ratio	Sex unspeci- fied No.	Sex unspeci- fied %	Total No.	Total %
< 1 year	4	3.5	2	2.5	200			6	3.1
1-4	35	31.0	21	25.9	170			56	28.9
5-9	34	30.0	31	38.3	110			65	33.5
10-14	12	10.6	10	12.3	120			22	11.3
15-17	7	6.2	5	6.2	140			12	6.2
18-19	11	9.8	6	7.4	183			17	8.8
20-24	6	5.3	3	3.7	200			9	4.6
25-29	3	2.7	2	2.5	150			5	2.6
30-49	0	0.0	1	1.2	—			1	0.5
50-100	1	0.9	0	0.0	—			1	0.5
Total of specified age	113	100	81	100	140			194	100
Adult	6		5					11	
Unspecified	157		53			16		226	
Total	276		139		199	16		431	

memorial.[33] But it may also mean that very young girls who, for one reason or another, had been deprived of natural parents were less likely to find a foster-parent to take care of them. If there were to be another mouth to feed, with little service obtained in return, a boy would be a better investment than a girl. But from the age of 5+[34] girls could perform domestic services as well as boys. The near balance in the sex ratio disappears again, however, in the upper teens. The fosterage bond disappears earlier for girls than for boys. The earlier marriage of girls probably accounts largely for this. Marriage would usually (but not always — see below) dissolve the bond of dependence which seems intrinsic to the *alumnus* relationship.[35]

In the legal texts, all the *alumni* for whom we have age indications are minors. Thus testators sometimes made elaborate provisions for their heirs or close friends to see to the support of *alumni*. This is often in the form of expenses until the age of maturity (usually 25) and then some capital.[36] The age of foster-parents is rarely specified on inscriptions. Those whose age is known are all adults and are the dedicatees.

The law and inscriptions thus give a picture very largely of *alumni* as dependants and minors, many of whom died before reaching adulthood. But the inscriptions give some glimpses of them as adults with their own dependants; and the law took this possibility into account in its reference to the children or heirs that an *alumnus* might have.[37] Of the 11 *alumni* attested with children, only two record both a spouse and a child and thus suggest a fairly settled family life. One of these (*CIL* 6.1964) may owe this to his imperial connections: M. Livius Aug. l. Secundio was an *accensus* and *alumnus* of Drusus Caesar, and his wife Iulia Tertulla was probably also connected with the imperial *familia*. Their son was a freeborn Roman citizen: M. Livius M. f. Pol. Macedonic(us).

That the law does not speak of adult *alumni* in relation to their foster-parents, and that examples of this in inscriptions are rare, might be due in part to the foster-parent dying before the *alumnus* grew up, but this did not always happen. A *filius* continued to think of himself as such for the duration of his parents' lives; did the *alumnus* lose all sense of his bond with foster-parents as soon as he reached adulthood? This is unlikely. Presumably the term was not considered appropriate for an adult, and grown *alumni* would have been subsumed in the general body of a person's *liberti* or clients. It is somewhat surprising, however, that there is no reference to charges of 'disloyal' behaviour (being *inofficiosus*) against *alumni*, such as applied to sons and freedmen. It suggests that the relationship was quite informal on both sides, i.e., that neither had any formal responsibility to the other. But the record of actual benefits is very one-sided, with the *alumnus* almost always on the receiving end.

Status and Age

The status attested for *alumni* in legal and inscriptional sources is sometimes slave, sometimes free. Manumission of slave *alumni* is mentioned in Gaius *Inst.* 1.19, D.40.2.13 (Ulpian), and 40.5.38 (Paulus). A *libertus et alumnus* receives a legacy from his patron in D.33.1.21.4 (Scaevola); and we have already referred to the question of marriage between a patron and his freedwoman-*alumna* (C.5.4.26). An *alumnus* is included with other free men (a son, a *libertus*, and a debtor of minor age) in D.43.29.3.4 (Ulpian); but the legal evidence which survives does not have need to distinguish between freeborn and freed *alumni*. A few freeborn *alumni* are attested in inscriptions. The foster-parents referred to in the law are presumably all of free status, as the

Table 7.2: *Alumni* by Age and Status

Status	< 1 year No.	%	1-4 years No.	%	5-9 years No.	%	10-14 years No.	%
S	0	0	1	1.8	1	1.6	1	4.5
S?	3	50.0	26	46.4	19	29.7	7	31.8
L	1	16.7	1	1.8	4	6.2	2	9.1
L?	0	0	1	1.8	3	4.7	0	0
Inc.	2	33.3	25	44.6	33	51.6	12	54.6
Ing.	0	0	1	1.8	2	3.1	0	0
Ing.?	0	0	1	1.8	0	0	0	0
Eques.	0	0	0	0	0	0	0	0
Unknown	0	0	0	0	2	3.1	0	0
Total	6	100	56	100	64	100	22	100
% of all *alumni*	1.4		13.0		14.8		5.1	

Notes:
S   = slave
S?   = probable slave
L   = freedman or freedwoman
L?   = probable freedman or freedwoman
Inc. = *incertus/a*, i.e. a citizen of either freeborn or freed status

context is usually property-ownership or testamentary disposition. Only in D.34.1.9 (Papinian) can we be more specific: there the foster-father is a *libertus* who leaves a fellow freedman as a co-heir and responsible for administering the provisions for the testator's *alumni*.

Table 7.2 shows the status distribution of *alumni* in inscriptions. Over half have some indication of citizenship. The table also shows the connection between status and age. Not surprisingly, probability of citizenship increases with age. But it is striking that in no age-group is the maximum possible proportion of slaves higher than 50 per cent, and already in the age-group 5–9 years the maximum possible proportion is less than one-third. If *alumni* began life as slaves, they seem to have had a good chance of early manumission, long before the legal age of 30.[38]

The distribution of age and status appears to be different for males and females, although the numbers involved in this breakdown of the figures are too small for confidence (and hence are not tabulated here). Under the age of 5, girls are more likely than boys to be slaves (68 per cent of girls, 37 per cent of boys). In the age-group 5-9, the proportion of girls who are slaves or

15-17 years		18-19 years		≥ 20 years		Age unspecified		Total	
No.	%	No.	%	No.	%	No.	%	No.	%
0	0	0	0	0	0	1	0.5	4	0.9
3	25.0	3	20.0	6	21.4	94	41.2	161	38.8
1	8.3	3	20.0	4	14.3	19	8.3	35	7.1
0	0	0	0	0	0	2	0.9	6	1.4
7	58.4	8	53.3	12	42.9	84	36.8	183	42.1
1	8.3	1	6.7	2	7.1	2	0.9	9	2.4
0	0	0	0	0	0	2	0.9	3	0.7
0	0	0	0	1	3.6	0	0	1	0.2
0	0	0	0	3	10.7	24	10.5	29	6.4
12	100	15	100	28	100	228	100	431	100
2.8		3.5		6.5		52.9		100	

Ingen. = freeborn
Ingen.? = probably freeborn
Eques. = equestrian
Sen.   = senatorial
Imp.   = imperial
Criteria for these status definitions
are basically those used in my 1974
article.

probable slaves is similar to the proportion of boys of such status (just under one-third). In the age groups 10-14 and 15-17 the proportion of girls of such status declines further, but this is not so for boys. In these age groups, the girls are more likely than boys to have some sign of citizenship. Perhaps boys are kept in slavery longer because they are in trainee positions and will not be manumitted until, in some sense, they have 'qualified'.[39]

Names

Of 431 *alumni*, 230 (53.4 per cent) have a *nomen*. (Of other persons in this set of inscriptions 75.4 per cent have a *nomen*.) Girls have a *nomen* more frequently than do boys (60 per cent of girls, 55 per cent of boys). This reflects the more rapidly rising status of girls after the age of 5. There is no such sex difference among the non-*alumni* in these inscriptions: about the same proportion of both males and females have a *nomen*.

It has sometimes been suggested that *alumni* were adoptees. If so, they should have shared the adopting parent's *nomen*. 86 *alumni* have the same *nomen* as one foster-parent (male), 41 have the same *nomen* as one foster-parent (female), and another

13 have the same *nomen* as both foster-parents. Of these *alumni*, 22 are certainly liberti[40] and another three are likely *liberti*. This reduces the possible adoptees from 140 to 118, probably to 115. As women could not adopt, the maximum number of *alumni* who might be adopted becomes 80, i.e. approximately 18 per cent of all *alumni* (there are three *liberti* among the 41 above with a female foster-parent, hence they have already been deducted). It may be objected, validly, that in some cases the *nomen* of *alumnus* or foster-parent has been omitted, and that the possible proportion consisting of adoptees is higher than 18 per cent. But the same likelihood applies to the records attesting natural children, and in these records almost 40 per cent (39 out of 98) of all natural children share a *nomen* with one or both parents. Thus the probability of *alumni* being adoptees is not very high. The sharing of a family name in 140 cases (32 per cent of the total) is to be explained either by manumission (by a foster-parent or by a common master/patron) or by a familial relationship other than parent–child.[41]

Only 12 *alumni* (8 boys, 4 girls; 2.8 per cent of all *alumni*) have the same *cognomen* as a foster-parent. By contrast, the children attested in this group of inscriptions with natural parents take a parent's *cognomen* much more frequently: 13.3 per cent of such children. This suggests that foster-parents were seldom responsible for the naming of *alumni* at birth, and confirms other indications that *alumni* were taken up by foster-parents at some time after infancy. There is a handful of cases (16) where natural parents are named along with foster-parents. The six of these *alumni* who took their *nomen* from their mother and were not themselves of freed status may have been illegitimate. In those cases the mother could have given the child the father's *cognomen* but without our knowing the father's identity we cannot test that.

Just under one quarter of the foster-parents recorded as couples share the same *nomen*: 23 out of 98 couples. In two of these couples, at least one partner can be certainly identified as of freed status. The others have been classified as *incerti*, but the suspicion that they are *liberti* must be strong.[42]

Order of Names

Were there criteria which normally determined whose name was placed first on the stone? Inscriptions attesting public careers normally observe a strict hierarchy in the order in which offices are recorded, and the Romans showed a highly cultivated sense of precedence and order according to status in other situations.[43]

Of the *alumni* on inscriptions 85 per cent are dedicatees, but a much lower proportion have their name inscribed in first position. A breakdown according to the number of people on the inscription (e.g. second out of three, third out of five) yields too many small groups to be useful. But more than half the *alumni* are recorded on stones carrying only two names, and of these 57.9 per cent (132 out of 228) have their name in first position. A distribution by status suggests that the higher the status of the *alumnus* the greater the chance of being named first (see Table 7.3).

Table 7.3: *Alumni* by Status and Position (inscriptions recording only two names)

Status	No.	Position 1 % (row)		No.	Position 2 % (row)		Total *alumni* in any position no.
S	1	25.0	} 27.9	0	0	} 26.7	4
S?	45	28.0		44	27.3		161
L	13	37.1	} 34.1	10	28.6	} 29.3	35
L?	1	16.7		2	33.3		6
Inc.	65	35.5		38	20.8		183
Ingen.	5	55.5	} 50	1	11.1	} 16.7	9
Ingen.?	1	33.3		1	33.3		3
Eques.	1	100.0		—	—		1
Sen.	—	—	—	—	—		—
Unknown	—	—	—	—	—		29
	132			96			431
		228					

S   = slave
S?   = probable slave
L   = freedman or freedwoman
L?   = probable freedman
         or freedwoman
Inc.   = *incertus/a*, i.e. a
         citizen of either free-
         born or freed status
Ingen. = freeborn
Ingen.? = probably freeborn
Eques. = equestrian
Sen.   = senatorial
Imp.   = imperial
Criteria for these status definitions are basically those used in my 1974 article.

Being a dedicatee gives a good chance of having one's name first, but less so for *alumni* than for others. Only 61.8 per cent of *alumni* dedicatees in the above group come first, whereas 96 per cent of non-*alumni* dedicatees in that group are inscribed first. This reinforces the picture of *alumni* as a socially inferior group: young and of comparatively low status.

Vernae

There has been more general agreement and clarity about the application of the term *verna* than for *alumnus*. The usually accepted definition is 'a home-born slave', i.e. a slave born in the house of its master, as opposed to slaves bought in or otherwise introduced to the *familia*. Home-born slaves had economic importance, being an addition to the master's property and being an important source of supply of slaves in the imperial period. They seem also to have sometimes had familial importance in substituting for or complementing a master's own child(ren). It is generally agreed that *vernae* held a special position in the household and could expect better treatment than other slaves.

The slave-child's master was its slave-mother's master. The status and whereabouts of the father were irrelevant. If one took literally Berger's definition (1953:761) of *verna*, 'a slave born in the house of his parents' master', one would have to assume that both parents belonged to the same household. But evidence for natural parents of *vernae* is scarce: fewer than 6 per cent of those attested on Roman inscriptions make any mention of two parents, and even when specific names are given little more can be established about the parents. It is true that when only one parent is named it is sometimes the father, but such numbers are small, and the overwhelming majority of *vernae* are attested in a relationship with one or more persons who appear to be their master(s) or ex-master(s).

Some doubts have been expressed about the normal definition, given above, of *vernae*. Starr (1942) reminded us that *verna* could also mean 'native of a town', but he conceded that this meaning was probably no longer used by 'the cultivated speaker of Latin' in the early Empire. He did, however, give some examples from non-Roman inscriptions, and suggested, rather gratuitously, that there might be many others 'in the great mass of Roman inscriptions'.[44] My own examination of the Roman *vernae* (helped, of course, by the Jory index which was not available to Starr) does not support that hypothesis. It does, however, show that the term *verna* might continue to attach to a slave after manumission (cf. the similar retention of terms such as *contubernalis*, which characterised the original relationship, into a later, modified relationship).

Imperial *vernae* play an important part in Weaver's study of the imperial household, *Familia Caesaris* (1972). He uniformly takes them to be slave-born, except for one moment (p. 207) where he wavers and includes 'freeborn children of *liberti*' in the term. However, the two possible examples cited (*AE* 1903, no. 338; *CIL* 6.12948) are at best inconclusive: the children have a *nomen* but no indication of status. The same applies to the apparently formidable list given by Chantraine (1967:171, n. 137). The parentage of imperial *vernae* remains controversial, as Weaver's discussion in Chapter 6 reveals; but the slave-born status of the *vernae* themselves is strongly supported by epigraphical and legal sources. The literary use of *verna* is, predictably, looser; but most examples confirm that 'slave-born' is the normal meaning.[45]

There are 564 *vernae* attested in usable inscriptions from Rome (all references to *CIL* 6). Another 30 persons use Verna as a *cognomen* and have not been included. Some of the *alumni* characteristics are shared by *vernae* in inscriptions and legal sources, e.g. young age, mixed status (free or slave), and a quasi-familial relationship with a foster-parent (a term which will again be used to compensate for the lack of a correlative to *verna*). But the status distribution is heavily weighted at the slave-end of the scale; and far more *vernae* than *alumni* have only a single foster-parent. Further, it looks at first as if there are many more male than female foster-parents (sex ratio 153); but on closer inspection one sees that 18.5 per cent of all foster-parents are an emperor (or, fairly rarely, another member of the imperial family). If one excludes the *vernae* under direct imperial authority, the sex ratio of foster-parents is 105, almost as many female foster-parents as male.

Terms associated with *vernae* give a glimpse of what may be a special relationship in the household. One is *collacteus*, i.e. he was reared together with Drusus, son of Rubellius Blandus, in the house of the imperial lady Antonia (16057); others are called

Table 7.4: *Vernae* by Age and Status

Status	< 1 year		1-4 years		5-9 years		10-14 years	
	No.	%	No.	%	No.	%	No.	%
S	0		0		1	1.0	0	
S(Imp)	0		4	4.2	6	6.0	4	8.3
S?	7	100	73	76.0	61	61.0	28	58.3
L	0		1	1.0	4	4.0	2	4.2
L(Imp)	0		0		0		0	
L?	0		11	11.5	19	19.0	7	14.6
Inc.	0		5	5.2	8	8.0	7	14.6
Ingen.	0		1	1.0	0		0	
Ingen.?	0		0		0		0	
Unknown	0	0	1	1.0	1	1.0	0	
Total	7	100	96		100		48	
% of all *vernae*		1.2%		17.0%		17.7%		8.5%

Notes:
S   = slave
S?   = probable slave
L   = freedman or freedwoman
L?   = probable freedman or
        freedwoman
Inc. = *incertus/a*, i.e. a citizen of
        either freeborn or freed
        status

delicium; and various diminutives are used (usually feminine) such as *vernacla*, *vernula*. Two *vernae* are identified as stepsons (*filiaster*, 19412, 28519) and two others as *alumni* (4412, 24112).

Status and Age

Table 7.4 shows the status distribution of *vernae* in inscriptions. By contrast with the *alumni*, far fewer than half have any indication of citizenship. There are 21 per cent clearly-attested slaves (nearly all slaves in the emperor's service), and another 53 per cent are probably slaves. There is further indication of slave origin of *vernae* in that another 13.7 per cent are *liberti*. Few of these are imperial freedmen: imperial *vernae* moved on to more distinguished and distinctive titles after obtaining their freedom. Only 2.6 per cent of foster-parents are certainly slaves, and another 6.7 per cent are probably slaves.

The correlation between improved status and greater age that was observed for *alumni* can be observed for *vernae* if one takes together as a whole the certain slaves and the probable slaves. The percentage of possible slaves in each age-group declines until

15-17 years		18-19 years		≥ 20 years		Adult		Unknown		Total	
No.	%	No.	%	No.	%	No.	%	No.	%	No.	%
0		0		2	5.4	0		1	0.5	4	0.7
4	21.1	3	20.0	23	62.2	20	80.0	50	23.0	114	20.2
10	52.6	8	53.3	5	13.5	1	4.0	105	48.4	298	52.8
1	5.3	1	6.7	1	2.7	0		11	5.1	21	3.7
0		0		0		1	4.0	4	1.8	5	0.9
2	10.5	3	20.0	4	10.9	1	4.0	25	11.5	72	12.8
2	10.5	0		2	5.4	1	4.0	13	6.0	38	6.7
0		0		0		0		0		1	0.2
0		0		0		0		0		0	
0		0		0		1	4.0	8	3.7	11	2.0
19		15		37		25		215		564	
	3.4%		2.7%		5.5%		4.4%		38.5%		100%

Ingen. = freeborn
Ingen.? = probably freeborn
Eques. = equestrian
Sen. = senatorial
Imp. = imperial
Criteria for these status definitions
are basically those used in my 1974
article.

the age of 14. After that, the percentage of possible slaves increases. If, however, the imperial slave *vernae* are removed, the decline continues for other groups. By contrast, the imperial slave *vernae* become proportionately more numerous with each increasing age cohort of *vernae*. This confirms other indications that the *familia Caesaris* is a special case and may not represent trends in broader Roman society. The overall increase in likely slave status from age 15 is due to the disproportionate representation of imperial *vernae* in the upper age-brackets. This is probably a reflection of their increasing importance as their job responsibilities increase, whereas other slaves outgrow the *verna* designation or gain freedom. Imperial slaves were unlikely to be freed before the legal age of 30, and the term *verna* was almost a career designation for older imperial slaves. But most of them must have got their freedom (or been dispensed with?) at the age of 30: only 7.9 per cent of imperial slaves have ages attested of 30 or more years.[46]

Although no imperial *vernae* are recorded in the inscriptions as being freed below the age of 30, many other *vernae* won freedom at lower ages, as Table 7.4 shows. Of 21 certain *liberti*, 9 are known to have been freed younger than 20 and of 72 others who were probably *liberti* 42 would have been freed before reaching the age of 20. This confirms other evidence that outside the imperial service age limits on manumission were not applied rigidly. The somewhat higher proportion of females under 20 who seem to have been freed (29 per cent females, 22 per cent males) is also consistent with other indications that women were freed more easily. One could test the specially favoured position of *vernae* by comparing their rate of early manumission with that of other slaves.

The one freeborn *verna* (20040) was an illegitimate child who lived less than two years: C. Iulius Sp. f. Hedynon derived his family name from his mother. His dedicator, C. Iulius Primus, bore the same family name but it is impossible to know whether he was the natural father or whether the common name reflects another link within a large (perhaps imperial) household.

The legal evidence for *vernae* is much less extensive than for *alumni*. In most cases, what applied to slaves in general (*servi*) applied to *vernae*. It is clear that *vernae* are slaves in the passages where they are bequeathed to another owner, e.g. 'Plotiae vernas meos omnes, praeterquam quos alii legavi, lego'.[47] In two cases a bequest is made to *vernae* themselves. In one of these cases the *vernae* seem to include *liberti* and may even be synonymous with them, e.g. the *vernae* may have been manumitted in the testator's will. The passage runs,

> A man had inscribed his daughter as his heir, with this proviso: 'I do not wish my house [*aedificium*] to pass out of my family name [*nomen*]; I want it to go to my *vernae* whom I have named in this will.' The question was, when the daughter and testamentary *vernae* had died, whether the whole *fideicommissum* applied to the one freedman who remained. The reply was that, in accordance with the facts adduced, the individual share should go to the one who survived from among the *vernae*.[48]

Age and Sex

Nearly half of the *vernae* attested on inscriptions have no indication of age, as Table 7.5 shows. Of those whose age is specified, almost two-thirds are aged 9 years or younger. The median age of all those whose age is known is 6.3 years; the mode is 5 years. This pattern is very similar to that established above for the *alumni*. There is the same over-representation of the 1–9 years group and the same under-representation of infants.

Table 7.5: *Vernae* by Age and Sex

Age	Male No.	%	Female No.	%	Sex ratio	Sex unspecified No.	%	Total No.	%
< 1 year	5	2.4	2	1.8	250			7	2.2
1-4	66	31.6	30	26.6	220			96	29.8
5-9	60	28.7	40	35.4	150			100	31.1
10-14	28	13.4	20	17.7	140			48	14.9
15-17	11	5.3	8	7.1	138			19	5.9
18-19	11	5.3	4	3.5	275			15	4.7
20-24	12	5.7	5	4.4	240			17	5.3
25-29	6	2.9	3	2.6	200			9	2.8
30-39	6	2.9	1	0.9	600			7	2.2
40-49	3	1.4	0	0				3	0.9
50-100	1	0.5	0	0	—			1	0.3
Total of specified age	209	100.1	113	100	185	0	0	322	100.1
Adult	21		4					25	
Unspecified	151		66					217	
Total	381		183		209			564	

A possible additional reason for the under-representation of infants is revealed in a legal passage[49] which considers the position of a child 'who has been born of a slave woman of the city household and sent to the country estate for rearing [*nutriendus*]'. The question was whether the child belonged to the urban or rural household, or neither. Paulus thought it best to consider the child part of the urban household, thus implying that he could be expected to return there after rearing. Treggiari (1979b:189-90) has suggested that the Romans' appreciation of a healthy country environment for pregnant women and small children led to their sending some of their pregnant slaves to the country for the birth and early rearing of *vernae*. She further suggests that boy slaves were recalled to the city earlier than girls because of greater job opportunities for boys in large households, especially for very young boys.

The sex ratio shows boys outnumbering girls overall by

approximately 2 to 1. These are also the proportions in the 1–4 years age-group. Girls improve their representation in the 5-9 year and 10-14 age-groups, although they are not as well represented here as *alumnae* (a ratio of 112 for *alumni*, 147 for *vernae*). Female *vernae* continue to improve their representation (marginally) into the 15-17 year age-group, but from the upper teens they are comparatively rare.

There are somewhat more *vernae* than *alumni* attested over the age of 30. Only one of these is a woman. As was true for the *alumni* records, the *vernae* are a much younger group than are the other people represented on their inscriptions. And female *vernae* are less well represented than are other women on these stones (32 per cent of *vernae* are female, 46 per cent of other persons are female).

It is rare to find the age of foster-parents specified. Those whose age is known are all adults and (with one indeterminate exception) dedicatees.

Legal references to *vernae* make no mention of any children they might have. A *verna* in the strictest sense, i.e. a slave, could have no children in the eyes of the law. But inscriptions give glimpses of the social reality of adult *vernae* who are parents, rare though these glimpses be. Six *vernae* (all imperial) are attested with children.[50] In five of these cases, only one child is attested; in the other there are four children. Of these nine children, five are probable slaves, and four have a *nomen* indicating citizenship. The mothers of the four all have a *nomen* (except for 8825a, where the wife's name is not given). In only one case is the female spouse the imperial *verna*:

D M

TROPHIME

AVG N VERNAE

VIXIT ANN XXI MENS II DIEB XXVIII

MARTIALES TRES PATER

ET CONTVBERNALIS ET FILIVS

B M F   (27674)

By a coincidence played on in the inscription, the woman's father, spouse and son were all called Martialis: 'the three Martial men'. They must all be classified as probable slaves. The family with four children (9077) shows something of the mixture of status possible amongst siblings. The daughters have a *nomen*, leading me to classify them as *incertae* (i.e. either freed or freeborn). The mother has the same *nomen*, but because her two sons are probable slaves I have classified her as *liberta* (?). The family tree can be represented thus:

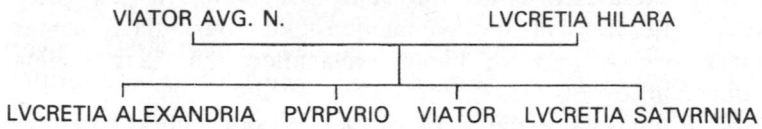

VIATOR AVG. N.   LVCRETIA HILARA

LVCRETIA ALEXANDRIA   PVRPVRIO   VIATOR   LVCRETIA SATVRNINA

The father has a clerical position in the imperial service: he is *adiut(or)* *tabul(ariorum)*, an assistant to the accountancy staff. Weaver (1972:143) thinks that the sons are to be taken as freeborn, with *nomen* omitted. But are they not more likely examples of the emperor's concern to recruit his slave's sons into the civil service — and thus his claim on them as his own slaves — and his lack of concern with daughters, who could enjoy a superior legal status?

In addition to the inscriptions attesting children of *vernae*, there are 31 others where there is some evidence of a *verna* being married. Many of these have a specific job or career position attested. The only 'two-career' couple is attested in 8958: (Iulia) Dorcas and (Iulius) Lycastus have both been freed by Livia; Dorcas is an *ornatrix* and her spouse a *rogator*.

Names

Of 564 *vernae*, 133 have a *nomen*, i.e. 23.6 per cent. By contrast, 72.2 per cent of non-*vernae* in these inscriptions have a *nomen*. Slightly more girl *vernae* than boys have a *nomen*. The ratio is approximately the same as for the rest of the population represented on the stones.

There are 100 *vernae* recorded (with 97 foster parents) who share a *nomen* with one foster-parent or both (34 with the male foster-parent, 56 with the female, and 10 with both). Of these *vernae*, 18 were certainly *liberti* and another 67 probably *liberti*. This indicates that manumission by a foster-parent or by a common master/patron is the most likely explanation. This is made explicit in those cases where the title *patronus* is used. In one case (36167) both foster-parents are the patrons:

DIS MANIBVS
PONTIAE TVNDARIS VIXIT
ANN XII M IX D XXVII FEᴄER
D PONTIVS ALCIDES ET
PONTIA THISBE VERNAE IDEM LIB

In only six cases does a *verna* share a *cognomen* with a foster-parent. In view of the commonness of some slave names, coincidence is a more likely explanation than any familial connection.

In 70 inscriptions the name of one or both natural parents is given. By far the biggest group of such *vernae* is composed of imperial slaves. This reduces the possibility of *nomen* linkage; and only five *vernae* in all share a *nomen* with a natural parent. (Two of them and seven others share a *cognomen*.) Comparatively few though the references to natural parents be, the imperial household seems to have provided a better chance than other environments for a *verna* to retain contact with natural parents. Mothers are named a little more frequently than fathers, but in nearly half the 70 cases both natural parents are mentioned. Their status is varied, but the preponderance is towards slave and ex-slave.

The imperial household also provided the most sympathetic environment for *vernae* to 'marry'; at least, most of the small number with unions attested (31 out of 37, proportionately more than for *alumni*), are imperial *vernae*. The most common pattern is for a male imperial slave to have a spouse of citizenship status (whether freeborn or freed is not usually clear). This is the pattern put forward and analysed in detail by Weaver. Children are infrequently attested for married *vernae*, and in only one case (9077) is more than one child attested.

Most of the *vernae* who have job titles belong to the imperial household. These jobs are either of a domestic kind or junior administrative posts and have been analysed by Weaver (1972). The only non-imperial jobs attested for *vernae* in the inscriptions are those of *cubucularius* (6262), *decurio conlegii centonoriorum* (7863), *empticus* (8919), *a cubiculo* (9286) and *musicarius* (9649). The law code records weavers and a cobbler (see n. 47). These job titles must have conferred some standing; their holders were expert enough, or the household affluent enough, to justify specialisation. Many other *vernae* would have carried out undifferentiated and humble, even degrading, duties.

Order of Names

We might have expected the prestige of imperial *vernae* to confuse the status order which we saw for *alumni*; but, as Table 8.6 shows, the chance of being recorded first was better for *vernae* of free status than for those of slave status. Nevertheless, not much more than a third of all *vernae* were recorded in first position: a picture similar to that described for *alumni*.

Table 7.6: *Vernae* by Status and Position (inscriptions recording only two names)

Status	No.	Position 1 % (row)		No.	Position 2 % (row)		Total *vernae* in any position No.
S	4	100.0	⎫	0	0	⎫	4
S(Imp)	36	31.6	⎬ 33.9	16	14.0	⎬ 19.0	114
S?	101	33.9	⎭	63	21.1	⎭	298
L	9	42.9	⎫	2	9.5	⎫	21
L(Imp)	2	40.0	⎬ 41.8	1	20.0	⎬ 18.4	5
L?	30	41.7	⎭	15	20.8	⎭	72
Inc.	16	42.1		1	2.6		38
Ingen.	1	100.0		0	0		1
Unknown	—	—		—	—		11
	199			98			564
		297					

Notes:
S   = slave
S?   = probable slave
L   = freedman or freedwoman
L?   = probable freedman
          or freedwoman
Inc.   = *incertus/a*, i.e. a
          citizen of either free-
          born or freed status
Ingen. = freeborn
Ingen.? = probably freeborn
Eques. = equestrian
Sen.   = senatorial
Imp.   = imperial
Criteria for these status definitions are basically those used in my 1974 article

Summary

The above analysis of two sets of children, *alumni* and *vernae*, reveals the surrogate family structure and relationship available to some of the more humble children in Rome who were separated (by death or other circumstances) from natural parents. It has not provided the detail necessary to answer the questions posed about such children's origin. We have seen glimpses of illegitimates and step-children but the evidence does not suggest that these were the norm in these categories. Many must have been orphans in some sense, either through parents' death or through separation due to slave sales and transfers or through exposure of the children. Of 431 *alumni*, only 16 record a natural parent's name; of 564 *vernae*, 70 do so. Natural kin may have come to the rescue to raise some of the children, but neither nomenclature nor other evidence gives much hint of this. The legal status of *alumni* was sometimes ambiguous, but a great many of the *alumni* and *vernae* studied seem to have worked largely as slaves but enjoying some of the better circumstances of foster-children — some affection, some expectation of family inheritance, some responsibility for carrying on the family name. There is virtually no evidence that at this level of society formal adoption was used.

Romans over many centuries used adoption as a method of continuing the family when no natural son had been born of a marriage and survived to adulthood. The financial and political motives for adoption will have affected the upper classes more than others, and Augustus's legislation (see Chapter 1) strengthened these motives. The incentive for formal adoption is likely to have been less in the lower classes, who had little concern for political careers, little property to bequeath, and little need for formal *patria potestas*. Moreover, it seems usually to have been young adult males who were adopted in place of natural sons. For all these reasons, adoption is unlikely to be a useful explanation for the foster-children discussed above. The evidence for nomenclature confirms this.[51]

For some children, the result — or perhaps purpose — of the foster relationship was the learning of a trade. Treggiari (1979b) has discussed the occupations documented for females and shown that the range is more limited than for males. Some, however, were specialised enough to make it likely that girls were sent outside the household for training (she suggests this for midwives and doctors and even *ornatrices*, 'dressers'). For others it was more likely that skills could be acquired within a large household (readers, clerks, secretaries and those with more domestic or personal duties).

Not enough is yet known about professional training in Rome and the role of children in it. It is clear, however, that the period of childhood — at least for the lower classes — was short, as it was for children in most western societies until comparatively recently.[52] It may also have been grim, and we must beware of romanticising the general picture on the basis of the close bonds attested for those who have left memorials behind. Nevertheless, the Roman *familia*[53] did serve as a community which could accommodate not only the nuclear family but a range of quasi-familial and other relationships and in which children seem to have had some intrinsic value and were able not only to survive but even to prosper.

Notes

1. On the effects of remarriage, see Humbert (1972), especially chapter 2.
2. As will be seen, these sometimes have one or both natural parents attested.
3. Few of the inscriptions or legal sources pre-date the first century AD, and the bulk of them refer to the late first century and the second century AD. A few inscriptions belong to the third century. (The datable *vernae* studied in this paper seem to belong largely to the first century AD, whereas Weaver's imperial *vernae* are largely second century (1972:51). This may be one of a number of aspects in which the imperial *familia* differed from the broader population. It may be that as the emperor's service took over the term other people began to drop it.) The legal sources continue to the age of Justinian (sixth century), but those used here will be the ones referring to the period of most of our other evidence, i.e. the first two and a half centuries AD.
4. For references, see Bibliography under 'Children' and 'Medicine'.
5. Two notable examples are given by Suetonius, *De grammaticis* 7, 21. These freeborn men were exposed, raised as slaves, educated, and became successful teachers. Each won freedom and Roman citizenship by manumission. One had declined to recover his freedom through his mother when she appeared on the scene (impressed by her son's influential contacts) to testify to his free birth.
6. Scaevola (D.40.4.29) gives an example of an exposed boy who was able later not only to recover his freeborn status but claim his father's estate as the legitimate heir.
7. e.g. Paulus (D.25.3.4): 'Responsible for killing is not only he who smothers a child but also he who abandons it and he who denies it sustenance and he who exposes it in a public place in order to arouse pity which he himself does not feel.'
8. The Emperor Claudius had adopted a similar policy in the first century for exposed slaves (Suetonius, *Claudius* 25).

9. These documents were published in a number of issues of *Parola del Passato* between 1946 and 1953: see articles on *Tabulae Herculanenses* by Pugliese Carratelli, Maiuri and Arangio-Ruiz. For a recent comment, see Boyé (1959:29-48).

10. The masculine will be used to include the feminine. If sex is significant, that will be made explicit.

11. I shall use this term for the 'nurturer' of all *alumni*, irrespective of the relationship between them. See below for comment on the lack of a single term correlative with *alumnus*.

12. Cameron (1939) took the *threptoi* of Roman Asia Minor as equivalent to *alumni* rather than to *vernae*. He divided *threptoi* into three groups: foster-children, adopted children, and children of servile status. He used *alumni* as analogies from time to time, but not in any systematic way. Brunt, in a review in 1958, commented that 'modern writers are apt to take *alumni* to be always foundlings', and expressed scepticism about this; but the examples he cited proved little about the origin or status of *alumni*. Sherwin-White, in his commentary (1966) on the question of exposed children in Pliny, *Letters* 10.65 and 66, commented that *alumni* in the western provinces may have something in common with the *threptoi* of the East, 'but the term in Roman legal texts covers a wider field than that of *expositi*'. *Threptoi* have also been studied by Nani (1943-44), and were alluded to by Hopkins (1978:158). Lemosse 1975:264 referred to the anomalous legal status of *alumni*, neither clearly free nor clearly slave, which in his view must have led to a very bleak lot. Manson (1983:151) referred to literary uses of *alumnus*. Boswell (1984:15) thought most *alumni* were foundlings. The article *alumnus* in *Thesaurus Linguae Latinae* merely lists the literary usages, without discussion. Most of these are metaphorical and none of those listed advances the definition of the children at present under discussion. Leclercq's article '*alumni*' in *Dictionnaire d'archéologie chrétienne et de liturgie* (1907), 1288-306 has some discussion of pagan *alumni* as a background to Christian usage, but most of the discussion concerns the practice of exposure at Rome. The article '*alumnus*' by De Ruggiero in *Dizionario epigrafico I* (1895), 437-40 is good on the inscriptional evidence; but it is not exhaustive, and inscriptions from many parts of the Roman world are cited indiscriminately. Social and legal backgrounds varied considerably within the Roman Empire, and different economic circumstances may also have influenced the condition of children. Thus each area should be studied separately, and the city of Rome is the largest centre and, arguably, the most important one on which to begin. (Note Trajan's reluctance, in Pliny, *Letters* 10.66, to apply to exposed children in Bithynia rulings handed down for other parts of the Empire.)

13. D.20.1.6, 8 (Ulpian); Paulus *Sent.* 5.6.16.

14. Gaius *Inst.* 1.19; D.40.2.11-13 (Ulpian); Justinian *Institutes* 1.6.5.

15. D.27.1.32 (Paulus); 33.2.34.1 (Scaevola).

16. D.33.27.2 (Paulus); cf. D.35.1.71 pr. (Papinian).

17. D.33.2.34.1, 33.7.20.2, 31.88.6 (Scaevola); D.32.78.3 (Paulus).

18. D.33.1.18.1, 33.1.21.4 (Scaevola); D.34.1.9 (Papinian); D.34.1.15 pr., 34.4.30 pr., 36.1.64.1, 36.2.26.1 (Scaevola).

19. D.34.2.18.1, 32.41.12 (Scaevola).

20. D.32.102.2 (Scaevola).

21. D.36.1.80.12 (Scaevola).

22. Cf. C.2.3.10, from the time of Alexander Severus, where a man provides a dowry for his *alumna*.

23. D.29.5.1 (Ulpian).

24. Domitian: Suetonius, *Domitian* 7; D.48.8.6 (Venuleius Saturninus). Hadrian: D.48.8.4.2 (Ulpian), 48.8.3.4 (Marcianus).

25. I have taken *patronus* in its technical sense as a correlative of *libertus* in these inscriptions. It is possible that it is used more loosely as a correlative of *alumnus*, implying no more than foster-parent or protector, but I think it unlikely that such a technical term would be used so loosely. Berger (1953) lists only the technical meaning.

26. D.43.29.3.4 (Ulpian). Cf. the reference to *pietas* in D.34.1.14 (Ulpian) to explain the generously high definition of the age of puberty — 18 for boys, 14 for girls — for the purpose of payment of support, *alimenta*.

27. Cf. D.27.1.32 (Paulus), where a person leaving his *alumni* as heirs is referred to as an *extraneus*.

28. Syme (1960) discusses the rarity of references to illegitimates in the upper classes.

29. D.34.9.16.1 (Papinian).

30. Cf. Tables 4 and 5 in Hopkins (1966). Of 8065 persons recorded in Rome with age of death (4575 males, 3490 females), just under one-third died at ages 0–9 years. In the inscriptions studied for this chapter, some persons whose age is unspecified can be assumed to be adults (e.g. if they have children of their own). Few such persons are *alumni* 11 out of 147: or, 2.6 per cent of all *alumni* are 'adult' on these criteria, compared with 23.1 per cent of all other persons.

31. But not infants? Only six *alumni* are recorded younger than 1 year. This probably reflects a lack of recognition of the identity of infants, but this very outlook and the high risk of infant mortality probably deterred the taking up of infants as *alumni*. Children in the 5–9 years age-group could find useful occupations, especially in large affluent city households. Stone (1979:295) speaks of children being gainfully employed after the age of 7 in the eighteenth and early nineteenth centuries in England. Horsburgh (1980:33) refers to an English statute of 1536 authorising the apprenticing of pauper children between the ages of 5 and 14 years. He gives an example (p. 46) of a girl apprenticed at the age of 9 in New South Wales in 1940.

32. The sex ratio expresses the number of males compared to 100 females. Thus a sex ratio of 100 would indicate exactly equal numbers of males and females.

33. See Hopkins (1966), who argues that in general girls had the greatest likelihood of being commemorated between the ages of 15 and 29 because they were then esteemed as both daughters and wives. He had also shown previously (1965a:309-27) that parents' responsibility for daughters' memorials declined sharply from the age of 15 and even more sharply after the age of 19. But I know of no analysis of girls' ages between 0 and 14 for children commemorated by their parents. For *alumni*, where the dramatic increase in the proportion of girls who are commemorated occurs soon after the age of 5, marriageability cannot alone explain the increase.

34. In this group of *alumni* the near equalisation of the sexes occurs at age 6.

35. I use the term 'marriage' for any continuing conjugal union, even if the partners are ineligible for legal Roman marriage, e.g. because of slave status. The change of relationships would still be likely to weaken the concept of being an *alumna*.

36. D.27.1.32 (Paulus); 32.102.1; 33.1.18.1; 33.1.21.4; 33.2.34.1; 34.1.15 pr. (all Scaevola); 36.2.26.1 (Papinian).

37. Papinian (D.36.2.26.1) found in favour of the heir of an *alumnus* although the *alumnus* (referred to also as a *puer*) had died before reaching the age of 25 when he might himself have entered fully on his own inheritance. For other envisaged heirs of *alumni*, cf. D.32.27.2 (Paulus) and 36.1.64.1 (Scaevola).

38. Cf. n. 14 above for the law which allowed early manumission of *alumni*.

39. Cf. the pattern in the imperial service, when it was unusual for male slaves

to be manumitted before the age of 30. But females and those further removed from the emperor's service got early manumission more frequently (Weaver 1972:97-104).

40. e.g. in 8930 (=33754a) the *alumnus* P. Aelius Aug. lib. Calippus shares the same *nomen* as his foster-parents and their natural son, all imperial *liberti* (the son, however, freed by Antoninus Pius rather than Hadrian).

41. In the preceding chapter Weaver suggests that some imperial freedmen on manumission formally adopted their illegitimate children and thus legitimised them. This is a plausible hypothesis, although no more; but, as seen in other situations, the practice of the imperial household was not that of the wider community.

42. See n. 40 above for spouses both manumitted by Hadrian.

43. e.g. seating in the theatre or amphitheatre. Flory's recent article (1984) has explored the question of the order of names in Roman epitaphs.

44. He cited two Roman inscriptions, both of doubtful relevance. There are, however, four *vernae* who use the description '*natione verna/vernacula*'. Two of these (10049a and b) refer to participants in the Circus games, whom I take to have been born in Rome, perhaps in the gladiators' barracks. This geographic meaning seems also to apply to *AE* 1972 no. 14, and may apply to 14208. I have excluded these four from this study.

45. e.g. Horace, *Epodes* 2.65, where the *vernae*, 'ditis examen domus', relax around the Lares in an idyllic picture of the end of a farmer's day.

46. Cf. n. 39 above. One example of a slave who did not make it is Euphemus Caes.ñ. ex ration(ibus) volu(ptariis), who died aged 42 (8564). His mother had been more successful than he: she was a citizen, Ulpia Aphrodite, who survived to commemorate her son.

47. D.30.36 pr. (Pomponius). (Some of these *vernae* were weavers.) Cf. D.32.99.5 (Paulus) (some *vernae* are couriers); D.36.1.78.12 (Scaevola) (a *verna* who is a cobbler). For another artisan *verna*, cf. n. 21 above.

48. D.32.38.2 (Scaevola). Cf. D.34.2.15 (Scaevola), where through a *fideicommissum* a wife is to pass on jewellery to the testator's *vernae* after her death.

49. D.32.99.3 (Paulus); cf. D.50.16.210 (Marcianus).

50. 8472, 8825a, 9077, 11186, 27674, 33776.

51. In Roman Egypt the adoption of male foundlings was forbidden: *Gnomon of the Idios Logos* 41, 107.

52. See Ariès (1962). For upper-class children, especially boys, there does seem to have been a concept of adolescence between childhood and adulthood: see Eyben's writings (e.g. 1981).

53. As discussed by Flory (1978).

8 WET-NURSING AT ROME: A STUDY IN SOCIAL RELATIONS

Keith R. Bradley

I

In his biography of the elder Cato, Plutarch records that Cato's wife, Licinia, breastfed her own son (*Cato the Elder* 20.3). Plutarch evidently approved the fact, because in several parts of the *Moralia* he makes clear his belief that maternal nursing of infants was preferable to the use of a wet-nurse.[1] Yet his remark about Licinia suggests that her example was unusual, or at least that it could be considered unusual in a later age, an inference which is supported by a number of remarks made by authors from the late Republic and early Empire. Thus for example Cicero, in a morbid piece on the evil nature of the world, remarked that 'it seems as if we drank in deception with our nurse's milk', while Tacitus, when commenting on the prevalence of maternal nursing among the tribes of Germany, implied that in his own society nursing was a job commonly done by surrogates.[2] Moreover, although Plutarch's view that maternal nursing was better than wet-nursing finds a parallel in opinions attributed by Aulus Gellius (12.1) to the sophist Favorinus, both Plutarch and Favorinus show that actual practices by no means coincided with their theories, and the same is true of the medical writer, Soranus, whose lengthy recommendations on how to select a wet-nurse presuppose a widespread audience for such advice (*Gynaecology* 2.19.24-5).

It can safely be assumed that the various writers who have been mentioned so far were reflecting or referring to the use of wet-nurses at their own social level, that is among the upper classes of Roman or, increasingly under the Empire, Graeco-Roman society. But a further item of evidence may be taken to indicate that wet-nursing was also practised at lower social levels. In an epitaph commemorating a woman named Graxia Alexandria, her husband Pudens, an imperial freedman, thought it important to record that his wife had breastfed her children,[3] an unusual distinction which suggests that maternal nursing

201

among the servile classes at Rome may have been exceptional rather than the rule. If then this evidence offers a reliable guide, the early care of infants in Roman society of the classical period,[4] especially the way infants were nursed, differed markedly from most modern western practices. The purpose of this chapter accordingly is to examine wet-nursing practices at Rome and to see what consequences for social history emerge from them. Within an assumed context of high infant mortality and high female mortality in childbirth, an attempt will be made to delineate the conditions which governed wet-nursing at the upper and lower levels of society and to explain the custom in terms of Roman social organisation.

II

A body of evidence that can be profitably explored is provided by epitaphs from the city of Rome in which women who are styled *nutrix* appear, and which permit something to be seen of the social background of both nurses and their nurslings.[5] The evidence contains several limitations. First, it must be recognised that the word *nutrix* may mean a wet-nurse or a nursemaid, so all the women known from inscriptions were not necessarily wet-nurses. However, there is firm evidence that wet-nurse was the primary meaning of *nutrix* (whereas the phrase *assa nutrix* could be used to designate a dry-nurse).[6] Thus to assume that *nutrix* generally means wet-nurse is not unreasonable. Secondly, it is often difficult to ascertain precisely the status of an individual mentioned on an epitaph if a clear indication of such is absent from the inscription itself (the usual case) or if independent evidence is unavailable. Reliance has then to be made on criteria conventionally followed in epigraphical studies for the attribution of status,[7] but inevitably a certain degree of uncertainty and imprecision subsists. Thirdly, the inscriptional sample is relatively small, numbering only 69 items,[8] and it cannot be assumed to give an accurate portrayal of practices in Roman society as a whole. Nevertheless the epitaphs constitute an important source of information not previously examined and deserve scrutiny.

Literary sources give several indications about the social status of the *nutrix*. Cato's Licinia is said to have breastfed the children of her slaves as well as her own child,[9] but there seems to be no other evidence for an upper-class woman acting as wet-nurse. A passage from Dio Chrysostom (7.114), not perhaps entirely irrelevant to Rome, shows that wet-nursing was a respectable job for women of free but poor status, and this receives support from some of the nursing contracts and receipts which have survived from Roman Egypt (Bradley 1980:321). Soranus too prescribes exercises for nurses in a way suggesting they were usually of humble rank, whereas Juvenal and Favorinus refer to the hiring of nurses, perhaps understanding free women.[10] But Tacitus characterises the nurse as a slave or ex-slave,[11] and predictably this is borne out by the inscriptions where in the majority of cases, as shown in Table 8.1, the nurse seems most often a slave or *liberta*. For the women in the inscriptions servile status has been assumed for those with only one name (unless there is evidence to the contrary); freed status is certain for those whose names are accompanied by the designation *l.* or *lib.*, and is reasonably certain for women whose *nomen* is the same as that of an identifiably upper-class family for which they worked. However, allowance has to be made for the possibility that some apparent freedwomen were in fact *ingenuae*, and these have been placed in a separate category in the table. Immediately, what seems to be the common use by upper-class families of a nurse from the servile classes points to an exploitative element in the life of the nurse occasioned by the birth of her own child or children and sets the direction for subsequent discussion.

The table also indicates the status of the nurslings so far as it can be determined. The impression created by the literary sources — that wet-nursing of upper-class infants was common — receives some confirmation from this material: nearly half of the nurslings belong to identifiable senatorial or equestrian families. It is equally clear, however, that a good proportion of nurslings seem to be slaves or children of freed status. Allowance must again be made for the possibility that some nurslings who could be *libertini/ae* may actually have been *ingenui/ae*, and they are included in the freed/freeborn category without asterisks. But at least one-fifth of the nurslings are of recognisably servile background, and the proportion may in fact be higher. Yet if wet-nursing cut clearly across class lines and was not confined to upper-class infants, it cannot be imagined that the motives which determined the use of a nurse were necessarily the same at all social levels. While upper-class parents could freely decide how

Table 8.1: Status of Nurses and Nurslings

Note	Name of Nurse	Status of Nurse			Name of Nursling	Status of Nursling			Reference
		slave	freed	freed/freeborn		slave	freed	freed/freeborn	
1	Asinia Victoria			x	Asinia Crispina			x*	1354
2	Aur. Publiana Elpidia			x	L. Septimia Pataviniana …			x*	1516
3	ignota				ignotus				3413
4	Prima		x		Iulia Germanici filia			x*	4352
5	Valeria Zos[i]ma		x		ignotus			x*?	4457
6	Rubria Eutychia			x	Helvia			x ?	5063
7	Iulia Iucunda		x		Drusus, Drusilla			x*	5201
8	Arruntia Cleopatra		x		ignotus			x*?	5939
9	[Clor[n]elia Quinta		x		[L]entulus Cethegus			x*	6072
10	Echonis	x			Statiliae minoris filius			x*	6323
11	Stacte	x			Sisennae f(ilius)			x*	6324
12	Cacia Restituta			x	Ti. Claudius Neothyrsus		x		6686
13	Spurinnia Nice		x		Ti. Iulius Antigonus		x		7290
14	Volusia Philete		x		Volusia Ru———		x		7355
15	Volusia Stratonice		x		L. Volusi…filius			x*	7393
16	Apollonia	x			L. Silanus			x*	7618
17	Botrys	x			[P]ompeia Thallia		x		7741
18	——— Alce		x		Faustina			x*	8941
19	Tatia Baucyl[is]			x	see Table-note			x*	8942
20	Valeria Hilaria		x		Octavia Caesaris Augusti			x*	8943

No.	Name				Name				CIL
21	Rubria Ichmas		x	x	Quinta Barbari filia			x*	9245
22	Asinia Ho ——		x	x	Agrippina			x*	9901b
23	Restituta	x			Acte filia Soterichis (?)	x?			10554
24	[Ae]lia Germana		x	x	divus [Had]rianus			x*	10909
25	Agrilia Comice		x	x	Agrilia Asprenilla			x	11265
26	ignota				L. Apisius . . .			x	12133
27	Naevia Cleopatra	x			Argaeus		x		12299
28	Filete (?)		x	x	Cn. Arrius Agapetus			x	12366
29	Hilara		x	x	Athenais		x		12600
30	Cacilia Marcia			x	ignotus				13683
31	ignota				Claudia Celerana			x	15377
32	Claudia Vitalis		x		Ti. Claudius Sabinianus			x	15655
33	Pedania Alce		x		M. Coelius Ampliatus			x	15952
34	Cornelia Prima			x	Scipio			x*	16128
35	Furia Silvina	x			Ummidianus			x	16329
36	Cornelia Quetula		x		Ti. Cl. Saet(h)ida Cet(h)egus			x*	16440
37	Ser. Cornelia Sabina		x		Ser. Cornelius Dolabella . . .			x*	16450
38	Cornelia Urbana		x		Faust(a)			x*	16470
39	Flavia Helena				A. Crispinus Caepionianus			x*	16587
[40]	Crispina	x			senatores duo			x*	16592
41	Valeria Hygia		x		Emin(e)ns	x	x		17157
42	ignota				Fabianus	x	x		17490
43	Zosime	x			Fab. Silvanus			x	17564
44	Flavia Euphrosyne		x	x	P. Flavius Crescens			x	18032
45	Flavia Nais		x	x	Flavius Gamus			x	18073
46	Hateria Hellas			x	ignotus		x		19155
47	Tryphaena	x			C. Iulius Helenus		x		20042
48	Iunia Glaphyra				Iunius Iulianus			x*	20883
49	Erasena Libas			x	Iuvenalis	x	x		20938
50	ignota				Lasciva	x	x		21151

continued

Table 8.1 continued

Note	Name of Nurse	Status of Nurse			Name of Nursling	Status of Nursling			Reference
		slave	freed	freed/freeborn		slave	freed	freed/freeborn	
[51]	[L]icinnia [P]rocessa		x		Cre[s]cens	x			21347
52	Lucretia Lais		x		ignotus			x*?	21661
53	Lusia Ampelis			x	ignotus				21710
54	Manlia Iucunda		x		Manlia Severa			x	21988
55	Numisia Fort[u]nata			x	Fl. Daphnes filius			x*	23128
56	Fabia Eutychis		x		Paullina			x*	23458
57	Oscia Sabina			x	Threptus	x			23589
58	Philaenis	x			L. Livius			x*	24073
59	Parthenope	x			C.Q. Hermias			x	25301
60	Sabina	x			Martina	x			25728
61	Sextia Thais		x		T. Sextius Magius …			x*	26539
62	Terentia Thisbe		x		Terentia Selicia			x	27262
63	Mellitissima	x			L. Valerius Stachyus			x*?	28120
64	Vatronia Arbuscula		x		Cercenia			x**	28381
65	Volussia Felicla		x		Torquata			x	29550
[66]	Novellia Atticilla			x	Q. Novellius Callinicus	x			34143b
67	Memmia Ephesia			x	Ammonius			x	34383
68	Pumidia Attica		x		A. Cornelius Pumidius Magnus			x	35037
69	Trophime	x			Domitia Felicitas			x	35123

Note: *Nursling of upper-class status. See end of chapter for numbered notes.

to care for their own newborn infants, parents of slave children could not, and the use of a nurse is more likely to have followed from the intervention of a slave-owner. The same is true of freed parents whose children were born into slavery before the parents' manumission, even though the children may subsequently have been set free. Detailed examination of the various categories of nurslings may help to clarify distinctions of motivation in wet-nursing procedures.

There are 11 nurslings who can be classified as slaves, though one of them (no. 51) is best omitted from consideration.[12] Lasciva (no. 50) was certainly a slave, because she is described as *verna* in her inscription, but it is possible that at least some of the remainder were not slaves. They may conceivably have had *nomina* which were identical to those of other individuals mentioned in their respective inscriptions but which were omitted from the stones; thus for instance Argaeus (no. 27) may have been Naevius Argaeus, Eminens (no. 41) may have been Valerius Eminens, and so on. The balance of probability is against this, however, since the appearance of a single name alone often connotes servile status, and so on this basis these nurslings may be considered to form a distinct category.

In three instances the inscription gives only the name of a child who died at an early age and that of the nurse who commemorated the infant (nos. 27, 41, 60): Argaeus, who died in his sixth year, was commemorated by Naevia Cleopatra; Eminens, who died at 11 months, by Valeria Hygia; and Martina, dead in her fourth year, by Sabina. The parents of these children are obviously unknown. It may be that the children needed nurses because their own mothers were already dead, or because they were infants who had been exposed at birth by their parents but who had been reclaimed by slave-owners. Martina, for instance, is called *alumna* by her nurse. Equally, however, their mothers may have been alive but unavailable for nursing.

This last possibility emerges from a group of cases where the names of other people than the nurse and nursling are given in the inscription. The case of Lasciva (no. 50) is of special interest because she was the subject of an unusually long memorial. Her inscription gives the name of her owner, Q. Sulpicius Abascantus, and also refers, but without naming them, to Lasciva's parents, her nurse, and the nurse's husband (*coniunx*). All seem to have been still alive when Lasciva died, in her seventh year, and all (but particularly the nurse's husband) seem to have been deeply affected by the event. It must be the case that Q. Sulpicius Abascantus had provided a nurse for Lasciva, despite her mother's probable availability, and a special circumstance may have been responsible because Lasciva was blind. However, the nurse had breastfed Lasciva and the handicap does not necessarily account for that fact.[13] The age at death of Threptus (no. 57) is not recorded, but he received a memorial from his nurse, Oscia Sabina, and his mother, Lamyra, apparently a slave woman. Again it looks as if Threptus's owner provided a nurse for a child whose mother could theoretically have nursed the child herself, but again a special circumstance may have been at work: Threptus is called *alumnus* in his inscription, and he may thus have been separated from his mother at birth and reared by a nurse in a household different from his mother's.[14]

Athenais (no. 29) was another slave who died in infancy, a little over 1-year-old, and she received a dedication from three people, her nurse, Hilara, her father, Eutychus, and a certain Thesmus, whose relationship to the others is not made clear by the inscription. The absence of the mother's name suggests that she was already dead when the inscription was set up, and if she had died in childbirth a nurse would have been essential for the child's survival. The same consideration might also apply in the case of Ammonius (no. 67), who was commemorated when he died aged 2 by his nurse, Memmia Ephesia, and whose father is known but whose mother is not. But unless the nurses were the *vicariae* of the two fathers, both of whom look like slaves, they must have been found by the owners of the nurslings Athenais and Ammonius. Iuvenalis (no. 49) died in his third year and his inscription was set up by his nurse, Erasena Libas, and his grandmother, Canuleia Tyche, so once more the child's mother is missing and may have predeceased her child. But in none of these instances can it be stated with certainty that the nursling's mother *was* no longer alive when the child died.

In these five examples then a slave appears to have been nursed by a woman other than its mother when the mother was physically available in two instances and perhaps all five. Special circumstances can be invoked to explain the use of the nurse in all the examples, but they are only theoretical circumstances. In all the cases so far considered it is implicit that the owner of the slave nursling wanted the child to be reared and that he thus had a special interest in the child's welfare. Fabianus (no. 42), whose age at death is unattested and who was commemorated just by an anonymous nurse, is a comparable example. It seems therefore that the inscriptions reflect a process at work of slave children being deliberately reared by their owners, a process for which further evidence comes from the cases of freed nurslings who, though free by the time their respective inscriptions were set up, had originally been born into slavery.

Three of the five cases here have been discussed by Treggiari and her views can be summarised. Thus Ti. Claudius Neothyrsus (no. 12), who received a dedication from his own *libertus* Ti. Claudius Stephanus and his nurse Cacia Restituta, was, on the basis of the nurse's different *nomen*, either raised as a child by a woman from a household other than his own, or else raised in one household and then transferred to another where he was manumitted. Similarly Ti. Iulius Antigonus (no. 13) was raised either in the household of the Emperor Tiberius by a nurse, Spurinnia Nice, from a different *familia*, that of the Volusii, or else in the household of the Volusii, before later finding his way into the emperor's *familia*. Volusia Ru—— (no. 14) was nursed by Volusia Philete: 'both nurse and nurseling are now free [i.e. in their inscription], but are likely to have been slaves, and they belong to the same family group.'[15] In none of these three instances is the identity of the nursling's mother known. But Pompeia Thallia (no. 17), who died in her twelfth year, was commemorated not only by her nurse, Botrys, but also by both parents, Martialis and Veneria, all three of whom seem to have been slaves (unless all were Pompeii); apparently a slave child set free before her death was nursed by a slave wet-nurse, and in this instance the nurse's presence cannot be explained away by imagining that the mother died in childbirth. Some other contingency may perhaps have been at work, such as the separation of mother and infant due to sale or inheritance. Finally the inscription of C. Iulius Helenus (no. 47) shows that he made a dedication to his father, Eros, his mother, Zmyrna, and his nurse, Tryphaena. Again all three were slaves, but not imperial slaves, whereas Helenus was *Aug(usti) l(ibertus)* when he set up the dedication. He must therefore have been reared in one household before entering the imperial *familia* where he was set free.[16]

The freed status of the preceding five nurslings can be taken as virtually certain. But there are other nurslings from the freed/freeborn column in the table for whom freed status is probable, but who have been separated from the true *liberti/ae* for safety's sake. If they are regarded as freed, then more evidence accrues for the nursing of slave children. Four nurslings can be considered freed, on the analogy of the Volusiae above (no. 14), because they share a common *nomen* with their nurses, but are not children of upper-class parents: Ti. Claudius Sabinianus, Agrilia Asprenilla, Manlia Severa, Terentia Selicia (nos. 32, 25, 54, 62). The parents of these four are all unattested, so information is limited. Other cases are more complex, but it is possible for example that Cn. Arrius Agapetus, Flavius Gamus, C. Q(uintius) Hermias, and Fabius Silvanus (nos. 28, 45, 59, 43) all started their lives as slaves.[17]

It should not require emphasis that the epigraphical material contains many problems of interpretation. But with all due allowance for its tenuous nature, the conservative conclusion is none the less justified that the *nutrix* inscriptions from Rome provide clear evidence of slave infants who were cared for by women other than their mothers. It would be rash to state that it was always more common for slave infants to be breastfed by wet-nurses than by their mothers. Nor should it be true of necessity that the servile proportion of all nurslings in Rome at any one time was the same as that in evidence here. But among the nurslings available from the *nutrix* inscriptions slave children comprise an element sufficiently significant to warrant investigation of the factors controlling the process.

Some of those factors have indeed been touched on in the description of specific cases above. The provision of a nurse for a slave infant may have been due to the very practical reason that the child's mother had died while giving birth or soon thereafter, so that a nurse was vital for the child's survival. Yet although maternal death in childbirth was common in antiquity, it would be unrealistic to believe that maternal death was always the cause of using a wet-nurse for a slave child. Separation of the child from its mother following exposure or transfer of slave property from one household to another will also have made the nurse a practical necessity. In addition some mothers may have found themselves physically or emotionally unable to nurse their children. Plutarch (*De liberis educandis* 5) was able to justify recourse to a wet-nurse if the mother was too weak to breastfeed her infant, for example, and such debilitation is as likely to have affected slave mothers as the upper-class women to whom Plutarch referred. The mother's milk supply may have been inadequate,[18] while a slave woman whose pregnancy was the outcome of sexual abuse by a *dominus* or the son of a *dominus* may have been psychologically unable to cope with her child once born, but predictably there is no evidence to corroborate this speculation.

It is possible then to enumerate reasons of expedience which controlled the wet-nursing of slave infants, but as was noted above behind reasoning of this sort there lies the implication that slave-owners were concerned to ensure that their slave children had a decent chance of survival and that it was thus to their advantage to create that opportunity. Humanitarianism may of course have played a part here but, given the ubiquitous practice of infant exposure in antiquity, the nursing of slave infants cannot be explained solely by recourse to the notion that every infant had a right to survival;[19] rather profit, or potential profit, was involved. Accordingly, it can be proposed that slave-owners' provision of wet-nurses for infant slaves is to be related to the process of slave-breeding, visible in the early Empire if not earlier.

Slave-breeding is a difficult subject to define because conceptually it conjures up a picture of systematic, coerced human reproduction comparable to the breeding of livestock. Such an image is hard to accept, because whereas the reproduction of livestock can be manipulated with a fair degree of control, human reproduction, even in a slave society, cannot be contrived with an equal measure of control. Consequently perhaps the most that can be said is that slave-owners were able to encourage rather than compel reproduction among their slave property. Nevertheless it is unquestionable that by the early imperial period natural increase had become an important means of providing new slaves at Rome, and that slave-breeding (in a loose sense) contained advantages for slave-owners beyond a simple increase of numbers:

Despite high infant mortality, it was probably much more economical to breed slaves than to buy adults. . . . *Vernae* were thought to be, and probably were, more attached to their

owner's family; they might have close family ties of their own
within the *familia*, and they could be trained to suit the
owner's tastes and needs. . . . If a *dominus* purchased slaves
from a dealer or private owner, he ran the risk of making a
bad bargain and getting a slave who had some disease or
vice — and even though he returned him to the seller, he
still had to find a slave. Or, no doubt more commonly, he
acquired a new slave, *novicius*, docile but ignorant, or a slave
already trained in some other employment, *veteranus*, who
would have to be re-formed to suit his own needs. *Vernae*
were much more attractive.[20]

It is a fact, however, that once *vernae* had been born they had
to be cared for. Yet scant attention has been paid to this aspect
of slave-breeding in scholarly discussions of the subject, so that it
can be assumed without question that slave mothers usually took
charge of their own infants. Thus Ste Croix, arguing the view that
slave-breeding lowered the general rate of servile productivity,
states that slave women 'at least will have part of their time and
energy diverted from normal work to bearing *and rearing*
children', even though he recognises that 'many slave mothers
will die in childbirth'.[21] But the slave-owner interested in
acquiring *vernae* must have been aware that he risked potential
loss of one slave, the mother, if he encouraged breeding; he must
have been aware that the mother's 'normal work' would be
interrupted once her child was born, whether she survived or not;
and he must have been aware that the newborn infant had to be
looked after. The *dominus* may thus have considered it far more
efficient for the child of one slave woman to be nursed by another
who had already given birth (and thereby already increased the
stock of *vernae*) so that as small a number of women as possible
were 'diverted' from their usual occupations. Moreover, while
the care of a nurse for an infant whose mother did not survive
childbirth was essential to protect the owner's interest in his new
property, separation of an infant from a mother who did survive
not only allowed her to return to work quickly but also increased
the chances that she would conceive again sooner than if she
nursed the child herself: the contraceptive effect of lactation was
appreciated in antiquity because Plutarch gives as another reason
for the use of a wet-nurse the mother's wish to have more
children.[22]

By the judicious use of nurses therefore the *dominus* could guarantee care for infants whose mothers were dead, and for infants whose mothers survived childbirth but who could be put back to work quickly, and he also increased the possibilities of further reproduction among surviving women. All of this was clearly to his advantage. It does not follow that slaves were deprived of all contact with their infants, since if nurse and parents belonged to the same household no great physical separation was involved. But there may have been greater emotional separation than the parents wished for and the nurse herself, when a slave, may often have had no choice in the matter of nursing a foster-child. It needs to be emphasised here that among the nurses known from the inscriptions there is none who was definitely freeborn: all were, had been, or could have been slaves, and their job of nursing depended on the owner's capacity to turn the circumstances of the nurses' own recent delivery to his further benefit. Such signs of compulsion in the lives of slaves, especially with regard to their familial ties, were not unique to the process of infant care as reconstructed here, but were characteristic of the whole manipulative nature of both slave-breeding in particular, and the Roman slavery system in general. As such, they provide little evidence for the display towards slaves of disinterested humanitarian attitudes on the part of owners.[23]

III

Nurslings of upper-class status constitute the largest group of all nurslings in the *nutrix* inscriptions, and it would seem that more often than not their nurses were family freedwomen or slaves. This is perfectly clear for example in the case of Prima (no. 4), the nurse of Julia Livilla and a *liberta* by the time her inscription was set up; or in the case of Valeria Hilaria (no. 2), the nurse of Octavia, also freed by the time of her death. It can be taken that a nurse whose *nomen* derived from the upper-class family for which she worked was a servile member of the household, such as Cornelia Sabina (no. 37), the nurse of Ser. Cornelius Dolabella Metilianus Pompeius Marcellus, cos. 133; or Cornelia Prima (no. 34), *nutrix Scipionis*, or Cornelia Quetula (no. 36) who nursed Ti. Claudius Saethida Cethegus Frontinus. Some nurses of course may have been hired by upper-class parents. It has been suggested that Tatia Baucylis (no. 19), the nurse of Flavia Domitilla's children, was a freeborn mercenary nurse,[24] and other nurses whose *nomina* seem not to derive from the families for which they worked may also have been mercenary *ingenuae* or *libertae* working independently after emancipation. A probable nurse not included in the table, a woman named Aurelia Soteris, perhaps falls into this category. She turns up in no less than three inscriptions, together with a male companion, Mussius Chrysonicus. The couple described themselves as *nutritores lactanei* in dedications they set up to nurslings of upper-class background, but whose names are different from their own, Gellia Agrippiana, *clarissima puella*, Q. Licinius Q. fil. Florus Octavianus, *eques Romanus*, and Licinia Q. f. Lampetia Basilioflora, perhaps the sister of Florus Octavianus.[25] Mussius Chrysonicus's role as *nutritor lactaneus* can only be guessed at; he may have fed infants from a bottle, though the evidence that bottle-feeding was practised at all is very slender,[26] or he may simply have assisted the nurse proper in such tasks as dressing, changing and bathing the children they looked after. Other plain *nutritores* are well attested.[27] In any case the hiring of nurses is in evidence from literary sources, as well as a passage from the *Digest* which refers to disputes over wages for wet-nursing services (*nutricia*), while the *columna lactaria* may have been a spot at Rome where nurses for hire could be found when needed.[28] It must have happened at times that even in large *familiae* slave or ex-slave lactating mothers were not to be found.

Whether a family servant or a mercenary, however, a wet-nurse seems commonly to have fed and looked after infants of upper-class parentage in Roman society of the classical period, despite criticism hurled against wet-nursing from other upper-class quarters. Plutarch objected because wet-nursing prevented emotional bonding between mother and child.[29] Favorinus agreed, and added the argument that it had a corrupting influence on children, especially if the nurse was a foreign slave woman, because the nurse's milk transmitted her moral characteristics to the child.[30] The corruptive opinion was shared by Quintilian (1.1.4-5) and Tacitus (*Dialogus* 29.1), perhaps less for biological reasons than as a result of sheer snobbery. Moreover, complaints about the inadequacy of nurses are heard which cannot be totally unrealistic even if some of them come from jaundiced authors. It was not just a question of morality, the fact that the nurse, as Favorinus says, might be dishonest, ugly(!), unchaste or a drunk; she might also be negligent, from drunkenness, ill-temper or religious devotions, not properly exercised, her diet all wrong, so that the child was not properly fed, its swaddling bands, on the foul odour of which Soranus could comment, not changed often enough; thus the infant might suffocate or be strangled while nursing or sleeping in the nurse's bed.[31] Soranus, indeed, who cannot be accused of having an excessively moralistic bias, counsels that for the sake of the child's proper care the nurse should not be permitted to drink or to have sexual intercourse; and the wet-nursing contracts from Roman Egypt similarly stipulate that the nurse must take good care of herself and the nursling, that she must not nurse other infants or have intercourse or become pregnant.[32] Such regulations suggest that meticulous child-care could not automatically be counted on when a child was entrusted to a wet-nurse, and in this regard Soranus's remark on Rome itself is of particular note: 'For the women in this city,' he says, 'do not possess sufficient devotion to look after everything as the purely Grecian women do' (*Gynaecology* 2.44).

Why then, if the dangers, both moral and practical, could be so articulately stated, was the practice of wet-nursing maintained at Rome? One simple solution could be that those who voiced opposition were in a very small minority and so were unrepresentative of upper-class feeling at large. But even with allowance made for the repetition of conventional platitudes, the chronological range of the opposition seems against this. A second solution could be found in the same reasons of expedience that were formulated *à propos* of slave nurslings: a mother may have died in childbirth or have been emotionally or physically unable to nurse, as was perhaps the case with Plutarch's wife who underwent some form of breast surgery after nursing one of her own children.[33] It happens to be recorded that L. Iunius Silanus Torquatus, the probable nursling of Apollonia (no. 16), was raised in the house of an aunt and so his mother (who is unknown) may have died when he was born.[34] Vanity, moreover, may have induced a woman to use a wet-nurse if she wanted not to disfigure herself or to restrict her social activities.[35]

At a deeper level, however, aristocratic mentality may have played a part. The essential purpose of the Roman grandee's *familia* after all was to perform certain kinds of service which by social convention the aristocrat could not perform himself, and in a society where the *dominus* or *domina* did not and did not expect to labour for their economic support or maintenance wet-nursing could be regarded as a form of work which the upper-class women often considered outside the limits of what she should or could properly do.[36] To this extent (and despite moralistic arguments to encourage emotional bonding between mother and child) wet-nursing was a consequence of the hierarchical structure of Roman society in which the élite exploited the labour of the less privileged to their own narrow advantage.

But a further possibility is also raised or implied by the evidence. Was wet-nursing practised or largely unopposed because the Roman élite were indifferent to the welfare of their children in early infancy? Was there in Roman society a general lack of concern for newborn infants and avoidance of emotional commitment until the children had provided some evidence of durability by surviving through their first two or three years? These questions are important not only because their answers might help explain wet-nursing as a social phenomenon, but also because in turn they have implications for Roman conceptions of the role of the family in upper-class society.

Infant death in antiquity was a part of everyday reality. Epitaphs set up by nurses to their nurslings who died at tender ages would be sufficient proof of this, even if there were no other evidence. It is therefore not at all surprising to find statements in literary sources which suggest that there was widespread indifference to young children, whose lives might end at virtually any moment. Plutarch for example wrote of the excessive grief some mothers demonstrated when their children died, grief which was without justification since they expended no effort in looking after the children while alive (*Consolatio ad uxorem* 6). In Tacitus's *Dialogus* (28.4-29.2) the orator Messalla contrasted the old custom whereby the aristocratic mother reared her own son with the contemporary use of the nurse and disreputable slaves, the result of which was a breakdown of moral standards in children. And Favorinus had to deal with the contention that it did not matter who nursed a child as long as someone (i.e. other than the mother) did (Aulus Gellius 12.1.10).[37] Behind such passages as these it would not be unreasonable to postulate a basis of parental indifference to children, while a letter written by Seneca, presenting the argument that a parent who has lost a child should exhibit restrained grief only, because the loss of a son is far less a calamity than the loss of a friend, is much more explicit (*Letters* 99).

Seneca's letter consists of advice supposedly given to a certain Marullus whose son had recently died and whose consequent grief he thought extreme. Seneca does not reach the point of maintaining that no grief at all should be felt, but in urging the usefulness of philosophy as its antidote his tone is detached and far from sympathetic. The boy, he says, might eventually have amounted to something but would probably have turned out a disappointment to his father; and Marullus will have been well served by philosophy if he is able to bear with courage the loss of a boy better known to his nurse than his father. The implication that the *nutrix* was closer to the child than the parent here is as interesting as the harshness of Seneca's attitude in the letter as a whole.[38]

It could be objected at once, however, that there are many passages from literature in total contrast to those mentioned above, passages which suggest true parental attachment to children and which express genuine emotion, especially in the circumstances of children's deaths. Marullus quite clearly had reacted to his loss far differently from the manner advocated by the dispassionate Seneca. The younger Pliny could write sarcastically of M. Aquilius Regulus's display of grief when his son died (though Pliny redeemed himself slightly by remarking that even a political enemy did not deserve to lose his son); and Pliny wrote also of the feelings of C. Minicius Fundanus on the death of his daughter Minicia Marcella.[39] There is no reason to doubt in either case that parental sadness was attributable to affection for the lost children. Earlier Cicero was deeply affected by the death of his daughter, Tullia.[40] Nevertheless a qualification must be attached to these examples because they concern deaths not of infants but of older children, and so, although their parents' emotional response need not be minimised, the response itself was conditioned not only by affection for the child concerned but also by the parents' unfulfilled hopes of what the child might have accomplished for the family in upper-class society at large. The Emperor Nero reacted with deep emotion first to the birth of his daughter by Poppaea and then to her almost immediate death (Tacitus, *Annals* 15.23), but this was not just an excess of sentiment: the two events respectively raised and dashed hopes for the continuation of the Julio-Claudian dynasty. Pliny records that when Minicia Marcella died she was already betrothed (at the age of 14) to an *egregius iuvenis*; and that Regulus had already emancipated his son from *patria potestas* so that the boy could inherit his mother's estate and preserve the family control of property.[41] Ser. Sulpicius consoled Cicero with the argument that Tullia had died at a time when the prospects of a brilliant marriage and of bearing sons to maintain the family property and to enter public life were overshadowed by the demise of political freedom.[42] Behind all of this the conjunction of parental affection and aristocratic preoccupation with family repute and wealth is clear; the kinds of interest, that is, which made adoption of adult heirs so prominent an aspect of Roman upper-class life. If indifference to children is lacking, concern was not based on love alone.

The complexity of upper-class parental attitudes towards children is illustrated particularly well by Plutarch's sensitive essay *Consolatio ad uxorem*, a work written on the death of his two-year-old daughter, Timoxena, the third of his children to die in childhood.[43] While Plutarch's love for the girl is unmistakable, his description of her with her nurse reads more like a description of an adult than of a two-year-old, and it forms a contrast with another passage in which Plutarch makes the point that the lack of fulfilment in Timoxena's life should not be regretted since, as a child, she had no conception of the course her adult life would have taken. Even so, Plutarch and his wife were clearly troubled that Timoxena had not lived long enough to marry and to have children; their affection for their daughter was bound up with their own traditional expectations of her. Finally Plutarch counsels demonstration of the restrained grief he says was conventional in his own society at the loss of an infant, because excessive grief was unnecessary for one who had barely belonged to society. Here the interplay of parental love with both concern for the future of the family and suppression of grief comes through, demonstrating the intricacy of affective attitudes to children at the upper levels of Graeco-Roman society.[44]

Those attitudes then were governed by factors of natural affection and anticipation of children's new contributions to the family's traditions, accomplishments and prestige, and they constitute evidence against the possibility of widespread indifference towards children in upper-class society. Further evidence comes from recognition of the concept of parental, and especially maternal love in the works of those authors who had something to say about the ills of wet-nursing. Favorinus believed in the existence of *materna flagrantia*, which he thought threatened with extinction if a mother gave her child to a nurse, and Plutarch believed that maternal breastfeeding brought a natural increase of *philostorgia*. As part of an argument to prove the affective tie between mother and child, he maintained that a mother had to love her newborn infant because she was the only one willing to handle such a repulsive, distasteful object.[45] Moreover, *amor maternus* could be characteristic of the ideal wife and mother when her virtues were enumerated for posterity.[46] Yet a reservation must still persist, for when Plutarch contended further that children were reared out of love and not because their parents were anticipating their children's future utilitarian value, and when Favorinus argued for the preservation of motherly love through breastfeeding, both were obviously pleading cases which were not self-evident; otherwise their arguments would have been superfluous.[47] The death of a child before his parents could be regarded as contrary to nature,[48] but such an unnatural event could easily become part of any parent's experience and indifference might easily result.

The conditions which caused a high death rate among infants, particularly in the city, are easily stated: poor hygiene, dietary insufficiencies, uncontrolled disease, inadequate medical knowlege.[49] In addition, child-care practices associated with the nurse may also have made a contribution. Premastication by the nurse of solid food for weaned infants for instance was far from hygienic, but was apparently a common procedure.[50] The ubiquitous use of swaddling-bands may or may not have retarded the child's physical development by restricting the movement of limbs; but while the child's passivity which resulted from the lowered heart beat and confinement was convenient for the nurse, the infant could simply stew in its own excrement unless the bands were changed frequently.[51] Since the women who nursed the children of upper-class status seem mainly to have belonged to the parents' *familiae*, and since there is little sign that children were boarded out away from the city (as happened extensively in France in a later period of history), presumably the mother was able, if she wished, to scrutinise and to exercise some control over the care given to her child.[52] But the child's chances of survival were not necessarily improved if the mother cared for her own infant because status could not bring immunity against disease or significant improvements in hygiene. Nor was there any guarantee that the mother would be less negligent than the nurse. The factors which led to a high death rate among infants were subject to little or no control, and it would be logical to conclude that wet-nursing of upper-class children resulted from parental indifference to children whose survival had largely been left to chance.

On balance, however, there is perhaps too much evidence against the parental indifference view to make this conclusion justifiable, no matter how complex parental feelings towards children were. Wet-nursing was practised extensively among the upper classes, and while not every relationship between child and mother will ultimately have resembled that between Nero and Agrippina a certain distancing impact must often have made itself felt. It is within this area of class mentality that perhaps the best explanation for the prevalence of wet-nursing is to be found, therefore, because the custom provided parents with a mechanism which operated against the over-investment of emotion in their children, or a cushion against the foreseeable loss of children and the accompanying emotional trauma. By driving a wedge between parent and child, wet-nursing fulfilled for the parent a self-protective function, diminishing the degree and impact of injury in the event of loss in a society where such loss was commonly experienced (cf. Stone 1979:83).

IV

To maintain the view that wet-nursing of upper-class children gave their parents an emotional safeguard is to strengthen the case for seeing the wet-nurse in Roman society as an exploited commodity. To the aspect of physical manipulation seen earlier now has to be added the dimension of emotional exploitation because as surrogate parent the nurse was forced into a relationship with a child by virtue of her inferior status. It is clear not least from the *nutrix* inscriptions that the relationship between nurse and nursling was sometimes close and warm, enduring at times far beyond the nursling's early years. An adult nursling could commemorate with an epitaph a *nutrix merens, pientissima, carissima*, or *dulcissima*, and a nurse could commemorate a child who was *dulcissima et amantissima* or *dulcissimus*.[53] Literary sources offer further material. The nurses of both Nero and Domitian took care to dispose properly of the remains of their former nurslings when they died, many years of course after the actual time of nursing, and the devotion implicit in their actions is quite remarkable.[54] The younger Pliny gave his nurse a small farm to guarantee her economic support in old age, a generous and kindly act which presupposes affection between nurse and nursling maintained across time.[55] In a more generalised way the nurse becomes in literature the symbolic comforter figure, telling stories to her nursling, rocking the cradle and singing the child to sleep,[56] and from evidence of this sort some historians have constructed an almost romantic view of the parent–child–nurse triangle, and have given a view of the urban *familia* as a secure and comfortable world, free from the tensions and strains that might otherwise be expected in the master–slave relationship. Thus, at the birth of Julia Livilla, 'Livia and Tiberius jointly supplied a *nutrix* for Germanicus' daughter. . . . As befitted her position of trust and familiarity with a child of the imperial house, she was freed.'[57] The nurse was Prima (no. 4), certainly a freedwoman in her inscription, though not necessarily so when she first became Livilla's nurse. However, the evidence of affective terminology in the inscriptions and of literary anecdotes cannot be taken to give a truly representative picture of relationships between nurse and nursling because it is subject to a fundamental weakness: there is no means of establishing its typicality. In terms of sheer probability negative or neutral relationships are likely to have been as common as the positive ones attested. But nurses who had no concern for their nurslings and nurslings who had no affection for their nurses have left no commemorative evidence of their attitudes, and so it cannot be simply assumed that the nurse's relationship with a child was always warm and loving. Whatever the measure of sentiment involved it has to be stressed that, within the world of the *nutrix* inscriptions and supporting literary material examined here, all relationships between nurse and nursling had compulsive origins: the wish of a slave-owner to maximise the potential of newborn *vernae* or foundlings, or the refusal or inability of an upper-class mother to take direct responsibility for her child's early care. As far as can be told, the nurse herself, whether Prima or anyone else, had little choice in the matter of whom she nursed or if she nursed, and it might be imagined that she regarded a new infant as a nuisance as often as she welcomed it. Above all her availability as a nurse depended on her subject, inferior status and her manipulation by a superior party: that element of manipulation and the constraints upon freedom it brought cannot be glossed over by the superimposition of a veneer of historical romanticism.[58]

Notes

1. Plutarch, *De liberis educandis* 5; *Consolatio ad uxorem* 5-6; *De amore prolis* 3-4. Although *De lib. educ.* is spurious, I shall refer to it here as Plutarch's composition for the sake of convenience; the views on mothering it contains are consistent with Plutarch's ideas elsewhere.

2. Cicero, *Tusculanae disputationes* 3.1-2; Tacitus, *Germania* 20.1. Lucretius, 5.222-230, took for granted the presence of a *nutrix* with the newborn infant, and Quintilian, 1.1.4-5, assumed that it was a matter of course for the infant to be in the charge of *nutrices*.

3. CIL 6,19128, 'Graxiae Alexandriae insignis exempli ac pudicitiae, quae etiam filios suos propriis uberibus educavit. Pudens Aug. lib. maritus merenti, vix, ann. XXIIII m. III d. XVI.'

4. I use the phrase 'classical period' to mean late Republic and early Empire.

5. I shall use the word 'nursling', again for the sake of convenience, even if the person who was nursed was an adult by the time a particular epitaph was set up.

6. For *nutrix* as wet-nurse, see *Thesaurus Linguae Latinae* (*TLL*) s.v.; among clear examples note (in addition to Cicero, Tacitus and Favorinus above) Propertius 4.1.55-66; D.50.13.1.14; cf. Nisbet and Hubbard (1970:271), 'a *nutrix* was primarily a wet-nurse'. For *assa nutrix*, see Scholion on Juvenal 14.208, *assa nutrix dicitur, quae lac non praestat infantibus, sed solum diligentiam et munditiam adhibet*. Cf. *CIL* 6.29497. The word *altrix* could also be used for wet-nurse, as at Aulus Gellius 12.1.20 and Columella, *De re rustica* 3.10.16, *velut altricis uberibus eductus*, but is less common and does not appear in *CIL* 6; cf. *TLL* s.v. Greek accommodated the distinction between wet-nurse and nursemaid with the terms τίτθη, τιτθήνη and τροφός; cf. *RAL* I, 381.

7. See Weaver (1972:42-92); Treggiari (1975a:393-4; 1981b *passim*); and n. 58 below.

8. The inscriptions are all from *CIL* 6 and are referred to in Table 9.1 by serial number alone. A few fragmentary or otherwise unclear examples have been omitted. For reasons given in table notes 40, 51, 66, three items are questionable, but they have been included for the sake of completeness.

9. Plutarch, *Cato the Elder* 20.3.

10. Soranus, *Gynaecology* 2.25; Juvenal 6.352-4. (À *propos* of *nutricem* here Courtney (1980:303) comments: 'The presence of this old family servant implies a respectable old family.' But it seems clear that Ogulnia hires [*conducit*] a mercenary nurse, not that the nurse belongs to Ogulnia's *familia*.) Cf. Aulus

Gellius 12.1.17, where Favorinus also mentions the servile status of the nurse. See also below p. 214 and n. 28.

11. *Germania* 20.1; *Dialogus* 28.4-29.2.
12. See Table - note 51.
13. Lasciva's inscription (21151) is best given in full:

Lasciva verna Q. Sulpici Abascanti, quae nondum septem [vitae] compleverat annos, quae caruit luce et tenebris se miscuit atris. Lasciva nimium fatis crudelibus orta est. liquit et orbatos miseros fidosque parentes, uberibus pressis nutricem liquit amantem. coniunx nutricis infelix ille relictus maeret et ad cineres plangit sua pectora palmis, nec satis ereptam lucem sibi.

For 'uberibus pressis' cf. Propertius 2.34.70 which I owe to J.G. Fitch.

14. The possibility that Threptus was a foundling is supported by his name, but the term *alumnus* does not necessarily connote this. There is always an ambiguity involved, since a foster-child need not have been a foundling. Cf. Sherwin-White (1966:650-1).
15. See Treggiari (1976:88) and Table - note 13.
16. See also Table - note 8 on L. Arruntius Dicaeus.
17. See Table - notes 28, 45, 59, 43, and n. 58 below.
18. *RAL* I, 381.
19. On infant exposure see Harris (1980:123). Soranus (*Gynaecology* 2.12) assumed that infants had no inherent right to be reared, but was amazingly punctilious about the care of those worth preservation.
20. Treggiari (1979b:188). On slave-breeding in general, see Harris (1980: 118-21); Ste Croix (1981:229-37). Note also Plautus, *Miles* 698, 'nutrici non missuru's quicquam, quae vernas alit?', which is suggestive.
21. Ste Croix (1981:231), my emphasis.
22. *De liberis educandis* 5, which seems not to be commented on by Hopkins (1965b).
23. On the lack of humanity in ancient slavery, see Finley (1980:93-122), arguing against the apologists. See further below.
24. Treggiari (1976:88). See Table - note 19.
25. *CIL* 6.1424; 1623; 21334. On independent freedmen in general see Garnsey (1981).
26. Etienne (1976:149-50).
(Editor's note: The Classics Museum at the A.N.U., Canberra, contains a clay infant-feeder: see the catalogue *Antiquities*, published by the A.N.U. 1981, item 66.39.)
27. Cf. Bonner (1977:41); *CIL* 6, Index s.v. 'nutritor'.
28. See n. 10 above; D.50.13.1.4; Platner and Ashby (1929), s.v. 'columna lactaria'.
29. *De liberis educandis* 5; cf. also Soranus, *Gynaecology* 2.18.
30. Aulus Gellius 12.1.17-23; cf. Soranus, *Gynaecology* 2.19; Macrobius, *Saturnalia* 5.11.15-18.
31. Aulus Gellius 12.1.17; Sextus Empiricus, *Contra rhetores* 2.42; Soranus, *Gynaecology* 2.19, 24, 25-26, 37, 38.
32. Soranus, *Gynaecology* 2.19. See the contract references collected in Bradley (1980), to which add van Lith (1974:145ff).
33. Plutarch, *Consolatio ad uxorem* 5.
34. Tacitus, *Annals* 15.52; 16.7. See Table - note 16.
35. Aulus Gellius 12.1.8; Juvenal 6.352-4 (cf. n. 10 above).
36. On attitudes to work see Finley (1973:40-60).
37. The subject of indifference to children in pre-modern societies appears in Ariès 1962 (on which see Vann 1982:279-97), and is taken up by, for example,

Shorter (1977), Stone (1979) and Degler (1980). It has received little attention from ancient historians, though note Etienne (1976:144) on 'indifference regarding the sick child'.

38. See especially *Letters* 99.2, 12-13, 14. Marullus was probably the Q. Iunius Marullus of Tacitus, *Annals* 14.48 (PIR^2 I 769); cf. Griffin (1976:92).

39. *Letters* 4.2; 4.7; 5.16.

40. Cicero, *Ad familiares* 4.5; 4.6.

41. *Letters* 5.16.6; 4.2.4. Minicia Marcella's age at death is given as almost 13 by *CIL* 6.16631; cf. Sherwin-White (1966:347).

42. Cicero, *Ad familiares* 4.5.3. Cf. 5.16.

43. For Timoxena's age, Plutarch, *Consolatio ad uxorem* 8. On the work and Plutarch's family, see Russell (1973:5-6, 78-9, 90); Martin and Phillips (1978:394-441); cf. Jones (1971:26-7). On consolation literature in general, see Kassel (1958) and Johann (1968).

44. See especially Plutarch, *Consolatio ad uxorem* 2, 3, 9, 11.

45. Aulus Gellius 12.1.22; Plutarch, *Consolatio ad uxorem* 5; *De amore prolis* 3.

46. *CIL* 6.10230, lines 4-5.

47. Plutarch *De amore prolis passim*; Aulus Gellius 12.1.21-3. On the history of the utilitarian reason for procreation, see Lambert (1982).

48. See Lattimore (1942:187-90).

49. See Brunt (1966; 1971a:135-6). The description of basic living conditions given for sixteenth- and seventeenth-century England by Thomas (1980:3-24) is relevant at many points for antiquity.

50. Cicero, *De oratore* 2.162; Sextus Empiricus, *Contra rhetores* 2.42; Soranus, *Gynaecology* 2.46.

51. On the effects of swaddling see Shorter (1977:196-9); Stone (1979:115); for swaddling in antiquity, see Etienne (1976:145-6) with accompanying photographs, and especially Soranus, *Gynaecology* 2.14-15 and 2.42, where two months is said to be the most conventional length of time for maintaining the practice.

52. Treggiari (1979b:189-90) presents the view that *vernae* from urban households were boarded out in the country in sufficient numbers for the procedure to be recognised by the Roman jurists though she hesitates to call this 'a general practice'. Further investigation is necessary. But one would imagine that the practice increased the incidence of wet-nursing among slave children; unless all the mothers were transported out of the city also, which is unlikely. Even so, there is no evidence that children of upper-class status were similarly boarded out. For France, see Shorter (1977:175-90).

53. See the inscriptions of items no. 1, 2, 27, 32, 48, 51 in Table 8.1; and cf. the affective terminology of the *contubernales* inscriptions collected by Treggiari (1981b:59).

54. Suetonius, *Nero* 50; *Domitian* 17.3.

55. Pliny, *Letters* 6.3.1.

56. Persius 3.18, 2.39; Tibullus 1.3.85; Lucretius 5.230; Galen, *De sanitate tuenda* 1.8; Horace, *Epistles* 1.4.8; Lucian, *Hermotimos* 82; cf. *RAL* I, 383.

57. Treggiari (1975b:56); cf. Vogt (1975:105-9). The quotation from Treggiari contrasts strongly with the human manipulation implicit in the quotation given at pp. 211-2 above.

58. It must be emphasised finally that the attribution of status given in the Table for both nurses and nurslings is often arguable, so that although plausible interpretations are offered the results must be considered tentative at most in many instances. It might well be the case that certain nurses (e.g. nos. 21, 65) considered family *libertae* were in actuality freeborn descendants of such, and that certain nurslings considered ex-slaves (e.g. nos 25, 32, 54,62) were also freeborn

descendants of former slaves. Thus caution is necessary. However, despite the uncertainties, nursing of infants at the upper and lower levels of Roman society is still visible. If it then becomes necessary to add wet-nursing at an 'intermediate' social level, the same reasons of expedience and self-protection for parents of moderate means may still apply. Similarly, service for the household from which freedom had first been gained by a freeborn nurse descended from slaves still points to personal constraint, though perhaps less intensively than with slaves and ex-slaves themselves.

I should like to express my thanks to Samuel E. Scully and Susan M. Treggiari for their generous comments on an earlier version of this chapter.

Notes to Table 8.1

1. Asinia Crispina is styled 'c(larissima) f(emina)' on her inscriptions and was thus of senatorial status; but nothing else of her is known; cf. *PIR*² A 1258. The nurse was evidently a family freedwoman.
2. The nursling's full name is L. Septimia Pataviniana Balbilla Tyria Nepotilla Odaenathiana; cf. *PLRE* I s.v. She is styled 'c(larissima) p(uella)' in her inscription and was thus of senatorial status, and was also her nurse's patron. But the nurse may have been freed following Caracalla's extension of the citizenship in 212, or even have been freeborn. Clearly her *nomen* did not derive from the nursling's family.
3. An anonymous nurse appears here, unless conceivably she was the 'Ulpia M. lib.' mentioned on the inscription.
4. Prima is styled an imperial freedwoman in her inscription (despite the appearance of only one name). The nursling is Julia Livilla, the youngest daughter of Germanicus; cf. *PIR*² I 674; Treggiari 1976: 88, who believes the nurse was inherited by Tiberius and Livia from Augustus.
5. Cf. Treggiari (1976:102, n. 40): 'Zosima may owe her *nomen* to Messalla (son of Marcella the younger) or to his daughter, Valeria Messallina.' The inscription does not give the nursling's name, but it was perhaps Marcella's son or granddaughter, or perhaps a member of the family which freed her apparent husband, M. Aemilius Paulli l. Demetrius; cf. Treggiari (1976:102, n. 40); *PIR*² A 396; C 1103. Alternatively it is possible that she nursed slave children in an upper-class household.
6. The phrase 'nutrici Helviae' is used on the inscription to identify Rubria Eutychia, which on the analogy of similar examples (e.g. no. 7, 'Iulia Iucunda nutrix Drusi et Drusillae'; no. 65, 'Volussiae Feliclae Torquataes nutrix') may mean that Helvia was a Rubria Helvia of upper-class status; but no suitable Rubria Helvia is attested.
7. Cf. Treggiari (1976:102, n. 39): 'Drusus was born in 7, Drusilla probably in 16. Iucunda is freed and derives her *nomen* from a Julius or Julia, who could be either of the children, or Germanicus or Tiberius or Livia.'
8. Arruntia is styled 'l(iberta)' on her inscription and she is recorded together with L. Arruntius L.l. Dicaeus *conlacteus*. The couple were perhaps the ex-slaves of L. Arruntius, cos. 6 (cf. *PIR*² A 1130), who, or whose child, may have been the nursling. If Arruntia nursed the consul, Dicaeus may have been her son. But again she may conceivably have nursed slave children in the household. Dicaeus must be regarded as a home-bred slave in any case.
9. The nursling's name appears in his inscription as '[L]entulus Cethegus'; he should be a relative of Ser. Cornelius Cethegus, cos. 24, or is perhaps that very man; *PIR*² C 1388. ']orelia Quinta', the reading of the text, is thus obviously

Cornelia Quinta and his, or his father's, *liberta*.
10. The nursling belongs to the family of the Statilii Tauri; cf. *RE* III A, 2 col. 2208.
11. The nursling was probably son of Sisenna Statilius Taurus, cos. 16, cf. *RE* III A, 2 col. 2207; Treggiari (1976:103, n. 42). The inscription commemorates his *conlacteus*, Atticus, Stacte's son, who died aged 4 and who seems to have predeceased the nursling.
12. See further below.
13. Cf. Treggiari (1976:88-9): 'Ti. Iulius Antigonus (a freedman of Tiberius or a freedman or son of a freedman deriving his name from Tiberius) is the son-in-law of a Volusian domestic and the nurseling of Spurinnia Nice. . . . If Amati really saw "*Torquatianae*" on the stone. . . . Nice will then have belonged at one stage of her life to a Torquata, apparently wife of Q. Volusius, consul in 56. She was subsequently freed by a Spurinnius or Spurinnia.'
14. See further below.
15. The nursling appears in the inscription as 'L. Volusi L. f. Saturnini ponti. f'. The *pontifex* is son of L. Volusius Saturninus, cos. 3; cf. *RE* Supp. IX col. 1862; Treggiari (1976:103, n. 43). The nurse was clearly a family freedwoman; her son L. Volusius Zosimus married a woman named Tampia Priscilla.
16. The nursling appears in his inscriptions as 'L. Silani M. f.' and is perhaps the L. Iunius Silanus Torquatus who was put to death under Nero; cf. *PIR*[2] I 838; *RE* X, 1 col. 1105.
17. See further below.
18. Alce is likely to have been a freedwoman, since she appears on her inscription as 'a]e Alce.' But the *nomen* is clearly unknown. The nursling could be the wife of either Antoninus Pius or Marcus Aurelius; cf. *PIR*[2] A 715; A 716; Treggiari (1976:103, n. 45).
19. According to the restored inscription, Tatia nursed the 'septem lib[erorum proneptum] divi Vespasian[i, filiorum Fl. Clementis et] Flaviae Domitil[lae uxoris eius, divi] Vespasiani neptis.' Cf. Treggiari (1976:103, n. 44), 'Tatia as a gentile name is rare in Roman annals after T. Tatius, but occurs in the urban inscriptions of humble people. Baucyl—— may be a variant of *Baúkalos* and we may make it fem. nom., though Baucyl[i uxor] is possible.' See however *IG* 14.1851 for Tatia Baucylis, noted by Dessau *ad ILS* 1839.
20. Valeria Hilaria was probably set free by Octavia's mother Messallina, her husband, Ti. Claudius Fructus, by the Emperor Claudius; Treggiari (1976:102, n. 41).
21. Quinta was the daughter of P. Rubrius Barbarus, prefect of Egypt, 13/12 B.C.; cf. *RE* I A, 1 col. 1171; Brunt (1975:142). The nurse was thus probably a family freedwoman, or a descendant of such (see n. 58).
22. Asinia was the 'nurse of Asinia Agrippina, freed probably by her or by her father, Asinius Celer, son of Asinius Gallus and Vipsania'; Treggiari (1976:102, n. 38); cf. *PIR*[2] A 1256.
23. The inscription was set up 'Acteni filiae Soterichi,' who died in her seventh month, by the *nutirices* (*sic*) Olympus and Restituta. All the individuals seem to be slaves and Olympus would appear to be a *nutritor*.
24. The nurse's name comes from an inscription that is heavily restored; she is otherwise unknown.
25. The nursling is otherwise unknown, but the nurse was probably her *liberta*; see above p. 210.
26. The nursling appears in his inscription as 'L. Apisius C. f. Scaptia Capitolinus' and makes clear his freedman descent; he built a tomb for his family. The inscription mentions a nurse, but is too damaged for her name to appear. She was most probably a family freedwoman.

27. See further below.

28. Cn. Arrius Agapetus died in his fourth year and was commemorated by his mother Arria Agapete, his father Bostrychus, his *mamma* Helpis and his nurse Fieie = Filete (?). His status cannot be established precisely. Bostrychus was probably a slave, unless he was Arrius Bostrychus, which is unlikely since Agapetus's *cognomen* may be derived from his mother's name. Agapetus could have been *ingenuus* if born after his mother's manumission or if his mother was *ingenua*. Since she was married to a slave husband, however, she is not likely to have been *ingenua*. Thus mother and son may have been slaves set free before Agapetus's death, in which case the slave infant was nursed by a slave nurse even though his mother was alive. Cf. n. 17.

29. See further below.

30. The nurse's *nomen* should perhaps be Caecilia. But the inscription gives no information beyond her name and function.

31. The nursling is otherwise unknown and the nurse's name does not appear on the inscription.

32. The nursling may have derived his name from the second century Vedii Antonini of Ephesus, who included a M. Claudius P. Vedius Antoninus Sabinus and his son M. Claudius P. Vedius Antoninus Phaedrus Sabinianus; cf. *RE* VIII A, 1 cols. 563-8. But this is only a guess. See above p. 210.

33. Although upper-class Coelii and Pedanii are attested, neither nursling nor nurse can safely be associated with any known individual. The different *nomina* of nurse and nursling could indicate that (i) the nurse was *ingenua* or a *liberta* who was hired; (ii) she was a slave freed by a Pedanius or Pedania but nursed as a slave in a household other than her own; (iii) if a slave, her owner was related by marriage to the nursling's owner (if the nursling was in fact a freed slave), or to the nursling's family (if freeborn). 'Ampliatus' can be a slave name, but not exclusively; see *CIL* 6 Index, s.v.

34. The nurseling may be P. Cornelius Scipio, cos. 16, or his son, or P. Cornelius Lentulus Scipio, cos. 2; cf. *PIR*² C 1438; C 1397. In either case the nurse is probably a family *liberta*.

35. The nursling's father, L. Cornelius Ummidianus, is otherwise unknown.

36. The nursling is Ti. Claudius Saethida Cethegus Frontinus, son of Ti. Claudius Frontinus Niceratus; cf. *PIR*² C 1005, where Groag conjectures from the nurse's name that the father married (Gavia) Cornelia Cethegilla, sister of M. (Gavius) Cornelius Cethegus, cos. 170. The nurse would thus be a family *liberta* on the mother's side.

37. The nursling appears in his inscription as 'Ser. Cornelius Dolabella Mettilianus', identifiable as the consul of 113; cf. *PIR*² C 1350. The nurse is styled 'Ser. Cornelia Ser. l. Sabina', so was set free either by the nursling, or his father, Ser. Cornelius Dolabella Petronianus, cos. 86 (cf. *PIR*² C 1351).

38. The nurse appears in her inscription as 'Cornelia Fausti l. Urbana', her former owner being apparently Faustus Cornelius Sulla, cos. 31; cf. *PIR*² C 1459. For Fausta (Cornelia), the consul's probable daughter, cf. *PIR*² C 1482. The nurse's husband was possibly a slave, Dio; cf. *CIL* 6. 12765, 16868, 23016.

39. The nursling is a descendant of A. Caepio Crispinus, quaestor in Bithynia c. 15; cf. *PIR*² C 149; Szramkiewicz (1976:II, 382; 520). The nurse may have been a family freedwoman through a marriage connection, or a hired nurse.

40. Crispina was commemorated by her husband, Albus, when she died aged 30. The couple were evidently slaves and had been married 17 years. Unless she had given birth at a very early age, Crispina could not have wet-nursed two senators by the time of her death, so she had perhaps been, as a girl before her marriage, only a dry-nurse or babysitter. The senators' names are not given on the inscription.

41. See further below.
42. See further below.
43. The nursling is otherwise unknown.
44. According to his inscription P. Flavius Crescens was the son of P. Flavius Amarantus and probably *ingenuus*. The nurse is styled 'mamma idem nutrix'. If *mamma* here means mother, Flavia Helena was Amarantus's wife and so not a wet-nurse; but more likely *mamma* is a synonym for *nutrix*. Either way the nurse is best considered a freedwoman.
45. Flavius Gamus died aged 13 and was commemorated by his grandfather, T. Flavius Abascantus, his father M. Cocceius Philetus, and his nurse, Flavia Nais. His mother's name is absent from the inscription, and so she perhaps predeceased her son. Gamus and his father have different *nomina*, so servile origins are indicated and they must have belonged to different owners at some stage. (If Philetus, for example, was married to a slave wife, he must have been transferred from an original common household to another where he was later set free.) Abascantus could have been the paternal or maternal grandfather, and Gamus's mother could have been a slave, freed or freeborn. On the whole it is most likely that Gamus was born a slave, however, and was set free in his grandfather's household. Cf. n. 17.
46. The inscription gives only the nurse's name and occupation. She may have been a freedwoman of Q. Haterius, cos. 5, who has known *liberti*, or of his sons; cf. *PIR²* H 24; H 25; H 26.
47. See further below.
48. The nursling may be the man of the same name who is known to have been proconsul of Sicily and who, in the early second century, owned potteries; cf. *PIR²* I 762. The nurse can then be regarded a family freedwoman.
49. See further below.
50. See further below.
51. The nurse's name is restored in her inscription as '[L]icinnia [P]rocessa', and the nursling's as 'Cre[sc]ens', who set up the inscription 'matri piae [n]utrici dulcissimae'. Since Crescens was probably a slave, the mother cannot have been *ingenua* (though he may have omitted his *nomen* in the dedication). Whether she was his mother *and* nurse or his mother and *a* nurse is not clear. If the former then she cannot properly be called a wet-nurse, but will have nursed her own child.
52. The nurse is styled 'Lucretia C. l. Lais nutrix' in her inscription. C. Lucretius Rufus, proconsul of Cyprus under Tiberius, could be the patron and nursling; cf. *PIR²* L 411; but this is very tentative. Lucretia may equally have nursed slave children in her *familia*.
53. The inscription gives only the nurse's name and occupation.
54. See above p. 210.
55. The nurse and nursling's mother could both be *libertae*, but certainty is impossible. This case may be one where a parent not of upper-class status or a slave-owner used a nurse for her own child, and would thus give a rare example of nursing outside the two main categories discussed in the text.
56. The nursling appears to be (Fabia) Paullina, daughter of Q. Fabius Maximus, cos. 45 BC, and wife of M. Titius, cos. 31 BC; cf. *PIR²* F 80. The nurse was thus probably a freedwoman, especially since she appears in her inscription with her husband, who was definitely a *libertus*.
57. See further below. If Oscia Sabina was a freedwoman, there *may* be a connection with Oscia Modesta Cornelia Patruina Publiana, wife of C. Arrius Calpurnius Frontinus Honoratus, cos. probably under Septimius Severus; cf. *PIR²* A 1095; *RE* XVIII, 2 cols. 1578-9.
58. The nursling is probably the emperor Galba; cf. *PIR²* L 299, L. Livius

Ocella = L. Livius Ocella Ser. Sulpicius Galba; Syme (1966:58).
    59. C. Q(uintius ?) Hermias died in his fifth year and was commemorated by
C. Q(uintius ?) Eufemus; the latter's wife died aged 14, and so is unlikely to have
been Hermias's mother (though the possibility remains open). The inscription
records two other dedicants, the nurse Parthenope, and P. Farsuleius Isidorus,
tata. If Eufemus was Hermias's father, he may have married twice, and Hermias's
mother presumably died before him since she does not appear as a dedicant in the
inscription; since Hermias's name contains no filiation, he may not have been
Eufemus's freeborn son, but was perhaps freed by the same owner (unless his
mother was already free[d]). If Isidorus was the father (i.e. if *tata* = father),
Hermias, born a slave, will have been freed in a different household from that of
Isidorus. More likely, however, Isidorus was a *nutritor* and assistant to (or even
the husband of) Parthenope. Cf. n. 17.
    60. See further below.
    61. The nursling appears in his inscription as 'T. Sexti Mag[i] [L]atera[ni]'. He
is the consul of 94; cf. *RE* II A, 2 cols. 2049-50. The nurse was thus clearly a
family freedwoman.
    62. The nursling is otherwise unknown. The nurse is styled *nutrix lactaria*. See
above p. 210.
    63. The nurse commemorated her *alumnus*, who lived only nine months and
who thus may have been *ingenuus* rather than *libertus*.
    64. The nurse is styled 'nutrix Cerceniae' in her inscription, which suggests
that the nursling was of upper-class status (cf. above Table - note 6). But
Cercenia is otherwise unknown. The nurse had a son, Primus, and, since he was
probably a slave, is not likely to have been *ingenua* (though see n. 58). The name
Vatronius is rare; cf. *RE* VIII A, 2 col. 2395.
    65. The nursling Torquata was the daughter of Q. Volusius Saturninus, cos.
56; cf. *RE* Supp. IX col. 1865. The inscription was set up by the nurse's son,
Verecundus, evidently a slave, so the nurse was clearly a family freedwoman.
    66. The nursling commemorates in this inscription his 'mater et nutrix', a case
similar to no. 51. The nurse may have nursed her own son and was thus not
strictly a wet-nurse. Her name was perhaps derived from Torquatus Novellius
Atticus, a Tiberian senator; cf. *RE* XVII, 1 col. 1179.
    67. Ammonius appears in his inscription as 'Ammoni f.', and so looks like the
slave son of a slave father. If so his owner may have been a Memmius and the
nurse a *liberta*.
    68. The identical *nomen* suggests that the nurse was a family freedwoman, but
the nursling cannot be shown to be of upper-class status.
    69. The nursling was the daughter of Cn. Domitius Helius and Helpis Domitia
(*sic*); both appear freed, the daughter possibly freeborn.

Abbreviations

IG Inscriptiones Graecae (1873-1890) G. Reimer, Berlin
    ILS Inscriptiones Latinae Selectae (1954-5) ed. H. Dessau, 2nd edn,
Weidmann, Berlin
    *RAL Rendiconti della Classe di Scienze Morali, Storiche e Filologiche dell'
Accademia dei Lincei*, Rome

9 THEORIES OF CONCEPTION IN THE ANCIENT ROMAN WORLD

Jan Blayney

Ancient speculation about the process of conception began early in the fifth century BC with the Presocratic philosopher, Alcmaeon of Croton. Alcmaeon's attempt to define certain aspects of the process formed but the beginning of a long and lively series of discussions, not only by a number of late Presocratics (Parmenides, Empedocles, Hippon of Samos, Anaxagoras, Diogenes of Apollonia and Democritus), but also by the tragedians, Aeschylus and Euripides, the philosophers, Plato and Aristotle, the philosopher-poet, Lucretius, and by the medical writers, Hippocrates and Galen.[1] By the late second century AD, a whole range of distinct approaches had evolved, the more sophisticated of which presented extremely perceptive analyses of the process of conception.

Four separate aspects of conception were delineated by the Presocratics. These were:

1. the nature of the male and the female contribution to the child;
2. the nature and/or origin of semen;
3. the determination of the sex of the child; and
4. the transmission of hereditary characteristics.

In subsequent times, these four aspects became what may be termed traditional areas of concern, being discussed individually, in various combinations, or *in toto*, by successive authors. For the purposes of this study (of theories of conception in the ancient *Roman* world), it is appropriate to utilise these four traditional aspects of conception as the foundation for discussion of the two key sources for the period, Lucretius and Galen.

Lucretius

It is to the *De rerum natura* — the didactic poem in which Lucretius expounded the atomic view of the universe that Epicurus had adopted, with some modification, from Democritus — that we must turn for information on Lucretius's views concerning the early stages of generation. Here, in a short passage of 20 to 30 lines (4.1209-32), Lucretius discusses the transmission of hereditary characteristics, a discussion from which we can compile at least a general outline of the Lucretian (and Epicurean) approach to the process of conception.

From the passage in question, we learn that Lucretius's view on the subject of the male and the female contribution to the child was that both parents produced semen, and that, since every child was fashioned from the two seeds, a female child could derive from the paternal seed and, conversely, a male child could derive from the maternal seed.

Lucretius's belief in the existence of both a paternal and a maternal seed was by no means innovative. From as early as the fifth century BC, Presocratic speculation about the contribution of the male and the female to the process of conception had given rise to the suggestion that both partners contributed semen: this was the approach adopted by Alcmaeon (Censorinus 5.4 [Diels/Kranz 24 A 13]);[2] Parmenides (Caelius Aurelianus, *Morb. Chron.* 4.9 [D/K 28 B 18]; Censorinus 5.4 [D/K 24 A 13]); Empedocles (Censorinus 5.4 [D/K 24 A 13]; Aristotle, *De generatione animalium* 722 b 10 [D/K 31 B 63], *ibid.* 723 a 23 [D/K 31 B 65]); possibly by Anaxagoras (Censorinus 5.4 [D/K 24 A 13], but cf Aristotle, *De generatione animalium* 763 b 30 [D/K 59 A 107]); and certainly by Democritus (Aëtius 5.5.1 [D/K 68 A 142]). The so-called 'doctrine of the two seeds' (as it later came to be termed) was also supported in the fourth century BC by the Hippocratic writer of *The Seed* (*passim*).

Given Lucretius's indirect debt (via Epicurus) to the Atomist, Democritus, it is worthwhile examining this particular predecessor in greater detail. So far as can be ascertained from the fragmentary evidence, Democritus was the earliest of the Presocratics to develop a comprehensive approach to the subject of conception. He was responsible for formulating what is known as the doctrine of pangenesis, a doctrine that provided the basis for all his sexual theories, from the male and female contribution and the origin of semen, through to sex differentiation and heredity. One of the essential features of pangenesis was that both the male and the female were thought to produce seed (Aëtius 5.5.1 [D/K 68 A 142]). This theory, supporting the existence of both the maternal and the paternal seed, was closely related to that concerning the source of semen, for in Democritus's view semen derived from the whole body, particularly the important parts such as bones, flesh and sinews (Aëtius 5.3.6 and Censorinus 5.2-3 [D/K 68 A 141]). To be more explicit, Democritus envisaged the paternal and maternal seeds as consisting of small particles or atoms drawn from every part of the male and female body respectively. This meant, in effect, that each seed contained within it a complete set of those parts necessary for the development of a child.

It is to the heredity of bodily characteristics that we must now turn our attention, for it forms the central focus of the Lucretian passage under study. According to Lucretius, if the female seed prevailed over the male seed, then the child would resemble the mother, and similarly, if the paternal seed prevailed, then the child would resemble the father. If, however, neither seed prevailed, but both seeds mixed equally, then the child would resemble both parents (4.1209-17).

There can be no doubt that Lucretius viewed the principle of predominance as the major factor in the transmission of hereditary characteristics. In so doing, he followed in the footsteps of a number of his predecessors: amongst the Presocratics, Empedocles (Aëtius 5.11.1 [D/K 31 A 81]) and possibly Anaxagoras (Censorinus 6.8 [D/K 59 A 111]) adopted this approach, whilst in the fourth century BC the Hippocratic author of *The Seed* (section 8) likewise promoted the principle of predominance.

The Hippocratic discussion of the problem of heredity is of particular interest on two counts. First, the theory of heredity proposed therein is rather more complex than that found in Lucretius. Thus, we find in the text of *The Seed* the statement that since sperm was a product which came from the whole body of each parent, weak sperm coming from the weak parts, and strong sperm from the strong parts, the child necessarily had to correspond; and so, if from any part of the father's body a greater quantity of sperm was derived than from the corresponding part of the mother's body, the child would, in that part, bear a closer resemblance to the father, and vice versa. That is to say, the child would resemble in the majority of its characteristics that parent who had contributed a greater quantity of semen from the greater number of bodily parts. Secondly, and more importantly, this theory of heredity confirms that the approach adopted by the Hippocratic writer of *The Seed* was based on the doctrine of pangenesis (whereby both the male and the female seed were drawn from the entire body of each parent respectively). It can be no coincidence that yet another source utilised by Lucretius was an adherent of this particular doctrine.

Lucretius's theory of heredity was not, however, limited to resemblances between children and their parents. He suggested that children sometimes resembled their grandparents or more distant ancestors because ancestral characteristics were transmitted (in atom groups within the seed) from generation to generation, surfacing haphazardly from time to time. Thus, children might resemble their ancestors in face or body or limb, look or voice or hair, none of which was created from a seed that was determined (4.1218-26).

Prior to Lucretius, only one serious attempt to define resemblances between children and their more distant ancestors had been made (Aristotle, *De generatione animalium* 767 a 36-768 b 5). Lucretius's own attempt, based as it is on the atomic approach, is not only quite distinct from that of his forerunner, but also deceptively simple, and decidedly modern in outlook.

Given the correspondences between the theories of Lucretius and those of Democritus and the Hippocratic writer, it seems reasonable to suggest that Lucretius, even as these predecessors, subscribed to the doctrine of pangenesis. Lucretius's views on the maternal and paternal contribution to generation and on the transmission of bodily characteristics show no disagreement with that pangenetic approach; indeed, they could easily be interpreted as the product of such an approach.[3]

Galen

Of the numerous works produced by the late second century AD medical writer Galen, it is the *De usu partium*, or more precisely, the fourteenth book thereof, and the *De semine* which contain material of particular importance to this study.

The first point that we should note is that Galen made an anatomical discovery which undermined the very basis of Aristotle's sexual theories, namely, the Aristotelian concept of form and matter. To briefly elaborate: in Aristotle's view, the male contribution to generation was semen, whilst that of the female was menstrual fluid; and given that the male was the one who generated, and the female the one out of whom the male generated, and that the male was naturally the active partner, whilst the female was the passive partner, then, in Aristotle's mind, it was only reasonable that the male provided the movement and form, the female the body or matter (*De generatione animalium* 729 a 20-33).

The anatomical discovery made by Galen may be summarised as follows: he determined that from the female testes (i.e. ovaries) — discovered in the post-Aristotelian period by the Alexandrian anatomist, Herophilus — spermatic ducts led directly to the sides of the uterus, and that because of the connection testes — ducts — uterus, female semen necessarily passed straight from the testes through the spermatic ducts to the uterus, where it contributed to the generation of the child (*De usu partium* 14.11; *De semine* 1.7, 2.1). By thus supporting the doctrine of the two seeds, Galen distanced himself from the Aristotelian viewpoint, and adopted a similar solution to the problem of the male and female contribution to generation as that proposed by a number of his predecessors, most notably, the Hippocratic author of *The Seed*.

Although Galen promoted the existence of both a maternal and a paternal seed, he believed that the former was less perfect than the latter: due to the female's lesser supply of heat, her seed was necessarily less substantial, colder, thinner and weaker than that of the male (*De usu partium* 14.6; *De semine* 2.5). Moreover, the main function of the female seed, in the early stages after its fusion with the male seed, was to provide the latter with nourishment; a function which, in the later stages of embryonic growth, was taken over by the menstrual blood (*De semine* 1.7, 2.1, 2.4). What is particularly striking here is the influence of Aristotle. Characteristically Aristotelian is Galen's insistence on the lesser significance of the female, his ascription of a smaller share of heat to the female, and his attribution of a nutritive role to menstrual blood.

On the question of the production of semen, Galen suggested

that in the numerous windings of the vessels that led to the male and female testes, blood was transformed into a semen-like liquid, and that this liquid was in turn transformed into real semen by the testes themselves (*De usu partium* 14.10; *De semine* 1.16, 2.5). The view that blood formed the origin of semen had been proposed in the fifth century BC by the Presocratic, Diogenes of Apollonia (Vindicianus q.f.3 [D/K 64 B 6]), and then in the fourth century BC — in a more complex form — by Aristotle (*De generatione animalium* 724 b 23-726 b 18). Whilst Galen could not divorce himself from this traditional theory that semen derived from blood, he none the less attributed a major role in the production of semen to the testes.

If we turn to the matter of sex differentiation, we find that Galen posited heat as the determining factor. He argued that since the spermatic vessels leading to the right male and female testes and to the right side of the womb had a different origin from those on the left, and therefore carried warmer blood than the left-hand vessels, the right male and female testes and the right side of the womb were necessarily warmer than the left, which, in turn, meant that the male and female semen deriving from the right testes and arriving in the right side of the womb was warmer and would produce males, whilst females were engendered on the left (*De usu partium* 14.7).

In suggesting warmth as the essential factor in the differentiation of sex, Galen was undoubtedly inspired by the Empedoclean theory of sex determination whereby a warm womb produced a male child, a cold womb, a female child (Aristotle, *De generatione animalium* 723 a 23 [D/K 31 B 65]), ibid. 764 a 1 [D/K 31 A 81]; Aëtius 5.7.1 [D/K 31 A 81]). Yet, the Empedoclean theory was not the only one that influenced him: Galen also adopted elements of the right/left theory of sex differentiation attributed to Anaxagoras (Aristotle, *De generatione animalium* 763 b 30 [D/K 59 A 107]), thus creating a composite theory which equated male/female with both hot/cold and right/left. His original contribution, however, was to substantiate his arguments with anatomical data.

The mechanism proposed by Galen for the transmission of individual characteristics relied on the principle of predominance. Galen suggested that different portions of the male and female semen contained different qualities of semen: thus, the first portion ejected might be of a thicker substance, whilst the second or third portions might be thinner, colder or weaker, and vice versa. When the two seeds combined, the male seed prevailed in some portions, the female seed in others, in accordance with the quality of those portions and, as a result, the child resembled the father in some parts of the body, and the mother in others (*De semine* 2.5).

This mechanism devised by Galen differs from that found in the Hippocratic work, *The Seed*, in that the latter involves the predominance of certain portions of the male or female seed in accordance with their quantity, whilst, with the former, it is a question of the quality of the portions concerned. It is notable that the viewpoint expressed by Galen does not entirely accord with his own general description of the nature of the maternal and the paternal seed.[4]

In conclusion, there can be no doubt that Galen drew heavily on the work of his predecessors, often adopting or adapting their views, but at the same time he added his own personal insights, frequently derived from his more extensive knowledge of anatomy. Of the many advances made by Galen, the most significant (from the point of view of this study) was undoubtedly his anatomical substantiation of the existence of an effective female seed.

Notes

1. For specific references see below. All references to Lucretius are to the poem *De rerum natura*.

2. *Die Fragmente der Vorsokratiker*, ed. H. Diels; 9th edn ed. W. Kranz, Berlin, Wiedmann, 1960; hereafter abbreviated as D/K.

3. Cf. here Lesky (1950:1316-17).

4. This contradiction is, in fact, but one of many which may be found in the material relating to heredity in Galen's *De semine*; see Lesky (1950:1410-17).

10 CONCLUSION

Some threads have recurred through the preceding chapters, some of substance, some of methodology.

A general concept of 'the Roman family' has emerged: the small, nuclear family residing in one household, sometimes embracing extensions such as slaves, ex-slaves and foster-children. The strength of the conjugal family comes through in legal, epigraphical and literary sources. There are hints of links between further kin, but more work — including linguistic work on terminology — is necessary to define and understand those links.

Family relations have been placed firmly within the larger social structure. We have canvassed not only what the law formally required or prohibited, but also how family members operated within that context to behave 'properly' or 'naturally' towards spouses and children. Upper-class families made wills, used dowry and otherwise disposed of property to this end; lower-class families often commemorated themselves as such and they adopted familiar terminology and attitudes even when formally excluded from Roman marriage. We have seen something of the role of the family in the workings of the imperial bureaucracy, in politics and in education. More remains to be done on other possible functions of the family — as an economic unit, as a support group for the elderly, widows, orphans, etc. It is clear that the family was one of the strong cohesive principles of Roman society, in spite of considerable mobility and perhaps instability. Chapter 5 argues that this principle was in fact the central one in Roman society.

Other structures sometimes replaced the natural family — e.g. fostering, wet-nursing, the large slave *familia*. The interrelation of these with the natural family has been touched on but would bear further investigation.

Within the family structure tensions may be identified. Women had an important role in their conjugal family, but maternal and paternal property were kept distinct. Marriage continued to be the norm, but divorce was frequent. Children were prized and government offered incentives and encouragement to fertility, but there seems to have been a high degree of childlessness. Moreover, death must have been ever-present in most people's lives. All of this must have affected personal expectations and attitudes, and we must continually set formal ideals and rules against actual practice.

This need has been highlighted by the study of legal matters in several chapters. One of the important methodological lessons to be learned from these studies is the need to know what the law said, and then to try to assess how representative or atypical the legal examples are. The law code is a rich source of case history and discussions of principle, not to be ignored because of its difficulties; but it must be tested against historically attested practice wherever possible. Discussions above of the roles of women and children have highlighted the difference between rule and practice for a *paterfamilias*: it should be a warning against the loose usage of 'patriarchal' which has developed in recent social science and politics.

We have seen the historical asymmetry reflected in claims about the decline of traditional values and the dates associated with this. This highlights the need identified several times of a better understanding of chronological indicators in our evidence. Our study of the Roman family has not provided much insight into development and change: it too often has to deal with several centuries as if they were one socially static period. One area that might provide a key to the problem is nomenclature: it is to be hoped that current efforts to determine better a chronology of the Roman name will be successful. This work is closely related to the study of inscriptions. We have already seen what a systematic study of inscriptions in bulk can yield for our understanding of Roman society and especially for an extension of that to the humbler classes. Weaver has referred in Chapter 6 to the 'profound silence' which has ensued from his 1972 study of evidence — legal, epigraphic, onomastic — for 'mixed marriages' (for which he has coined the term *c.c.c., contubernium cum cive*). We cannot afford to ignore such studies, difficult and even intractable though the evidence may be.

The question of status has arisen in many of the preceding studies. We have acknowledged the difficulty in differentiating the *incerti*: who were freeborn and who freed? Several of us have suspected that amongst our Roman citizens there may be camouflaged some of lesser status, e.g. Latins and *peregrini*.

We must continue to try to differentiate, but one must also ask the question, 'Did it matter?' If the surviving evidence makes it so difficult to make status distinctions, one suspects that for everyday purposes the great mass of people at Rome lived lives not greatly affected by such distinctions. There were, of course, enormous economic gaps between inhabitants of Rome, and indeed class differences, but formal status might have been called into question only on comparatively rare occasions. We have seen that in their family lives people often behaved as if such differences did not exist, crossing status barriers to 'marry' and have children. But we have also seen some evidence to suggest that within the family members of higher status took precedence.

The focus of these studies has been the city of Rome. Future work could usefully focus on other areas, so that we build up a series of regional studies which will permit comparative analyses of the family across the Roman empire, trying to relate regional differences to local cultural traditions. At Rome itself there was a wide range of cultural and ethnic backgrounds in the population: can we identify their influence in family practices and ideals, without recourse to old prejudices and preconceptions?

As Chapter 1 pointed out, family studies must proceed on the basis of all the evidence available to us and all the skills and approaches available to analyse that evidence. There is a lesson to be learnt here for the training of future Roman historians. There is also an incentive for those trained in the traditional study of language and literature to use their insights and apply their experience to the study of an institution which must have influenced the development of Latin and Greek language and literature, i.e. the family in the Roman world.

BIBLIOGRAPHY

BIBLIOGRAPHY I:

SOURCES FOR THE STUDY OF THE ROMAN FAMILY

Edyth Binkowski and Beryl Rawson

This section is intended both as a point of reference and as a guide and stimulus to further research. It is of necessity very selective and for reasons of limitation of space most modern works cited are in English. These will often lead the reader to work being done in other languages.

The primary sources for the study of the Roman family are of course the records — literary and non-literary — left by contemporaries. (See Chapter 1 on the range and limitations of these sources.) Of the literary figures, there is much to be learnt not only from the primary source material of Cicero, Pliny, Horace, Martial, Juvenal and Quintilian, but also from Roman and Greek writers such as Tacitus, Suetonius, Plutarch and Cassius Dio who lived later than the events they recounted. References to much of the ancient material will be found in other chapters of this book. This chapter is concerned with modern material.

Until recently material on the Roman family was at best embedded in general books on the classical world, with the exception of two books specifically on the family: R. Paribeni, *La famiglia Romana* (1929, with subsequent editions in 1939, 1940 and 1948) and P. Lacombe, *La famille dans la société romaine: étude de moralité comparée* (1889). Both of these are now inadequate, owing largely to the times and conditions in which they were written and to the progress made since then in the fields of anthropology, archaeology, psychology, sociology and historical demography as well as in the study of ancient sources themselves.

Amongst general social histories of Rome, two by Balsdon reflect progress made during the 1960s. Balsdon (1962) was a useful handbook of recorded details about individual women and some institutions, but it offered little explanation and undertook no sustained analysis of women's roles and relationships in Roman society. Balsdon (1969) had a chapter entitled 'Family

243

Life' which incorporated some of the most recent ideas on that topic and was a considerable improvement. Of other general studies the following are basic and comprehensive: Johnston (1957), Cowell (1961), Dilke (1975), Paoli (1963, translated from the Italian text of 1940) and Liversidge (1976).

Older social histories which are still often referred to are those of S. Dill (2nd edn 1905), W.W. Fowler (1908), L. Friedländer (translated from the German 7th edn 1908-13, 4 vols) and J. Marquardt (2nd edn 1886). The picture of Roman society presented in these books has remained unchanged for many years. Some of them, especially those by German authors, perhaps influenced by Mommsen's work on inscriptions (see Chapter 1), showed a greater readiness to use non-literary evidence than many of their successors have done; but more of this evidence is available now than in their times, and we have learned to use it more accurately and with greater understanding.

For ancient Greece, whose society influenced and interacted with that of Rome in many ways, there has been an excellent standard work since 1968, that of W.K. Lacey. A comparative work which throws some light on Greek and Roman ideals and morality is that of den Boer (1979): there are chapters on 'Women' and on 'Abortion and Family Planning'.

Although the society of Roman Egypt had many special features and cannot be taken as representative of other parts of the Roman world, recent work in that area is of interest. Bardis (1966a, 1966b) and Hopkins (1980) are useful on marriage; Bojaval (1978) warned against correlating the high representation of women in epitaphs with a high mortality rate in the years of fecundity; and Préaux and Hombert (1952) used the uncommonly rich census data to deduce household structure and other demographic conclusions.

There are now many modern works on the history of the family. Thirsk's review article (1964) and Hareven's method-ological and bibliographical article (1971) provided a useful overview of work done before the 1970s on pre-modern societies. Ariès (1960, English translation 1962) and de Mause (1976) are important for any studies of the historical role of children and childhood. The Cambridge Group for the History of Population and Social Structure has been most productive of studies of pre-industrial societies: Laslett (1972) aroused much controversy with his use of household data to rebut the myth of the dominance of the extended family; Wall (1983) takes account of intervening discussion and work on this topic. Laslett (1977, 1980) is also good on the history and concept of illegitimacy. Stone (1977) is probably the best-known work on aristocratic family life in pre-industrial England.

The United Nations Department of Economic and Social Affairs has published manuals on methods of estimating population, of which no. 3, *Methods for population projection by sex and age* (New York 1956) includes model tables which can be useful for comparative purposes.

In recent years many books and journal articles have been written on aspects of Roman social history which have a bearing on the family. The range of topics which might be thought relevant to the family is enormous, but we have listed below the most useful works under these headings: children, death and burial, demography, education, housing, law, marriage, medicine, nomenclature, *patria potestas*, religion, slaves and freedmen, social classes, and women.

Children

Little has been written specifically on children in Roman society, although discussion of legal issues often relates to children. An article by Manson (1983) gives a glimpse of interesting work on the development of the concept of the small child in Roman society.

Bertman (1976) dealt with the 'generation gap' (and its comparative lack of importance in Rome) not only in cases presented in the legal code and by ancient historians but also in literature. Daube (1969) emphasised the power of the purse-strings in keeping a son in harmony with his father. Neraudau's compilation of material concerning children and adolescents (1979) from literary and non-literary evidence, particularly the legal code, focused on the 'ages of life' and the passage between them, and on the religious and political role of adolescents. Eyben has written a good deal on the concept and practices of youth in the Roman world (e.g. 1972; 1973; 1981).

The fluidity of Roman society because of many factors (e.g. slavery, premature death, divorce and remarriage, class mobility) makes topics such as 'the household', nurture, adoption, exposure, infanticide, illegitimacy and orphans important for the study of children. Rawson (1966), Weaver (1972) and Flory (1978) have all discussed the position of slave children, especially in large households. Humbert (1972) discussed the rights and treatment of children when a parent remarried. Etienne (1976) provides one of the very few modern accounts of the care of newborn and developing infants, based partly on the second-century *Gynaecology* of Soranus and partly on archaeological evidence such as cradles. Bourne (1960), Duncan-Jones (1964), and Garnsey (1968) have discussed the 'alimentary' system which provided funds for the sustenance of needy children in Italian country towns in the second century.

Schulz (1942; 1943) drew together the discussion of the preceding 20 years on registration of births in the Roman world: birth certificates had been found in Egypt which confirmed other evidence of this practice from the early first century.

Prévost (1949) dealt with the political motives of adoptions in the upper classes. The legal aspects of adoption were dealt with in Chapter 3 of Buckland (1963), and Horvat (1974) dealt with social aspects. Goody (1969) provided excellent comparative material, discussing reasons for adoption in various societies, including Rome.

Charpentier (1967) discussed exposure of children in the context of developing French law, and Hands (1968) touched on the question of exposed children and orphans. The topic needs further work (cf. Rawson in Chapter 7), but Boswell's recent article (1984) is valuable. There has been a lively debate on infanticide, especially for female infants, with Engels (1980) arguing that the practice was not widespread but Golden (1981) and Harris (1982) have disagreed.

It is likely that illegitimacy was often the result of formal incapacity to marry and therefore carried less moral stigma than in some modern societies: Rawson (1974). Syme (1960) commented on the ancient silence on this subject, and there has been little modern discussion. Wolff (1974) described earlier laws on illegitimacy as a background to Justinian's legislation.

A useful methodological article, dealing mainly with modern texts, is that of Stewart, Winter and Jones (1975).

Death and Burial

The sociological and historical importance of customs and

concepts relating to death and burial has been increasingly recognised in recent scholarship on diverse societies. Ariès, whose earlier work on childhood was so influential, has now produced a work on death which has already been translated into English (1981). For Rome, Hopkins (1983) collected his papers under the title *Death and Renewal* and for Greece Humphreys (1983) published *The Family, Women and Death*.

As so often, Roman law has been the basis of an important work, that of de Visscher (1963) on legal aspects of burial places. Archaeologists, too, have provided valuable information, as in Toynbee (1971). Cumont was interested in ideals and concepts of the after-life as early as 1922 and returned to the theme with a second book in 1942.

Demography

Under this heading are included works on population and depopulation estimates, age structure, mortality, census statistics and similar topics.

There have been many attempts to estimate the population of Rome and the Roman world, and a figure of about 1 million for the city of Rome in the second century would have many supporters. Russell (1958) dealt with the 'late ancient and mediaeval' periods. The most comprehensive work on our central period is Brunt (1971a), a detailed and well-tabulated study which covers all the above mentioned topics, as well as reproduction and fertility, emigration, land allotments, etc. for Rome itself, Italy in general and the Empire as a whole. The major review of this work is by W. den Boer (1973). He praised most of Brunt's conclusions, but was critical of some (e.g. the reasons for census-collecting, the marriage patterns of the poor). Salmon (1974) discussed population movements throughout the Roman Empire; Lassère's work (1977) dealt with Roman Africa but provided many insights into general features of the Roman world. Frier (1982) discussed general demographic problems as well as specific evidence on life-expectancy,

Burn (1953), Henry (1957; 1959) Durand (1959–60) and Etienne (1959) used funerary inscriptions to try to construct estimates of mortality and expectation of life, but Hopkins (1966) is the most valuable. He argued that the funerary inscriptions are misleading, because infants and young children are under-represented, as are the poor who could not afford tombstones, and that the relatively high mortality of young women is misleading. He used the UN model life-tables (see above) to try to work out more realistic figures for the age structure and average age of death of the Roman population.

Kajanto (1968) discussed problems inherent in trying to estimate average duration of life, and made comparisons between Rome and Africa.

Packer (1967) used archaeological evidence to try to deduce from the domestic buildings in Rome and its nearby port Ostia what the population of these centres might have been.

There is a wealth of material on more modern historical demography. Glass and Eversley (1965) is still a valuable point of reference.

Education

The standard general account of Roman and Greek education has long been Marrou (1956). It is still the most comprehensive, but Clarke (1971) showed more awareness of the social implications of the educational system. Bonner (1977) is more specialised on the Roman side, and sound on descriptive detail; but his social judgements rely on out-of-date works. He still sees concubinage as a sign of unstable family life, he generalises about the large number of unmarried and childless persons, he relies on literary sources for the view that Roman youth was characterised by 'idleness, effeminacy and extravagance', and blames contemporary society and lack of parental control for this. His whole picture is summed up in the chapter heading 'Education in a Decadent Society'.

Many works on Roman education have concentrated on technicalities of rhetoric and oratory, but Parker (1946) looked at the education of boys in the Julio-Claudian family as a preparation for political and perhaps imperial power.

The importance of training and education for slaves who would have responsible positions in their households was recognised in Möhler (1940), Forbes (1955), and Booth (1979).

Although schooling seems to have been quite widespread in Rome, and available to both girls and boys, many lower-class children must have had little more than the informal education provided within the family. Provision for trade apprenticeship has not been much discussed, and it is as yet unclear whether parents normally provided this or whether there were external arrangements. Rawson suggests in Chapter 7 that *alumni* and *vernae* might sometimes have been apprentices.

Housing

The nature of domestic architecture and the functions of public buildings influence family life in many ways. Archaeologists have not given much attention to this dimension of their work. Finley (1975), Chapter 5, made a trenchant attack on the difficulties involved in using archaeologists' reports to answer historians' questions.

Yavetz (1958) discussed living conditions in Republican Rome; Packer (1967) saw the implications for population statistics; Frier (1980) discussed the legal aspects of tenants' relationships with landlords.

Of more general works, D'Arms (1970) and McKay (1975) help put houses and villas into a wider social context. Hermansen (1982) does the same thing for the private and public buildings of Ostia.

Law

As stated in Chapter 1, the most substantial work on the Roman family has been based on legal texts. Much of this derives from the sixth-century compilation of Latin texts commissioned by Justinian. The three parts (*Digest, Institutes, Codex*) are often referred to collectively as the *Corpus Iuris Civilis*.

A useful summary reference is Berger's dictionary of legal terms and topics (1953). Standard textbooks include Schulz (1936), Jolowicz (1957), de Zulueta (1946–53), Nicholas (1962), Buckland (1963), Watson (1967) and Käser (1980). Crook (1967b) and Daube (1969) were more concerned with the social implications of the law than were the textbook authors. Two early works on legal texts relating to aspects of family life were Rivier (1891) and Leathley (1922), both now difficult to find (we are grateful to a friend in Cambridge for the loan of his personal copies). Bauman (1980) provided a detailed account of Roman trials and legislation affecting them: some of this related to family matters.

References to legal aspects of more specific topics will be found in other sections of this chapter. They do not do justice to the wealth of material in languages other than English, especially in Italian.

Marriage

Legal textbooks all have sections on marriage, and Corbett (1930) devoted a book to the Roman law of marriage. Durry's article (1956) provided a briefer general account. Susan Treggiari's *Roman Marriage* will provide a much needed new account when available. See her 1984 article on betrothals.

Augustus's legislation to encourage marriage and parenthood has been discussed in Chapter 1: it has aroused considerable debate. Csillag (1976) is the most detailed work available; Brunt (1971a) in Appendix 9 and Frank (1975) provided concise and useful summaries of the legislation, its causes and its effects. Raditsa's account (1980) was emotional and moralising and misunderstood some of the previous work being surveyed.

There are many more specialised articles on aspects of Roman marriage. The question of age at marriage has been discussed in Chapter 1. Hopkins (1965a) is still essential reading on the question, although Chapter 1 above suggests that the normal age of marriage was higher than he argued. Durry (1955; 1969) and del Castillo (1977) have also discussed pre-pubertal marriage of girls.

Matringe (1971) discussed the power of the *paterfamilias* over children's marriages and divorces; Pomeroy (1976) the relationship of married women to their blood relatives; Williams (1958) the ideals reflected in marriage ceremonies.

Legal Roman marriage was normally available only to Roman citizens; thus the partnerships of some non-citizens (especially slaves) were technically concubinage or *contubernium* in Roman eyes. Rawson (1974) and Treggiari (1981a; 1981b) discussed this, and Rawson showed that the studies by Meyer (1895) and Plassard (1921) on extra-legal marital unions are now quite unreliable.

Adultery, especially trials under Augustus's legislation, has attracted attention. It is included in Bauman's survey (1980) and has been treated by Dorey (1962), Garnsey (1966) and Daube (1972).

There is little available on divorce and widowhood beyond the legal textbooks, but Humbert's work on remarriage (1972) is valuable. Kajanto's investigation of divorce in the lower classes (1969) yielded little evidence for the practice.

Medicine

The Romans relied heavily on the Greeks for medical expertise. With few exceptions, all the doctors in Rome were Greek, and almost all the surviving medical texts were written by Greeks, with the exception of Pliny the Elder (whose *Natural History* includes sections on medicine) and Celsus, both Roman but both laymen. One of the most useful surviving works is a textbook for midwives by Soranus of Ephesus, *Gynaecia*, written early in the second century AD. This has been translated as Soranus of Ephesus, *Gynaecology*; translated (from the Greek) and with an introduction by Temkin (1956). Richardson (1979) provided a summary of Celsus's multi-volume work *On Medicine*, all that remains of the encyclopaedia which Celsus wrote in the first century.

Scarborough (1969) is the most recent general work on Roman medicine. Nutton has written many articles on the topic, often focused on army and navy practice. His 1977 paper argued that the *archiatros* was often physician to the city, providing a municipally-funded public service.

The age and concept of puberty were discussed by Eyben (1972); and Amundsen and Diers have written two articles on the onset of menstruation and menopause (1969; 1970).

In Roman society, as in ours, abortion and contraception were controversial topics, though for different reasons. Roman law saw abortion not as a crime against the foetus, but against the father, as it deprived him of an heir and the continuation of his family line. These topics are mentioned in general medical and legal texts and in more specialised articles by Krenkel (1971), which lists abortifacients used in antiquity, and Nardi (1980). Nardi's earlier book (1971) was reviewed and summarised by

Dickison (1973). Watts (1973) dealt with the subject from the standpoint of the poem of Ovid written when his mistress had had an abortion without telling him.

On contraception, Hopkins (1965) is the authoritative article. Brunt (1971a:131-55) is useful on 'Reproductivity in Ancient Italy'. See also Etienne (1976). Wilkinson (1979) included a chapter on population and family planning.

Nomenclature

Chapter 1 explained some of the implications of the Roman name forms for status and family relationships.

Much of the recent work on nomenclature has been done by Finnish scholars. To be especially noted are Kajanto (1963a; 1963b; 1965; 1966; 1972; 1973) and Solin (1971; 1973; 1974). Both these scholars contributed papers to the 1975 conference on Latin nomenclature whose proceedings were published as *L'onomastique latine* in 1977. A predecessor of this work on nomenclature and epigraphy was Thylander: his brief summary (1952:128-33) is still very useful; in 1954 he discussed the forms of names used by Cicero in his letters to Atticus.

Weaver (1972) based much of his work on close examination of name forms. Other discussions include Adams (1978), who examined Cicero's speeches as well as his letters; Douglas (1958), a brief account of the *cognomen*; Morris (1963); and Reinhold (1971) who set out the penalties imposed on people who used names to which they were not entitled. Older works which are still of interest for more specialised study are Schulze (1904), Baumgart (1936) and Doer (1937).

Patria Potestas

Chapters 1 and 5 discuss further this power of the head of household, and all legal textbooks have some account of it.

Crook (1967c) is still the most useful point of reference, but Daube's witty and perceptive essay on *Filiusfamilias* (1969) is also noteworthy.

Bertman (1976) dealt with examples in life and literature of conflicts in the family between older and younger members, caused by this power. Nisbet (1964) argued that this power was subjected to the force of a more powerful institution, the Empire and the emperor. Volterra (1948) believed that the power of the *paterfamilias* to force, prevent or interfere with children's marriages was used sparingly; and Matringe (1971) showed its decline throughout the imperial period. Rabello (1972) was concerned with the power of life and death in the case of adultery.

Religion

Kraemer (1983) has given a useful survey of work done on women in ancient religions.

Orr's dissertation (1978) is one of the few studies of Roman domestic religion: it is based largely on archaeological evidence from Pompeii and Herculaneum. Heyob's work (1975) on the cult of Isis also deals with women's roles and the association of Isis with birth, marriage and death. Scullard (1981) discusses the festivals and ceremonies associated with each part of the Roman calendar.

Slavery

Roman Italy and classical Athens must both be termed slave societies because of the proportions of slaves to free persons, and the extent to which these societies were dependent on slave labour. Only three other civilizations have been comparable: the West Indian islands (including Cuba), Brazil, and the southern states of North America until the 1860s. The proportion of free (i.e. freeborn or freed) to slave in Rome is sometimes estimated as 2:1.

Many of the slaves in Rome appear to have been foreign-born or of foreign extraction. The contempt for foreigners in some Roman literature (e.g. Juvenal's contempt for the dregs washed in from the Orontes, i.e. Greek-speaking natives of Asia Minor) probably reflects class or status prejudice rather than race prejudice. There is considerable evidence in the ancient sources of humane treatment of slaves and even of a certain independence and prosperity amongst some. Many of them, especially in large, urban, affluent households, were probably better off and better protected than the poorest of the free citizens. But there is also evidence of ill-treatment and primitive living conditions, and the conditions of those for whom there is no evidence were probably grim.

Slaves were, as Chapter 1 explains, part of the *familia*. Rawson (1966), Weaver (1972) and Flory (1978) have all shown that the *familia* provided some kind of family life for slaves, and in Chapter 7 Rawson suggests that some slaves were regarded as part of the master's family. When slaves were freed, they took on the family name of their master (now patron) and inherited some of the privileges and obligations of family membership.

From the large bibliography on slaves and freedmen, major books by Duff (1958), Finley (1960; 1980), Hopkins (1978), Treggiari (1969), Vogt (1974) and Westermann (1955) stand out. Wiedemann's collection of sources in translation (1981) is very useful.

Bradley (1978a) believed that the age of reproduction was important in the timing of sales of female slaves, especially in Roman Egypt; but Dalby (1979) contested that. Harris (1980) is the most recent discussion of the slave trade in Roman sea-borne commerce. Of Treggiari's many articles on aspects of the lives of slaves, that of 1975a is specifically on the family life of slaves in one large household.

Social Classes

Social class is difficult to categorise firmly in ancient Rome, as in most societies. There was a clear hierarchy of status, with freeborn citizens superior to freed (i.e. ex-slave) citizens and both superior to slaves. Foreigners are harder to place in this hierarchy: they probably mixed in circles comparable to those of their place of origin. Many of them were probably involved in trade and commerce. Amongst freeborn Roman citizens, the approximately 600 senators and their families held pride of place. Equestrians ('knights') were closest to them in status, but to call them 'the middle class' is misleading. Both senators and equestrians had much of their capital invested in land, but senators were not allowed to take part directly in trade or commerce. These two groups might be described as the 'upper classes'. Some freedmen, especially those in the imperial bureaucracy, attained positions of considerable wealth and influence and, as Weaver argues in Chapter 6, often married freeborn partners; but there was always a stigma attached to slave birth. (Cf. Chapter 1, n. 6.)

Brunt (1971a) discussed struggles for power within the upper classes as well as the living conditions of the lower classes which led to protests and riots. Bush (1982) dealt with questions of social structure such as marriage patterns and status. Castrén (1975) broke new ground in studies of Pompeii by examining closely the roles of various families in the administrative, political and social life of the town.

De Ste Croix (1981) has ranged wide over 'the ancient Greek world' to present a Marxist analysis of class struggle, and there is much of interest to Rome. Gelzer (1969), an English translation of much earlier German work, was referred to in Chapter 1 as an early example of family history; its focus was politically prominent families. Hopkins (1965c) discussed reasons for the considerable class mobility in the Roman Empire. Huttunen (1974) is one of those who have seen the potential in Roman epitaphs for analysing social stratification. MacMullen (1974) saw the need for discussing rural–urban conflicts of interests in any study of social relations. Weaver (1972), already often referred to, is essential to any study of social class; and his earlier article (1967) was a succinct account of the social mobility of imperial freedmen and slaves.

Women

Women have a role in all the other topics already listed as being relevant to family studies. There is little ancient evidence which derives directly from women themselves (although epitaphs are a valuable source), but in recent years scholarly writing on women's roles in the ancient Greek and Roman worlds has increased enormously.

Two useful bibliographies are those of Pomeroy (1973)[1] and Goodwater (1975). Pomeroy focused mainly on Greece; Goodwater was more comprehensive and included ancient as well as modern sources, other bibliographies and works of reference. Both these women included useful annotations. Because these bibliographies exist, none of the following references is earlier than 1975; even so, they are very selective.

Two recent collections of essays have been those of Cameron and Kuhrt (1983) and Foley (1981). The revised edition (1982) of Lefkowitz and Fant provides a useful set of sources in translation.

Africa (1978) is a study of the powerful Roman women who had great influence on Brutus, Caesar and other political figures of the late Republic, especially Brutus's mother Servilia. Clark (1981) was written for students of classics: it is basic but comprehensive. Dixon (1983) stressed the influence women had in patronage and indirectly in politics. Giacosa (1977) contains excellent illustrations of coin portraits of imperial women. Kampen (1981) described six reliefs of working women and the kinds of job they did. Kaplan (1979) discussed the imperious and influential Julio-Claudian women in Tacitus's *Annals*. Lefkowitz (1981) is an entertaining series of essays on women in antiquity covering various aspects of their lives. Lightman and Feisel (1977) discussed the respect accorded to a woman married only once. MacMullen (1980) argued that though lower-class women may have gone veiled, upper class women did not, and were influential enough to hold offices, particularly that of priestess. Marshall (1975a; 1975b) discussed wives accompanying their husbands to the provinces.

Phillips (1978) gave examples of mothers' influence in all aspects of their daughters' lives. After compiling her bibliography on women in antiquity, Pomeroy produced one of the most comprehensive books on the subject (1975). Syme (1981) is a discussion of the influential women in Tacitus's *Annals* by the world's foremost Tacitean scholar. Treggiari has written much on the women of Rome, particularly on their household life and jobs. Articles of 1976 and 1979(a) and (b) are of particular interest in this context. Wilkinson (1979) contains a chapter on 'Women's Liberation'.

In a select bibliography there is no space to list the books and articles written about specific women, many of whose names, whether virtuous or notorious, will readily spring to mind. One exception must be made, for a woman known to us as Turia who seems to embody all the virtues of a Roman matron. Her monument, erected by a grieving husband, tentatively identified as Q. Lucretius Vespillo, is no mere epitaph, but a virtual funeral oration. She avenged the murder of her parents, saved her husband's life during the proscriptions of 43-42 BC, and offered her husband a divorce so that he could have children by another wife. The text of this eulogy (the *Laudatio Turiae*) is often found in anthologies (e.g. translated in Lewis and Reinhold, vol. 1, 1951:484-7); and there are annotated editions by Durry (1950) and Wistrand (1976), the latter with parallel Latin and English text.

Notes

1. The up-date of this to 1981 in Peradotto and Sullivan (1984), which collects earlier papers on women in the ancient world, has just come to my notice.

BIBLIOGRAPHY II:

LIST OF REFERENCES

Ancient Sources

Any standard edition may be consulted, except for the following which are specifically referred to in the text.

Apokrimata. Decisions of Septimius Severus on Legal Matters; ed. W.L. Westermann and A.A. Schiller (1954), Columbia University Press, New York. Sometimes referred to as P. Col. 123.

Asconius, *Q. Asconii Pedanii Orationum Ciceronis quinque enarratio*; ed. A.C. Clark (1907), Clarendon Press, Oxford. Reprinted 1936.

Bailey, D.R. Shackleton (1865-70), (ed.) *Cicero's letters to Atticus*, Cambridge University Press, Cambridge, 7 vols.

—— (1977), (ed.) *Epistulae ad Familiares [of] Cicero*, Cambridge University Press, Cambridge.

Festus, Sextus Pompeius, *De verborum significatu*; ed. W.M. Lindsay (1913), Teubner, Leipzig. Reprinted 1965, Olms, Hildesheim.

Fronto, Marcus Cornelius, *The correspondence of Marcus Cornelius Fronto with Marcus Aurelius Antoninus, Lucius Verus, Antoninus Pius and various friends*; ed. C.R. Haines (1919-20), Heinemann, London, 2 vols. (Loeb Classical Library, 112-13.)

Ovid, *Publii Ovidii Nasonis Fastorum libri sex: the Fasti of Ovid*; ed. with a translation and commentary by J.G. Frazer (1929), Macmillan, London, 5 vols.

Tyrrell, R.Y. and L.C. Purser (1885-1901) *Commentary on the Correspondence of Cicero*, Hodges, Foster & Figgis, Dublin.

Reference Works

AE, L'année épigraphique. Presses Universitaires de France, Paris.

CIL, Corpus Inscriptionum Latinarum (1876-1933). Academia Litterarum Regia Borussica; G. Reimer, and after 1926, W. de Gruyter, Berlin; including vol. 6, pt. 7, *Indices*, ed. E.J. Jory and D.G. Moore, 1974.

Corpus iuris civilis (1877-1968). Editio stereotypa altera. Weidmann, Berlin. vol. 1. *Institutiones*, recognovit P. Krueger: *Digesta*, recognovit Th. Mommsen, 1877; vol. 2. *Codex Iustinianus*, recognovit P. Krueger, 1880; vol. 3. *Novellae*, recognovit R. Schoell . . . [et] G. Kroll, 9th edn, 1968.

D: *Digesta*.

C: *Codex Iustinianus*.

FIRA, Fontes Iuris Romani Antejustiniani (1968-9). In usum scholarum ediderunt S. Riccobono . . . [et al.]. Barbèra, Florence, 3 vols. Includes:

Gaius *Institutes* (Gaius *Inst.*)

Paulus *Sententiae* (Paulus *Sent.*)

Ulpian *Regulae* (Ulpian *Reg.*)
Ulpian *Tituli* (Ulpian *Tit.*)
Gnomon of the Idios Logos.
Inscriptiones Graecae ad res Romanas pertinentes (1906-27) . . . edendum curavit R. Cagnat, auxiliantibus J. Toutain et P. Jouguet; Leroux, Paris. Reprinted 1964, 'L'Erma' di Bretschneider, Rome.
PIR¹, *PIR²*, *Prosopographia Imperii Romani* (1897-98). Reimer, Berlin. 3 vols.; *Prosopographia Imperii Romani* (1933-), 2nd edn, De Gruyter, Berlin.
PLRE, Jones, A.H.M., Martindale, J.R. and Morris, J. (1971-80). *The prosopography of the later Roman Empire*. Cambridge University Press, Cambridge, 2 vols.
P.Oxy., *The Oxyrhynchus Papyri*, vol. XXXVI, ed. R.A. Coles et al., British Academy, London, 1970.
RE, Pauly, A.F. von (1893-1967) *Paulys Realencyclopädie der classischen Altertumswissenschaft*. Neue Bearbeitung unter Mitwirkung zahlreicher Fachgenossen, hrsg. von G. Wissowa, [W. Kroll et al.]. Druckenmüller, Stuttgart. 34 vols. in 77. Reprinted 1958-67.
Ruggiero, E. de (1895-1906) *Dizionario epigrafico di antichità romane*. 'L'Erma' di Bretschneider, Rome, 1961- reprint.
Thesaurus Linguae Latinae (1900-58); (editus auctoritate ex consilio Academicarum quinque Germanicarum, Berolinensis, Gottingensis, Lipsiensis, Monacensis, Vindobonensis.) Teubner, Leipzig.

Modern Works

Adams, J.N. (1978) 'Conventions of naming in Cicero'. *Classical Quarterly*, n.s. 28, 145-66.
Adcock, F.E. (1959) *Roman political ideas and practice*. University of Michigan Press, Ann Arbor.
Africa, T.W. (1978) 'The mask of an assassin: a psychohistorical study of M. Junius Brutus'. *Journal of Interdisciplinary History*, 8, 599-626.
Aitkin, D. (1982) *Stability and change in Australian politics*, 2nd rev. edn. Australian National University Press, Canberra. 1st edn 1977.
Amundsen, D. and Diers, C.J. (1969) 'The age of menarche in classical Greece and Rome', *Human Biology*, 41, 125-32.
—— (1970) 'The age of menopause in classical Greece and Rome', *Human Biology*, 42, 79-86.
Anshen, R.N. (ed.) (1959) *The family: its function and destiny*. Harper, New York.
Arangio-Ruiz, V. (1948) 'Il processo di Giusta', *Parola del Passato*, 3, 129-51.
—— (1951) 'Nuove osservazioni sul processo di Giusta', *Parola del Passato*, 6, 116-23.
Ariès, P. (1962) *Centuries of childhood: a social history of family life*. Cape, London. Translated from the French original, 1960.
—— (1981) *The hour of our death*. Knopf, New York. Translated from the French original, 1977.
Astin, A.E. (1978) *Cato the Censor*. Clarendon Press, Oxford.
Badian, E. (1958) *Foreign clientelae, (264-70 B.C.)*. Clarendon Press, Oxford.
Bailey, D.R. Shackleton (1960) 'The Roman nobility in the second civil war'. *Classical Quarterly*, n.s. 10, 253-67.
Balsdon, J.P.V.D. (1962) *Roman women, their history and habits*. Bodley Head, London. Reprinted 1983, Barnes & Noble, New York.
—— (1969) *Life and leisure in ancient Rome*. Bodley Head, London.

Bardis, P.D. (1966a, 1967) 'Marriage and family customs in ancient Egypt: an interdisciplinary study', *Social Science*, 41, 229-45 and 42, 104-19.
—— (1966b) 'Selected aspects of family life in ancient Egypt'. *International Review of History and Political Science*, 3, 1-16.
Bauman, R.A. (1980) 'The "leges iudiciorum publicorum" and their interpretation in the Republic, Principate and Later Empire', in *Aufstieg und Niedergang der römischen Welt*, H. Temporini (ed.), De Gruyter, Berlin. *Principat, Recht*, II, 13, pp. 103-233.
Baumgart, J. (1936) *Die römischen Sklavennamen*. Dissertation, Breslau.
Beard, M. (1980) 'The sexual status of Vestal Virgins', *Journal of Roman Studies*, 70, 149-65.
Beaucamp, J. (1976) 'Le vocabulaire de la faiblesse féminine dans les textes juridiques romains du troisième au quatrième siècle', *Revue Historique de Droit Français et Etranger*, 54, 485-508.
Berger, A. (1953) *Encylopedic dictionary of Roman law*. American Philosophical Society, Philadelphia (its Transactions, n.s. 43, 2).
Bertman, S. (1976) *The conflict of generations in ancient Greece and Rome*. Grüner, Amsterdam.
Blackstone, Sir Wm (1821-2) *Commentaries on the laws of England*. Sweet, London. 4 vols.
Boer, W. den (1973) 'Demography in Roman history: facts and impressions'. *Mnemosyne*, 26, 29-46.
—— (1979) *Private morality in Greece and Rome*. Brill, Leiden.
Bojaval, B. (1978) 'Surmortalité et fécondité féminines dans l'Egypte gréco-romaine'. *Zeitschrift für Papyrologie und Epigrafik*, 28, 193-200.
Bonner, S.F. (1977) *Education in ancient Rome: from the elder Cato to the younger Pliny*. Methuen, London.
Booth, A.D. (1979) 'The schooling of slaves in first-century Rome'. *Transactions of the American Philological Association*, 109, 11-19.
Boswell, J.E. (1984) '*Expositio* and *oblatio*: the abandonment of children and the ancient and medieval family'. *American Historical Review*, 89, 10-33.
Boulvert, G. (1974) *Domestique et fonctionnaire sous le haut empire romain. La condition de l'affranchi et de l'esclave du Prince*. Les Belles Lettres, Paris. (Centre de Recherches d'Histoire Ancienne, 9.)
Bourne, F.C. (1960) 'The Roman alimentary program and Italian agriculture'. *Transactions of the American Philological Association*, 91, 47-75.
Boyé, A.J. (1959) 'Pro Petronia Iusta', in *Droits de l'antiquité et sociologie juridique: Mélanges Henri Levy-Bruhl*. Sirey, Paris, pp. 29-48.
Boyer, G. (1950) 'Le droit successorial romain dans les oeuvres de Polybe'. *Revue Internationale des Droits de l'Antiquité*, 4, 169-87. (Mélanges de Visscher III.)
Bradley, K.R. (1978a) 'Age at time of sale of female slaves'. *Arethusa*, 11, 243-52.
—— (1978b) 'Claudius Athenodorus'. *Historia*, 27, 336-9.
—— (1980) 'Sexual regulations in wet-nursing contracts from Roman Egypt' *Klio*, 62, 321-5.
Briscoe, J. (1981) *A commentary on Livy, Books XXXIV-XXXVII*. Oxford University Press, London.
Broughton, T.R.S. (1951-2; 1960) *The magistrates of the Roman Republic*, T.R.S. Broughton with M.L. Patterson. American Philological Association, New York, 2 vols. (its Philological monographs, no. 5).
Brunt, P.A. (1958) Untitled review of works on slavery by Westermann, Tudor and Vogt. *Journal of Roman Studies*, 48, 164-70.
—— (1966) 'The Roman mob'. *Past and Present*, 35, 3-27.
—— (1971a) *Italian manpower, 225 BC–AD 14*. Clarendon Press, Oxford.
—— (1971b) *Social conflicts in the Roman Republic*, Chatto & Windus, London.

—— (1975) 'The administrators of Roman Egypt'. *Journal of Roman Studies*, 65, 124-47.

Buckland, W.W. (1908) *The Roman Law of Slavery: the condition of the slave in private law from Augustus to Justinian*. Cambridge University Press, Cambridge. Reprinted 1969, AMS Press, New York.

—— (1963) *A text-book of Roman law from Augustus to Justinian*, 3rd edn rev. P. Stein. Cambridge University Press, Cambridge.

Burgess, E.W., Locke, H.J. and Thomes M.M. (1963) *The family: from institution to companionship*. American Book Co., New York.

Burn, A.R. (1953) '*Hic breve vivitur*: a study of the expectation of life in the Roman Empire'. *Past and Present*, 4, 1-31.

Bush, A.C. (1982) *Studies in Roman social structure*. University Press of America, Washington, D.C.

Butler, D.E. and Stokes, D. (1970) *Political change in Britain: forces shaping electoral choice*. Macmillan, London.

Cameron, A. (1939) 'ΘΡΕΠΤΟΣ and related terms in the inscriptions of Asia Minor', in *Anatolian studies presented to William Hepburn Buckler*, ed. W.M. Calder and J. Keil. Manchester University Press, Manchester, pp. 27-62.

Cameron, Averil and Kuhrt, A. (1983) *Images of women in antiquity*, ed. A. Cameron and A. Kuhrt. Croom Helm, London.

Campbell, A., Converse, P.E., Miller, W.E. and Stokes, D.E. (1960) *The American voter*, Wiley, New York.

Cancelli, F. (1957) *Studi sul censores e sull' arbitratus della lex contractus*. Giuffrè, Milan.

—— (1960) 'Postilla sul potere dei censores', *Labeo*, 6, 225-7.

Carcopino, J. (1940) *Daily life in ancient Rome*. Yale University Press, New Haven. Translated from the French original, 1939.

Castillo, A. del (1977) 'Sobre la controversia entre matrimonio romano y pubertad femenina. *Rurius*, 4, 195-201.

Castrén, P. (1975) *Ordo populusque pompeianus: polity and society in Roman Pompeii*. Bardi, Rome. (Acta Instituti Romani Finlandiae, 8.)

Champlin, E. (1980) *Fronto and Antonine Rome*. Harvard University Press, Cambridge, Mass.

Chantraine, H. (1967) *Freigelassene und Sklaven im Dienst der römischen Kaiser*. Steiner, Wiesbaden.

Charpentier, J. (1967) *Le droit de l'enfance abandonnée: son évolution sous l'influence de la psychologie*. Presses Universitaires de France, Paris.

Clark, G. (1981) 'Roman women'. *Greece and Rome*, ser. 2, 28, 193-212.

Clarke, M.L. (1971) *Higher education in the ancient world*. Routledge & Kegan Paul, London.

Corbett, P.E. (1930) *The Roman law of marriage*. Clarendon Press, Oxford. Reprinted 1969.

Courtney, E. (1980) *A commentary on the satires of Juvenal*. Athlone Press, London.

Cowell, F.R. (1961) *Everyday life in ancient Rome*. Putnam, New York.

Crook, J.A. (1955) *Consilium principis: imperial councils and counsellors from Augustus to Diocletian* . . . Cambridge University Press, Cambridge.

—— (1967a) 'Gaius, *Institutes*, i, 84-86'. *Classical Review*, 17, 7-8.

—— (1967b) *Law and life of Rome*. Thames & Hudson, London.

—— (1967c) '*Patria Potestas*', *Classical Quarterly*, n.s. 17, 113-22.

—— (1973) 'Intestacy in Roman society'. *Proceedings of the Cambridge Philological Society*, 19, 38-44.

Csillag, P. (1976) *The Augustan laws on family relations*. Akademiai Kiado, Budapest.

Cumont, F. (1922) *Afterlife in Roman paganism: lectures delivered at Yale University on the Stillman Foundation, 1922.* Yale University Press, New Haven. Reprinted 1959, Dover, New York.
—— (1942) *Recherches sur le symbolisme funéraire des romains.* Geuthner, Paris. Reprinted 1966.
Dalby, A. (1979) 'On female slaves in Roman Egypt'. *Arethusa*, 12, 255-63.
D'Arms, J.H. (1970) *Romans on the bay of Naples: a social and cultural study of the villas and their owners from 150 B.C. to A.D. 400.* Harvard University Press, Cambridge, Mass.
Daube, D. (1965) 'Licinnia's dowry', in *Studi in onore di Biondo Biondi.* Giuffrè, Milan. 4 vols. v. 1, pp. 197-212.
—— (1966) 'Dividing a child in antiquity'. *California Law Review*, 54, 1630-7.
—— (1969) *Roman law: linguistic, social and philosophical aspects.* Edinburgh University Press, Edinburgh.
—— (1972) 'The *Lex Julia* concerning adultery'. *Irish Jurist*, n.s. 7, 373-80.
Degler, C.N. (1980) *At odds: women and the family in America from the revolution to the present.* Oxford University Press, New York.
Degrassi, A. (1952) *I Fasti consolari dell' Impero Romano dal 30 avanti Cristo al 613 dopo Cristo.* Edizioni di Storia e Letteratura, Rome.
De Mause, L. (ed.) (1976) *The history of childhood: the evolution of parent–child relationships as a factor in history.* Souvenir Press, London.
Develin, R. (1977) '*Lex curiata* and the competence of magistrates'. *Mnemosyne*, 30, 49-65.
Dickison, S. (1973) 'Abortion in antiquity'. *Arethusa*, 6, 159-66.
Dilke, O.A.W. (1975) *The ancient Romans: how they lived and worked.* David & Charles, Newton Abbott, England.
Dill, S. (1905) *Roman society from Nero to Marcus Aurelius.* 2nd edn. Macmillan, London.
Dixon, S. (1983) 'A family business: women's role in patronage and politics at Rome, 80-44 BC'. *Classica et Mediaevalia*, 34, 91-112.
—— (1984) '*Infirmitas sexus*: womanly weakness in Roman law', *Tijdschrift voor Rechtsgeschiedenis*, 52, 343-71.
Doer, B. (1937) *Die römischen Namengebung, ein historischer Versuch.* Kohlhammer, Stuttgart.
Dorey, T.A. (1961) 'Adultery and propaganda in the early Roman Empire'. *University of Birmingham Historical Journal*, 8, 1-6.
Douglas, A.E. (1958) 'Roman *cognomina*'. *Greece and Rome*, 5, 62-6.
Duff, A.M. (1958) *Freedmen in the early Roman Empire.* Rev. edn. Heffer, Cambridge. 1st edn 1928.
Dumézil, G. (1979) *Mariages indo-européens, suivi de quinze questions romaines.* Payot, Paris.
Duncan-Jones, R.P. (1964) 'The purpose and organisation of the *alimenta*'. *Papers of the British School at Rome*, 32, 123-46.
Durand, J.D. (1959-60) 'Mortality estimates from Roman tombstone inscriptions'. *American Journal of Sociology*, 65, 365-73.
Durry, M. (1950) *Éloge funèbre d'une matrone romaine.* Les Belles Lettres, Paris.
—— (1955) Le mariage des filles impubères dans la Rome antique'. *Revue Internationale des Droits de l'Antiquité*, ser. 3, 2, 263-73.
—— (1956) 'Sur le mariage romain'. *Revue Internationale des Droits de l'Antiquité*, ser. 3, 3, 227-43.
—— (1961) 'Réhabilitation des *Funerariae*'. *Revue archéologique*, 1, 14-15.
—— (1969) 'Le mariage des filles impubères à Rome', in *Revue des Etudes Latines: Mélanges Marcel Durry, 47 bis*, 17-25, and 'Autocritique et mise en point', 27-41.

Earl, D. (1967) *The moral and political tradition of Rome*, Thames & Hudson, London.
Eck, W. (1978) 'Zum neuen Fragment des sogenannten testamentum Dasumii', *Zeitschrift für Papyrologie und Epigraphik*, 30, 277-95.
Engels, D. (1980) 'The problem of female infanticide in the Greco-Roman world'. *Classical Philology*, 75, 112-20.
Esmein, A. (1893) 'La nature originelle de l'action *rei uxoriae*', *Nouvelle Revue Historique de Droit Français et Etranger*, 17, 145-71.
Étienne, R. (1959) 'Démographie et épigraphie', in *Atti del Terzo Congresso Internazionale di Epigrafia Greca e Latina, Roma, 1957*, 'L'Erma' di Bretschneider, Rome, pp. 415-24.
—— (1976) 'Ancient medical conscience and the life of children', *Journal of Psychohistory*, 4, 131-61. Translated from the French original, 1973.
Eyben, E. (1972) 'Antiquity's view of puberty'. *Latomus*, 31, 677-97.
—— (1973) 'Roman notes on the course of life'. *Ancient Society*, Louvain, 4, 213-38.
—— (1981) 'Was the Roman "youth" an "adult" socially?', *L'Antiquité Classique*, 50, 328-50.
—— (1984) 'Youth in Roman antiquity'. *Classicum*, no. 24, 10, 18-20.
Finley, M.I. (1960) *Slavery in classical antiquity: views and controversies*. Heffer, Cambridge.
—— (1968) 'The silent women of Rome', in his *Aspects of antiquity*. Chatto & Windus, London, pp. 128-42.
—— (1973) *The ancient economy*. Chatto & Windus, London.
—— (1975) *The use and abuse of history*. Chatto & Windus, London.
—— (1980) *Ancient slavery and modern ideology*. Chatto & Windus, London.
Flory, M.B. (1978) 'Family in *familia*: kinship and community in slavery'. *American Journal of Ancient History*, 3, 78-95.
—— (1984) 'Where women precede men: factors influencing the order of names in Roman epitaphs', *Classical Journal*, 79, 216-24.
Foley, H.B. (ed.) (1981) *Reflections of women in antiquity*. Gordon & Breach, New York.
Forbes, C.A. (1955) 'The education and training of slaves in antiquity'. *Transactions of the American Philological Association*, 86, 333-59.
Fowler, W.W. (1908) *Social life at Rome in the age of Cicero*. Macmillan, London.
Frank, R.I. (1975) 'Augustus' legislation on marriage and children'. *California Studies in Classical Antiquity*, 8, 41-52.
Freedman, M. (1958) *Lineage organization in Southeastern China*. Athlone Press, London.
Friedländer, L. (1908-13) *Roman life and manners under the early Empire*. Routledge, London, 4 vols. Translated from the 7th German edn.
Frier, B.W. (1980) *Landlords and tenants in imperial Rome*. Princeton University Press, Princeton, N.J.
—— (1982) 'Roman life expectancy: Ulpian's evidence'. *Harvard Studies in Classical Philology*, 86, 213-51.
Gallivan, P.A. (1974) 'Confusion concerning the age of Octavia'. *Latomus*, 33, 116-17.
Garnsey, P. (1966) 'The *Lex Julia* and appeal under the Empire'. *Journal of Roman Studies*, 56, 167-89.
—— (1967) 'Adultery trials and the survival of the *Quaestiones* in the Severan age'. *Journal of Roman Studies*, 57, 56-60.
—— (1968) 'Trajan's *alimenta*: some problems'. *Historia*, 17, 367-81.
—— (1981) 'Independent freedmen and the economy of Roman Italy under the

Principate'. *Klio*, 63, 359-71.
Gelzer, M. (1912) *Die Nobilität der römischen Republik*. Translated into English, 1969.
Giacosa, G. (1977) *Women of the Caesars: their lives and portraits on coins*. Edizioni Arte e Moneta, Milan.
Gide, P. (1867) *Étude sur la condition privée de la femme dans le droit ancien et moderne et en particulier sur le senatusconsulte Velléien*. Durand et Pedone-Lauriel, Paris. Reprinted 1885.
Glass, D.V. and Eversley, D.E.C. (1965) *Population in history: essays in historical demography*. Arnold, London.
Golden, M. (1981) 'Demography and the exposure of girls at Athens'. *Phoenix*, 35, 316-31.
Goodwater, L. (1975) *Women in antiquity: an annotated bibliography*. Scarecrow Press, Metuchen, N.J.
Goody, J. (1969) 'Adoption in cross-cultural perspective'. *Comparative Studies in Society and History*, 11, 55-78.
Gould, J. (1980) 'Law, custom and myth: aspects of the social position of women in classical Athens'. *Journal of Hellenic Studies*, 100, 38-59.
Griffin, M.T. (1976) *Seneca: a philosopher in politics*. Clarendon Press, Oxford.
Hallet, J.P. (1984) *Fathers and daughters in Roman Society: women and the elite family*. Princeton University Press, Princeton, N.J.
Hands, A.R. (1968) *Charities and social aid in Greece and Rome*. Thames & Hudson, London. Ch. 5, The poor, pp. 62-76.
Hareven, T.K. (1971) 'The history of the family as an interdisciplinary field'. *Journal of Interdisciplinary History*, 2, 399-414.
Harris, W.V. (1980) 'Towards a study of the Roman slave trade', in *The seaborne commerce of ancient Rome*, ed. J.H. D'Arms and E.C. Kopff. American Academy in Rome, pp. 117-40. (its Memoirs, v. 36.)
—— (1982) 'The theoretical possibility of extensive infanticide in the Graeco-Roman world', *Classical Quarterly*, 32, 114-16.
Harrison, A.R.W. (1968-71) *The law of Athens*. Clarendon Press, Oxford. 2 vols; v.1, The family and property, v.2, Procedure.
Henry, L. (1957) 'La mortalité d'après les inscriptions funéraires'. *Population*, 12, 149-52.
—— (1959) 'L'age du decès d'après les inscriptions funéraires'. *Population*, 14, 327-9.
Herlihy, D. (1972) 'Mapping households in medieval Italy'. *Catholic Historical Review*, 58, 1-24.
Hermansen, G. (1982) *Ostia: aspects of Roman city life*. University of Alberta Press, Edmonton, Canada.
Hess, S. (1966) *America's political dynasties*. Doubleday, New York.
Heyob, S.K. (1975) *The cult of Isis among women in the Greco-Roman world*. Brill, Leiden. (Etudes préliminaires aux religions orientales dans l'Empire romain, 51.)
Hodge, A.T. (1981) 'Virtuvius, lead pipes and lead poisoning', *American Journal of Archaeology*, 85, 486-91.
Hopkins, K. (1965a) 'Age of Roman girls at marriage'. *Population Studies*, 18, 309-27.
—— (1965b) 'Contraception in the Roman Empire'. *Comparative Studies in Society and History*, 8, 124-51.
—— (1965c) 'Élite mobility in the Roman Empire'. *Past and Present*, 32, 12-26.
—— (1966) 'On the probable age structure of the Roman population'. *Population Studies*, 20, 245-64.
—— (1978) *Conquerors and slaves: sociological studies in Roman history 1.*

Cambridge University Press, Cambridge.
—— (1980) 'Brother–sister marriage in Roman Egypt'. *Comparative Studies in Society and History*, 22, 303-54.
—— (1983) *Death and renewal: sociological studies in Roman history 2*. Cambridge University Press, Cambridge.
Horsburgh, M. (1980) 'The apprenticing of dependent children in New South Wales between 1850 and 1885'. *Journal of Australian Studies*, 7, 33-54.
Horvat, M. (1974) 'Les aspects sociaux de l'adrogation et de l'adoption à Rome', in *Studi in onore di Guiseppe Grosso*, Giappichelli, Torini, vol. VI, p. 45-53.
Huchthausen, L. (1974) 'Herkunft und ökonomische Stellung weibliches Adressaten von Reskripten des Codex Iustinianus (2. und 3. Jh. u.Z.)', *Klio*, 56, 199-228. Running title: 'Frauenreskripte des Codex Iustinianus'.
Humbert, M. (1972) *Le remariage à Rome: étude d'histoire juridique et sociale*. Giuffrè, Milan.
Humphreys, S.C. (1983) *The family, women and death: comparative studies*. Routledge & Kegan Paul, London.
Huttunen, P. (1974) *The social strata in the imperial city of Rome: a quantitative study of the social representation in the epitaphs published in the* C.I.L.v.VI. University of Oulu, Oulu, Finland.
Johann, H.T. (1968) *Trauer und Trost: eine Quellen- und struktur-analytische Untersuchung der philosophischen Trostschriften über den Tod*. Fink, Munich.
Johnston, M. (1957) *Roman Life*. Scott, Foresman, Chicago.
Jolowicz, H.F. (1952) *Historical introduction to the study of Roman Law*. 2nd edn. Cambridge University Press, Cambridge. Reprinted 1961, 1965.
—— (1957) *Roman foundations of modern law*. Clarendon Press, Oxford.
Jones, A.H.M. (1957) *Athenian Democracy*. Blackwell, Oxford. Reprinted 1964.
Jones, C.P. (1971) *Plutarch and Rome*. Clarendon Press, Oxford.
Kajanto, I. (1963a) *Onomastic studies in the early Christian inscriptions of Rome and Carthage*. Helsinki, 1963. (Acta instituti romani finlandiae, 2, 1.)
—— (1963b) *A study of the Greek epitaphs of Rome*. Helsinki, 1963. (Acta instituti romani finlandiae, 2, 3.)
—— (1965) *The Latin cognomina*. Societas Scientiarum Fennica, Helsinki.
—— (1966) Supernomina: *a study in Latin epigraphy*. Societas Scientiarum Fennica, Helsinki.
—— (1968) *On the problem of the average duration of life in the Roman Empire*. Suomalainen Tiedeakatemia, Helsinki.
—— (1969) 'On divorce among the common people of Rome', *Revue des Etudes Latines: Mélanges Marcel Durry*, 47 bis, 99-13.
—— (1972) 'Women's *praenomina* reconsidered', *Arctos*, 7, 13-30.
—— (1973) 'On the first appearance of women's *cognomina*', in *Akten des VI. Internationalen Kongresses für Griechische und Lateinische Epigraphik, München, 1972*, Beck, Munich, pp. 402-4.
Kampen, N. (1981) *Image and status: Roman working women in Ostia*. Mann, Berlin.
Kaplan, M. (1979) '*Agrippina semper atrox*: a study of Tacitus's characterization of women', in *Studies in Latin literature and Roman history I*; ed. C. Deroux. Latomus, Bruxelles, pp. 410-17. (Collection Latomus, v. 164.)
Käser, M. (1980) *Roman private law*. 3rd edn. Butterworths, Durban. Based on the 10th revised German edn. 1st English edn 1965.
Kassel, R. (1958) *Untersuchungen zur griechischen und römischen Konsolationsliteratur*. Beck, Munich.
Kleiner, D.E.E. (1977) *Roman group portraiture: the funerary reliefs of the late Republic and early Empire*. Garland, New York.
Koschaker, P. (1930) 'Unterhalt der Ehefrau und Früchte der Dos', in *Studi in*

Onore di P. Bonfante 4, Milan, pp. 3-27.

Kraemer, R.S. (1983) 'Women in the religions of the Greco-Roman world', *Religious Studies Review*, 9, 127-39.

Krenkel, W.A. (1971) 'Erotica I: der Abortus in der Antike', *Wissenschaftliche Zeitschrift der Universität Rostock*, 20, 442-52.

Lacey, W.K. (1974) 'Octavian in the Senate, January 27 BC'. *Journal of Roman Studies*, 64, 176-84.

—— (1968) *The family in classical Greece*. Thames & Hudson, London.

—— (1980) '2 BC and Julia's adultery'. *Antichthon*, 14, 127-42.

Lacombe, P. (1889) *La famille dans la société romaine: étude de moralité comparée*. Vigot, Paris.

Lambert, G.R. (1982) *Rhetoric rampant: the family under siege in the early western tradition*. University of Western Ontario, London, Ontario.

Laslett, P. (1971a) 'Age at menarche in Europe since the eighteenth century'. *Journal of Interdisciplinary History*, 2, 221-36.

—— (1971b) *The world we have lost*. 2nd edn. Methuen, London.

—— (ed.) (1972) *Household and family in past time: comparative studies in the size and structure of the domestic group over the last three centuries*, ed. P. Laslett with R. Wall. Cambridge University Press, Cambridge.

—— (1977) *Family life and illicit love in earlier generations: essays in historical sociology*. Cambridge University Press, Cambridge.

Laslett, P., Oosterveen, K. and Smith, R.M. (eds.) (1980) *Bastardy and its comparative history: studies in the history of illegitimacy and marital nonconformism in Britain, France, Germany, Sweden, North America, Jamaica and Japan*. Ed. P. Laslett, K. Oosterveen and R.M. Smith with the assistance of other[s]. Arnold, for the Cambridge Group for the History of Population and Social Structure, London.

Lassère, J.M. (1977) *Ubique populus: peuplement et mouvements de population dans l'Afrique romaine de la choute de Carthage à la fin de la dynastie des Sévères, 146 a.C — 235 p.C.* CNRS, Paris.

Last, H. (1923) 'Family and social life', in C. Bailey (ed.) *The legacy of Rome*, Clarendon Press, Oxford, pp. 209-36.

Lattimore, R. (1942) *Themes in Greek and Latin epitaphs*. Illinois University Press, Urbana, Ill. Reprinted 1962.

Leathley, S.A. (1922) *The Roman family and De Ritu Nuptiarum: Title XXIII (2) from the Digest of Justinian*. Blackwell, Oxford.

Leclercq, H. (1907) 'Alumni', in *Dictionnaire d' archéologie chrétienne et de liturgie*, publié par F. Cabrol . . . 1907-53, Letouzey et Ané, Paris, 15 vols. in 30, v.1, pt.1, cols. 1288-306.

Lefkowitz, M.R. (1981) *Heroines and hysterics*. Duckworth, London.

Lefkowitz, M.R. and Fant, M.B. (1982) *Women's life in Greece and Rome. A source book in translation*, ed. and trans. M.R. Lefkowitz and M.B. Fant. Rev. edn. Duckworth, London.

Lemosse, M. (1975) 'L'enfant sans famille en droit romain', in *L'enfant, première partie: Antiquité, Afrique, Asie*. Editions de la Librairie Encyclopédique, Brussels, pp. 257-70. (Société Jean Bodin. Recueils, 35.)

Leonhard, R. (1905) 'Dos'. *RE* 5.2, cols. 1591-3.

Lesky, E. (1951) *Die Zeugungs- und Vererbungslehren der Antike und ihr Nachwirken*. Akademie der Wissenschaften und der Literatur, Mainz. (Akademie der Wissenschaften und der Literatur. Abhandlungen der Geistes- und Sozialwissenschaftlichen Klasse, Jahrg. 1950, Nr. 19.)

Lewis, N. and Reinhold, M. (1951) *Roman civilization*, Columbia University Press, New York, vol. 1, The Republic.

Lightman, M. and Feisel, W. (1977) '*Univira*: an example of continuity and change in Roman society'. *Church History*, 46, 19-32.

Liversidge, J. (1976) *Everyday life in the Roman Empire*. Batsford, London.

McKay, A.G. (1975) *Houses, villas and palaces in the Roman world*. Thames & Hudson, London.

MacMullen, R. (1974) *Roman social relations 50 B.C. to A.D. 284*. Yale University Press, New Haven. Reprinted 1981.

—— (1980) 'Women in public in the Roman Empire'. *Historia*, 29, 208-18.

Magdelain, A. (1983) 'Les mots *legare* et *heres* dans la loi des XII Tables', in H. Zehnacker and G. Hentz (eds.) *Hommages à Robert Schilling*, Les Belles Lettres, Paris, pp. 159-73.

Maiuri, A. (1946) 'Tabulae ceratae Herculanenses: testi e documenti', *Parola del Passato*, 1, 373-9.

Manson, M. (1983) 'The emergence of the small child in Rome (Third century B.C. – First century A.D.)'. *History of Education*, 12, 149-59.

Marquardt, J. (1886) *Das Privatleben der Römer*. 2nd edn. Hirzel, Leipzig. Reprinted 1964, Darmstadt.

Marrou, H.I. (1956) *A history of education in antiquity*. Sheed & Ward, London. Translated from the 3rd French edn. Reprinted 1977.

Marshall, A.J. (1975a) 'Roman women and the provinces'. *Ancient Society*, Louvain, 6. 109-27.

—— (1975b) 'Tacitus and the governor's lady: a note on Annals iii.33-4'. *Greece and Rome*, ser. 2, 22, 11-18.

Martin, H. and Phillips, J.E. (1978) '*Consolatio ad uxorem*', in *Plutarch's ethical writings and early Christian literature*, ed. H.D. Betz. Brill, Leiden, pp. 394-441.

Matringe, G. (1971) 'La puissance paternelle et le mariage des fils et filles de famille en droit romain (sous l'Empire et en Occident)'. *Studi in onore di Eduardo Volterra*. Giuffrè, Milan, vol. 5, pp.191-237.

Mattingly, H. and Sydenham, E.A. (eds.) (1923-81) *The Roman imperial coinage*. Spink, London. 9 vols. in 12.

Medicus, D. (1957) *Zur Geschichte des senatusconsultum Velleianum*. Bohlau, Cologne. (Forschung zum römischen Recht, 8. Abh.)

Megarry, R.E. (1973) *A Second Miscellany-at-law: a diversion for lawyers and others*. Stevens, London.

Meyer, P.M. (1895) *Der römischen Konkubinat nach den Rechtesquellen und den Inschriften*. Teubner, Leipzig. Reprinted Aalen, Scientia Verlag, 1966.

Mohler, S.L. (1940) 'Slave education in the Roman Empire'. *Transactions of the American Philological Association*, 71, 266-79.

Mommsen, T. (1887-8) *Römisches Staatsrecht*. Hirzel, Leipzig. 3 vols. in 5.

—— (1899) *Römisches Strafrecht*. Duncker & Humblot, Leipzig. Reprinted 1955, Akad. Druck-u.Verlagsanstalt, Graz.

Morris, J. (1963) 'Changing fashions in Roman nomenclature in the early Empire'. *Listy filologicki*, 86, 34-46.

Münzer, F. (1920) *Römische Adelsparteien und Adelsfamilien*. Metzler, Stuttgart.

Nani, T.G. (1943-4) 'ΘΡΕΠΤΟΙ'. *Epigraphica*, 5-6, 45-84.

Nardi, E. (1971) *Procurato aborto nel mondo greco romano*. Giuffrè, Milan.

—— (1980) 'Aborto e omicidio nella civiltà classica', in *Aufstieg und Niedergang der römischen Welt*, H. Temporini (ed.), De Gruyter, Berlin. *Principat, Recht*, II, 13, pp. 366-85.

Nash, E. (1962) *Pictorial dictionary of ancient Rome*. 2nd edn. Praeger, New York, 2 vols.

Neraudau, J.P. (1979) *La jeunesse dans la littérature et les institutions de la Rome républicaine*. Les Belles Lettres, Paris.

Nicholas, B. (1962) *An introduction to Roman law*. Clarendon Press, Oxford.

Nisbet, R.A. (1964) 'Kinship and political power in first century Rome', in *Sociology and history: theory and research*, W.J. Cahnman, and A. Boskoff (eds.), Free Press of Glencoe, New York, pp. 257-71.

Nisbet, R.G.M. and Hubbard, M.A. (1970) *A commentary on Horace: Odes Book I*. Clarendon Press, Oxford.

Nutton, V. (1977) '*Archiatri* and the medical profession in antiquity'. *Papers of the British School at Rome*, 45, 191-226.

Ogilvie, R.M. (1965) *A commentary on Livy, books 1-5*. Clarendon Press, Oxford.

L'onomastique latine (1977) *L'onomastique latine, Paris, 13-15 Octobre, 1975*. CNRS, Paris. (Colloques internationaux du CNRS, no. 564.)

Orr, D.G. (1978) *Roman domestic religion: a study of the Roman household deities and their shrines at Pompeii and Herculaneum*. University Microfilms International, Ann Arbor, Michigan. Degree date 1972.

Packer, J.E. (1967) 'Housing and population in imperial Ostia and Rome'. *Journal of Roman Studies*, 57, 80-95.

Paoli, U.E. (1963) *Rome, its people, life and customs*. McKay, New York. Reprinted 1975, Greenwood Press, Westport, Conn. Translated from the Italian original, 1940.

Paribeni, R. (1948) *La famiglia Romana*. 4th edn. Cappelli, Bologna. 1st edn published 1929.

Parker, E.F. (1946) 'The education of heirs in the Julio-Claudian family'. *American Journal of Philology*, 67, 29-50.

Peradotto, J. and Sullivan, J.P. (1984) *Women in the ancient world: the* Arethusa *papers*. State University of New York Press, Albany.

Phillips III, C.R. (1984) 'Old wine in old lead bottles: Nriagu on the fall of Rome', *Classical World*, 78, 29-33.

Phillips, J.E. (1978) 'Roman mothers and the lives of their adult daughters'. *Helios*, 6, 69-80.

Plassard, J. (1921) *Le concubinat romain sous le haut Empire*. Tenin, Paris.

Platner, S.B. and Ashby, T. (1929) *A topographical dictionary of ancient Rome*, by S.B. Platner, completed and revised by T. Ashby. Oxford University Press, London.

Pomeroy, S.B. (1973) 'Selected bibliography on women in antiquity'. *Arethusa*, 6, 125-57.

—— (1975) *Goddesses, whores, wives and slaves: women in classical antiquity*. Schocken Books, New York.

—— (1976) 'The relationship of the married woman to her blood relatives in Rome'. *Ancient Society*, Louvain, 7, 215-27.

Préaux, C. and Hombert, M. (1952) *Recherches sur le recensement dans l'Egypte romaine*. Brill, Leiden.

Prévost, M.H. (1949) *Les adoptions politiques à Rome sous la République et le Principat*. Sirey, Paris.

Pugliese Carratelli, G. (1946, 1948, 1953) 'Tabulae Herculanenses: testi e documenti, I, II, III'. *Parola del Passato*, 1, 379-85, 3, 165-84; 8, 455-63.

Rabello, A.M. (1972) 'Il *ius occidendi iure patris* della *Lex Julia de adulteriis coercendis* e la *vitae necisque potestas* del *paterfamilias*', in *Atti del seminario romanistico internazionale*, Libreria Editrice Universitaria, Perugia, pp. 228-42.

Raditsa, L.F. (1980) 'Augustus' legislation concerning marriage, procreation, love affairs and adultery', in *Aufstieg und Niedergang der römischen Welt*. H. Temporini (ed.), De Gruyter, Berlin. *Principat, Recht*, II, 13, pp. 278-339.

Rawson, B.M. (1966) 'Family life among the lower classes at Rome in the first two centuries of the Empire'. *Classical Philology*, 61, 71-83.

—— (1974) 'Roman concubinage and other *de facto* marriages'. *Transactions of the American Philological Association*, 104, 279-305. (See also under Wilkinson, B.M.)

Reinhold, M. (1971) 'Usurpation of status and status symbols in the Roman Empire'. *Historia*, 20, 275-302.

Richardson, W.F. (1979) 'Celsus on Medicine'. *Prudentia*, 11, 69-93.

Riesman, D. in collaboration with N. Glazer and R. Denney (1950) *The lonely crowd: a study of the changing American character.* Yale University Press, New Haven, Conn.

Rivier, A.P.O. (1891) *Précis du droit de famille romain, contenant un choix de textes.* Rousseau, Paris.

Roby, H.J. (1902) *Roman private law in the time of Cicero and of the Antonines.* Cambridge University Press, Cambridge. 2 vols.

Rose, H.J. (1926) '*De virginibus vestalibus*'. *Mnemosyne*, 54, 440-8.

—— (1948) *Ancient Roman religion.* Hutchinson, London.

Rostagni, A. (1956) *Suetonio* 'de poetis' *e biografi minori*, restituzione e commento di A. Rostagni. Loescher, Torino.

Russell, D.A. (1972) *Plutarch.* Duckworth, London.

Russell, J.C. (1958) *Late ancient and medieval population.* American Philosophical Society, Philadelphia. (its Transactions, n.s. 48, 3.)

Sachers, E. (1943) '*Tutela*'. *RE* 7A. 2, 1498-501.

Ste Croix, G.E.M. de (1970) 'Some observations on the property rights of Athenian women'. *Classical Review*, n.s. 20, 273-8.

—— (1981) *The class struggle in the ancient Greek world: from the archaic age to the Arab conquests.* Duckworth, London.

Salmon, P. (1974) *Population et dépopulation dans l'Empire romain.* Latomus, Bruxelles. (Collection Latomus, v. 137.)

Scarborough, J. (1979) *Roman medicine.* Thames & Hudson, London.

Schaps, D. (1979) *Economic rights of women in ancient Greece.* Edinburgh University Press, Edinburgh.

Schmidt, O.E. (1893) *Der Briefwechsel des M. Tullius Cicero.* n.p., Leipzig.

Schulz, F. (1936) *Principles of Roman law.* Clarendon Press, Oxford. Reprinted 1951.

—— (1942-43) 'Roman registers of births and birth certificates'. *Journal of Roman Studies*, 32, 78-91; 33, 55-64.

—— (1951) *Classical Roman law.* Clarendon Press, Oxford.

Schulze, W. (1904) *Zur Geschichte lateinischer Eigennamen.* Weidmann, Berlin. Reprinted 1966 (with original date of publication misprinted as 1964).

Scullard, H.H. (1981) *Festivals and ceremonies of the Roman Republic.* Thames & Hudson, London.

Shackleton Bailey, D.R. *See* Bailey, D.R. Shackleton.

Sherwin-White, A.N. (1966) *The letters of Pliny: a historical and social commentary.* Oxford University Press, Oxford.

—— (1973) *The Roman citizenship.* 2nd edn. Clarendon Press, Oxford.

Shorter, E. (1975) *The making of the modern family.* Basic Books, New York.

Solin, H. (1971) *Beitrage zur Kenntnis der griechischen Personennamen in Rom.* Societas Scientiarum Fennica, Helsinki.

—— (1973) 'Namengebung und Epigraphik', in *Akten des VI Internationalen Kongresses für Griechische und Lateinische Epigraphik, München, 1972*, Beck, Munich, pp. 404-7.

—— (1974) 'Onomastica ed epigrafia: riflessione sull' esegesi onomastica delle iscrizioni romane'. *Quaderni Urbinati di Cultura Classica*, 18, 105-32.

—— (1982) *Die griechischen Personennamen in Rom: ein Namenbuch.* De Gruyter, Berlin. 3 vols.

Soranus, of Ephesus (1956) *Gynecology*; translated from the Greek and with an introduction by O. Temkin. Johns Hopkins Press, Baltimore.

Starr, C.G. (1942) '*Verna*'. *Classical Philology*, 37, 314-17.

Stewart, A.J., Winter, D.G. and Jones, A.D. (1975) 'Coding categories for the study of child-rearing from historical sources'. *Journal of Interdisciplinary History*, 5, 687-701.

Stone, L. (1979) *The family, sex and marriage in England, 1500-1800*. Abridged edn. Penguin, Harmondsworth. Complete edn first published 1977, Weidenfeld & Nicolson, London.

Syme, R. (1939) *The Roman revolution*. Clarendon Press, Oxford.

—— (1956) 'Missing persons (P-W VIIIA)'. *Historia*, 5, 204-12.

—— (1958) *Tacitus*. Clarendon Press, Oxford.

—— (1960) 'Bastards in the Roman aristocracy'. *Proceedings of the American Philosophical Society*, 104, 323-7.

—— (1966) 'The consuls of A.D. 13', *Journal of Roman Studies*, 56, 55-60.

—— (1981) 'Princesses and others in Tacitus'. *Greece and Rome*. ser. 2, 28, 40-52.

Szramkewicz, R. (1976) *Les gouverneurs de province à l'époque augustéenne: contribution à l'histoire administrative et sociale du principat*. Nouvelles editions latines, Paris. 2 vols.

Taylor, L.R. (1960) *The voting districts of the Roman republic*. American Academy in Rome.

—— (1961) 'Freedmen and freeborn in the epitaphs of imperial Rome'. *American Journal of Philology*, 82, 113-32.

Taylor, L.R. and Scott, R.T. (1969) 'Seating space in the Roman senate and the *senatores pedarii*'. *Transactions of the American Philological Association*, 10, 529-82.

Thirsk, J. (1964) 'The family'. *Past and Present*, 27, 116-22.

Thomas, J.A.C. (1975) *The Institutes of Justinian*. North-Holland, Amsterdam/New York.

—— (1976) *Textbook of Roman law*. North-Holland, Amsterdam/New York.

Thomas, K. (1980) *Religion and the decline of magic: studies in popular beliefs in sixteenth- and seventeenth-century England*. Penguin, Harmondsworth.

Thylander, H. (1952) *Etude sur l'épigraphie latine: date des inscriptions, noms et dénomination latine, noms et origine des personnes*. Gleerup, Lund.

—— (1954) 'La dénomination chez Cicéron dans les lettres à Atticus'. *Opuscula Romano Acta Instituti Romani Regni Sueciae*, 18, 153-9.

Toynbee, J.M.C. (1971) *Death and burial in the Roman world*. Thames & Hudson, London.

Treggiari, S. (1969) *Roman freedmen during the late Republic*. Clarendon Press, Oxford.

—— (1975a) 'Family life among the staff of the Volusii'. *Transactions of the American Philological Association*, 105, 393-401.

—— (1975b) 'Jobs in the household of Livia'. *Papers of the British School at Rome*, 43, 48-77.

—— (1976) 'Jobs for women'. *American Journal of Ancient History*, 1, 76-104.

—— (1979a) 'Lower class women in the Roman economy'. *Florilegium*, 1, 65-86.

—— (1979b) 'Questions on women domestics in the Roman West', in *Schiavitu, manomissione e classi dipendenti nel mondo antico*, 'L'Erma' di Bretschneider, Rome, pp. 185-201. (Universita degli Studi di Padova, Pubblicazioni dell' Instituto di Storia Antica, v. 13.)

—— (1981a) '*Concubinae*'. *Papers of the British School at Rome*, 49, 59-81.

—— (1981b) '*Contubernales* in *CIL* 6'. *Phoenix*, 35, 42-69.

Treggiari, S. and Dorken, S. (1981c) 'Women with two living husbands in *CIL* 6'. *Liverpool Classical Monthly*, 6, 269-72.

Treggiari, S. (1984) '*Digna condicio*: betrothals in the Roman upper class'. *Echos du Monde Classique: Classical Views*, 28, 419-51.

United Nations Department of Economic and Social Affairs (1956) *Manuals on methods of estimating population. No. 3. Methods for population projection by sex and age*. New York.

Van Lith, S.M.E. (1974) 'Lease of sheep and goats: nursing contract with accompanying receipt'. *Zeitschrift für Papyrologie und Epigraphik*, 14, 145-62.

Vann, R.T. (1982) 'The youth of Centuries of Childhood'. *History and Theory*, 21, 279-97.

Van Oven, J.C. (1956) 'Le senatusconsulte Velléien et le P. Col. 123'. *Labeo*, 2, 85-9.

Versnel, H.S. (1970) *Triumphus: an inquiry into the origin, meaning and development of the Roman triumph*. Brill, Leiden.

Visscher, F. de (1963) *Le droit des tombeaux romains*. Giuffrè, Milan.

Voci, P. (1960) *Diritto ereditario romano I*. Giuffrè, Milan.

Vogt, H. (1952) *Studien zum senatus consultum Velleianum*. Rohrscheid, Bonn.

—— (1967) 'Micellanea ad Senatus consultum Velleianum'. *Tijdschrift voor Rechtsgeschiedenis*, 35, 90-124.

Vogt, J. (1974) *Ancient slavery and the ideal of man*. Blackwell, Oxford. Translated from the 2nd edn, 1972.

Voigt, W.V. (1905) '*Excursus*: eine vorläufige Bemerkung über die *transitio ad plebem*'. *Philologus*, 64, 362-6.

Volterra, E. (1948) 'Quelques observations sur le mariage des *filiifamilias*', *Revue Internationale des Droits de l'Antiquité*, 1, 213-42.

Waldstein, W. (1972) 'Zum Fall der "dos Licinniae" '. *Index: Quaderni Camerti di Studi Romanistici*, 2, 343-61.

Wall, R. (ed.) with J. Robin and P. Laslett (1983) *Family forms in historic Europe*. Cambridge University Press, Cambridge.

Wallace-Hadrill, A. (1981) 'Family and inheritance in the Augustan marriage laws: Appendix, *Exceptae Personae*', *Proceedings of the Cambridge Philological Society*, 207 (n.s. 27), 73-6.

Watson, A. (1965) 'The divorce of Carvilius Ruga', *Tijdschrift voor Rechtsgeschiedenis*, 33, 38-50.

—— (1967) *The law of persons in the later Roman Republic*. Clarendon Press, Oxford.

—— (1971) *Law of succession in the later Roman Republic*. Clarendon Press, Oxford.

—— (ed.) (1974) *Daube Noster: essays in legal history for David Daube*. Scottish Academic Press, Edinburgh.

—— (1975) *Rome of the XII Tables: persons and property*. Princeton University Press, Princeton, N.J.

Watts, W.J. (1973) 'Ovid, the law and Roman society on abortion'. *Acta Classica*, 16, 89-103.

Weaver, P.R.C. (1967) 'Social mobility in the early Roman Empire: the evidence of the imperial freedmen and slaves'. *Past and Present*, 37, 3-20.

—— (1968) 'Family dating criteria: *proximi* and "*provincia*" in the *Familia Caesaris*'. *Journal of Roman Studies*, 58, 110-23.

—— (1972) *Familia Caesaris: a social study of the emperor's freedmen and slaves*. Cambridge University Press, Cambridge.

—— (1979) 'Misplaced officials, 70-102'. *Antichthon*, 13, 70-102.

Weinstock, St (1934) 'Terentia'. *RE* 5A. 1, col. 710.

Weiss, E. (925) '*Leges Juliae*'. *RE* 12.2, cols. 2363-4.

Westermann, W.L. (1955) *The slave systems of Greek and Roman antiquity*. American Philosophical Association, Philadelphia. (its Memoirs, no. 40.)

Wieacker, F. (1970) 'Die römischen Juristen in der politischen Gesellschaft des zweiten vorchristlichen Jahrhunderts', in *Sein und Werden im Recht. Festgabe für Ulrich von Lubtow z. 70. Geburtstag am 21 Aug. 1970.* Hrsg. von W.G. Becker und L. Schnorr von Carolsfeld. Duncker u. Humblot, Berlin, pp. 183-214.

Wiedemann, T. (1981) *Greek and Roman slavery.* Croom Helm, London.

Wilkinson, B.M. (1964) 'A wider concept of the term *parens*'. *Classical Journal*, 59, 358-61. (For other works by this author see under Rawson, B.M.)

Wilkinson, L.P. (1975) *The Roman experience.* Elek, London.

—— (1979) *Classical attitudes to modern issues.* Kimber, London.

Williams, G. (1958) 'Some aspects of Roman marriage ceremonies and ideals'. *Journal of Roman Studies*, 48, 16-29.

Wistrand, E. (1976) *The so-called Laudatio Turiae.* Introduction, text, translation and commentary, by E. Wistrand. Acta Universitatis Gothoburgensis, Lund.

Wolff, H.J. (1944) 'Marriage law and family organization in ancient Athens: a study in the interrelation of public and private law in the Greek city'. *Traditio*, 2, 43-95.

—— (1974) 'The background of the post-classical legislation on illegitimacy: paper presented at the Riccobono Seminar on Roman Law, Washington, DC, 1945', in *Opuscula Dispersa*, Hakkert, Amsterdam, pp. 135-59.

Yaron, R. (1964) '*De divortio varia*'. *Tijdschrift voor Rechtsgeschiedenis*, 32, 553-7.

Yavetz, Z. (1958) 'The living conditions of the urban plebs in Republican Rome', *Latomus*, 18, 500-17.

—— (1969) *Plebs and princeps.* Clarendon Press, Oxford.

Zimmerman, C.C. (1947) *Family and civilization.* Harper, New York.

Zulueta, F. de (ed.) (1946-53) *The Institutes of Gaius.* Clarendon Press, Oxford. 2 vols.

SUBJECT INDEX

passim, 173, 174, 181, 182-4, 187, 190, 193
manus marriage 59, 61, 72, 73, 79, 84, 100, 105, 111, 128-9
marriage 1, 4, 5, 6, 9, 11, 14, 15, 18-22 *passim*, 26, 27, 30, 130, 180
  informal 15, 23-4, 27, 28, Ch. 6 *passim*
  patron-freed 24, 28, 149-50, 154, 157, 176-7, 181
  see also adultery; age at marriage; children; *contubernium*; divorce; dowry; *familia*; matrimonial property; widows
matrimonial property 91, Ch. 4 *passim*
ménage à trois 15
mixed marriage
  see marriage, informal
mothers 18-19, 24, 25
  bonds with children 111, 116, Ch. 8 *passim*
  rearing of children 18, 30, 36, 40
  status Ch. 6 *passim*

names
  see nomenclature
natural parents
  see parents
nomenclature 5, 8, 13, 18, 23, 42-3, 155-66ff, 179, 183-4, 192-5, 207, 213-14
  order on stones 184-6, 195
nurses (*nutrices*) 30, 178, Ch. 8 *passim*
oikos 121-3
Oppian law
  see lex Oppia
orphans 66, 196

pacta dotalia
  see dowry
pangenesis 231-2, 233
parent-child relationships 111, 116, Ch. 8 *passim*
parents 36, 37, 38, 171, 172, 194, 196
  see also fathers; foster-parents; mothers; step-parents
partibility 60, 62, 65, 76
paterfamilias 4, 7, 8, 14, 16-17, 30, 61, 62, 63, Ch. 5 *passim*
patria potestas 8, 48-9, 59, 84, Ch. 5 *passim*, 196, 218

patricians 20, 127, 132, 135-6
patron-freed relationships 13, 37, 137, 139-40, 176-8, 181
peculium 17, 77, 78, 127, 133, 134, 135
Penates 126, 128, 130
peregrini 23, 145, 155, 167, 238
plebeians 132, 135-6
pledges (law) 174
political attitudes 41
political careers 17, 136, 196
political groups 5, 6
pomerium 129
pontifex maximus 20, 126-9 *passim*, 139
praetors 129, 137
Presocratics 230, 231, 232
priesthoods 20, 135-6
primogeniture 65, 76
property 18-19, Ch. 2 *passim*
  confiscation of 93, 96-8, 101
  control 16-17, 58, 126-7, 130, 135
prostitutes 35

querela inofficiosi testamenti 65, 75, 78

religious ceremonies 4, 38, 40
remarriage 36, 77-78, 171
rents 109
retentiones 106-13 *passim*

schools 38, 40
semen Ch. 9 *passim*
senatusconsultum Claudianum AD 52 ix, 145, 149-54 *passim*, 165-6, 167
senatusconsultum Macedonianum 77
senatusconsultum Orfitianum 62, 67-8, 79, 123
senatusconsultum Tertullianum 62, 67, 79
senatusconsultum Velleianum Ch. 3 *passim*
sepulchral inscriptions
  see epitaphs
sex determination 230, 235-6
sex ratio 18, 179-80, 187, 191-2
slave-breeding 50-1, 157, 211-13
slave-owners 207-13 *passim*, 221
slaves 2, 12, 13, 14, 15, 17, 24, 37, 44, Ch. 7 *passim*
  education 39
  marriages 23, Ch. 6 *passim*
  occupations 191, 193, 194, 196-7, 212

INDEX OF NAMES

(Emperors' names are given in their common English form in block letters.)